# The Orientalists: Delacroix to Matisse

## THE ALLURE OF NORTH AFRICA
## AND THE NEAR EAST

# The Orientalists:
# Delacroix to Matisse

## THE ALLURE OF NORTH AFRICA
## AND THE NEAR EAST

*Edited by Mary Anne Stevens*

NATIONAL GALLERY OF ART, WASHINGTON

*Catalogue published in association with Weidenfeld and Nicolson London*

*Dates of Exhibition in Washington*
1 July–28 October 1984

*Cover Illustrations*
*Front* Renoir
          *Odalisque* (detail)
          (National Gallery of Art, Washington)
*Back* Bauernfeind
          *Market in Jaffa* (detail)
          (Private Collection, Houston, Texas)

House editor  Denny Hemming

Designed by Trevor Vincent for
George Weidenfeld and Nicolson Limited
91 Clapham High Street, London SW4 7TA
ISBN 0 89468 075 7

Set in Palatino
Printed in Great Britain by BAS Printers Limited, Over Wallop, Hampshire
Color separations by Newsele Litho Limited, Italy
Color printed by Printers Srl, Trento, Italy

# Contents

## Acknowledgements

The National Gallery of Art and The Royal Academy extend their thanks to the following individuals and institutions who have contributed in many ways to the organisation of the exhibition and the preparation of the catalogue.

Eve Alonso
Alex Apsis
The Library, Arizona State University
Rachel Astor
Wendy Baron
Agnès de la Baumelle
David P. Becker
Kenneth Bendiner
The Bodleian Library, Oxford
Eugene N. Borza
Richard Brettell
The Library of the University of
    British Columbia
British Council, Fine Art Department
Roger Cardinal
Tony Carroll
Roger Clarke
Timothy Clifford
Patrick Conner
A. Cohen Esq.
Claire Constant
Malcolm Cormack
Roy David
Paul Devautour
Joanna Drew
Lorraine Dyess
Simon Edsor
André El Zenny
The Fine Art Society
Anne Gilbert
Michael Gilsenan
Lucas Gloor
Helen Guiterman
Robin Hamlyn
Vicky Hayward
Denny Hemming
The Houghton Library, Harvard
The Huntington Library, San Marino
Richard Hussey
Francina Irwin
Kenneth Jay Lane
Lee Johnson
Sona Johnston
William Johnston
Samuel Josefowitz
Isabelle Julia
Robert Kashey
Margaret Kelly
Jill Knight
Vivien Knight
Geneviève Lacambre

Michel Laclotte
Ronald de Leeuw
Leggatt Brothers
Michael Levey
Major-General J.M.H. Lewis
Richard Lockett
Brian MacDermot
Caroline Mathieu
James and Else Melvin
Denis Milhau
Dewey F. Mosby
Jean-Marie Moulin
Alice Munro-Faure
Alexandra Murphey
John Myerscough
Gail Naughton
The New York Public Library
Patrick Noon
Richard Ormond
Mattieu Pinette
Princeton University Library
Benedict Read
Brenda Richardson
Joseph Richell
Phillippe Robert-Jones
Michael Rogers
Anne Roquebert
Melvin Rose
Pierre Rosenberg
Donald Rosenthal
John Rylands University Library of Manchester
Barbara Shapiro
Peyton Skipwith
Tom Sokolowski
Stephen Somerville
Claude Souviron
Ted Stebbins
Timothy Stevens
Peter Stocks
Geoffrey Stowe
Richard Thompson
Lynne Thornton
Gary Tinterow
Germain Viatte
Clive Wake
Michael Wentworth
Arnold Wilson
The Staff of the Witt Library
M. Xavier
Eric Zaffran

## Photographic Acknowledgements

*Map* produced by Constance and Brian Dear Ltd.

The exhibition organisers would like to thank the following
for making photographs available.
All other photographs were provided by the owners of the paintings.
Cliché des Musées Nationaux  3, 7, 11, 26, 51, 52, 78, 87
A.C. Cooper  66, 73
Birmingham City Art Gallery  fig. 10
Prudence Cuming Associates Ltd.  68, 70, 89
The Fine Art Society, London  61, 67, 71, 74, 79, 90, 93, 95
P J Gates Photography  90
Kunsthalle, Hamburg  fig. 14
Manchester City Art Gallery  fig. 12
Musée d'Orsay, Paris  fig. 15
Royal Academy of Arts  1, 21, 22, 25, 29, 30, 35, 37, 38, 40, 41, 44, 45, 94
Sotheby's Belgravia  62
Sotheby Parke Bernet, London  68, 74
Sterling and Francine Clark Art Institute, Williamstown  fig. 1
Herbert P. Vose  42
The Wallace Collection, London  figs. 2, 9

## List of Lenders

Aberdeen Art Gallery and Museums  100
The Art Institute of Chicago  12, 27
The Art Museum, Princeton University  32
The Baltimore Museum of Art  76
M. Pierre Bergé, Paris  64
The City of Bristol Museum and Art Gallery  81, 88
The Brooklyn Museum  60
The Chrysler Museum, Norfolk  24
Sterling and Francine Clark Art Institute, Williamstown  86
The Dayton Art Institute  31
The Denver Art Museum  92
The Detroit Institute of Arts  50
Mr. Jerald Dillon Fessenden, New York  43
The Fine Art Society, London  63
The Forbes Magazine Collection, New York  4
H. Fritz-Denneville Fine Arts Ltd., London  62
Guildhall Art Gallery, London  47
Harris Museum and Art Gallery, Preston  66
Maryland Institute, College of Art, Baltimore  5
Mr. Henry P. McIlhenny, Philadelphia  16
The Metropolitan Museum of Art, New York  6, 23, 34
The Minneapolis Institute of Arts  15, 39, 96
Moderna Museet, Stockholm  77a
Musée des Augustins, Toulouse  17
Musée Cantonal des Beaux-Arts, Lausanne  99
Musée des Beaux-Arts, Nantes  14, 28, 46, 48, 82
Musée Fabre, Montpellier  13
Musée National d'Art Moderne, Centre Georges Pompidou, Paris  78
Musée National du Château de Versailles  8
Musée National du Louvre, Paris  11, 75
Musée d'Orsay, Paris  3, 7, 26, 51, 52, 87
Musée Rolin, Autun  98
Museum of Fine Arts, Boston  97
National Gallery of Art, Washington  19, 77c, 84
National Portrait Gallery, London  83
Nationalmuseum, Stockholm  18
The Nelson-Atkins Museum of Art, Kansas City  9
Olana State Historic Site, Hudson  10
Mr. and Mrs. Tim Rice, London  79
Royal Academy of Arts, London  89
Royal Holloway College (University of London), Egham  91
David E. Rust, Washington  41a
Scottish National Portrait Gallery, Edinburgh  93
Southampton Art Gallery  53
Städtische Galerie im Lenbachhaus, Munich  58, 59
Mr. and Mrs. Eugene B. Sydnor, Jr., Richmond  42
The Trustees of the Tate Gallery, London  57, 69, 102
Gallerie degli Uffizi, Florence  55
The Walters Art Gallery, Baltimore  56
Worcester Art Museum  85
Yale Centre for British Art, New Haven  67

*and lenders who wish to remain anonymous*

# Glossary *Compiled by Peter Stocks*

Transliteration generally follows the old British Museum system. However, localities within the former French sphere of influence retain their French transliteration, except where it would cause confusion.

A = Arabic; T = Turkish; P = Persian.

*'ālmah* (A) lit. 'learned woman' but popularly in the nineteenth century a singer and entertainer and by extension a prostitute.

*Arnavut* (T) Albanian, a group particularly favoured by Muḥammad 'Alī for his army. He was in fact one himself, and used them to counter the strength of the *Bays* (q.v.) and their retainers.

*asāwir* (A) bracelet.

*babush* (T from P) slippers.

*baqshish* (A from P) a present, more commonly a gratuity.

*bashibazuk* (T) lit. 'headless', an irregular soldier, unpaid but allowed to partake of plunder.

*Bay* (T) highest rank among the *mamlūks* (q.v.) of Egypt from the sixteenth to the nineteenth centuries.

*burnūs* (A) voluminous, hooded cloak worn on desert journeys.

*cami* (T from A *jāmi'*) an assembly mosque.

*Copt* (from A *qibt*) a Christian of the Egyptian Monophysite Church.

*dahabiyyah* (A) house boat.

*daqq* (A) tattoo and the application thereof, usually performed on children.

*darābukah* (A) clay drum.

*dervish* (P) an itinerant *sufi* (q.v.).

*dhikr* (A) lit. 'remembrance', part of a *sufi* (q.v.) ceremony in which the name of Allah is invoked. These exercises take various forms among the many *sufi* brotherhoods.

*durqā'ah* (A) the central area of the *qā'ah* (q.v.) with a sunken central area often with a fountain, and an elevated tower rising above the *līwāns* (q.v.).

*dūsah* (A) lit. 'trampling', a ritual of the Sa'diyyah *sufis* (q.v.) of Egypt in which the Shaykh rode over the bodies of his followers. Banned in 1881.

*fellāḥ* f. *fellāḥah*, pl. *fellāḥīn* (A) a land worker, a farmer or peasant.

*frank* (from A. *franji*) a European.

*giaour* (from P from A) Kafir, a non-believer (in Islam).

*gūzah* (A) water pipe (from A for nut).

*ḥājj* (A) the pilgrimage to Mecca, therefore *ḥajj*, one who has made the pilgrimage.

*harem* (from A *ḥaram*) forbidden, the women's quarters in a house.

*hawsh* (A) an enclosure including the courtyard of a house.

*Islam* (A) lit. 'surrender', the religion having the *Qur'ān* (q.v.) as the revealed scripture and teaching that there is only one God and that Muḥammad is his prophet.

*jihād* (A) lit. a war of Muslims against non-believers.

*jinn* (A) being created of fire by Allah whose destiny is other that that of man.

*kamangah* (A) two-stringed viol.

*kātib* (A) scribe.

*katirji* (T) muleteer.

*khān* (A from P) hostel for merchants and their goods.

*kavas* (T from A) an armed policeman.

*khamsīn* lit, 'fifty', hot sand-laden wind of spring in Egypt, so-called because it lasts about fifty days.

*khānqah* (P) a mosque built specifically for *sufis* (q.v.).

*khirka* (T) black cloak worn by *Malawiyyah* (q.v.) *sufis* (q.v.).

*kiosk* (from T *koshk*) a light, open-sided pavilion.

*kohl* (A) powdered antimony used as mascara in the Near East.

*ksour* (from A *qusūr*) fortified villages in oases.

*līwān* (A from P) vaulted chamber leading from the *durqā'ah* (q.v.)

*lokhanda* (A from Italian) inn, hotel for travellers.

*madrasah* (A) a mosque built specifically for teaching, usually belonging to one or more of the four schools of law.

*maq'ad* (A) lit. 'sitting place', a pillared loggia overlooking the courtyard of a house.

*mashrabiyyah* (A) a decorative lattice formed of turned wooden units assembled without the use of glue and made up into casements and screens.

*Malawiyyah* (A) a *sufi* (q.v.) brotherhood founded by Jalāl al-Dīn Rīmī (d.1273), known to Europeans as the whirling dervishes (T. *Mevlevi*). Their name is derived from their title for Rīmī, *mawlā*, 'master'.

*mamlūk* (A) lit. 'owned', one of the innumerable slaves brought from S. Russia and Europe into the armies of Egypt and Syria. They ruled Egypt from 1250–1517 and after the Ottoman conquest still formed the single most powerful group. Finally extinguished during the reign of Muḥammad 'Alī.

*Medina* (A Madīnah) city to the north of Mecca to which Muḥammad escaped and where he made his home and died. His tomb is often visited after the pilgrimage.

*Mecca* (A Makkah) a city in W. Arabia containing the Ka'bah, the object of the pilgrimage, and the holiest city of Islam, where Muḥammad was born.

*miḥrāb* (A) niche in the wall of a mosque indicating the direction of Mecca.

*minbar* (A) a stepped chair to the right of the *miḥrāb* from which the *khutbah* (Friday sermon) is given.

*mu'adhdin* (A) the man who calls (*adhān*) the faithful to prayer five times each day.

*Muḥammad* (?570–632 AD) The last prophet of Islam. Born in Mecca he received the first revelation in 610 but, after much privation, persecution forced him to escape to Medina in 622. After several battles Mecca was opened to him and Islam was established throughout Arabia.

*Muslim* (A) a believer in the religion of Islam (q.v.), adj.

*nargīlah* (P) a water pipe (from P. for nut).

*nizām* (A) a regular soldier.

*odalisque* (from T *odalik*) lit. 'belonging to the chamber'.

*Orientalist* (from French) denoting, during the nineteenth century, that pertaining to North Africa and the Near East.

*Ottomans* Turkish tribe who, in 1453, conquered the shrunken Byzantine Empire by taking Constantinople. They established themselves as the most powerful force in the Near East until modern times.

*pasha* (T) high Ottoman official of the second rank; provincial governors were usually appointed from this class.

*qā'ah* (A) main chambers of a house usually consisting of the *durqā'ah* (q.v.) off which lead the *līwāns* (q.v.).

*qangah* (A) a long boat used on the Nile.

*qanūn* (A from Greek?) a framed stringed instrument played with a soft hammer.

*qiblā* (A) the direction of Mecca.

*quftān* (A) a coat-like robe, sometimes of rich fabric usually worn with a belt.

*qullah* (A) a wide-mouthed, unglazed water pot.

*Qur'ān* (A) lit. 'recitations', collected texts of the revelation to Muḥammad, believed by Muslims to be the infallible 'word' of God.

*quṣūr* (A) fortified villages in oases.

*safa* (A) hair ornaments.

*sarvel* (T) baggy trousers.

*shaykh* (A) from the root *shakh* 'to age'. It therefore has many meanings eg. head of tribe or family, elder, master of a *sufi* (q.v.) brotherhood etc.

*shibriyyah* (A) arched camel litter.

*shibbuk* (T) long pipe.

*sikke* (T) high felt hat worn by Malawiyyah *sufis* (q.v.).

*simoun* (from A. *simūm*) hot, suffocating wind.

*sirocco* (Italian, from A. *sharqī*), name for the hot winds of southern Europe.

*sufi* (A) a member of one of innumerable brotherhoods following a *tariqah* (way) in an active search for knowledge of Allah under the guidance of a *shaykh*. Examples are Bayūmiyyah, 'Isawiyyah, Malawiyyah.

*sultān* (A) ruler.

*takhtabush* (T) as *maq'ad* (q.v.).

*takhtrawān* (T) two-camel vehicle.

*tarbouka* (A) see *darābuka*.

*tarbūsh* (A from P) lit. head covering; a felt cap originally worn under a turban.

*ṭarḥah* (A) a veil.

*'uqd* (A) necklace.

*valide sultān* (T. from A.) lit. 'mother of the ruler', i.e. queen mother.

*yelek* (T) a light coat either short or long.

*zummarah* (A) double reed pipe.

# Editorial Note

Works indicated with an asterisk (*) are exhibited at the National Gallery of Art, Washington only; those indicated with a dagger (†) are exhibited at the Royal Academy of Arts only.

Artists appear in alphabetical order and their works are arranged in chronological sequence, with watercolours listed before works in oil.

Titles of works in the exhibition are given first in English, followed by the title in the original language. Where possible, pictures are given the title by which they were originally known, or otherwise that by which they are best known. Contemporary spelling of proper nouns has been followed in all cases.

A single date after a title indicates that the work was executed, or completed, in that year. Two dates separated by a hyphen indicates that the work was definitely executed between these two years, thus: 1860–65. Two dates separated by an oblique stroke indicates that the work was definitely executed at some point during this time span, thus: 1860/65. A date preceded by 'c.' indicates that the work was executed at around this date, thus: c. 1865. When no date occurs, insufficient evidence is available to suggest an accurate date within the system given above.

All works are in oil on canvas unless otherwise stated.

Dimensions are given in centimetres; height precedes width.

Inscriptions on a picture, on the verso or on a label attached to the work are transcribed literally, and their location specified. They are recorded below the dimension of the work and always given in italics.

Provenances of the works have been checked as far as possible.

Published sources referred to throughout the catalogue have been abbreviated as follows:

Lane 1836      E.W. Lane, *An Account of the Manners and Customs of the Modern Egyptians*, London, 1836

Lenoir 1872      P. Lenoir, *Le Fayoum, le Sinaï et Petra. Expéditions dans la Moyenne Egypte et l'Arabie Petrée sous la direction de J. L. Gérôme*, Paris, 1872 (English translation, London 1873)

Steegmuller, ed., 1979      F. Steegmuller, ed. and transl., *Flaubert in Egypt: A Sensibility on Tour*, Chicago, 1979

Thornton 1983      L. Thornton, *Les Orientalistes. Peintres voyageurs 1828–1908*, Paris, 1983

Sources referred to frequently within the catalogue entries of an artist have also been abbreviated and are given in Abbreviated References immediately below the artist's biography. When a source occurs both in the text and in the Reference section of an individual catalogue entry, it is referred to in the text by the author's surname and the date of the publication. All references are given in chronological order, Abbreviated References preceding those given in full.

Exhibition details have been given in full wherever possible. For exhibitions listed as 'Paris, Salon' which occurred after 1884, 'Salon des Champs-Elysées' refers to the Salon de la Societé des Artistes Français, reorganised in 1881, and 'Salon du Champ de Mars' refers to the Salon of the exhibition body, La Societé Nationales des Beaux-Arts, founded in 1890.

The transliteration of Arabic words generally follows the old British Museum system (for further details, see *Glossary*) and in the text, they occur in italics.

The authors of the catalogue entries are noted by the following initials:

J.E.B.      Judith Bronkhurst
C.B.      Caroline Bugler
G.L.C.      Gerald L. Carr
D.C.      Deborah Chotner
N.C.      Nicolai Cikovsky, Jr.
B.L.      Briony Llewellyn
J.M.      Jane Munro
MA.S      MaryAnne Stevens
J.T.      James Thompson
P.V.      Peter Vergo
M.W.      Malcolm Warner

*Arab Advisor*
Peter Stocks

*Exhibition Assistants*
Stephanie Belt
Ann Bigley
Annette Bradshaw
Simonetta Fraquelli
Cameran Greer
Kathleen Kelley
Elisabeth McCrae

*Exhibition Designers*
Mark Leithauser
Gaillard Ravenal

*Editorial Office*
Frances Smyth

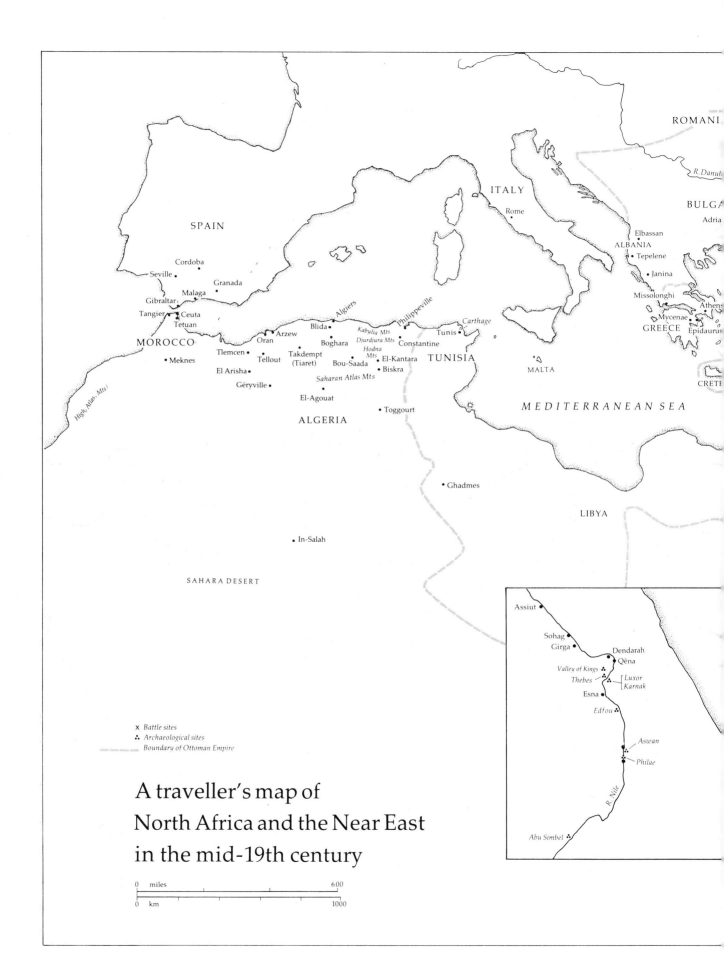

ROMANI

R.Danub

BULGA

Adria

ITALY

Rome

Elbassan

ALBANIA

Tepelene

Janina

Missolonghi

Athens

Mycenae

GREECE  Epidaurus

SPAIN

Cordoba

Seville

Granada

Malaga

Gibraltar

Tangier  Ceuta

Tetuan

MOROCCO

Meknes

High Atlas Mts

Algiers

Blida

Kabylia Mts

Philippeville

Carthage

Tunis

Oran  Arzew

Boghara

Djurdjura Mts

Constantine

Tlemcen

Hodna
Mts

Tellout

Takdempt
(Tiaret)

Bou-Saada

El-Kantara

TUNISIA

El Arisha

Géryville

Saharan Atlas Mts

Biskra

MALTA

El-Agouat

ALGERIA

Toggourt

MEDITERRANEAN SEA

CRETE

Ghadmes

LIBYA

In-Salah

SAHARA DESERT

Assiut

Sohag

Girga

Dendarah

Qēna

Valley of Kings

Thebes

Luxor
Karnak

Esna

Edfou

Aswan

Philae

R. Nile

Abu Simbel

x  Battle sites

∴  Archaeological sites

⸺⸺⸺  Boundary of Ottoman Empire

# A traveller's map of
# North Africa and the Near East
# in the mid-19th century

0   miles                    600

0   km                      1000

CRIMEA

BLACK SEA

CASPIAN
SEA

Constantinople
Bosphorus

TURKEY

ANATOLIA

PERSIA

• Teheran

Tlos

Xanthus

Rhodes

SYRIA

R. Euphrates

R. Tigris

CYPRUS

• Palmyra

• Baghdad

LEBANON    • Baalbec

Beirut    • Damascus

Acre

PALESTINE

• Jerusalem

PERSIAN GULF

Damietta

Rosetta

Port Said

Abū Qīr

Alexandria

Ismalia    — Suez Canal

∴ Petra

Gizah    • Cairo    Suez

SINAI

EGYPT

Minya

R. Nile

Mt Sinai
∴ St. Catherine's monastery

Nazareth

Nablus

Jaffa

Jericho

Jerusalem    Mt
Olivet

Bethlehem

Mts of Moab

Dendarah

Medina •

Dead Sea

1st cataract

IDUMAEA

ARABIA

2nd cataract

THE HIJAZ

R. Nile

Jeddah •    • Mecca

3rd cataract

RED SEA

4th cataract    5th cataract

THE SUDAN

6th cataract

Khartoum •

Aden •

11

# Preface

A few years ago, we held at the National Gallery an exhibition called 'The European Vision of America'. The present exhibition might have been called 'The European (and American) Vision of North Africa and the Near East'. It was a vision based on allure, and this exhibition illustrates not only the subject-matter which fascinated these artists, but also the profound effect that it had upon their art. It covers the origins of what came to be known as 'Orientalist' painting in the works of Baron Gros and Delacroix, and concludes at the beginning of this century with the redefinition of Fauvism in the art of Matisse and the remarkable voyage to abstraction in that of Kandinsky. (In the interest of limiting ourselves to paintings on canvas, the work on paper of such artists as Macke and Klee had to be excluded.)

Orientalist painting must have been known to Mark Twain, who recorded his enthusiastic yet awestruck response to Tangier at the beginning of his voyage to the Holy Land in 1867 in these words: 'The pictures used to seem exaggerations – they seemed too weird and fanciful for reality. But behold, they were not wild enough – they were not fanciful enough – they have not told half the story. Tangier is a foreign land if ever there was one, and the true spirit of it can never be found in any book save *The Arabian Nights*'. Indeed, as Sir Hugh Casson wrote in the Foreword to the catalogue of the Royal Academy version of our exhibition, a visit to North Africa and the Near East in the nineteenth century involved both dangers and delights for intrepid travellers determined to experience and to record these exotic lands. Flaubert gazed transfixed by the sight of the sun rising over the Pyramids at Gizah; Belly went up the Nile on a boat to the strains of Glück played on a grand piano specially hired for the journey; William Holman Hunt sat by the Dead Sea with a paint brush in one hand and a loaded rifle in the other – to ward off wild animals and curious Bedouins.

The political and commercial involvement of Britain, France and the United States in the Near East and North Africa, from Napoleon's Egyptian campaigns of 1798 and Stephen Decatur's sortie in Tripoli in 1815, to the opening of the Suez Canal and the establishment of the British Protectorate over Egypt, encouraged artists to explore, record and celebrate these predominantly non-Christian lands.

Armed with sketches, photographs and myriad Islamic objets d'art to decorate their studios, these artist-travellers returned to the West to create paintings, lithographs and albums of daguerreotypes which illustrated the monuments of ancient civilisations, bazaars, harems and mosques. Some were unmoved, their work retaining quintessentially Western characteristics. For others, however, the strangeness of the terrain and the unfamiliar light provoked both a rethinking of Western artistic conventions and a discovery of brilliant colour.

This exhibition is a variation and augmentation of the show presented at the Royal Academy of Arts, London, between March and May 1984. We are grateful to that institution's president, Sir Hugh Casson, to its secretary, Piers Rodgers, and to its exhibitions secretary, Norman Rosenthal. It is, however, to the talented British scholar MaryAnne Stevens that this show primarily owes its existence. With the assistance of many dedicated people, and in particular, two members of the National Gallery staff, D. Dodge Thompson and Florence E. Coman, she has been responsible for the selection of the works of art and the editing of the catalogue.

To all of these people, and to the many lenders on both sides of the Atlantic who have so generously parted with their paintings for this undertaking, we are enormously grateful.

*J. Carter Brown*
*Director, National Gallery of Art*

MARYANNE STEVENS

# Western Art and its Encounter with the Islamic World 1798–1914

*'The question amounts to knowing whether the Orient yields to interpretation, to what extent it is open to this and, if to interpret it is not to destroy it . . . The Orient is extraordinary . . . It escapes conventions, it lies outside all disciplines, it transposes, it inverts everything, it overturns the harmonies with which landscape painting has for centuries functioned. I do not talk here of a fictional Orient'.*[1]

Eugène Fromentin, *Une Année dans le Sahel*

The Orient to which Fromentin, the French painter and writer, was referring in 1858 was not the Far East of China and Japan, but the lands of North Africa and the Ottoman Empire, Turkey and Asia Minor, Egypt and Syria, including the Holy Land, Palestine and the Lebanon.[2] Fromentin, in his struggle to come to terms with the Orient which so tantalised him, expresses many of the paradoxes and challenges that artists from Europe and America faced in their encounter with this alien culture.[3] Between 1798 and 1914, North Africa and the Near East, as the closest non-Christian region to Europe, exercised a fascination upon the West, which responded in a variety of ways: the scholarly study of ancient civilisations and of contemporary cultures, imaginary evocations in poems and novels, literary descriptions and tourists' enthusiasms, as well as representations by artists.

Whilst for many of the numerous painters who visited the Orient the encounter had no lasting effect, the concern of this exhibition is with the succession of artists who for more than a century found their work fundamentally influenced by the experience of at least one visit to the Near East. The repercussions of such visits can be seen in their effects on two broad areas of artistic concern, subject-matter and technique. Whereas Gérôme, Lewis and Bauernfeind, for example, found themselves returning regularly to the distinctive scenes and subjects of the Near East, in the case of Delacroix, Fromentin, Renoir and Matisse, the influence of the Orient was on their technical development as painters, specifically in their handling of light and colour.

Whilst there are many ways of exploring an encounter between two cultures, and many issues might be raised thereby,[4] this exhibition adopts an historical, European viewpoint in its approach to the study of artists, not limited necessarily to great masters, in contact with a foreign culture. It illustrates the range of subject-matter depicted by the Orientalist painters: landscapes of ancient sites, the Holy Land, the River Nile, the desert, caravans and encampments, the bustling life of the cities, harems, baths and odalisques, and the religious manifestations of Islam. It excludes, however, history paintings, such as Poynter's *Israel in Egypt* (1867),[5] since they involved the historical reconstruction of the Orient rather than a commitment, in varying degrees, to direct observation of the contemporary culture. The exhibition also explores the relationship between Orientalist painting and movements in European art during the nineteenth century. The shift from Romanticism to Realism, and then to Impressionism and early Modernism, sees its reflection in the Orientalist works of Delacroix, then of Holman Hunt, Lewis and Gérôme, and finally in the Orientalist paintings of Renoir, Brangwyn and Matisse. The exhibition also confronts the issues raised by Orientalism, which cut across the chronology of European painting, such as the various attempts to evoke an exotic, remote world, and the artistic solutions to the challenge of depicting unfamiliar terrain, customs, light and colour.

Prior to the Napoleonic campaigns of 1798–99,[6] Western interest in the Near East and North Africa had been fostered mainly through the medium of trade, intermittent political contact and a small quantity of travel books and imaginative literature concentrated primarily on the Ottoman Empire.[7] The early nineteenth century saw a particular conjunction of political events and artistic concerns which brought a rapid expansion of the West's contact with the Near East.[8] Whilst the development of the Picturesque aesthetic extended the interest in topography to the visiting and recording of unfamiliar lands, the growth of scientific and historical curiosity also called for accurate surveys and careful depictions of peoples and places in strange lands. This scientific impetus further produced a more empirical approach to the exploration of the Holy Land and to the understanding of the events of the Bible.[9] Finally, the political and commercial aspirations notably of France and Britain established their territorial hegemony over Egypt and North Africa, and saw the settlement of the Greek War of Independence, their support for the semi-autonomous ruler of Egypt, Muḥammad 'Alī, reforms within the Ottoman Empire and extensive investment in public utilities, including railways and the Suez Canal.[10]

The gradual penetration of the Near East and North Africa by an expansive Europe increased the variety of contacts with the Islamic lands. Some Europeans, like the writer, Trollope, were in the employ of pashas and potentates. Others swelled the growing ranks of tourists who found Thomas Cook's package tours, steamboats on the Nile and a burgeoning railway network at their service in the quest for visual, religious and historical experience.[11] Yet others went to the Near East with the intention of transmitting to Europe, in either paint or the written word, a world culturally remote, though physically increasingly accessible. Some artists – Delacroix, Bonnat, Makart, Roberts and Gleyre – visited the Orient only once in their careers. Others chose to return, sometimes frequently, as was the case with Gérôme, Holman Hunt, L. C. Müller and Horace Vernet. A few became addicted to the Islamic lands and stayed for long periods: Lewis lived in Cairo for ten years, Bauernfeind spent the end of his life in Jerusalem and Fromentin undertook protracted visits to the Sahara and the Sahel in North Africa,[12] as did Girardet and Guillaumet.[13]

American commercial interests and missionary programmes in the region likewise encouraged a small, but significant number of artist-travellers from the New World. During the first half of the nineteenth century, despite the establishment of trading relations with the Day of Algiers as early as 1805,[14] artistic involvement was very limited.[15] During the decade of the 1860s, however, organised travel, as described by Mark Twain in *Innocents Abroad*,[16] and guide books by authors such as Washington Irving, made the Near East and North Africa more generally accessible. In 1860, the landscape painter, Samuel Colman, travelled to Grenada and celebrated his discovery of Moorish architecture in works such as the *Hill of the Alhambra, Grenada*.[17] The success of this painting when it was exhibited at the National Academy of Design in New York in 1865, encouraged Colman's students, Robert Swain Gifford and Louis Comfort Tiffany, to undertake their own artistic ḥajj in 1870.[18] Frederic Edwin Church, the most important American landscape painter of the mid-nineteenth century, set out for Europe, the Mediterranean and the Holy Land in 1867,[19] and Sanford Robinson Gifford travelled to Egypt and the Near East in 1869.[20] Elihu Vedder visited Egypt in 1889,[21] although he had set his mystical paintings executed in the 1860s in landscapes purporting to be those of North Africa.

While these American-trained artists were recording the topography of lands more luminous and strange than those of the American West, a younger group of painters were studying in Paris, notably under Gérôme who had been appointed Professor

at the Ecole des Beaux-Arts in 1863. Of the large number of American artists whom Gérôme trained, Frederic Arthur Bridgeman and Edwin Lord Weekes adopted most comprehensively the French artist's characteristic Orientalist style.[22] In addition, American collectors, such as William H. Stewart, bought works by Gérôme,[23] and Stewart's son, Julius, also an artist, lived with Gérôme in Egypt for several months 'in a house that was an inspiration in itself, being, like the French Consulate in Cairo, constructed from the fragments of ceilings, ruins, and quaint Arabic monuments.'[24] Although not a pupil of Gérôme, John Singer Sargent had studied in Paris and travelled twice to the Orient, visiting North Africa in 1880 and Egypt and the Holy Land a decade later. The latter journey provided material for the artist's twenty-five-year project to decorate the walls of the Boston Public Library[25] while the former produced one of the most scintillating, mysterious images of American Orientalist art, the *Fumée d'Ambre Gris* (fig. 1).[26]

Alexandre-Gabriel Decamps (1803–1860), who went only once to Asia Minor but whose Oriental experience was so powerful that it established him as a leading Orientalist of his day, is omitted from the exhibition.[27] Decamps had travelled to Greece and then settled in Smyrna (Izmir) for over a year in 1828–29. He made a dramatic mark upon the Salon of 1831 with a group of Turkish scenes which shaped the pattern of most of his subsequent oeuvre

fig. 1 Sargent *Fumée d'Ambre Gris* 1880
[Sterling and Francine Clark Art Institute, Williamstown, Mass.]

(fig. 2). Praised at the time for their rich colour and varied Turkish subject-matter, most of his works have suffered badly from deterioration of their surfaces due to Decamps's extensive use of bitumen varnish, mixed into a coarse, thick impasto.[28]

The works of two artists, Baron Gros and Jean-Auguste-Dominique Ingres, who never travelled to North Africa or to the Near East, are nevertheless included in the exhibition because their particular visions of these regions profoundly marked Europe's expectations and interpretations of the Orient. Gros had been the 'propagandist' of Napoleon's military campaigns in northern Italy during the 1790s, and he was thus the obvious choice to produce a favourable, official interpretation of the ultimately-doomed Egyptian campaign. He painted three pictures which celebrate the exploits of Napoleon's armies, *The Battle of Nazareth* (Cat. 48), *The Battle of Abū Qīr* (Cat. 50) and *The Pesthouse at Jaffa* (Cat. 49), but he was prevented from travelling to the Near East to survey the sites of these events by the British naval control of the eastern Mediterranean. Instead, he relied upon eye-witness accounts through which he conjured up an exotic world of brilliant colour, dramatic turmoil and unfamiliar settings, which was to fix certain European preconceptions about the Near East. In addition, Gros recorded the events which instigated a lasting French cultural interest in the Near East: the exploration of archaeological sites under Vivant Denon (Cat. 20), the geographical survey of Egypt and the foundation of the Institut d'Egypte (1798), as well as many subsequent manifestations, such as the Egyptian Revival style in the decorative arts and Champollion's deciphering of the Rosetta stone.[29]

Like Gros, Ingres never went further south or east than Italy and yet, despite the position he was accorded as the leader of the French classical school, he had already displayed a more catholic taste early in his career. His interest in archaeologically-correct settings for his classical history paintings extended to the use of appropriate backgrounds and technique for his portraits and genre scenes.[30] Furthermore, his detailed rendering of the texture and colour of fabrics gave to his paintings a rich tone and a luxurious tactile surface. These two elements in his work were ideally suited to adding an Oriental dimension to the influential sequence of bathers (fig. 3) and odalisques (Cat. 56), which he created throughout his career. These nudes were derived from antique sculpture and delineated in clean, pure outline, but were given an exotic, Orientalist context by the magical colours and textures of Islamic interiors, derived from eighteenth-century illustrations and the descriptions found in the letters of Lady Mary Wortley Montague[31] and in Montesquieu's *Lettres persanes* (1721).

Ingres was not alone in gaining his understanding of the Islamic world through eighteenth-century images which had been shaped, with certain notable exceptions, more by exotic imagination than by fact.[32] Together with Gros's paintings of tumultuous drama and heightened colour, Ingres's representations of the Orient were to shape the expectations of both artists and the public throughout much of the nineteenth century. For some, even a visit to the Near East failed to displace these expectations. For others, the encounter with the Orient forced a modification of these expectations, the effects of which upon the resulting works of art were often radical.

One of the preoccupations which profoundly affected the Western understanding of the Near East was the belief that this region could satisfy the West's urge for exotic experience. Exoticism meant the artistic exploration of territories and ages in which the free flights of the imagination were possible because they lay outside the restrictive operation of classical rules. Despite the

fig. 2 Decamps *Sortie de l'école* 1841 [Wallace Collection, London]

existence of 'Turqueries' in the eighteenth century, Romanticism's celebration of the primacy of the imagination, together with the pattern of early nineteenth-century political and scholarly interests, guaranteed a position for the Islamic lands as one of the most effective locations for Western expressions of exoticism. Before he actually went to Algeria and Morocco in 1832, Delacroix, for example, had been attracted by an exotic Orient conjured up in the poems of Byron and in Hugo's *Orientales* (1829). In a sequence of powerful Oriental paintings he also drew upon the brutal events of the Greek War of Independence as well as a collection of Persian and Indian miniatures and Islamic objets d'art assembled by the traveller and artist, Jules-Robert Auguste (1789–1850).[33] Delacroix's works such as *The Combat between the*

fig. 3 Ingres *Le Bain turc* 1862 [Musée du Louvre, Paris]

*Giaour and the Pasha* (Cat. 12) and *The Death of Sardanapalus* (Salon of 1827; see Cat. 16)[34] were flamboyant confirmations of the imaginary force of the exotic idea in art, which he shared with other artists in his circle, notably Géricault and Bonington, all of whom sought to extend their subject-matter and technique beyond the classical sphere.

The vision of an exotic Orient – passionate, cruel and intoxicating – which fired Delacroix to accept with alacrity an invitation to visit North Africa in 1832, was shared by many Western visitors to the Near East. In 1868, Paul Lenoir, the artist who gives one of the most revealing accounts of a visit to the Near East, confirmed the persistence of the idea of the exotic Orient when he embarked upon his journey to Egypt, Sinai and Petra, in the company of Gérôme, Edmond About[35] and Frédéric Masson. He described it as *'cette grande féerie* [enchantment] *qu'on appelle un voyage en Orient'*, the beginning of which he likened to the 'raising of the curtain',[36] as if he were setting forth on a voyage into a theatrical world where illusion rather than reality was to be the guiding principle. The imaginary exotic Orient was also given a more particular focus in the fascination which Western visitors had for the women of the East. These unobtainable women, with their veils and secretive lives, haunted the Western visitor and goaded him to seek access, if only in his imagination, to the forbidden quarters of the harem and the bath.[37] Renoir, when in Algiers, noted that Arab women were 'clever enough to know the value of mystery. An eye half-seen through a veil becomes really alluring!',[38] while Gérard de Nerval related his own fascination in more literary terms: 'Does one not dream of adventure and mysteries at the sight of these tall houses, these latticed windows, where so often one sees the sparkle of the inquiring eyes of young girls?'[39] It is symptomatic of the strength of this image that, despite the heightened interest in the truthful representation of the Near East and North Africa during the nineteenth century, the harem, the bath and the guard to the seraglio remained amongst the most popular manifestations of Orientalism in both painting and literature. While Gérôme (Cat. 33), Ingres (Cat. 56), Lewis (Cat. 73) and Benjamin-Constant (Cat. 5) could produce infinite variations on these themes, so too the subject could be celebrated in the imaginary literature of de Molines[40] and the Princesse Belgiojoso,[41] and in the lyrical novel of Pierre Loti, *Aziyadé*,[42] part fact and part fiction.

Parallel to such popular images of an exotic Orient, which coloured many Western perceptions of the Near East, was a range of hostile opinion which found much to condemn in particular facets of Muslim culture. The critic Emile Galichon, for example, discussed Gérôme's *Le Prisonnier du Nil* (fig. 4) as a painting which possessed 'all the Orient', by which he meant 'implacable fatalism', 'passive submission' and 'blatant cruelty',[43] a conclusion with which the artist, Benjamin-Constant, concurred in his work, *L'Exécution des rebelles*, which deliberately lingers on the wanton cruelty of an Arab potentate (see Cat. 4). J. C. M. Bellows,[44] Lamartine[45] and E. W. Lane[46] all deplored the indolence which they saw as the prime cause of the ruinous state of the contemporary Ottoman Empire. The painter, David Roberts, went further and blamed indolence, in conjunction with Islam, as the root cause of the deplorable condition of Egypt: 'Splendid cities once teeming with a busy population and embellished with temples and edifices, the wonder of the world, now deserted and lonely, or reduced by mismanagement and the barbarism of the Muslim creed to a state as savage as wild animals by which they are surrounded. Often have I gazed on them till my heart actually sickened within me.'[47] The theme of the 'barbarism of the Muslim creed' was taken up by Lenoir in his description of the departure of the great caravan of pilgrims from Cairo to Mecca as an example of *'une religion idiote et barbare'*.[48] By the same token, K. Bendiner[49] has pointed out how, in the many views of Jerusalem painted during the nineteenth century, the Mosque of Omar frequently appears to stand like a predatory animal over the destroyed Temple of Solomon (see Cat. 23, 61).

At the same time, many artists travelling in the Near East and North Africa found much to admire. When Delacroix made his brief trip in 1832, he willingly adjusted his imaginary preconceptions in the face of the unsurpassed beauty of Morocco and Algeria and the nobility of their peoples, who became for him,

fig. 4 Gérôme *Le Prisonnier du Nil* 1861 [Musée des Beaux-Arts, Nantes]

paradoxically, the reincarnation of the classical ideal of Greece and Rome:

*'I am truly sorry for the artists gifted with imagination who can never have any idea of this virgin, sublime nature . . . I can only look forward with sadness to the moment when I shall leave forever the land of beautiful orange trees covered with flowers and fruit, of the beautiful sun, of the beautiful eyes and of a thousand other beauties . . . Rome is no longer in Rome . . . Imagine, my friend, what it is to see figures of the Age of the Consuls, Catos, Brutuses, seated in the sun, walking in the streets, mending old shoes . . . The Antique has nothing that is more beautiful.'*[50]

Similarly Gautier, a most perceptive commentator on the Orient, noted the discrepancy between his own exotic preconceptions of a Muslim husband's relationship with his wives and the dignified reality as he saw it:

*'If one becomes aware of the dignity and even the chastity which exist between a Muslim and his wives, one would renounce all this voluptuous mirage which our writers of the eighteenth century have created, the idea of these harems described by the author of the* Lettres persanes.*'*[51]

Sympathetic observation could also be found in Lady Duff Gordon's letters, written during her five-year sojourn in Egypt (1863–69), which repeatedly refer to the excellence, the industry and the nobility of modern Egyptians.[52] Above all, many Westerners responded with awe and considerable respect to the practices of the Muslim faith. The scenes of mosque interiors by Gérôme (Cat. 34, 40) and Deutsch (Cat. 22) stress the equality of worshippers in the sight of Allah and the solemnity of the religious celebrations. Belly's *Pilgrims going to Mecca* (Cat. 3) and Gérôme's *Mu'adhdin's Call to Prayer* (Cat. 38) illustrate Islam's regulation of all aspects of the believer's life.

Some visitors carried their enthusiasm for the Orient even further and saw the influence of the West as potentially disastrous to North Africa and the Near East. The artist Guillaumet, who spent a considerable time in the remote, southern regions of Algeria, deplored the march of modernisation in that country, especially the 'frenchification' of the capital, Algiers: 'They demolish without letting up in Algiers, the mauresque peristyles, the gateways of sculpted marble . . . Life here no longer seems as before, held together by dreams and bringing life to the shadows.'[53] For many commentators,[54] the pastoral primitive life and the biblical atmosphere of the Arab villages appealed to an almost Rousseauesque desire to escape from the debasement of the human spirit supposedly brought about by Western civilisation.

The degree to which Orientalist painters ever fully comprehended the Muslim world or considered the consequences, if any, for the indigenous population of their celebration of primitivism is problematical. Some commentators have tried to view all Orientalist manifestations as an aspect of cultural imperialism.[55] Yet, the evidence would suggest that this is too simplistic an interpretation of both Western visitors' intentions and their artistic work. The Western approach to the Orient was neither unchanging, without its own inconsistencies, nor closed to the influence of observation. Flaubert attempted in 1850 to analyse the shift which had taken place in his own attitudes to the Orient since his arrival in Egypt in late 1849. His comment is most revealing:

*'You ask me whether the Orient is up to what I imagined it to be. Yes it is; and more than that, it extends far beyond the narrow idea*

*I had of it. I have found, clearly delineated, everything that was hazy in my mind. Facts have taken the place of supposition.'*[56]

Flaubert's encounter with Egypt illustrates the meeting point of Western prejudice and the observation of the Orient, and his response was to redefine certain of his attitudes. By the same token, many painters faced the need to modify their artistic conventions, which they brought with them from Europe, such as the Picturesque approach to landscape and the established means for notating light and colour. This process may be closer to a 'dialogue' between cultures than a 'discourse', to pick up Edward Said's terminology as laid out in his book *Orientalism*.[57] In this sense Delacroix had already engaged in a 'dialogue' with North Africa, albeit idiosyncratically. The emergence in the next generation of European painters in the 1850s of a more Realist approach to subject-matter, further developed this 'dialogue', coinciding as it did with the first flood of artists to the Near East and North Africa.[58]

One of the major impulses for artists travelling to the Orient in the wake of the Napoleonic campaigns had been to provide a record of the topography and the customs of places and peoples unfamiliar to the West.[59] During the eighteenth century, European artists had already undertaken such an exercise with the landscapes of Italy and northern Europe, and had devised the artistic conventions of the Picturesque, whereby a landscape painting was composed according to the rules of the ideal landscapes of Poussin and Claude. At first sight, the Oriental landscapes of Dauzats (Cat. 11), Marilhat (Cat. 75), Lear (Cat. 60), Roberts (Cat. 90) and Frère (Cat. 23) seem perfectly to exemplify the application of Picturesque conventions. The spectator's eye is carefully directed to proceed from a foreground composed of native figures or fragments of ruined monuments, framed by trees, buildings or a projection of higher land, toward the middle distance containing the main subject of the view (a monastery, a ruined mosque, the Island of Philae, the City of Jerusalem), and finally to the background where land meets sky in a misty horizon. However, on closer inspection, it can be seen that in order to accommodate these strange landscape subjects each of these artists has modified in various ways the conventions of the Picturesque. David Roberts, for example, in *The Island of Philae, Nubia* (Cat. 90) adopts a 'fish-eye' lens view as the only means by which he is able to frame an object in the middle distance of an empty landscape devoid of 'natural' Picturesque elements. For Lear, in his view of the same subject (Cat. 60), it is the Picturesque handling of light which he modifies rather than the composition, emphasising, by means of translucent glazes over a thick, smooth, white ground, the range and intensity of a landscape lit by an Egyptian sunset.

The need to invent new compositional structures to compensate for the absence of conveniently placed vegetation and undulating hills in a vast, often barren and featureless landscape, was a major formal problem for Orientalist painters, which Belly and Guillaumet above all confronted. In his 1857 Salon review, Gautier had remarked upon the impressive increase in the number of pictures depicting strange lands and peoples and concluded that, while these outnumbered the traditionally dominant subjects of classical nudes and history paintings, their presence did not necessarily threaten the future of French painting. He argued that the need to come to terms with foreign subject-matter might indeed prove to be the basis for exciting aesthetic innovations:

*'From these effortless journeys is born a varied art, changeable, many faceted, whose chief characteristic is not to have one. What master can be consulted for models as yet unexpressed? What tradition can be*

*followed where there is no tradition? Each artist searches, invents and renders in his own way that which he sees and that which he feels. Where there is no ready-made formula for a subject, individualism is truly forced to come to the fore.'*[60]

The transcription of a flat, featureless desert, a subject handled by both Belly and Guillaumet, reveals the willingness of artists to invent their own visual vocabularies. Guillaumet's *The Desert* (Cat. 51) blatantly accepts the emptiness, the extreme horizontality and the remarkable light effects of his subject. He makes no concessions to existing Western conventions, apart from the inclusion of the camel's carcass in the foreground as a *'memento mori'*. Belly, in his *Pilgrims going to Mecca* (Cat. 3), takes the pilgrims as the compositional anchor for the work, piling them pyramidally at the centre of the composition and letting the flat desert slip off the edges of the canvas, a device which conveys the limitless expanse of the landscape. Furthermore, by placing the figures against the blinding light of the desert, he monumentalises the group in their solemn, arduous and hazardous journey and, at the same time, stresses the impact of the burning sun which catches the line of pilgrims winding back through the composition.

Belly's concern with capturing strange light as much as with compositional innovation points to a second area in which artists were challenged by what they found in the Near East: the relationship between an Oriental light and a Western palette. For a number of Orientalist painters, exoticism and Orientalism were synonymous with brilliant, explosive colour. In the wake of Gros, artists such as Dehodencq, Decamps, Benjamin-Constant and to a certain extent Lewis and Bauernfeind, all adopted the kind of palette which Gautier had in mind when he observed that 'normally one represents hot lands in a flamboyant, torrid manner'.[61] But Gautier then added the important qualification that 'extreme light under its streaming whiteness drains colour from the sky, from the land'.[62] It was indeed no new proposition to be reminded that the intensity of light in the sky determined the hue of the landscape. But under the extreme illumination of the Oriental latitudes, the palette of the artist had to be that much more responsive. This awareness of the properties of light and its translation into paint were already seen in France, in 1864, as the most prominent contribution of Orientalist painting to French art. Five years

before the emergence of a fully-fledged Impressionist style, Hector de Callias could declare: 'French painting owes a great debt to the passion for the Orient. This passion has given it what until now has been lacking, light and the sun. What is, in effect, missing from the French gallery at the Louvre? It is neither style in drawing nor the science of composition, nor again the harmony of colour. It is the rays of the sun.'[63]

Orientalist painters did not respond uniformly to their encounter with this alien light. Delacroix, for example, found in the light and colour of North Africa the justification of his system of complementary colours by which he intensified the tonal range of his palette and introduced pure colour into shadow, as in the remarkable shadow areas of *Les Femmes d'Alger* (fig. 5) and the *Sultān of Morocco* (Cat. 17). It was the example of Delacroix that encouraged Renoir twice to visit Algeria. He wished to test the efficacy of Delacroix's colour system as well as hoping to find new inspiration which might help him escape from the apparent limitations of Impressionism. Although he produced only a small number of pictures during his brief visits, Renoir reveals his exuberant response to the distinctive landscapes, townscapes and people, interpreted by a renewed enthusiasm for pure colour and a serious commitment to the modification of the handling of his paint.

However, both Delacroix and Renoir also discovered that the light of North Africa contained a whiteness which cloaked all colours in a delicate grey film. Baudelaire, in his 'Salon de 1845', noted this effect in Delacroix's *Sultān of Morocco*: 'In spite of the splendour of its hues, this picture is so harmonious that it is grey – as grey as nature, as grey as the summer atmosphere when the sun spreads over each object a sort of twilight film of trembling dust.'[64] Indeed, this was the very quality which Fromentin also observed in his extensive discussion of the problems of painting in North Africa and which he attempted to express in his own works, such as *Windstorm on the Esparto Plains of the Sahara* (Cat. 25): 'I talk of this country, dusty, bleached, somewhat raw when it becomes coloured, rather gloomy when no live colour awakens it, thus uniform and hiding an infinite number of particles of nuances and values under this apparent unity of tones . . . In fact, never before us, as far as I know, has anyone bothered to do battle with this capital obstacle, the sun, nor dreamt that one of the aims of painting was to be able to express, with the poor means that you know we have, the excess of solar light, enhanced by its diffusion.'[65]

Fromentin's forthright acceptance of the challenge presented by the light of North Africa points to a further ingredient in Orientalist painting, namely the influence of Realism. For Delacroix and Decamps, the careful recording of incidental detail in North Africa and Asia Minor was not their primary concern. But, by the midnineteenth century, the truthful representation of the external world, based upon objective observation, set an aesthetic standard for artists and patrons alike. Flaubert[66] and Richard Burton[67] noted with meticulous detail their respective Near Eastern journeys. When Lenoir discussed the purpose of his 1868 Egyptian trip, he said: 'Without having pretentions to seeing everything, we wanted to look carefully in order to paint *dal vero* that which we saw.'[68] Similarly, William Holman Hunt, writing from Jerusalem, counselled humility in a foreign land: 'I have a notion that painters should go out, two by two, like merchants of nature, and bring back precious merchandise in faithful pictures of scenes interesting from historical considerations or from the strangeness of the subject itself.'[69]

The influence of Realism on Orientalist painting was felt

fig. 5 Delacroix *Les Femmes d'Alger* 1834 [Musée du Louvre, Paris]

throughout the second half of the nineteenth century. On the one hand, it generated a new school of religious painting. No longer content with religious images derived from Renaissance models, artists such as Tissot and Holman Hunt travelled in the Holy Land to search out the peoples and landscapes which could provide material for a more authentic reconstruction of the events and locations described in the Bible.[70] On the other hand, Realism called forth a new category of art, known as 'ethnographic' painting. By 1850, European painters had already developed an interest in the study of social and regional types which encouraged them to differentiate more precisely the landscapes and inhabitants of specific geographic locations. The Orientalists carried this concern into less familiar territory.[71] While Pierre Loti carefully located his novels, *Aziyadé* (1877) and *Le Roman d'un spahi* (1881), in Asia Minor and the Sahara respectively, Gérôme headed a school of painters who took pride in being able to distinguish between the physiognomies of Circassians, Turks and Egyptians as well as between the finer shades of Mauresque, Mamlūk, Ottoman and Byzantine architecture and decorative detail.

The high finish and meticulous rendering of detail in most 'ethnographic' paintings encouraged the spectator to accept them as literally truthful images. Yet closer inspection of pictures in this genre can reveal some observational inaccuracies. Despite the fact that since 1834 all 'ālmahs, or prostitutes, had been banned from Cairo, Gérôme's *Dance of the 'Ālmah* (1864; Cat. 31) still includes a glimpse of the characteristic pink- and yellow-banded buildings of Cairo through the door. Lecomte-du-Nouÿ's *Guard of the Seraglio* (1876; Cat. 64) introduces jumbled architectural elements in the manner of a *capriccio* into a painting subtitled 'Souvenir of Cairo'. And, as Linda Nochlin has pointed out, there are no images which describe the poverty, dirt and disease which almost all travellers to the region commented upon with varying degrees of sympathy.

Both *Dance of the 'Ālmah* and *The Guard of the Seraglio* proved to be immensely popular images. The latter found a purchaser even before it was exhibited at the Salon of 1876, whilst the former received ecstatic public acclaim and a generally favourable response from the critics when it was shown at the Salon of 1864. The enthusiastic taste for such Orientalist paintings yields no ready explanations.[72] These paintings were available in increasing numbers during the nineteenth century in keeping with other genres through annual exhibitions at the Royal Academy and at the Paris Salon.[73] They were displayed at the International Exhibitions, through dealers — both those who owned galleries, such as Goupil in Paris and Gambart in London and those who worked privately, such as George Lucas in Paris — and in widely-circulated engravings. Some Orientalist painters certainly commanded high prices for their works, notably Fromentin,[74] Lewis,[75] Gérôme[76] and Decamps, a factor which might also explain the frequent production of copies or variants of popular paintings. There seemed to be no end to the combinations of light filtering through latticed screens into cool interiors replete with graceful, pale women and Oriental bric-à-brac which Lewis could conjure up. Equally, Gérôme and Deutsch could produce endless variations on the theme of *bashibazuks* carousing, *ālmahs* dancing, Arnavuts smoking and Muslims praying. In terms of the demand for Oriental paintings, several significant collections were assembled at the time, notably those of John Walters in Baltimore, the Marquis of Hertford (later the Wallace Collection), the Duc d'Aumâle at Chantilly and David in Nantes. Yet the reasons for such concentrations of Orientalist works are far from simple. All four men collected a variety of nineteenth-century paintings and, while the

fig. 6 Maxime du Camp, Baalbec, Lebanon   Daguerreotype   1850

Duc d'Aumâle had ample reason for collecting Orientalist works, since he had actually campaigned in North Africa, and Wallace was ambassador in Constantinople, neither Walters nor David appear ever to have set foot in the Orient.

Orientalism also touches upon two further artistic issues of the period, namely the protracted search for 'modern' painting and the relationship between art and photography. The difficulty of finding an artistic idiom capable of expressing the aspirations of the contemporary world became a matter of great urgency in mid-nineteenth-century Britain and even more so in France. Both Jules Janin[77] and Théophile Gautier[78] proposed that Orientalist painting might have an answer to this problem. Realism demanded that the artist should paint in front of nature. Yet, in contemporary Europe, this laid Realism open to the possibility of including low subject-matter rendered in coarse technique, evident in the art of Courbet, which prevented any reference to the principles of eternal beauty. The advantage of Orientalist painting was that by depicting living scenes in a world sufficiently remote and timeless the artist could make a record according to the principles of Realism and simultaneously intend the result to stand as an example of eternal beauty.

The debate over the relationship between art and photography (fig. 6) in the nineteenth century centred primarily on the degree to which the one would usurp the role of the other. For the Orientalist painter, however, the photograph was early accorded an important position. On his trip to Egypt in 1839, Horace Vernet became one of the first artists to employ the daguerreotype as a faster and more accurate method of sketching.[79] His example was followed by almost all the Orientalist painters, from Holman Hunt and Seddon to Gérôme, Deutsch, Roberts and William Müller. The advantages of the mechanical eye were considered overwhelming and Gautier was quick to recognise this fact:

'[Art] has set off in all directions on the wing of steam: new countries, unexplored climates, unknown types, unrecorded races present themselves to it in all parts. After 6000 years, it takes possession of a real world which up until now it had only viewed indistinctly. The photograph, this humble servant, takes notes for [art], and the sun draws upon its travel notebooks the men, the animals, the plants, the rocks, the monuments, the statues, the remarkable sites with an infallible certainty and a mathematical precision; vast quantities of *material, sketches almost devoid of labour, are at the disposition [of art]'.[80]*

In this regard, Orientalist painting also fostered the professional photographer. Individuals such as Le Gray, Maxime du Camp, Beato and Francis Frith, together with survey teams under the auspices of the Ordnance Survey and the Palestine Exploration Fund provided accurate delineations of ancient sites and local customs for a diverse public of archaeologists, anthropologists, tourists, and even artists themselves.[81]

The last two decades of the nineteenth century saw a significant diversification in Orientalist painting. To be sure, Gérôme, and his followers Aublet, Ernst and Deutsch, continued to produce their highly wrought transcriptions of the Near East, but as early as 1876, the critic Castagnary was fervently looking forward to the demise of Orientalist painting: 'In a few years, we shall be able to erect a stone and engrave upon it these comforting words: "Orientalism has lived in French painting".'[82] Castagnary's wish was not, however, fully granted. The Orientalist painters in France were sufficiently numerous and well-organised to arrange from 1894[83] an annual salon devoted to their work, and the discoveries of Impressionism encouraged a school of 'colonialist' painters in North Africa which survived until the Second World War.[84]

In addition, there was a younger generation of artists whose encounter with the Orient ensued from a set of new artistic objectives. Renoir, Sargent, Brangwyn, Emile Bernard, Matisse and Kandinsky had all cast their art within the new pictorial tradition in Europe which asserted that painting should achieve something more than the mere transcription of the external world. For some of these artists, the trip to North Africa and the Near East provided the basis for the discovery of fresh ways to handle paint and a new perception of colour, as in the case of Renoir, Brangwyn and Sargent. For Matisse and Kandinsky, the Orient confirmed a style which, through reference to a combination of the primitive elements and the intense colour of the Oriental world, consolidated the radical innovations introduced earlier in their artistic careers, which were to prove central to the evolution of Modern art.

Matisse's and Kandinsky's individual responses to the Orient represent one aspect of the encounter of the West with the Near East and North Africa. The resulting works of art tell us less about the 'reality' of North Africa than they inform us about each artist's own position on the issues facing European art at the beginning of the twentieth century. In contrast, Fromentin's admission of his technical and intellectual impotence, when confronted with the Orient, reveals the degree to which Western artists could conscientiously seek adequate visual formulations by which the essence of these strange lands could be captured on canvas. Apart from the exploration of the exotic idea in art and the interaction with Realism as an artistic principle, perhaps the encounter with light is the most enduring quality of Orientalist art. Hector de Callias, in his article of 1864, correctly identified this particular characteristic of the Orientalists.[85] So too Flaubert awoke to the intense colour provoked by the light of these lands in his description of the sun rising over the Great Pyramids of Gizah:

*'The sun was rising just opposite; the whole valley of the Nile, bathed in mist, seemed to be a still white sea; and the desert behind us with its hillocks of sand, another ocean, deep purple, its waves all petrified. But as the sun climbed behind the Arabian Chain the mist was torn into great shreds of filmy gauze; the meadows, cut by canals, were like green lawns with winding borders. To sum up: three colours — immense green at my feet in the foreground; the sky pale red — worn vermilion; behind and to the right, a rolling expanse looking scorched and irridescent . . . Finally the sky shows a streak of orange where the sun is about to rise. Everything between the horizon and us is white and looks like an ocean; this recedes and lifts. The sun, it seems, is moving fast and climbing along the oblong clouds that look like swan's down of an inexpressible softness. . . . The light increases. There are two things: the dry desert behind us and before us an immense, delightful expanse of green.'[86]*

Indeed, whatever their motives, the fact that artists chose to explore the Near East and North Africa during the nineteenth century opened up a vast store of pictorial motifs and presented a challenge to the conventions of their Western artistic learning. And to be sure, almost all the paintings which emerged from this encounter between two cultures speak of an enthusiasm for these foreign lands, witnesses to their splendour, their enchantment and their powerful fascination.

NOTES

1 E. Fromentin, *Une Année dans le Sahel*, Paris, 1858, 1981 ed., pp. 174–75, 177.

2 The phrase 'Middle East' was coined only in 1902, by the American historian, A. T. Mahon, to distinguish the region of the eastern Mediterranean from the Far East; see A. Williams, *Britain and France in the Middle East and North Africa*, London, 1968, chap. 1. Prior to that date, the terms 'Near East' and 'Orient' were used to describe this region.

3 K. P. Bendiner, 'The Portrayal of the Middle East in British Painting, 1835–1860', Ph. D. thesis, Columbia University, 1979, gives a careful discussion of the problems of defining the term 'Orientalism'. He concludes that, although Greece could be included within the term, 'Classicism is too intimately connected to the culture and history of Western Europe to be classified as an Orientalist subject' (p. iii).

4 These range from the strictly art historical issues, through the study of art within its cultural context to the analysis of art as an aspect of politics, whereby the encounter is seen as the domination of one culture by another. See L. Nochlin, 'The Imaginary Orient', *Art in America*, May 1983, pp. 119–31, 187–91; E. Said, *Orientalism*, New York, 1978.

5 Guildhall Art Gallery, London.

6 See Irwin, p. 24, Cat. 32, 48, 49, 50.

7 See S. Searight, *The British in the Middle East*, London, 1969, Part I; P. Martino, *L'Orient dans la littérature française au XVIIᵉ et au XVIIIᵉ siècles*, Paris, 1908; P. Hughes, *Eighteenth-century France and the East* (Wallace Collection Monographs, 4), London, 1981; Rochester, New York, Memorial Art Gallery, *Orientalism*, catalogue by D. Rosenthal, chap. 1.

8 Both political and cultural historians have seen the arrival of Napoleon in 1798 as an event of dramatic consequence for Europe and Near East alike; see B. Lewis, *The Middle East and the West*, London 1964, p. 34; J. Alazard, *L'Orient dans la peinture française au XIXᵉ siècle*, Paris, 1930, chap. 1, especially p. 21.

9 See Warner, pp. 32–35.

10 See D. S. Landes, *Bankers and Pashas*, London, 1958.

11 See Bugler, pp. 29–30.

12 Fromentin recorded his experiences in two books, *Un Eté dans le Sahara*, Paris, 1856, and *Une Année dans le Sahel*, Paris, 1858.

13 See G. Guillaumet, *Tableaux algériens*, Paris, 1888.

14 The United States Senate signed a trade agreement with the Day of Algiers on 2 March 1797, whereby safety of American shipping in the Mediterranean was guaranteed in exchange for the delivery of a frigate, 'The Crescent'. The treaty failed to hold, and commercial relations were only finally established with the capture of Tangier by the United States in 1805.

15 The Philadelphian sculptor and a founder of America's first art academy, William Rush, was commissioned to design the figurehead and decorative scheme for the frigate, 'The Crescent' (1982, Philadelphia, Pennsylvania Academy of Fine Arts, *William Rush, American Sculptor*, p. 102). Michèle Felice Corné, the protegé of the Salem merchant, Elias Hasket Derby, created a sixty-foot panorama entitled *The Seige of Tripoli*, which was exhibited in the Boston region (M. M. Swan and L. Karr, 'Early Marine Painters of Salem', *Antiques*, 1940, p. 64).

16 Mark Twain (Samuel Langhorne Clemens), *Innocents Abroad; or, the New Pilgrims Progress*, Hartford, 1869.

17 Metropolitan Museum of Art, New York; see W. Craven, 'Samuel Colman (1832–1920): Rediscovered Painter of Far-Away Places', *American Art Journal*, May, 1976, p. 19.

18 *R. Swain Gifford 1840–1905*, Old Dartmouth Historical Society, New Bedford, 1974, p. xiv.

19 D. C. Huntington, *The Landscapes of Frederic Edwin Church*, New York, 1963, pp. 93–101.

20 I. Weiss, *Sanford Robinson Gifford, 1823–1880*, New York, 1970, p. 276.

21 1979, Washington D.C., National Collection of Fine Arts, *Perceptions and Evocations: The Art of Elihu Vedder*, p. 58.

22 1976, Dayton, Art Institute, *American Expatriate Painters of the Late Nineteenth Century*, pp. 88, 142.

23 Stewart owned Gérôme's *Mosque, El Assaneyn* (now in the Forbes Collection, New York); see also 1898, New York, American Art Association, *Catalogue of the Modern Masterpieces Gathered by the Late Connoisseur William H. Stewart*, no. 39.

24 L. McProud, *American Students' Census, Paris, 1903*, Paris, 1903, p. 111.

25 C. Radcliffe, *John Singer Sargent*, New York, 1982, pp. 55, 57, 126–55.

26 Sterling and Francine Clark Art Institute, Williamstown.

27 For a comprehensive study of Decamps, see D. Mosby, *Alexandre-Gabriel Decamps*, New York, 1977.

28 The best examples of Decamps's work are to be found in the Château de Chantilly and the Wallace Collection, London, neither of which institution is permitted to lend works from its collection.

29 See N. Pevsner and S. Lang, 'The Egyptian Revival', *Architectural Review*, May 1956, pp. 242–54; J. Stevens Curl, *The Egyptian Revival, an Introductory Study of a Recurring Theme in the History of Taste*, London, 1982.

30 See, for example, the use of Flemish fifteenth-century background and technique in *Mlle. Rivière* (1805; Louvre, Paris).

31 Lady Mary Wortley Montague, *Letters*, London, 1727.

32 Throughout the eighteenth century, the Orient was visually conveyed in 'turqueries', or 'fêtes galantes' transposed into a Turkish setting, for example, in the works of Van Loo and Nattier. It was also evoked in the turbaned figures introduced into the Western port scenes of Claude-Joseph Vernet. Exceptionally, there were the paintings by the Swiss artist, J.-F. Liotard, which were derived from actual observation, as were a few illustrated publications such as Comte de Fériol's, *Recueil de cents estampes représentant différentes nations du Levant*, Paris 1712, and L. F. Cassas, *Voyage pittoresque en Syrie*, Paris, c. 1785. See A. Maubert, 'L'Exotisme dans la peinture française du XVIIIᵉ siècle', dissertation, Paris, 1943; A. Boppe, *Les Introducteurs des ambassadeurs*, Paris, 1901; A. Boppe, *Les Peintres du Bosphore au XVIIIᵉ siècle*, Paris, 1911.

33 For a full study of Jules-Robert Auguste, see D. Rosenthal, 'Jules-Robert Auguste and the Early Romantic Circle', Ph.D. thesis, Columbia University, 1978.

34 Musée du Louvre, Paris.

35 Critic and writer whose novel, *Le Fellah, Souvenir d'Egypte*, Paris, 1869, was based upon his experiences on the 1868 trip and was dedicated to J.-L. Gérôme.

36 P. Lenoir, *Le Fayoum, le Sinaï et Pétra*, Paris, 1872, p. 3.

37 See Th. Gautier, *Constantinople*, Paris, 1853, pp. 164–65, 166, 189, 199–200.

38 Quoted J. Renoir, *Renoir*, Paris, 1962, p. 228.

39 G. de Nerval, *Voyage en Orient*, Paris, 1851.

40 P. de Molines, 'Aisha Rosa, Souvenirs des rives du Bosphore', *Revue des Deux Mondes*, 15 December 1856.

41 Princesse Belgiojoso, 'Récits turco-asiatiques', *Revue des Deux Mondes*, 1856–58.

42 *Aziyadé*, Paris, 1877.

43 E. Galichon, 'M. Gérôme, peintre ethnographe', *Gazette des Beaux-Arts*, 1ère période, XXIV, February 1868, p. 150.

44 J. C. M. Bellows, 'The Seven Churches of Asia Minor', *Art Journal*, February 1863, p. 36.

45 A. de Lamartine, *Souvenirs, impressions, pensées et paysages pendant un voyage en Orient*, Paris, 1835, vol. II, p. 8.

46 E. W. Lane, *An Account of the Manners and Customs of the Modern Egyptians*, London, 1836, 1895 ed., p. 285.

47 D. Roberts, quoted J. Ballantine, *The Life of David Roberts*, London, 1866, pp. 104–05.

48 P. Lenoir, *op. cit.*, p. 134.

49 K. Bendiner, *op. cit.*, p. 41.

50 E. Delacroix, *Correspondance générale de Eugène Delacroix*, A. Joubin ed., Paris, I, 23 February 1832, p. 313; I, 29 February 1832, p. 319.

51 Th. Gautier, *op. cit.*, pp. 164–65.

52 Lady Duff Gordon, *Letters from Egypt*, partial ed., London, 1865, 1983 ed., especially pp. 59, 79.

53 G. Guillaumet, *op. cit.*, pp. 312–13.

54 See P. Lenoir, *op. cit.*, pp. 123, 145; also Warner, pp. 32–33.

55 This is a position held notably by E. Said, *Orientalism*, New York, 1978. Said claims that the West's political and economic engagement in the Near East and North Africa during the nineteenth century constituted Imperialist domination of these regions and that all art, be it literary or pictorial, was created to reinforce Western superiority vis à vis these lands, rather than as an attempt to understand the multifarious aspects of their cultures. See also the reviews of E. Said's book, eg. Sadik Jalal al-'Azm, 'Orientalism and Orientalism in Reverse', *Khamsin*, No. 8, 1981, pp. 5–25, Basim Masallam, 'Power and Knowledge', *MERIP Reports*, no. 79, pp. 19–26. This question is also discussed in L. Nochlin, *loc. cit.* An alternative critique of E. Said is given in eg. A. Hourani, *New York Review of Books*, 8 March 1979, pp. 27–30.

56 *Flaubert in Egypt*, transl. and ed. F. Steegmuller, Chicago, 1979, p. 75.

57 E. Said, *op. cit.*, p. 3.

58 X. Marmier, *Les Voyageurs Nouveaux*, Paris, 1851, pp. 369–71, 390.

59 See Bugler, p. 27.

60 Th. Gautier, 'Salon de 1857–1', *L'Artiste*, 14 June 1857, p. 190.

61 Th. Gautier, 'Salon de 1857–IV: MM. Gérôme, Mottez', *L'Artiste*, 5 July 1857, p. 247.

62 *Idem.*

63 H. de Callias, 'Le Salon de 1864–XVII: Les Italiens et les orientaux', *L'Artiste*, 1864, vol. I, p. 198.

64 Ch. Baudelaire, 'The Salon of 1845', *Art in Paris 1845–1862*, transl. J. Mayne, London, 1965, p. 6.

65 E. Fromentin, *op. cit.*, p. 177.

66 G. Flaubert, *Notes de voyage*, Paris, 1910.

67 R. Burton, *Personal Narrative of a Pilgrimage to El-Medinah and Mecca*, 3 vols., London, 1855.

68 P. Lenoir, *op. cit.*, p. 1.

69 Letter dated 'Jerusalem, 12 August 1855', quoted K. Bendiner, *op. cit.*, p. 14.

70 See Warner, pp. 33–34.

71 Th. Gautier, 'Le Salon de 1857–IV: MM. Gérôme, Mottez', *L'Artiste*, 5 July 1857, p. 245.

72 It has been suggested that Orientalist painting contrived to make available experiences forbidden to the prurient West (see L. Nochlin, *loc. cit.*). E. Said, *op. cit.*, implies that the ownership of Orientalist painting denotes the desire of the West both to dominate the Near East and to reinforce the West's own sense of cultural superiority.

73 Further research is needed in analysing the quantity of Orientalist paintings shown at the major annual exhibitions as an indication of changing patterns of taste.

74 Eg. Cat. 24 fetched 19,000 francs in 1881.

75 Eg. Cat. 68 would not be sold by its owner in 1874, despite an offer of £10,000.

76 See L. M. C. Randall (ed.), *The Diary of George A. Lucas*, Princeton, 1979.

77 J. Janin, 'Le Salon de 1839: 5ᵉ article', *L'Artiste*, 1939, vol. II, p. 269.

78 Th. Gautier, 'Le Salon de 1857–IV :MM. Gérôme, Mottez', *L'Artiste*, 5 July 1857, p. 245.

79 H. Vernet, *Voyage daguerrienne*, Paris, 1841.

80 Th. Gautier, 'Le Salon de 1857–I', *L'Artiste*, 14 June 1857, p. 190.

81 See L. Vaczek and G. Buckland, *Travellers in Ancient Lands. A Portrait of the Middle East 1839–1919*, New York, 1981.

82 Castagnary, 'Salon de 1876', *Salons*, p. 224.

83 Société des Peintres Orientalistes Français, founded by Léonce Bénédite, 1893.

84 Société des Peintres Algériens et Orientalistes, founded in Algiers, 1897; the Villa Abd el Tif founded by M. Jonnart, Governor of Algeria in 1907, for French artists wishing to work in North Africa. Scholarships were offered to two artists for a year each and, from 1920, one of the Scholarships was extended to two years.

85 H. de Callias, *loc. cit.*

86 G. Flaubert, *op. cit.*, pp. 52–53.

ROBERT IRWIN

# The Orient and the West from Bonaparte to T. E. Lawrence

On 1 July 1798 Napoleon Bonaparte's flagship, the *Orient*, with an armada of ships of the line, frigates and transports, appeared off the coast of Egypt. Alexandria was swiftly occupied and three weeks later the French army won an easy victory over the disorderly cavalry of the Mamlūk Bays at the Battle of the Pyramids actually fought at Imbaba, almost nine miles away from the Pyramids (see Cat. 48, 49, 50). The Mamlūks, mostly Circassian, Turk or Slav, were of slave origin or descent and formed a caste of military aristocrats which had ruled Egypt since the thirteenth century. Although Egypt and Syria had been conquered by the Ottoman Turks in 1516–17, and were subsequently governed in the name of the Ottoman Sultān by the Pasha, the Bays, or heads of the Mamlūk household, retained their financial and military position, and by the late eighteenth century the jurisdiction of the Ottoman Sultān over Egypt was scarcely more than nominal. The military prestige of the Mamlūks was damaged by their defeat in 1798 at the hands of the armies of the French Directorate. An attempt in 1799 by the Ottoman army to land on the Nile delta, drive the French army out of Egypt and restore the Sultān's authority resulted in a defeat at Abū Qīr (see Cat. 50) which was even more humiliating for the prestige of Turkish arms.

Before the Battle of Abū Qīr Bonaparte told General Murat that 'this battle will decide the fate of the world'. It is not clear why he thought this would be the case. The aims of the French expedition were from the first ill-defined. The French Directorate had thought vaguely of threatening British possessions in India and the British naval presence in the Mediterranean, and certainly they wanted the troublesome Bonaparte out of France. Later, Napoleon was to talk grandiosely of his scheme to march through Syria and return to Europe via Constantinople. In the event, his invasion of Palestine in 1799 (see Cat. 48) turned into a disaster. Although 2000 of the Turkish garrison at Jaffa were massacred after surrendering, Jezzar Pasha, the warlord governor of Acre, undeterred, successfully resisted a two-month siege by the French. Meanwhile, plague ravaged the French army (see Cat. 49) and Bonaparte, before withdrawing to Egypt, gave orders at Jaffa that those too sick to be moved should be poisoned with overdoses of opium, orders which were not obeyed.

Muslim observers of the French occupation of Egypt were less impressed with the wonders of Western civilisation than might have been expected, though al-Jabarti did commend the discipline of the French army. Its readiness to obey orders had few parallels in the slave corps, war bands, tribal levies or militias of the Near East (see Cat. 30, 72). Whatever the intentions of the French in Egypt, their long-term tenure of the country was made impossible by Nelson's destruction of most of the French fleet at the Battle of the Nile (Bay of Abū Qīr) in August 1798, so that by 1801 the entire French force had been evacuated from Egypt. However, the multi-volume *Description de l'Egypte* (1808–29), subsequently produced by the *savants* whom Bonaparte had taken with him on his invasion force, stimulated in Europe a greater interest in Near Eastern matters, and the French expedition of 1798 proved the harbinger of future European interventions in the region and of the colonisation of North Africa.

In the first decade of the nineteenth century the Ottoman Sultān still ruled, or at least pretended to rule, Greece, Crete, Cyprus, the greater part of the Balkans, Asia Minor, the south-western provinces of the Caucasus, Iraq, Syria, Lebanon, Palestine, Egypt, Libya, Tunisia and Algeria. Millions of the Sultān's subjects in Europe and in Asia were Christians – Orthodox, Armenian, Jacobite, Maronite, Coptic or Catholic. Most of his subjects in the Near East and North Africa were Arab or Berber. But in all provinces the ruling élite, the pashas, viziers, bays, mamlūks and janissaries, were Muslims and were recruited for the most part from the Turks, Albanians and Circassians. The successful Greek revolt of 1821–29 began the erosion of Turkey's power in Europe, and by 1914 very little of the Balkans was still in Turkish hands, while the North African provinces had passed into the hands of France, Italy and Britain.

Although in the mid-nineteenth century Tsar Nicholas I may have observed of the Sultān that 'we have on our hands, gentlemen, a sick man, a very sick man', in fact the century saw a revival of the Sultān's central control over Anatolia, Syria and Palestine and the re-establishment of his suzerainty over the Muslim holy places of the Hijāz. Indeed the increased, though still imperfect, policing and administration of the Levant by the Sultān's servants was one of the factors which facilitated its penetration by European merchants, missionaries, pilgrims and tourists (see Bugler, pp. 27–31). Sir Andrew Ryan, last of the dragomans at the British embassy in Constantinople, looked back on the final decades of Ottoman rule, as an 'Indian summer'. To some extent the Ottoman revival resulted from the reform of its institutions. The sultāns laboured, in the first instance, to create a Turkish army with European standards of discipline and weaponry. With the massacre of the old janissary corps on the 'Auspicious Day' in June 1826, one of the most important obstacles to autocratic reform was removed. Broader constitutional reforms, notably the Tanzimat reforms, followed in the years 1839–78.

Reform and improvement drew in European advisers and necessitated European loans. As Kinglake's fantastical pasha told the Eastern traveller: 'My mind comprehends locomotives. The armies of the English ride upon the vapours of boiling cauldrons, and their horses are flaming coals! – whirr! whirr! all by wheels! – whiz! whiz! all by steam!' In the decade that followed the publication of Kinglake's *Eothen* (1844), the British began to build a railway along the coast of Asia Minor. Later, more ambitious projects, such as the Berlin–Baghdad Railway, were predominantly German in their engineering and funding. Similarly, the Germans, in due course, replaced the French as advisors and instructors of the Ottoman army, and the great munitions firms of Krupp and Mauser maintained important branches in Istanbul. Boards of health, staffed by European consuls and doctors, took control of medical and sanitary affairs in many Ottoman regions following the first appearance of cholera in the Near East in the 1830s. Plague had been endemic in this region for centuries and quarantine restrictions were still enforced on the frontiers of the Ottoman Empire in the nineteenth century.

By virtue of capitulatory or treaty rights, the nationals of many European powers enjoyed important commercial and legal privileges in the Ottoman lands. Their consuls were also able to offer such concessions to the indigenous Christians and Jews who worked for them, and indeed to other interested Turkish citizens who could afford to pay for them. Although beneficial to the European recipients, capitulatory rights were a corrosive phenomenon in Egypt and North Africa. At the same time the Russian Tsar claimed rights as the protector of all Orthodox Christians living under Ottoman rule, while France declared its special interest in the Maronites. In 1860 religious and economic resentments boiled over and Christians in Damascus and the Lebanon were massacred by Muslims and Druze. This provoked European intervention, and through the Organic Regulation of 1861, the special status of the Lebanon was established under Western supervision.

Modernisation and reform in the Ottoman Empire proved to be as costly a process as the persistent corruption and court extravagance. Turkish indebtedness to European banks led to the formation of the Public Debt Administration in 1881 and the supervision by foreigners of many areas of Turkish finance. A similar sequence of modernisation, indebtedness and surrender to Western demands for supervision or actual control, was followed in Egypt and the autonomous regencies of Tunis and Algiers. Indeed, many of the Ottoman reforms of the early nineteenth century followed Western models only at one remove and it was the reforms initiated in Egypt by Muḥammad 'Alī that furnished their more direct source of inspiration.

Muḥammad 'Alī, a military adventurer of Albanian origin, seized power in Egypt in 1805, after outmanoeuvring both the janissary garrison sent from Turkey and the Mamlūk Bays. In 1811 the Mamlūk Bays and their retinues were invited to a feast at the Cairo Citadel and were swiftly massacred. Mamlūk power was destroyed forever, though mamlūks continued to be imported and employed in Egypt, and even to sit for Western portraitists (see Cat. 72), until the late nineteenth century.

Under Muḥammad 'Alī's enlightened, if sanguinary, rule, in Egypt, land tenure was restructured and the tax burden increased. He called in European experts to establish new industries and to remodel the army, which undertook campaigns with some success in the Hijāz, Greece and Syria. In this way Sudan was made a province of Egypt.

Muḥammad 'Alī died in 1849, the founder of a khedivial dynasty which came to an end only with the expulsion of Farouk in 1952. Although financial returns, largely from irrigation improvements and vastly increased cotton exports, reinforced Muḥammad 'Alī's effective independence from the Turkish Sultān and the European powers, his successors, less ruthless and more extravagant, drifted into debt. The construction of the Suez Canal was a particularly heavy drain on Egypt's resources, as were the celebrations to mark its opening in 1869. These included the staging of the première of *Aida*. 'I've never travelled . . . but I dare say, dear, that you can't judge Egypt by *Aida*' (Ronald Firbank, *The Eccentricities of Cardinal Pirelli*), but in the nineteenth century many Europeans did. Growing insolvency induced the Ismail Pasha to sell his shares in the Suez Canal to Disraeli which, coupled with a concern for the security of British merchants resident in Alexandria, furnished the pretext for British intervention and the occupation of Egypt in 1882. Thereafter, Britain became involved in Egypt's attempts to retain and then regain control of the Sudan. The deaths of Hicks Pasha and General Gordon at the hands of the Mahdi's dervish following were only avenged by Kitchener at Ūmdurman in 1898.

Dervishes and Muslim mystics (see Cat. 41), furnished Western writers and artists with unedifying scenes of fanaticism and superstition. Less obvious was the role of some individual dervish orders, particularly in North Africa, in renewing and purifying the Islamic faith. At times the dervishes spearheaded resistance to colonialism as did the Qādiris in Algeria in the 1830s, or the Sanusis in Libya in the early twentieth century. However, resistance to colonialism was more usually tribal in character. After a complex series of wrangles about debts and consular privileges, and the notorious incident in 1827 when the Day of Algiers struck the French consul with a fly whisk, the French were able easily to occupy Algiers in 1830. The subjugation of the tribal interior took much longer. French generals and land-hungry colonists favoured different policies and Abd al-Qādir, leader of the tribal resistance in western Algeria until 1847, became a hero in the eyes of many in metropolitan France. The last major revolt was bloodily quelled in 1880, by which time there were almost a quarter of a million colonists in Algeria.

The suggestion in the 1887 edition of Murray's *Handbook for Travellers in Algeria and Tunis* that Tunis, once 'an independent Beylick', had since become 'as much an integral part of France as the neighbouring colony of Algeria', is misleading. Tunisia was only occupied by the French in 1881. However, before that date its independence had been heavily compromised by ineffective and expensive attempts to modernise its army and administration. Some reforms were undertaken under European pressure, and some precisely to pre-empt that pressure. Muslim authority in Tunis, as elsewhere along the coast, had been undermined by the privileged communities of French, Spanish and Maltese (British) subjects, who were resident there. Tunis, like Algiers and Morocco, had also been adversely affected by the decline of privateering in the early nineteenth century. On the other hand Tunisia was never as intensively colonised as Algeria and consequently was to regain its independence much more easily in the twentieth century.

Morocco had never formed part of the Ottoman Empire, and since the seventeenth century had been ruled by the Alawite Sharifs, claiming descent from the Prophet Muḥammad. Until 1830 the country, apart from Tangier, was largely inaccessible to foreigners. Thereafter French difficulties in western Algeria and the undefined frontier between Morocco and Algeria prompted the Sharif 'Abd al-Rahmān (see Cat. 17) to offer assistance against the French to the rebel Abd al-Qādir and protection to the town of Tlemcen. Such provocations came to an end when the Moroccan army was humiliatingly defeated by the French at Isly in 1844. Hardly less humiliating was the capitulatory treaty signed with the British in 1856. The more the Sharifs ceded to the Western powers the more their prestige declined in the eyes of their subjects, and when France declared Morocco a protectorate in 1912, it was primarily to protect the Sharif from his own rebellious tribesmen. Only the jealousy of other European powers had prevented the French from taking this step earlier.

In the second half of the century, Arabian deserts and Moroccan mountain passes provided appropriate backdrops for daring exploits. The French Foreign Legion, founded in 1831, performed most spectacularly at the Battle of Ischeriden (1857) during the conquest of the Kabylia region of eastern Algeria, when they took at bayonet point a high ridge defended by musketry. G. M. Young wrote: 'Still armies might march into the mountains and be lost for weeks, as Roberts marched on Kandahar: into the desert and be lost forever, as Hicks was lost at al-Obeid. Still false prophets might arise in the wastes beyond Wadi Halfa, still Lhassa was unvisited, and a man might make himself as famous in fact by riding to Khiva, as by discovering King Solomon's mines in fiction.'

A less romantic contact with the Orient was Thomas Cook's association with Egyptian tourism which began in 1869. The firm was granted in 1880 exclusive control of all passenger steamers on the Nile, which subsequently led to contracts for supply and transport of the British army in Egypt and the Sudan. Murray's *Handbook for Travellers in the Ionian Islands, Greece, Turkey, Asia Minor and Constantinople* first appeared in 1840, the volume for Egypt in 1847. The Librairie Hachette's *Itinéraire descriptif, historique et archéologique de l'Orient* was published in 1861. Baedeker guides to the region followed. Most serious tourists were attracted by pre-Islamic antiquities in the area (see Cat. 28, 60, 69, 88, 89, 97). When sand was removed from the base of the Great Sphinx during the festivities for the opening of the Suez Canal in 1869, intense public interest was aroused, as was the case with other great moments in Egyptology in the nineteenth century: Champollion's decipherment of the Rosetta Stone (1820s), Layard's excavations at Nineveh (1840s), Schliemann's in the Troad (1870s) and Maspero's work in Egypt (1880s). A clearer idea of what the antiquities actually looked like could also be gained from the new science of photography in such publications as Maxime du Camp's *Egypte, Nubie, Palestine et Syrie* (1852).

Interest in Islamic art grew more slowly. Prisse d'Avennes's *L'Art arabe d'après les monuments du Caire* appeared only in 1877, and, though Delacroix had told du Camp that 'the most beautiful pictures I have seen are certain Persian carpets', the first major carpet exhibition only took place in 1891 in Vienna. In the last quarter of the century there was a huge increase in the production of Anatolian rugs, which, thanks to the introduction of Western synthetic dyes, could now be produced more cheaply.

Other Westerners went to Africa and Asia to rescue bodies and souls. In the Levant, Christian missionaries, among whom American Presbyterians were particularly prominent, concentrated their efforts on the Jews and native Christians. In Algeria the more aggressive Cardinal Lavigerie and the White Fathers attempted to convert the Muslims, to their mutual peril. The Christian missions were of course closely involved in the anti-slavery movement. A particularly vigorous campaign was conducted against the white slave trade in Circassian women, for the Circassians were Christians and besides there was a certain prurient concern about the details of harem life (see Cat. 33, 56, 64). In 1846, the Tunis slave market had been closed, followed, in 1854–55, by the prohibition by the Ottoman Sultān of the white slave trade and two years later by the black slave trade. Nonetheless, slavery and the surreptitious trade in slaves survived into the twentieth century.

Since the Ottoman Empire had closest links with the German Empire and few reasons to trust Russia, Britain or France, Turkey entered the First World War on the side of Germany and the Sultān urged the Jihād against the infidel rulers of Muslim peoples. Despite fears of a Pan-Islamic conspiracy against the British Empire voiced in *The Times's* editorials and popular works of fiction such as Talbot Mundy's *King of the Khyber Rifles* (1916), the Turkish Jihād was no real threat to the Allies. Indeed, the British were successful in persuading the Sharif of Mecca, formerly a more or less loyal subject of the Sultān to declare a Jihād against the Turks. The Arab revolt which followed in the Hijāz and Syria drew upon British gold, and advisers like T. E. Lawrence. But it also fed upon the new belief in an Arab nation and a growing sense that the Arab and the Turk had different destinies, which was in part a reaction to the ethnocentrism of the Young Turks in Constantinople. During the First World War many hypothetical partitions of the Near East were proposed and many contradictory promises made. At the end of the war not only did the Allies retain all their possessions in Africa, but France became the 'protecting' power in Syria and the Lebanon, while Britain acquired the same responsibility in Palestine, Trans-Jordan and Iraq. The Ottoman Empire was dismembered and in November 1922 the British battleship *Malaya* took the last Ottoman Sultān to his exile in San Remo.

CAROLINE BUGLER

# 'Innocents Abroad': Nineteenth-Century Artists and Travellers in the Near East and North Africa

'Travelling here is the strangest mixture of fun, danger, inconvenience, good living, and starving', enthused William Bartlett about his journey through the Holy Land in 1834. 'One night we are entertained in a convent, and live in clover; the next finds us in a village khan, sleeping under a shed, and supping on milk and eggs; a third, we are dining and supping out. Sometimes kept all night awake by fleas – the next sleeping like a top on good sheets.'[1]

Bartlett was one of the earliest British topographical artists to tour the Near East with the express purpose of systematically recording its features, and his comments express succinctly the attractions that were to lure many of his fellow artists to the comparatively unknown regions of the Holy Land, the Levant, Egypt and North Africa. Despite the constant threats of plague and war, the trickle of visitors, which had begun in the eighteenth century with early expeditions led by gentlemen antiquarians, such as the Reverend Richard Pococke and James Bruce of Kinnaird,[2] grew steadily throughout the early years of the nineteenth century, transforming these countries into fashionable venues for tourism of a more popular nature (fig. 7).

For artists, there were particular reasons for visiting North Africa and the Near East. Initially, many went simply as topographical draughtsmen and as the chroniclers of military victories, attached to expeditions or armies. From Napoleon's Egyptian campaigns onwards the French were particularly good at furnishing some pretext of a political mission for sending their artists abroad. In 1830 Horace Vernet was sent to Algeria to document the battles leading to the French conquest of that country. Adrien Dauzats followed in his footsteps when he accompanied the Duc d'Orléans and his army to the towns of Philippeville and Constantine during the later stages of the French Algerian campaign. Delacroix went to Morocco in 1832 as part of the Comte de Mornay's diplomatic mission to negotiate with the Sultān of Morocco (see Cat. 17), who was encroaching upon French Algerian territory. Yet it soon became economically viable for artists to initiate their own travels, recouping their outlay in the sale of paintings and volumes of lithographs on their return. As early as 1835, the Swiss artist Gleyre commented upon the large numbers of painters in Cairo,[3] complaining that their presence had quite spoiled his stay in the city. By 1838, David Roberts was sufficiently confident of the financial rewards to undertake a journey in the Near East in order to collect material for the ambitious publishing project that became the highly successful *The Holy Land, Syria, Idumea, Arabia, Egypt and Nubia* (1842–49). Thackeray, on his visit to Cairo in 1844, was quick to identify the sources of such commercial success: 'There is a fortune to be made for painters in Cairo', he mused. 'I never saw such a variety of architecture, of life, of picturesqueness, of brilliant colour, of light and shade. There is a picture in every street, and at every bazaar stall'.[4]

But there were several difficulties that stood in the way of artists in the Near East, many of which stemmed from the Islamic aversion to graven images. Holman Hunt was accused of collecting the likenesses of people to sell to the devil,[5] and Edward Lear was denounced as Satan incarnate while drawing in Albania. His journals recall how, on a sketching expedition at Elbassān, a universal shout burst forth from the crowd surrounding him, and 'one of those tiresome dervishes – in whom, with their green turbans, Elbassān is rich – soon came up and yelled "Shaitan scroo! – Shaitan!" (the Devil draws! – the Devil!) in my ears with all his force; seizing my book also, with an awful frown, shutting it, and pointing to the sky, as intimating that heaven would not

fig. 7 Anon., Tourists with servants at Karnak, c. 1870

allow such impiety. It was in vain after this to attempt more.'[6] Even if artists were not always subjected to such witch-hunts, they had to suffer various inconveniences. While drawing in the dusty town streets, they might be jostled and stared at all day long. 'No-one in looking over my sketches will ever think of the trouble the collection of them has cost me',[7] complained David Roberts after one such day's drawing in Cairo. Nor was it easy to obtain models, especially female ones. However, the dearth could sometimes be remedied either by using Jewish female models (an expedient resorted to by artists such as Chassériau), or by bribery. As Delacroix put it, 'their prejudices against the art of painting are great, but a few coins here and there take care of their scruples.'[8] Renoir was later to complain bitterly that this procedure, especially amongst British artists, had made access to models financially prohibitive when he visited Algeria in 1882.[9]

It was also difficult to gain entry to most religious monuments. *Firmans*, or passes, generally had to be negotiated in advance, parties arranged and guides procured. In some areas of the Near East, modification of Western appearance was essential. David Roberts had to shave off his whiskers (and refrain from using hog's hair brushes) in order to sketch in the mosques in Cairo, but this was nothing compared to the elaborate disguise donned by Robert Catherwood. As part of Robert Hay's expedition to the Levant in 1833, Catherwood was commissioned by Muḥammad 'Alī, Pasha of Egypt (see Cat. 102) to inspect a number of mosques with a view to assessing what repairs were necessary, including the Mosque of the Dome of the Rock in Jerusalem. Despite the fact that Franks, or foreigners, had reportedly been put to death for merely entering the outer court, he twice went into the mosque dressed as an Egyptian officer. On the second occasion, an ugly scene ensued when Catherwood sat down to sketch. The suspicion and hostility of the crowds was aroused, and matters worsened when the cap of one of the dervishes was accidentally knocked off. It was only the personal intervention of the Governor of Jerusalem, who convinced the crowd of the value of Catherwood's mission, that saved his life.[10] Gradually, however, as the Western presence in the Near East grew, mosques and holy places opened up to the Christian visitor, and *baqshish* replaced the *firman* as a means of access to sacred buildings.

By the middle of the century, tourism was well established. Recognised itineraries and destinations were proposed, supported by a rapidly expanding corpus of travel literature.[11] Turkey was the starting point for many visitors, and the 1854 edition of Murray's *Guide to Turkey* gives details of a bewildering variety of routes available for travellers to Constantinople. They could sail down the Danube to the Black Sea to arrive ten days after leaving London; they could travel to Italy and embark on a steamer at Trieste; or they could sail direct from Marseille or Southampton. On their arrival at Constantinople, travellers were steered by their guidebooks round the Palace of the Ottoman sultāns, the mosques, the bazaars, baths, antiquities, and the shores of the Bosphorus where Europe and Asia met. While visitors to Constantinople were presented with a reasonable selection of hotels in that city, such facilities did not exist in the rest of Asia Minor, where they would have been obliged to stay in *lokandas* or *khāns* of dubious salubrity in the smaller towns. Bayard Taylor vividly describes the sight that frequently greeted the newly-arrived guest at one of these establishments in his account of his travels through Asia Minor. He recalled that while eating supper, 'in the midst of our enjoyment, happening to cast my eye on the walls, I saw a sight that turned all our honey to gall. Scores on scores — nay hundreds on hundreds — of enormous bed-bugs swarmed

up the plaster, and were already descending to our beds and baggage. To sleep there was impossible, but we succeeded in getting possession of one of the outside balconies, where we made our beds after searching them thoroughly.'[12]

Where there were no *khāns*, convents could usually be relied upon to provide accommodation, and sometimes the hospitality of the chief man in the village was extended to travellers. Nonetheless, it was generally advisable to take a tent, together with a cumbersome array of medicines, culinary utensils, umbrellas, straw hats, lamps, saddles, navigational aids and tea-making equipment. There were three modes of travel in the Near East as described in Murray's guide to Turkey: 'The most agreeable and comfortable is that adopted by a Turkish gentleman. It consists in having several native servants, tents, and either one's own horses or those hired from a *katirji*. The speed is slow, the caravan rarely accomplishing more than 20 or 25m. a day. The tents are pitched in the evening near some running stream or some pleasant gardens . . . This mode of travelling is comparatively cheap, but requires some acquaintance with the language and customs of the people . . . The second mode is that adopted by the Englishman of certain means. It consists in hiring one or two Greeks who speak some European language, paying so much a day, and leaving every arrangement in his or their hands. Some trouble may be spared, but the traveller will learn little of the manners and language of the people amongst whom he is travelling — will be imposed upon in every way — and will pay ten times the real price for everything . . . The third mode is the best for one who desires to become thoroughly acquainted with the country and people, and to learn something of the language. It consists in buying a couple of horses, one for a riding-horse, the other for a pack-saddle, on which his luggage — reduced to the smallest compass — can be placed, and, above it, a native youth hired as a servant.'[13]

Despite these attractive possibilities, the only really well-known parts of Turkey were Constantinople and Smyrna (now Izmir), mainly because of their convenient locations as stopping-off points for excursions further afield, generally south to the Holy Land, rather than east to Persia. In addition to the overland route to the Holy Land, there was the option of travel by steamer from Constantinople, Smyrna or Alexandria in Egypt. Jerusalem was only a day's ride on horseback from the port of Jaffa, and it was the most common destination of visitors to the Holy Land, especially around Easter, when thousands of pilgrims of all denominations converged on the city. Visits to the holy sites were recommended, but often these were spoilt by scenes of sectarian antagonism. It was a terrible scramble to get a place at the Easter service in the Church of the Holy Sepulchre, while each sect conducted its own observances under the same roof. The anonymous narrator of *Three Weeks in Palestine and Lebanon*, published in 1833, relates how his janissary was obliged to clear a path through the thronging masses 'after the manner of the Turks . . . laying his cane most lustily upon the heads and shoulders of all before him.'[14] The city itself did not always arouse much enthusiasm. Many commentators noted with distaste its curiously primitive, dismal appearance, and the melancholy air of its inhabitants. Edward Lear was not alone in recalling the interior of the city as 'horrid dreams of squalor & filth, clamour & uneasiness, hatred & malice & all uncharitableness.'[15] However, Lear went on to comment that the outside of the city was 'full of melancholy glory, exquisite beauty & a world of past history of all ages . . . The Arab & his sheep are alone the wanderers on the pleasant vallies and breezy hills round Zion: — the file of slow camels all that brings to mind the commerce of Tyre & other bygone merchandize.' The lack of picturesque subject matter, apart from the sacred monuments within the city itself, may help to explain the preponderance of panoramic views taken from the environs of the city (see Cat. 61), and the dearth of the bazaar and street scenes that countless artists painted in Cairo (see Cat. 74).

For those who were making the combined trip to the Holy Land and Egypt, and who were prepared to forego the comfort of the steamer, there was the overland route that passed through Petraea and the Sinai desert, following the journey of the Exodus. This route was particularly popular with artists, as it took them through such spectacular scenery. Preparations for the voyage were often elaborate; Gérôme's journal for his visit in 1868 to the Sinai desert reveals that he took forty-seven camels, twenty servants and six companions.[16] There was a certain safety in numbers as, despite the blithe assertions of some guidebooks[17] that travel in the desert was no more dangerous than in certain parts of Europe, predatory attacks by Bedouin Arabs, particularly around Petra, were by no means uncommon. Gérôme's own party had a narrow escape from a hostile tribe of that region[18], and Edward Lear found himself in the middle of a dispute between the Arabs who had agreed to act as his escort, and the local *fellāḥīn* of that area, who demanded an extortionate fee for letting him pass through their territories.[19]

On the other hand, some Europeans were fortunate enough to observe the elaborate code of hospitality that some Arabs could extend to strangers. Major Fridolin, travelling through Syria en route to Mecca, was invited by the *shaykh* of the Anésis Arabs to dine in his tent. Even the dread of the culinary experience failed to measure up to the reality. 'The torture began with a cup of coffee', he wrote, 'which I swallowed heroically, brandy and

liqueur. Followed by a plate of dates dressed with mutton fat, in front of which I felt my heart sink . . . but that was only the prelude to my tribulations. The crowd pressing round the tent came in, and I saw, carried on the shoulders of four men, something extraordinary and fabulous . . . On the gleaming slopes of a mountain of rice, a young camel, undoubtedly a suckling, an innocent victim slaughtered for my welcome, was lying with its legs folded and its neck straight, in the most realistic of attitudes.'[20]

Of all the countries of the Near East, Egypt undoubtedly provided the highest degree of comfort and sophistication for the traveller. Many Europeans rented houses in Cairo in the Frank quarter of the city (having first taken the precaution of sending three of four *fellāḥīn* through the apartments to carry off the worst of the fleas). For those who did not anticipate a long stay, there were always the well-equipped hotels. And there were no problems of access to the city. By the time Thackeray visited Cairo in 1844, he found it easy and convenient to have his journey arranged by the P & O Company. Had he waited another eleven years, he would have been able to take the train from Alexandria to Cairo on the railway line built between the two cities in 1855. Twenty-five years after Thackeray's trip it was possible to travel up the Nile in the comfort afforded by Thomas Cook's organised tours, which began in 1869. By the 1890s, Thomas Cook & Co. even had their own well-appointed steamships travelling up and down the river, complete with electric lights, a daily delivery of newspapers, porridge for breakfast, and afternoon tea.[21]

The diverse attractions of Egypt brought tourists of all descriptions. Amelia Edwards, whose journey up the Nile in 1873 is memorably recorded in *A Thousand Miles up the Nile*, remarked of her fellow guests at Shepheard's Hotel in Cairo (fig. 8) that 'nine-tenths . . . are English or American. The rest will be mostly

fig. 8  J. Pascal Sébah, Terrace of Shepheard's Hotel, Cairo, after 1868

29

German with a sprinkling of Belgian and French ... Here are invalids in search of health, artists in search of subjects, sportsmen keen upon crocodiles, statesmen out for a holiday, special correspondents alert for gossip, collectors on the scent of papyri and mummies, men of science with scientific ends in mind.'[22] As the summer months were unbearably hot, the majority of tourists visited Egypt between October and April, when the climate was deemed particularly beneficial to the health. The Prince of Wales participated in the fashion when he wintered in Egypt in 1872–73 for health reasons, and among the hotels that sprang up to cater for the tourist trade, there were a number that specialised in the treatment of the sick. Some invalids stayed far longer: Lucie Duff Gordon went to Luxor in 1864 hoping to alleviate the symptoms of her tuberculosis, and spent the last five years of her life chronicling the daily life of village Egyptians and British expatriates in her letters home.[23]

Organised tourism was not to everyone's taste, and its growth allowed those who travelled independently the luxury of a certain sense of superiority. Amelia Edwards maintained that one could distinguish at first sight between a Cook's tourist and the autonomous traveller. In the same way, those who went up the Nile as far as the second cataract could look down on those who only ventured as far as the first. Of the various types of boat available for hire on the Nile, the wooden *dahabiyyah* provided the most leisurely and delightful conveyance. Miss Edwards's *dahabiyyah*, the 'Philae', afforded the ultimate in gracious living. It was 100 feet long, possessed seven sleeping cabins, a spacious dining saloon with white panels picked out in gold and equipped with a piano, a bathroom, and a stern cabin saloon. None of these well-appointed rooms was reserved for the sleeping-quarters of the twenty members of crew, who simply rolled themselves up at night in rough blankets and 'lay about the lower deck like dogs'.[24] It was, of course, possible to hire craft of more modest dimensions. Gustave Flaubert and Maxime du Camp travelled up the Nile in a smaller *qangah*, with a crew of eight or nine, as did many artists of the time, including David Roberts, who insisted on having his craft submerged in the river to rid it of vermin before he set off.[25] By mid-century, it was not really necessary for a European to wear Eastern dress on the Nile trip, but Flaubert and Du Camp took great delight in putting on Nubian shirts trimmed with pompons, shaving their heads and wearing red *tarbooshes* (a form of fez), growing beards and smoking a *nargīlah* (a native pipe). Several artists, including J. F. Lewis, Carl Haag and Frederick Goodall, wore native dress in Cairo, but it seems to have been largely for the fun of dressing up, and perhaps as a means of distinguishing themselves from the more temporary visitors to the city. Certainly, by the 1870s, Murray's guides were strongly advising tourists against wearing Oriental clothes in Egypt unless they were fluent in Egyptian, recommending suits of flannel in their place.[26]

The prodigious growth of tourism in Egypt soon had the effect of making some parts of the country as over-familiar and as spoilt as certain picturesque parts of Europe. There were complaints that the old quarters of Cairo were disappearing and that the city was being 'Haussmannised'[27] due to the influx of foreigners and the pro-Western attitudes adopted by successive Egyptian pashas. Graffiti were appearing on many of the monuments: Flaubert lamented that after climbing to the top of the Great Pyramid, he was confronted with the name and address of a Parisian wallpaper manufacturer inscribed in block capitals on the stone.[28] Of course, all tourists habitually complain about the presence of other tourists, and artists and writers often exhibited no more respect

towards Egypt's heritage than the very people they despised. Flaubert's companion, Maxime du Camp, broke up mummies in the Crocodile Grotto and carried off pieces of the embalmed bodies,[29] and Gérôme committed a similar act of vandalism when he unravelled a mummy he had plundered from its tomb and watched the white bandages float down the Nile before removing the hands and feet for souvenirs.[30]

The most sensitive Western observers realised the potentially destructive character of this contact with the East, which brought not only the wanton defacement of monuments, but also a serious threat to the indigenous way of life. William Holman Hunt was concerned that 'traditional manners were threatening to pass away, together with the ancient costume and hereditary taste ... in another generation it would be too late to reconstruct the past, save in rural and desert life, if even then.'[31] The process of Westernisation was especially evident in the French colony of Algeria, where the colonial government, as part of its *mission civilisatrice*, was systematically re-organising the entire country, and successfully re-modelling the capital, Algiers, into a French provincial city. Only a day's journey from Marseille, the city soon boasted several good hotels, European doctors, French schools, a library, a museum, and a theatre. While the harbour, fortifications and Grand Mosque of Algiers provided subjects for painters, its warm climate recommended the city to sufferers from consumption, lung disease, coughs and rheumatism. Excursions to other coastal towns were facilitated by the construction of the coastal railway which, by 1873 (when Murray's published their first *Handbook for Travellers in Algeria*), ran between Algiers and Oran, Constantine and Philippeville.

Following the initial conquest of the north of Algeria in 1830, French control spread southwards in a series of military campaigns in the 1830s and 1840s. In their wake, visitors and artists began to venture into the heart of the country in search of an uncorrupted life and picturesque scenes. Eugène Fromentin's three Algerian journeys of 1846, 1847–48 and 1852–53 took him first to the Sahel, south of Algiers, and later to the oasis town of El-Agouat in the Sahara, where he stayed for some months.[32] In 1862, the artist Gustave Guillaumet went to live in the inland town of Bou-Saada, where he chose to share in the hard lives of the native Ouled-Niall.[33] These second generation artists made a far more concerted attempt to understand the landscape and the indigenous population of Algeria than either Delacroix and Dauzats before them, or Renoir and Matisse after them.

The two countries which flanked Algeria, Morocco and Tunisia, lacked the reassuring presence of European garrisons in their interiors and so presented a more daunting prospect to the mid-century traveller. Yet, while Tunisia was usually discussed in travel literature merely as an extension to Algeria, Morocco's cultural links with, and proximity to Spain, made it the subject of frequent visits. A desire to see Moorish buildings in their place of origin led David Roberts, in southern Spain in 1833, to undertake the easy trip across the narrow strait that separated Spain from the capital city, Tangier. J. F. Lewis made the same journey, also in 1833, to gain his first impressions of the Islamic world. The French artist E. A. A. Dehodencq (1822–1882) even established his family in southern Spain while he went on artistic excursions to Tangier in the 1850s, and Henri Regnault (1843–1871) and Mariano Fortuny (1838–1874) also approached Morocco through a knowledge of Spain. Initially, at least, visitors restricted themselves to Tangier, where the city's large Jewish population gave a warmer welcome to Christian travellers than did the Muslims of the interior. Delacroix, while on the Comte de Mornay's diplomatic expedition to the interior city of Meknes in 1832, found the experience of venturing into the streets intolerable. 'Christian dress and faces are anathema to those people', he wrote. 'One always has to be escorted by soldiers. I am escorted every time I go out by an enormous crowd of spectators who do not spare me the insults of dog, infidel, *caracco*, and who push towards me to grimace with contempt.'[34] Even as late as the 1890s, guide-books were still advising that the short journey between the coastal towns of Ceuta, Tangier and Tetuan could not always be guaranteed free from attack by hostile tribesmen.[35]

Religious fanaticism and anti-Western feelings may have created problems in North Africa for the traveller, but by far the most difficult feat that a European could accomplish was the annual pilgrimage to Mecca performed by thousands of Muslims. Given that recognition as an unbeliever would bring death, only a hand-ful of the most intrepid travellers ever managed to complete the journey. As early as 1812, J. L. Burckhardt had visited Mecca with a tribe of Bedouins. He lived to tell the story although he was obliged to hide the notes he was taking from his companions.[36] Sir Richard Burton, the inveterate adventurer, linguist, and sub-sequently consul, went on the pilgrimage in 1853. Dressed as an Arab *shaykh* but pretending to be a Pathan doctor, he supported his claims to Muslim identity with an excellent knowledge of Arabic and a fervent display of devotion to Islam.[37] Charles Doughty, who did not share Burton's fascination with Islam, also joined the Mecca caravan during his twenty months of wandering in the 'empty quarter' of north-western Arabia from 1876 to 1878. Such was the rashness of his undertaking in venturing into areas where no European had been before, that the Governor of Syria felt unable to give any guarantee of his personal safety. Nor did Doughty make life any easier for himself by attempting to disguise his Christian origins as Burton had done, a stubbornness that nearly cost him his life.[38]

The majority of travellers, however, stayed within the ter-ritories charted by guidebooks and popular literature. Imbued with the attitude of confident superiority embodied in the guidebook assertion that Arabs 'occupy a much lower grade in the scale of civilisation than most of the Western nations'[39], tourists were not able, or did not wish to participate in local life to any significant degree. There were notable exceptions, of course, such as Lucie Duff Gordon, who became a figure of some consequence among the Egyptians at Luxor through ministering to the sick. But the average visitor neither overcame the frustration of the language barrier, nor stayed long enough to gain more than a superficial impression of Near Eastern life.

NOTES

1 W. Beattie, *Brief Memoirs of the Late William Henry Bartlett*, London, 1855, p. 20.
2 The Reverend Richard Pococke visited the Near East from 1737 to 1740 and James Bruce of Kinnaird travelled to Egypt and Abyssinia from 1768 to 1778.
3 Gleyre's diary quoted in P. Jullian, *The Orientalists*, Oxford, 1977, p. 136.
4 W. M. Thackeray, *Notes on a Journey from Cornhill to Grand Cairo*, London, 1846, pp. 278–79.
5 W. Holman Hunt, *Pre-Raphaelitism and the Pre-Raphaelite Brotherhood*, London, I, 1905, pp. 387–88.
6 E. Lear, *Journals of a Landscape Painter in Albania and Ilyria*, London, 1851, p. 92.
7 J. Ballantine, *The Life of David Roberts R.A.*, Edinburgh, 1866, p. 107.
8 P. Burty, *Lettres de Eugène Delacroix*, Paris, 1878, p. 121.
9 Letter from Renoir to Durand-Ruel dated March 1882, reprinted in *Renoir en Italie et en Algérie*, Paris, 1955, n.p.
10 Letter from Catherwood published in W. Bartlett, *Walks about the City and Environs of Jerusalem*, London, 1844, pp. 148–65.
11 For a full English bibliography see R. Bevis, *Bibliotheca Cisorientalia: An Annotated Checklist of Early English Travel Books on the Near and Middle East*, Boston, Mass., 1973.
12 Bayard Taylor, *Pictures of Palestine, Asia Minor, Sicily and Spain or The Lands of the Saracens*, London, 1855, p. 291
13 *A Handbook for Travellers in Turkey*, 3rd ed., London, 1854, pp. 17–18.
14 pp. 25–26.
15 Lady Strachey, *Letters of Edward Lear*, London, 1907, p. 106.
16 See Morgan-Vauthier, *Gérôme, peintre et sculpteur*, Paris, 1906, p. 224.
17 Baedeker, Egypt. *Handbook for Travellers. Part First: Lower Egypt . . . etc.* Leipzig, 1878, p. 16.
18 P. Lenoir, *Le Fayoûm, Le Sinaï et Pétra*, Paris, 1872, pp. 315–20.
19 Sir Franklin Lushington, 'A Leaf from the Journals of a Landscape Painter,' *MacMillan Magazine*, 75, pp. 421–25.
20 Major Fridolin, 'Scènes de la vie religieuse en Orient', *Revue des Deux Mondes*, Nouvelle période, 2ᵉ série, 1854, VI, p. 90.
21 See S. Searight, *The British in the Middle East*, London, 1979 ed., p. 229.
22 A. Edwards, *A Thousand Miles up the Nile* (first published 1876), London, 1982, pp. 2–3.
23 Lady Duff Gordon, *Letters from Egypt*, partial ed., London, 1865, 1983 ed.
24 A. Edwards, *op. cit.*, p. 41.
25 J. Ballantine, *op. cit.*, p. 104.
26 S. Searight, *op. cit.*, p. 230.
27 Lady Brassey quoted in Norman Daniel, *Islam, Europe and Empire*, Edinburgh, 1966, p. 50.
28 F. Steegmuller, *Flaubert in Egypt*, London, 1972, p. 54.
29 *Ibid.*, p. 206.
30 C. Moreau-Vauthier, *op. cit.*, pp. 119–20.
31 W. Holman Hunt, *op. cit.*, I, p. 275.
32 See E. Fromentin, *Une Année dans le Sahel*, Paris, 1859, and *Un Eté dans le Sahara*, Paris, 1857.
33 See G. Guillaumet, *Tableaux algériens*, Paris, 1888.
34 P. Burty, *op. cit.*, p. 127.
35 See Murray's *Handbook to the Mediterranean*, London, 1890 ed., p. 5.
36 See J. L. Burckhardt, *Travels in Arabia, comprehending an Account of those Territories in Hedjaz which the Mohammedans regard as Sacred*, London, 1829.
37 Sir Richard Burton, *Personal Narrative of a Pilgrimage to El-Medinah and Mecca*, 3 vols., London, 1855–6.
38 C. Doughty, *Passages from Arabia deserta*, London, 1888, 1983 ed., pp. 290–92.
39 Baedeker, *op cit.*, p. 12.

MALCOLM WARNER

# The Question of Faith: Orientalism, Christianity and Islam

Most nineteenth-century travellers in the Near East, whether painters, writers, archaeologists or tourists, were also pilgrims, the high point of whose journey was a visit to the Holy Land. Seeking not just the divine aura of Chateaubriand's 'land weathered by miracles', but eye-witness knowledge that would explain and confirm the Scriptures, they were pilgrims very much of the scientific age. With the first thorough, critical investigation of biblical sites made by the American scholar Edward Robinson in 1838, the foundation of the Palestine Exploration Fund in London in 1865 and the publication of its *Survey of Western Palestine* in 1881–84, styled as 'the most valuable contribution to the illustration of the Bible since its translation into the vulgar tongue', the middle years of the century were a boom period for biblical archaeology.[1] But this was just the academic manifestation of a prevalent feeling that it was important to find the roots of the Christian truth in a concrete, observable reality. In art, it showed itself first in the views of biblical sites produced by British topographical artists: the draughtsmen whose on-the-spot sketches were redrawn by Turner and others, and engraved by the Findens in the *Landscape Illustrations of the Bible* (1836), W. H. Bartlett and Thomas Allom, who illustrated John Carne's *Syria, the Holy Land, Asia Minor, etc.* (1836–38) and David Roberts in his volumes of lithographs published in the 1840s. As makers of visual records, they played a part that was gradually taken over, as the century progressed, by photography.

For other artists, the people, dress and customs of the contemporary Near East were as important a link with its biblical past as its geography and archaeological remains. It was generally accepted that these had been left miraculously unaffected by the passing millennia. When David Wilkie said that the Arabs 'look as if they had never changed since the time of Abraham', he was stating a commonplace.[2] 'The unchanged habits of the East', wrote Dean Stanley, 'render it a kind of living Pompeii.'[3] The idea went together with a concern that this source of religious knowledge would soon be polluted by contact with the West, that 'in a short time the exact meaning of many things which find their correspondences in the Bible will have perished.'[4] Modernisation in the Near East seemed almost a travesty; as Gustave Guillaumet said, 'you can hardly imagine Abraham coming forth from his tent to mix up some tarmac.'[5]

From seeing the Near East as a timeless, albeit imperilled world, it was a short step to finding the living image of figures and incidents from the Bible in everyday sights. Horace Vernet looked at an Arab girl in Algeria giving a soldier a drink at a well and saw Rebecca and Eliezer; David Roberts watched a caravan leave Cairo and imagined the Israelites carrying the Ark through the wilderness; W. J. Müller declared that a Holy Family, just fled from Bethlehem presumably, was to be seen in every Egyptian village.[6] The artist, more than any other traveller, was bound to notice the discrepancy between the scenes before him and the way scriptural subjects had traditionally been represented in Western art, with European facial types and vaguely classical draperies. The first to be forcibly struck by this was Horace Vernet in the 1830s. As a result, he undertook a campaign for a new, authentic kind of biblical painting. The Arabs, he argued, provided an accurate idea of how characters in the Bible really looked and modern religious art should take account of the fact, as Raphael and Titian would have done if as much information had been available to them. 'Once the connection between Arab manners and customs and those of the ancient Hebrews takes hold of your thoughts ... then the richest vein is yours to be mined!', he exclaimed in a letter of 1840. 'Here is the way to do something

fig. 9   Vernet *Judah and Tamar*   1840   [Wallace Collection, London]

new that's not merely freakish'.[7] Vernet was primarily a military painter. He seems to have seen no contradiction in imagining the Arabs in Algeria as patriarchs and celebrating the French occupation of their country in a series of vast battle pictures. His own attempts to put his principle of veracity in biblical painting into practice are few and, despite what he said, more than a little freakish (fig. 9). But in his effort to bring religious art into line with modern knowledge, he set an important precedent.

Vernet concerned himself with Old Testament subjects. The first artist seriously to consider painting an authentic Near Eastern Christ, in an archaeologically accurate setting, was David Wilkie. He went to the Holy Land in 1841 but died on the return voyage to England, never bringing any of his projects for biblical pictures to completion. Wilkie translated Vernet's idea into Protestant terms, saying that 'a Martin Luther, in painting, is as much called for as in theology, to sweep away the abuses by which our divine pursuit is encumbered.'[8] But it is hard to imagine the leader of an artistic Reformation being as anxious as Wilkie was that the facts might turn out to be inconvenient. What if Christ and the disciples had eaten the Last Supper sitting in an undignified fashion on the floor? The task of the religious painter, he decided, must be to gather as much reliable information as possible, then 'to consider what will serve and what will not serve.'[9] He acknowledged that Christ ought to look Jewish but could not bring himself to show him as such, and in his unfinished *Christ before Pilate* used as his model a European-looking Persian prince.

Perhaps Wilkie would have recognised his Luther of painting in William Holman Hunt, member of the Pre-Raphaelite Brotherhood. Hunt's fellow Pre-Raphaelites, Rossetti and Millais, painted scenes from the lives of the Virgin Mary and Christ in London,

and their work, in its defiant refusal to idealise, can be called realistic. But Hunt went further, taking the Brotherhood's principles to their logical conclusion and insisting that to paint holy subjects, he must go to the Holy Land and see at first hand the places and the kind of people biblical painting purports to depict. To represent Christ among the doctors of the Temple, he must himself be among real Jews on the spot in Jerusalem (fig. 10). The resulting pictures were, like Hunt's previous work, replete with detailed, erudite symbolism that conveys their spiritual meaning. It was the amount of historical research, far beyond anything envisaged by Vernet or Wilkie, that made them innovatory. The word 'truth' is the keynote of everything Hunt said about his aims as a religious artist. 'Truth, wherever it leads, being above price, must increase the beauty of the story of the Divine Man', he told his friend Augustus Egg just before his first trip to the Near East in 1854. 'Art of the highest, illustrating it, has mostly dwelt upon the supernatural and ignored the human aspect.'[10] Hunt shared Wilkie's feeling that the painting of historically accurate biblical pictures was a distinctly Protestant endeavour. Here was an alternative to the decadent Italian tradition of Catholic devotional art, an advertisement to the world that Protestantism could accept scientific enquiry as a means of approaching God.

The Orientalist vision of the Scriptures became familiar not only through exhibition pictures at the Salon and Royal Academy (and engravings after them), but also through illustrated editions of the Bible. The first of these to pretend to some degree of historical authenticity was Gustave Doré's of 1866, which contained a great deal of fantasy but a certain amount of Orientalist observation too. The Dalziel Brothers' *Bible Gallery*, begun in the 1860s and eventually published in 1880, included engravings after a

fig. 10  Holman Hunt *The Finding of the Saviour in the Temple*  1854–55 and 1856–60  [Birmingham Museum and Art Gallery]

fig. 11 Tissot, 'Eloi, Eloi, Lama Sabachtani!', from
*La Vie de Notre-Seigneur Jésus Christ*,
1896–97

number of artists, some idealised, the majority in the style of Holman Hunt, or by Hunt himself. But the most whole-heartedly 'Orientalised' of all the illustrated Bibles was by James Tissot. This featured not only well-researched impressions of sacred events, but also landscape views, maps, sketches of architecture and vignettes showing Near Eastern ethnic types. The Preface carried Tissot's assertion, crusading in tone but hardly original in 1896, that 'the imagination of the Christian world has been led astray by the fancies of artists'. The man putting it back on the right track in this case was a spiritualist and his images of the supernatural, especially his angels, had the air of the séance about them. For the rest, the Near Eastern details were painstakingly authentic, which of course lent credibility to the supernatural side. Tissot was well aware of his forerunners in this kind of project and determined to take the level of accuracy higher, basing his illustrations on countless sketches and photographs made in the Holy Land, and on authoritative archaeological texts. Through his designs he would tell the misguided Christian world, as he told his astounded father on returning from one of his research missions, that Calvary was not the sizeable hill usually depicted, but only 'from 20 to 22 feet high at the most' (fig. 11).[11]

The argument often raised against the realist approach to the Bible was summed up by Charles Blanc when he criticised Vernet for 'sacrificing its broad, human side for the narrow, Arab side, replacing the substance with the shadow, the spirit of the thing with the letter of mere costume'.[12] A *Christ at the Pool of Bethesda* in the Orientalist manner by Charles Ronot, with 'fellāḥin being

healed by a Bedouin Jesus in an Arab Jerusalem', struck Théophile Gautier as undermining the whole dignity of the subject, moving him sternly to warn that 'those who islamicise sacred themes are on a dangerous path'.[13] Burne-Jones felt similarly that Tissot's authenticity got in the way of the real meaning of what he represented, that his *Annunciation* was all Arab costume and no Virgin Mary.[14] Eugène Fromentin, who devoted probably the fullest discussion to the issue in *Un Eté dans le Sahara*, concluded that 'to put the Bible into costume is to destroy it. It's like dressing a demi-god: you turn him into an ordinary mortal. Set the Bible in a recognisable location and it is no longer itself. You are making history of an anti-historical text. It is certainly necessary to find some kind of clothing for the essential idea, but, as the Old Masters realised, the best way to capture the truth is to simplify the form and eliminate all "local colour".'[15]

Though opposed to Orientalist paintings of Bible subjects, Fromentin could not but admit that the appeal of the Arabs was that they did retain 'that something we call "biblical", like a perfume of ancient times'.[16] Fromentin himself found this only in the very humblest scenes from Arab life, the 'Arab-ness' of which was not too insistent. For him, a Bedouin in full *burnūs* was a Bedouin and nothing more; a half-naked shepherd, on the other hand, might well turn his imagination to thoughts of Jacob tending the flocks of Laban. Most Orientalists were willing to see the shepherd as Jacob and the Bedouin as Abraham too. A great deal of Orientalist painting that is not explicitly biblical is none the less full of biblical resonances and to understand its meaning fully, the spectator must be willing, before the most contemporary-looking genre scene, to recognise its correspondence with some scriptural prototype.

The urge to find the Bible in the actuality of the Near East arose out of the crisis of religious faith in nineteenth-century Europe. The authority of Bible and Church, both Protestant and Roman Catholic, was being undermined, not just by famous controversies such as that surrounding Darwin, but by the spirit of scientific materialism that characterised the age. As Charles Lyell produced evidence against the biblical chronology in his *Principles of Geology* (1830) and Darwin against the Genesis account of the Creation in his *Origin of Species* (1859), thinking believers set about re-examining their faith, attempting, amidst much debate, disagreement and confusion, to sort out what they could still believe and what they could not. There was no shortage of critical writings on the Bible, the conclusions of which were all the more worrying for being supported by heavyweight German scholarship. In his *Geschichte des Volkes Israel bis Christus* (1843–52), for example, Georg Heinrich August von Ewald argued that Moses was the first historical figure in the Bible and that the patriarchs were entirely legendary. By 1900 this idea was to be widely accepted and not regarded as a serious threat to Christian belief, but in the mid century it seemed exactly that. There were any number of responses to the German school of biblical criticism and the general debate about religion and science. The most relevant to our theme is that of liberal Christians who accepted a little of the new learning but not too much, men such as H. H. Milman, Dean of St. Paul's, who prepared educated opinion in Britain for the impending shocks from Germany in his *History of the Jews* (1829) and would occasionally cause a stir during sermons by referring to Abraham as a *shaykh*.

The New Testament came in for the same kind of critical analysis and interpretation as the Old. For those whose faith rested on a conviction that the Gospels were historical fact, pure and simple, it was disturbing to read D. F. Strauss's *Leben Jesu* (1836) and be told they were just myths embodying spiritual truth. Conventional belief was hardly reassured when Ernest Renan gave Christ back his historicity in the widely-read and influential *Vie de Jésus* (1863) but stripped him of his divinity. Writing in the Holy Land, working from on-the-spot observation like an Orientalist painter, Renan portrayed Christ the man, greatest of the sons of man but no greater than that, allowing a place in religion for the insights of the heart but definitely not for the supernatural. In being free from 'old religious priest teaching', Holman Hunt felt that his picture of *The Shadow of Death* (fig. 12) was 'more fitted by itself for the Renan class of thinkers who have been studying the life of Christ as one particular branch of history'.[17] Without agreeing with Renan's wholly materialistic approach,

Hunt, Wilkie and Tissot were in the same business of trying to create an image of Christ for the scientific age. As Hunt said, 'we must show that we are not afraid of the truth.'[18]

Some Christian thinkers were led by the same spirit of inquiry that was exciting debate over the veracity of the Holy Book to take an interest in other religious beliefs. The period saw the rise of Comparative Religion as a respectable academic discipline and it is no coincidence that, at the same time, European painters began to represent non-Christian worship in a fairly accurate, serious manner. If the biblical subject, authentically treated, is the first contribution of Orientalism to religious art, the second is the scene of worship, occasionally Jewish but in the vast majority of cases Muslim: the call to prayer, the prayer in the mosque, at the tomb,

fig. 12  Holman Hunt *The Shadow of Death*  1870–73  [City of Manchester Art Galleries]

fig. 13  Gérôme *Prayer in the Mosque of 'Amr*   *c.* 1872   [Metropolitan Museum of Art, New York]

on the rooftop and in the desert, and the pilgrim caravan bound for Mecca (figs. 13, 14).

By and large, the European view of Islam was ignorant and bigoted. Muslims were traditionally held to be superstitious, immoral, corrupt, cruel, and liable to commit fanatical outrages against Christians, an impression that reports of Turkish conduct during the Greek War of Independence and the massacres of 1860 in the Lebanon and Damascus did much to reinforce. David Roberts, who equated Islam with barbarism, demonstrates another aspect of the usual picture of the Muslim – his extreme laziness

– when he shows Arabs idling away their time chatting and smoking as the great monuments behind them crumble from neglect. On the other hand, there was a movement in European thought towards a view of Islam that was sympathetic and occasionally, though by no means always, well-informed. While condemning the fatalism of Muslims, Lamartine praised the depth of their faith, their charity, tolerance and administration of justice, claiming that the teaching of the *Qur'ān* is essentially no different from Christianity.[19] For Thomas Carlyle, Islam was 'a bastard kind of Christianity but a living kind, with a heart-life in it', and Muḥammad, far from the evil impostor of the normal European conception, was a great religious leader of unquestionable sincerity.[20] Richard Burton argued that whereas Christianity debased Man by conceiving of him as a fallen being, Islam exalts and teaches respect for human dignity.[21]

For many, the principal attraction of the Islamic world was its supposed voluptuousness. Muslim men were thought to be dedicated sensualists (an idea that Muslims themselves would have found astonishing) and Islam a religion without morality. The harems and slave markets of Orientalist painting held a prurient fascination as places where Christianity did not apply, where the would-be adventurer could, in his imagination, indulge his every carnal desire. The degree of eroticism would have been unthinkable in images of life in contemporary Europe. But with the Near East there was an excuse, since the work of a 'peintre ethnographe' such as Gérôme was ostensibly a matter of scientific observation. It was the stuff of sexual fantasy with the appearance of a documentary record. It titillated its audience and at the same time confirmed 'objectively' their assumption that the people it depicted were morally inferior.[22]

The Orientalist portrayal of all-male gatherings of Muslims at prayer might seem just a corollary to the idea of the Muslim as lord of the harem, an apotheosis of the men's club. This may well have been part of the meaning of the subject, but it seems to have carried other, genuinely religious implications as well. In their devotion, as in their dress, Muslims were looked upon as a relic of another age, and it was quite usual to compare Islam with European Christianity in the Middle Ages. Eugène-Melchior de Vogüé, for example, declared that 'the intellectual and social horizons of the Islamic world are in many respects comparable to those of our medieval forefathers'.[23] The association was strengthened by the widely-held belief that Gothic architecture, enjoying revival as a link with the Age of Faith, was Islamic in origin. Some were moved to reflect on the Muslim kind of mentality as a good thing disastrously lost to modern Europe. Describing the evening prayer of pilgrims to Mecca, Major Fridolin wrote: 'There before your eyes is the East, just as Muḥammad left it so long ago, just as it will endure until the spirit of incredulity and revolt, the so-called Enlightenment, will undermine the edifice of Islam as it has undermined society and Christianity in Europe.'[24] Fridolin was expressing the mood of nostalgic religiosity that fostered countless paintings of 'primitive' devotion, images of Muslim worship by Orientalists as well as scenes of peasant piety in Europe, especially among Bretons in picturesque folk costume.

In 1839–40 the painter Frédéric Goupil-Fesquet visited the Near East with Horace Vernet and saw Muslims at prayer in a mosque. 'A holy respect comes over the spectator in the presence of this silent gathering', he wrote. 'The expression of humility and veneration imprinted on every face, which no distraction can alter, gives their features a stately grandeur that seems to harmonise with the building itself. Prayer makes all men equal: the half-naked *fellāḥ* next to the rich man in his silk *quftān* and

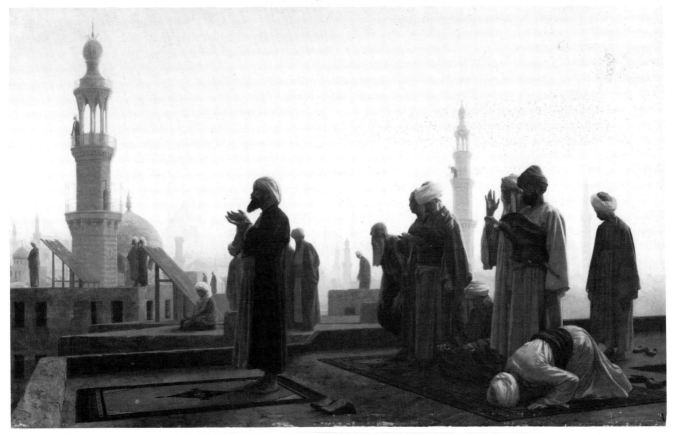

fig. 14 Gérôme *Prayer on the Rooftops* 1865 [Kunsthalle, Hamburg]

gold-embroidered turban, his ornate weapons removed for the moment, both believing in the same God, both come to worship with the same fervour.'[25] When Gérôme went to the area in 1868, he also took a friend and fellow artist who documented their travels. This was Paul Lenoir, whose account of their visit to the Mosque of Sultān Hasan in Cairo is of particular interest, not only because it sums up the sense of inadequacy that could be felt by the modern Christian at an exhibition of 'medieval' piety, but also because of Gérôme's special concern with the mosque interior as a subject. 'The thing that strikes you most when you visit mosques is their exclusively religious, almost poetic, atmosphere. These are not our pretty-pretty Parisian cathedrals, nor our phoney-Greek temples, which are just theatres where the performance is the Mass. Seeing quiet, serious Arabs prostrate themselves without affectation before the wall of the miḥrāb, I could not help thinking of my good old Madeleine, where the one-o'clock service is just like the opening night of a show . . . In Cairo, it's fanaticism if you like, but at least it's real religious faith, and it expresses itself without any of that elegant, frivolous piety that characterises the Roman Catholic mosque back home.'[26]

The Arab of the desert was even more likely to be regarded as shamingly devout than his urban counterpart. The desert of the European imagination is harsh but also purgative, conducive to deep religious thought, a place in which to communicate with the Godhead. The idea is an ancient one of course, and many are the prophets and saints who spent periods of meditation in the wilderness. Richard Burton found in the desert 'the type of Liberty, which is Life' and was constantly aware of 'the idea of Immensity, of Sublimity, of Infinity'.[27] The fact that the three great revealed religions of Judaism, Christianity and Islam originated in the Near East was attributed to the influence of the desert and men such as Burton assumed the Bedouin to be possessed of an instinctive godliness by virtue of his environment. The scene of Arabs praying in the desert was a stock Orientalist subject. In his *Tableaux algériens*, Gustave Guillaumet provided what could be an accompanying line for his own (fig. 15), or almost any other

treatment of the theme: 'The murmur of piety, which no temple imprisons, spreads its harmony into the infinity of the universe.'[28]

The image of the Arab at prayer appealed far more in Roman Catholic France than Protestant Britain, perhaps because of the Protestant's reluctance to set any store by the outward forms of worship. In France there was a traditionalist current of opinion within the Church that ran against those who would try to reconcile religion with modern science, advocating instead an uncompromising return to the rule of faith and transcendental revelation. By the 1870s it constituted a 'Catholic Revival'.[29] A conspicuous manifestation of this was the upsurge in pilgrimages, notably to the new centre of Lourdes, a parallel to the interest in the pilgrimage to Mecca shown by many Orientalist artists and writers. The Catholic Revivalists looked longingly to Islam, as they looked to the Middle Ages, as a pre-scientific society bound together by religious belief. Before becoming a leading scholar of Islam, Henri de Castries served during the 1870s as an officer in the colonial cavalry in Algeria. His feelings on seeing the Muslim troops under his command engaged in communal prayer came out of a yearning for religious identity felt by a large section of the Catholic community: 'I heard the invocation "Allah akbar!" ring out loud and clear. God is Supreme! That simple concept of divinity took on a meaning in my soul beyond anything theology or metaphysics had taught me. I was struck down by an inexpressible malaise, a mixture of shame and anger. I felt that, in this moment of prayer, these Arab cavalrymen, so subordinate just a short time ago, were asserting their superiority over me. How I wished I could have cried out to them that I too believed, that I too knew how to worship my God!'[30]

There was sympathy, respect, reverence and occasionally envy towards Islam, but very few conversions. Among painters, the case of Alphonse-Etienne Dinet, who settled in Algeria, became a Muslim, made the pilgrimage to Mecca and became Hadj Nasr Ed Dine Dini, may well be unique. For the most part, painters of devout Muslims no more thought of converting to Islam than painters of devout Bretons thought of becoming peasants. Given

fig. 15  Guillaumet *Evening Prayer in the Sahara*    1863    [Musée d'Orsay, Paris]

the traditional distaste of Muslims for the representation in art of living creatures, an attitude derived from verses in the *Qur'ān* forbidding idolatry, the idea of painting Islamic devotion was in a sense anomalous. Furthermore, the naturalistic style in which most scenes of Muslim worship were treated implied a scientific, fact-finding approach that was alien to the transcendental state of mind they depicted. They embodied a relationship between European and Muslim, some would say an essentially colonialist relationship, in which there was little or no potential for common experience or communication. Like the harem or slave market scene, they suggested both fascination with the subject and distance from it. They ostensibly held up Muslims as a model of devotion yet at the same time, by the means of representation, emphasised the gulf between 'us' and 'them'. The scenes of 'primitive' religion treated in a correspondingly 'primitive' style by Gauguin and his followers were a resolution of this contradiction. Developing from the idea that religious content could reside in style as much as subject, the main form of religious art in the twentieth century has been abstract.

The issue at stake in the portrayal of Islam in nineteenth-century art was not Islam at all, but Christianity. Both types of Orientalist religious subject, the Muslim and the biblical, illustrated arguments arising from the debate on what relationship, if any, could exist between Christianity and science in the modern world. Biblical Orientalism expressed the desire of the liberal Christian to reconcile his religion as far as possible with modern knowledge and show, to borrow Holman Hunt's phrase, that he was not afraid of the truth. The painter of Muslim devotion represented the more reactionary face of Christianity, the yearning for the old days when religion was a matter of Faith. This meant not trying to take science on at its own game but producing evidence of what the scientific mentality was destroying. The Orientalist painter was not an innocent eye. His vision of the Near East was conditioned by his own concerns as a European and a Christian. Looked at from the religious point of view, as from others, Orientalism tells us something about the Near East but far more about the state of mind of nineteenth-century Europe.

## NOTES

1 See Robinson's *Biblical Researches in Palestine, Mount Sinai and Arabia Petraea*, London, 1841, and F. Jones Bliss, *The Development of Palestine Exploration*, London, 1906.

2 A. Cunningham, *The Life of Sir David Wilkie*, London, 1843, III, p. 442.

3 *Lectures on the History of the Jewish Church*, Part I, London, 1863, p. 11.

4 Palestine Exploration Fund, *Twenty-One Years' Work in the Holy Land*, London, 1886, p. 19.

5 *Tableaux algériens*, Paris, 1888, p. 85.

6 See A. Durande, *Joseph, Carle et Horace Vernet. Correspondance et biographies*, Paris, 1864, p. 329; J. Ballantine, *The Life of David Roberts, R.A.*, Edinburgh, 1866, p. 109; N. Neal Solly, *Memoir of the Life of William James Müller*, London, 1875, p. 71.

7 Durande, *op. cit.*, p. 149. A brief survey of biblical Orientalism amongst French painters, beginning with Vernet, is given in J. Alazard, *L'Orient et la peinture française au XIXe siècle, d'Eugène Delacroix à Auguste Renoir*, Paris, 1930, pp. 131–34.

8 See Cunningham, *op. cit.*, p. 427. For a scholarly account of British Orientalism, with special reference to Wilkie, Roberts, Holman Hunt and J. F. Lewis, and containing many insights into the religious aspect of their work, see K.P. Bendiner, 'The Portrayal of the Middle East in British Paintings 1835–1860', Ph.D. thesis, Columbia University, 1979.

9 Cunningham, *op. cit.*, p. 376.

10 W. Holman Hunt, *Pre-Raphaelitism and the Pre-Raphaelite Brotherhood*, 2nd edition, London, 1913, II, pp. 255–56.

11 For a fuller account of Tissot as an Orientalist biblical painter, and his artistic and archaeological sources, see the exhibition catalogue *J. James Tissot, Biblical Paintings*, Jewish Museum, New York, 1982, especially the essay 'Tissot's Illustrations for the Hebrew Bible' by Gert Schiff.

12 *Une Famille d'artistes. Les Trois Vernets. Joseph – Carle – Horace*, Paris, 1898, pp. 160–63.

13 *Les Beaux-Arts en Europe*, 2nd series, Paris, 1855, II, p. 19.

14 G. Burne-Jones, *Memorials of Edward Burne-Jones*, London, 1904, II, p. 281.

15 1874 edition, pp. 79–80.

16 *Ibid.*, p. 81.

17 See Tate Gallery, *The Pre-Raphaelites*, 1984, cat. no. 143.

18 'Religion and Art', *Contemporary Review*, January 1897, LXXI, p. 50.

19 See his *Souvenirs, impressions, pensées et paysages pendant un voyage en Orient*, Paris, 1835.

20 See 'The Hero as Prophet. Mahomet: Islam' in *On Heroes, Hero-Worship and the Heroic in History*, London, 1841. For discussions of the image of Islam in Europe, with reference mostly to literature, see Byron Porter Smith, *Islam in English Literature*, Beirut, 1939; P.K. Hitti, *Islam and the West. A Historical Cultural Survey*, Princeton, 1962; N. Daniel, *Islam, Europe and Empire*, Edinburgh, 1966; S. J. Nasir, *The Arabs and the English*, London, 1976; and, most recent and most provocative, E.W. Said, *Orientalism*, New York, 1978. Said defines Orientalism as 'a Western style for dominating, restructuring, and having authority over the Orient' (p. 3).

21 See his essay 'El Islam, or the Rank of Muhammedanism among the Religions of the World', probably written in 1853, in *The Jew, the Gypsy and El Islam*, London, 1898.

22 Linda Nochlin has analysed Orientalist painting using the methods applied to literature by Edward Said in her article 'The Imaginary Orient', *Art in America*, May 1983, vol. 71, pp. 118–31, 187–91, to which the present author is indebted.

23 *Syrie, Palestine, Mont Athos: Voyage aux pays du passé*, Paris, 1876, p. 74.

24 'Scènes de la vie religieuse en Orient', *Revue des Deux Mondes*, 1 April 1854, nouvelle période, 2e série, 16, p. 96.

25 *Voyage en Orient fait avec Horace Vernet en 1839 et 1840*, Paris, 1843, p. 99.

26 *Le Fayoum, le Sinaï et Pétra. Expédition dans la Moyenne Egypte et l'Arabie Petrée sous la direction de J. L. Gérôme*, Paris, 1872, pp. 167–68.

27 *Personal Narrative of a Pilgrimage to El-Medinah and Meccah*, London, 1855-56 I p. 149. On the British fascination with the desert, see Kathryn Tidrick, *Heart-beguiling Araby*, Cambridge, 1981.

28 *Tableaux algériens*, Paris, 1888, p. 139.

29 See Richard Griffiths, *The Reactionary Revolution. The Catholic Revival in French Literature, 1870–1914*, London, 1966.

30 *L'Islam: Impressions et études*, Paris, 1896, p. 4.

*Color Plates*

80 Ingres *Odalisque and Slave*

12  Delacroix *Arab Chief visiting a Tribe*

13  Delacroix *The Fanatics of Tangier*

16 Delacroix *The Lion Hunt*

17  Delacroix *The Collection of Arab Taxes*

90  Lewis *In the Bezestein, El Khan Khalil, Cairo (The Carpet Seller)*

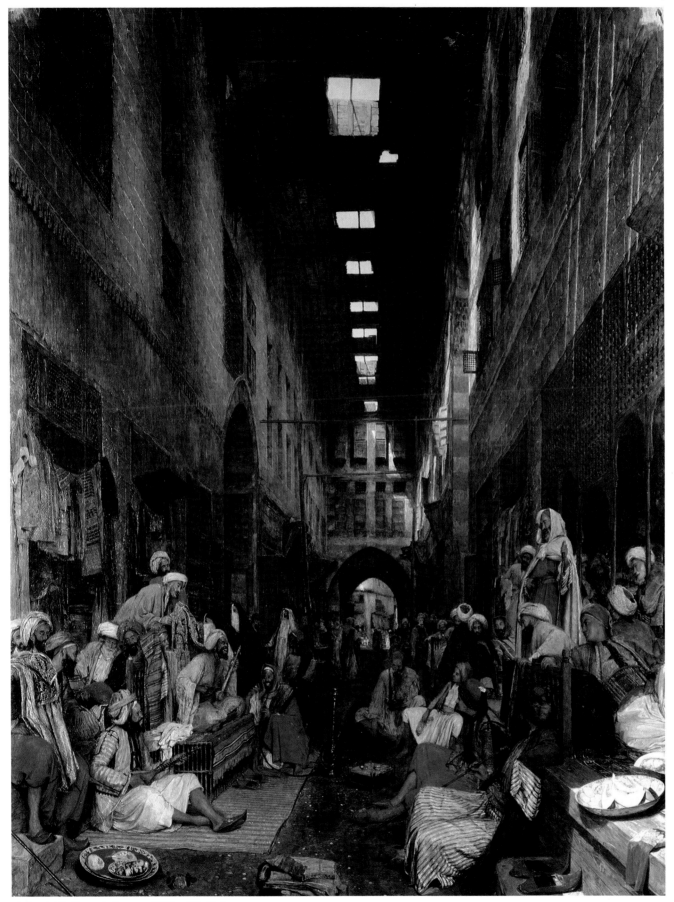

96 Lewis *The Bezestein Bazaar of El Khan Khalil, Cairo*

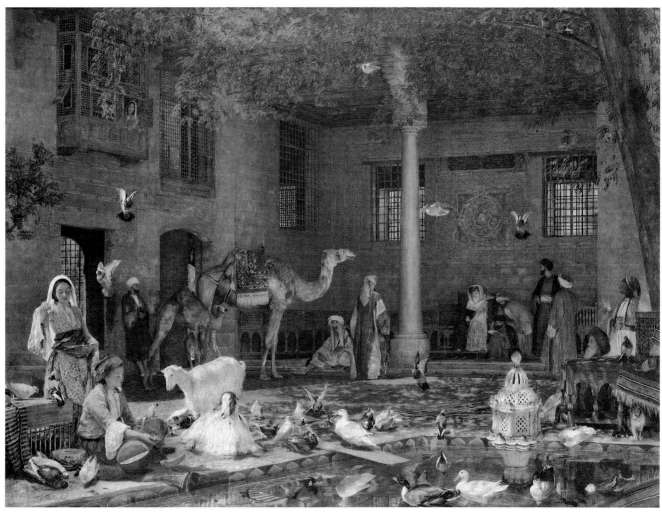

92 Lewis *The Hósh (Courtyard) of the House of the Coptic Patriarch, Cairo*

93 Lewis *A Turkish School in the Vicinity of Cairo*

95 Lewis *An Intercepted Correspondence, Cairo*

89  Lewis *A Frank Encampment in the Desert of Mount Sinai, 1842 – The Convent of St. Catherine in the distance*

91  Lewis *Edfou, Upper Egypt*

112  Roberts *The Island of Philae, Nubia*

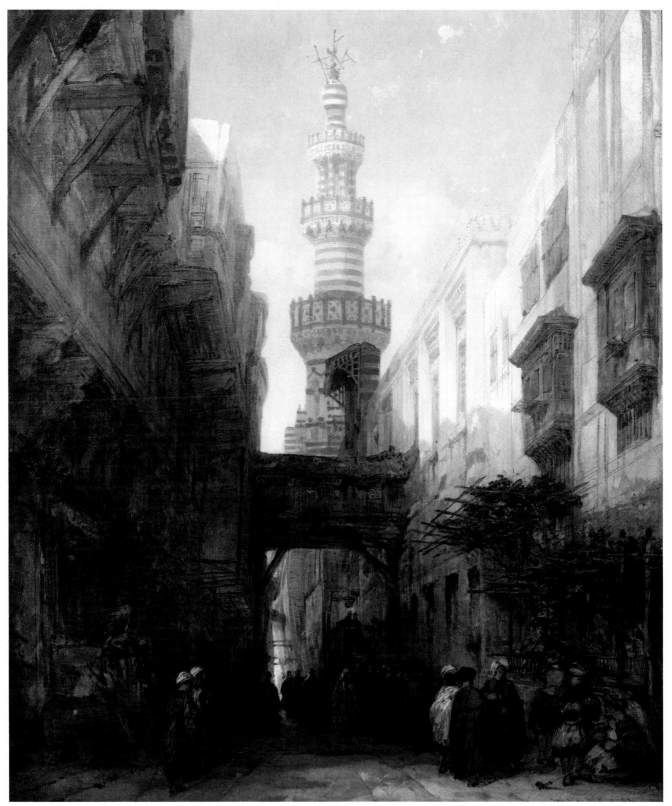

113  Roberts *A Street in Cairo*

110  Roberts *The Temple of Dendereh*

111 Roberts *The Gateway to the Great Temple at Baalbec*

85 Lear *The Pyramids Road, Gizah*

84 Lear *The Cedars of Lebanon*

83  Lear *Jerusalem from the Mount of Olives, Sunrise*

82  Lear *Philae on the Nile*

64  Gros *The Battle of Nazareth*

65  Gros *The Pesthouse at Jaffa*

119  Vernet *The Battle of Somah*

8  Chassériau *Ali Ben Hamed, Caliph of Constantine, followed by his Escort*

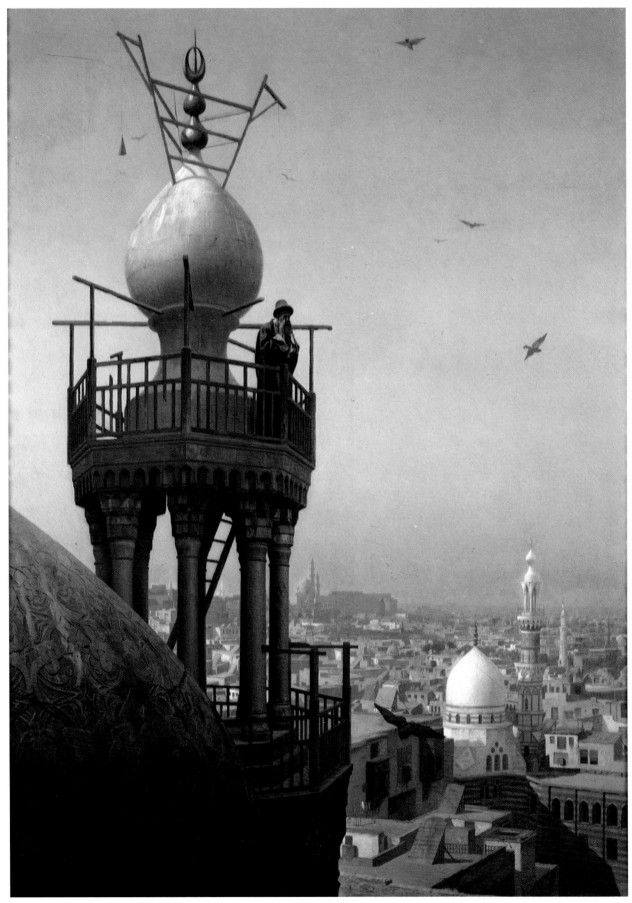

36  Gérôme *The Muezzin's Call to Prayer*

39  Gérôme *The Whirling Dervishes*

28  Gérôme *Prayer in the House of an Arnaut Chief*

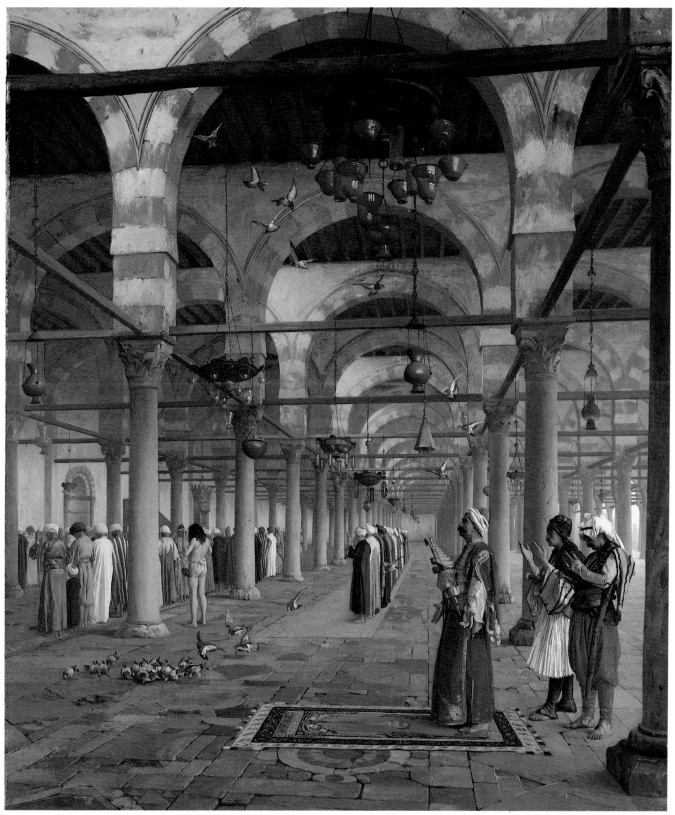

32  Gérôme *Prayer in the Mosque of 'Amr*

88 Leighton *Portions of the Interior of the Grand Mosque of Damascus*

38  Gérôme *Prayer in the Mosque of Qāyt-bāy*

20 Deutsch *The Prayer at the Tomb*

37  Gérôme *The Carpet Merchant*

1  Bauernfeind *Market in Jaffa*

103  W. J. Müller *The Carpet Bazaar at Cairo*

122 Wilkie *The Tartar Messenger Narrating the News of the Victory of St. Jean d'Acre*

121  Wilkie *The Turkish Letter Writer*

19 Deutsch *The Scribe*

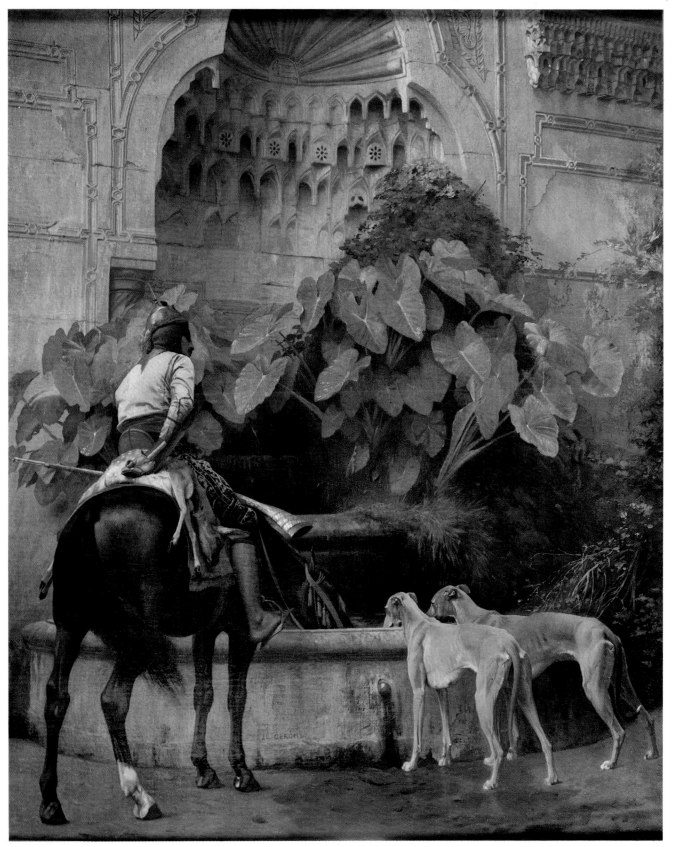

35  Gérôme *The Return from the Hunt*

22  Fromentin *Arab Falconer*

114  Schreyer *Arab Horsemen*

23 Fromentin *Windstorm on the Esparto Plains of the Sahara*

25  Fromentin *Dahabeeyah on the Nile at Luxor*

26 Gérôme *The Plain of Thebes, Upper Egypt*

27 Gérôme *Egyptian Recruits Crossing the Desert*

40 Girardet *Salt Caravans in the Desert*

42 Girardet *Caravans in the Dunes at Bou-Saada*

3  Belly *Pilgrims going to Mecca*

67 Guillaumet *The Desert*

41 Girardet *The Tailor's House in an Arab Town*

116 Seddon *Dromedary and Arabs at the City of the Dead, Cairo, with the Tomb of Sultan El Barkook in the background*

102 L. C. Müller *Encampment in the Desert at Gizah*

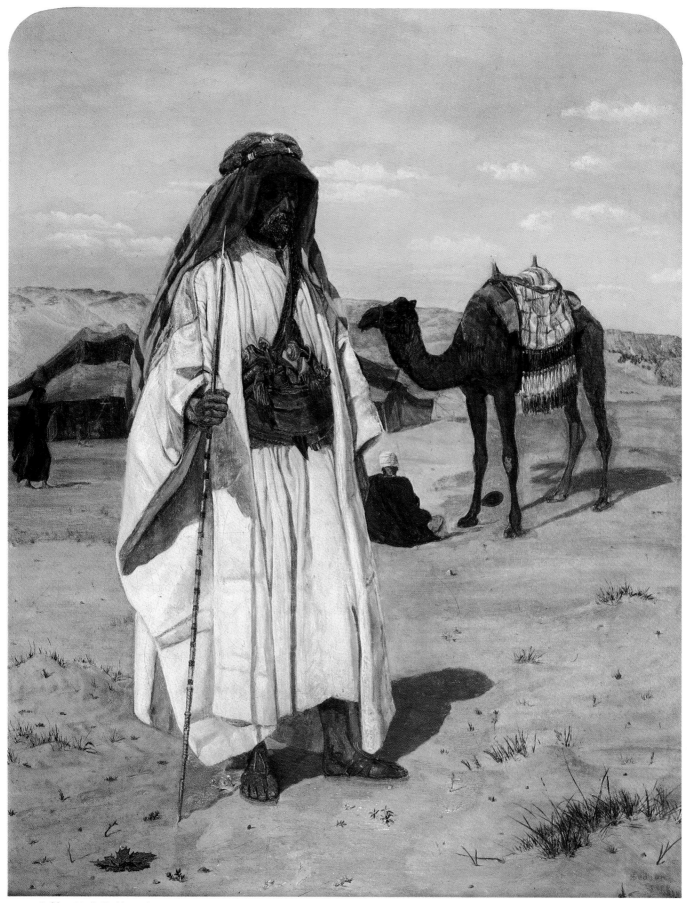

117  Seddon *'Arab Sheikh' (probably Richard Burton)*

30  Gérôme *General Bonaparte in Cairo*

115  Scott Lauder *David Roberts Esq. in the Dress he wore in Palestine*

105  Phillips *Portrait of Lord Byron*

34  Gérôme *A Bashi-Bazouk*

94 Lewis *A Memlook Bey, Egypt*

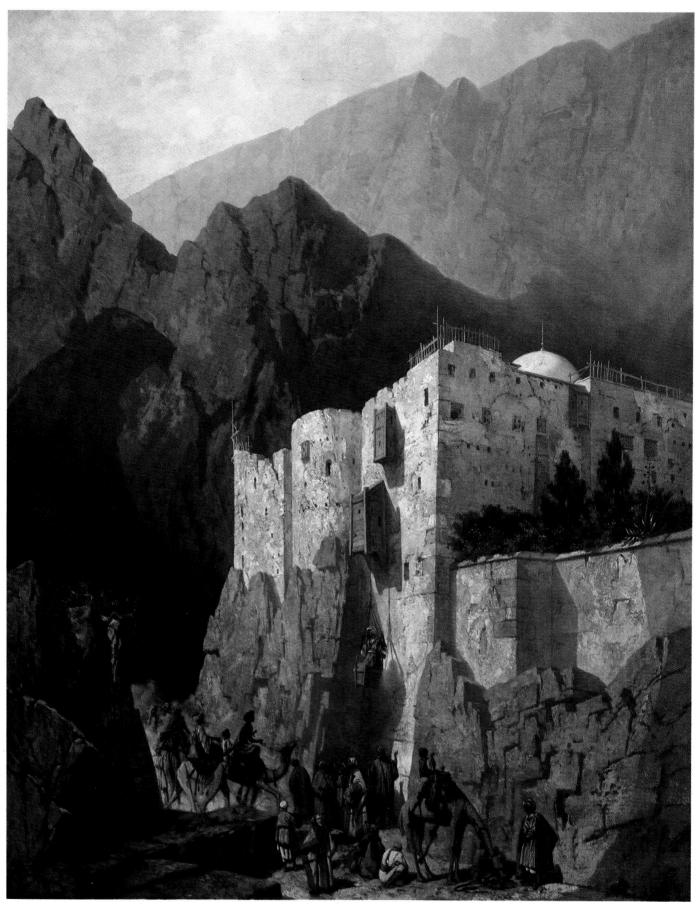

9 Dauzats *Monastery of St. Catherine, Mount Sinai*

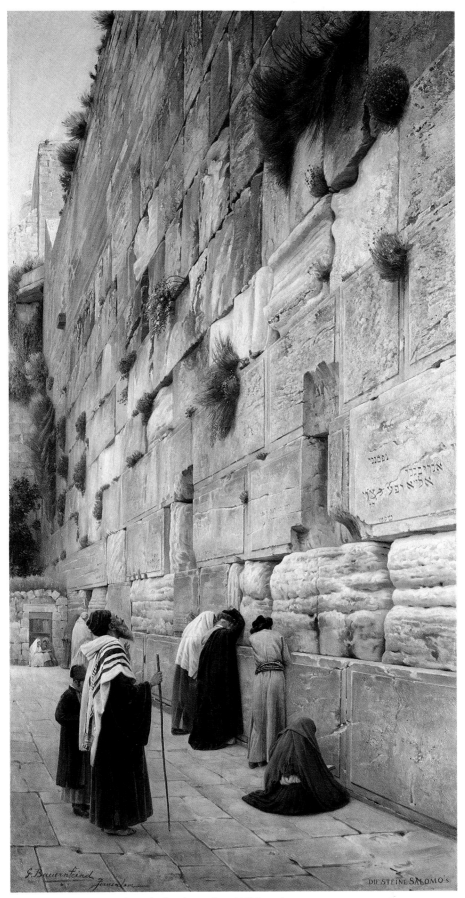

2  Bauernfeind *Lament of the Faithful at the Wailing Wall, Jerusalem*

68  Guillaumet *The 'Seguia', Biskra*

118  Tissot *The Journey of the Magi*

78  Holman Hunt *The Afterglow in Egypt (The Visitors of the Ashmolean Museum)*

77  Holman Hunt *The Afterglow in Egypt (on loan from Southampton Art Gallery)*

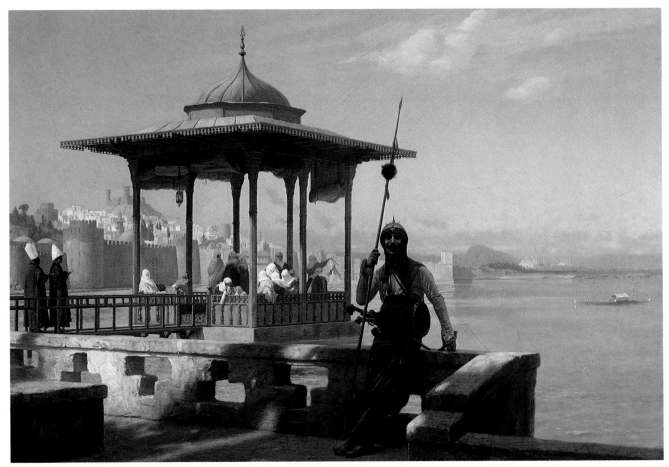

33  Gérôme *Harem in the Kiosk*

101  Melville *Awaiting an Audience with the Pasha*

86  Lecomte du Nouÿ *The Guard of the Seraglio (Souvenir of Cairo)*

31 Gérôme *The Moorish Bath*

29 Gérôme *Dance of the Almeh*

5 Benjamin-Constant *Odalisque*

7 Brangwyn *A Trade on the Beach*

106  Renoir *Woman of Algiers* or *Odalisque*

108  Renoir *Girl with a Falcon*

107 Renoir *The Jewish Wedding (after Delacroix)*

109  Renoir *Arab Festival*

98  Matisse *The Blue Nude – Souvenir of Biskra*

100 Matisse *Odalisque in Red Trousers*

99b Matisse *Moroccan Garden*

99c  Matisse *The Palm Leaf, Tangier*

99a Matisse *Moroccan Landscape*

*The Catalogue*

# Bauernfeind, Gustav   1848–1904

Bauernfeind's first career was in architecture, which he studied and practised in his native Stuttgart. On visits to Switzerland and Italy he began making topographical sketches and paintings, mostly townscapes, and eventually decided to pursue art professionally. He trained under Ludwig von Löfftz in Munich, where he afterwards set up his own studio. In 1880–82 he travelled extensively in the Near East, sketching street scenes in Cairo, Jaffa, Jerusalem and Damascus. In 1888 he visited Damascus again and Palmyra, and in 1898 settled in Jerusalem, where he died in 1904.

## 1*

## Market in Jaffa   1887

*Markt in Jaffa*

81 × 109 cm
Signed and dated bottom left: *G. Bauernfeind/Jaffa 1887*
Private Collection, Houston, Texas
[*repr. in colour on p. 70, plate 1*]

The ancient port of Jaffa (sometimes called 'Joppa'), now subsumed by Israel's main commercial and industrial centre Tel Aviv, was for centuries Jerusalem's natural outlet to the sea and the landing-point from which most pilgrims and travellers began their journeys into Palestine. It was devastated during the Napoleonic campaigns (1798–99; see Cats. 32, 48) and largely rebuilt in the early nineteenth century. The place was a favourite subject of Bauernfeind from the time he first visited it on his Near Eastern trip of 1880–82. This market scene may have been painted on the spot, as the inscription implies, or in Munich from sketches made in Jaffa at an earlier date. A work with the same title was shown by Bauernfeind at the International Exhibition in Munich in 1883. For another Jaffa street scene, dated 1890, see M. Verrier, *The Orientalists*, New York and London, 1979, no. 21, ill.   M.W.

PROVENANCE
1981, June, acquired by The Fine Art Society, London; acquired by Kurt E. Schon Ltd, New Orleans; Priv. Coll., Houston, Texas

REFERENCE
Coral Petroleum, *A Near Eastern Adventure*, n.d., n.p., ill.

## 2

## Lament of the Faithful
## at the Wailing Wall, Jerusalem

*Klage der Gläubigen an den Tempelmauern Jerusalems*

193·5 × 98 cm
Signed bottom left: *G. Bauernfeind/Jerusalem*
Inscribed bottom right: *DIE STEINE SALOMO'S*
Private Collection
[*repr. in colour on p. 93, plate 2*]

The Wailing Wall in Jerusalem is a stretch of the western side of the stone platform on which stood the Temple of Solomon, a site occupied since the eighth century by the Muslim Qubbat al-Sakhrah, or Dome of the Rock. It is traditionally where orthodox Jews come to pray and bewail the capture of the city by the Romans. Bauernfeind was resident in Jerusalem for the final six years of his life and a larger version of this subject (250 × 150 cm) is said to have been the last picture he completed.   M.W.

PROVENANCE
1983, 21 June, sale of the artist's grand-niece, Sotheby's, London (lot 25); acquired by the present owner
REFERENCES
Thornton 1983, ill. pp. 200–01
H. Schmid, *Der Maler Gustav Bauernfeind, 1848–1904*, Sulz, 1981, n.p., ill.

1

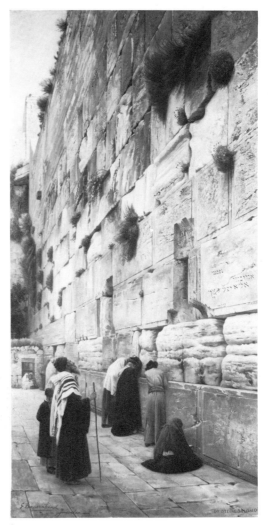

2

# Belly, Léon-Adolphe-Auguste    1827–1877

A native of Saint-Omer (Pas-de-Calais), Belly passed briefly through the studio of Picot (1786–1868) before receiving his formative training with Constant Troyon (1810–1865). Early in his career he was attracted to the work of Decamps and Marilhat (*q.v.*), and in 1849 visited Barbizon, where he came under the influence of Millet, Corot and especially Rousseau.

Belly made three trips to the Orient, the first in 1850–51, when he travelled to Greece, Syria and the Black Sea in the company of de Saulcy and Edouard Delessert. In 1855–56 he returned to Egypt with the painter Edouard Imer, and, with a piano, together made their way up the Nile to the strains of Mozart, Glück and Bach. A final voyage in 1857 was largely spent making preparatory studies for *Pilgrims going to Mecca*.

The four landscapes from the suburbs of Nablus and Beirut, and from the shores of the Dead Sea, with which he made his Salon debut in 1853, won him immediate critical acclaim, and thereafter he rose quickly to fame, gaining a first class medal in 1861, and a Croix de la Légion d'Honneur the following year.

From 1861 he held weekly soirées with his mother at their home on the Quai d'Orsay, which were frequented by leading artists of the 1860s, including Rousseau, Corot, Fromentin (*q.v.*) and Puvis de Chavannes. Though captivated by Egypt, Belly continued to execute portraits and landscapes of Normandy and the Sologne, and in 1867 acquired land at Montauban, where he spent an increasing amount of time in the forests and pasture lands of the Sauldre.

Belly was plagued by illness during the last five years of his life, and died in Paris at the age of fifty.

ABBREVIATED REFERENCE
Mandach 1913 Conrad de Mandach, 'Artistes Contemporains, Léon Belly (1827–1877)', *Gazette des Beaux-Arts*, January 1913, pp. 73–84; February 1913, pp. 143–57

## 3

## Pilgrims going to Mecca    1861
*Pèlerins allant à la Mecque*

161 × 242 cm
Signed and dated bottom left: *L Belly 1861*
Musée d'Orsay, Paris
[*repr. in colour on p. 82, plate 3*]

The initial idea for this painting came during Belly's second trip to Egypt in 1855–56. In a letter of 1 June 1856, he recorded his intention to paint a desert scene with Arabs and dromedaries, and to reproduce, like Courbet, 'the truly beautiful and interesting features of the everyday life of our fellow men' (Mandach 1913, p. 149).

The *Ḥājj* (pilgrimage to Mecca) is one of the five pillars of Islam, commanded by the *Qur'ān* to be made, if possible, at least once during a Muslim's life. The official caravan was a highly organised affair travelling between carefully placed water stations and taking thirty-seven days from Cairo. Belly faithfully depicts the social cross-section of the procession with the *Shaykh al-Ḥājj* (director of the pilgrimage) leading the way, followed by the poorer pilgrims, probably slaves or substitutes for the infirm rich; behind them the wealthy identified by the sumptuous *shibriyyah* (rounded) or *takhtrawān* (two camel) litters, with the most beautiful camel in the middle distance bearing the Khedive's gifts. In an original idea for the *Pilgrims going to Mecca* (Musée des Beaux-Arts, Tours; inv. 925-301-4), Belly experimented with a higher horizon line. Here it is considerably lowered to give greater force to the composition and to stress the awesome proportions of the foreground figures. The rhythmical diminution of the caravan to the very back of the canvas suggests both the inexorable progress of the pilgrims, and the

3

measureless expanse of desert and sky beyond. On the left of the procession, a hunched figure leading a woman and child on an ass, makes an allusion to the biblical flight into Egypt which, together with the ferocity of the sunlight, sparse landscape, and ascetic tonalities, contributes to the solemnity of the occasion, and the feeling that one is here participating in an ancient religious rite.

En route to Syria in 1850, Belly had noted the emotional sobriety of mural painting in Padua and Milan, and the calm rationality of Greek religious architecture. It was this grandeur of effect that he recaptured in the present painting creating a sense of respect and an admiration for what he considered to be a very humane religion. For Belly, the occasion represented more than a mere ethnographical curiosity, as his comments on the advanced intelligence of the Egyptians reveal: 'In what way are we superior to this people who precede us by three thousand years?' (Mandach 1913, p. 152). In this he reflected the concern of painters in the latter half of the century to describe not only the picturesque qualities, but the full realities of Oriental life.

Belly was very conscious of the significance of his visual experiences in the Near East and, as a result of his time spent there, his brushstroke became looser and his handling broader. Indeed, his Orientalist work effectively summarises the attractions of the East for the artist; divorced from the mainstream of European art, he found 'the most beautiful form all around! a complete spiritual freedom. The sole concern to paint well for the pleasure of being true, without worrying about the opinion of anyone else. Sometimes it even seems as if I might become a real painter' (Mandach 1913, p. 148).    J.M.

PROVENANCE
1861, acquired by the State from the Salon and placed in the office of Comte Waleski; 1863, August, transferred to Musée du Luxembourg; 1874, 3 May, attributed to Musées nationaux by decree, and added to the inventory of paintings; 1881, 10 February, transferred to the Louvre; 1949, deposited in Musée des Colonies after exhibition in *Histoire de l'Exotisme*; 1968, returned to the Louvre; transferred to the Musée d'Orsay

EXHIBITIONS
1861, Paris, Salon (no. 214)
1867, Paris, *Exposition Universelle* (no. 28)
1873, Vienna, *Exposition universelle internationale, Oeuvres d'art français*, Groupe 1, Classe 1 (no. 35)
1878, Paris, Ecole Nationale des Beaux-Arts, *Exposition des oeuvres de Léon Belly* (no. 39)
1928, Cairo, *Exposition d'Art Français* (no. 1)
1931, Paris, *Exposition coloniale, Beaux-Arts, section rétrospective* (p. 29)
1947, Paris, Musée des Colonies, *Histoire de l'Exotisme*
1974, Paris, Grand Palais, *Le Musée du Luxembourg en 1874* (no. 14)
1975, Marseille, Musée Cantini, *L'Orient en Question* (no. 6)
1977, Saint-Omer, Musée de l'Hôtel Sandelin, *Léon Belly 1827–1877 Rétrospective* (no. 38)
1982, Rochester, New York, Memorial Art Gallery, *Orientalism* (no. 72)

REFERENCES
Mandach 1913 pp. 148–49
Thornton 1983, pp. 96–97, ill.
Ch. Tardieu, 'Silhouettes d'artistes contemporains', *L'Art*, 1878, 10 February, pp. 132, 133
J.K. Huysmans, 'Art Contemporain – Belly', *Les Chefs d'oeuvre d'art au Luxembourg*, Paris, 1881, pp. 61, 62
Ch. Timbal, *Notes et causeries sur l'art et les artistes*, Paris, 1881, pp. 395, 396, 400, 401
E. Michel, *Les Maîtres du paysage*, Paris, 1906, pp. 500–02

# Benjamin-Constant, Jean-Joseph    1845–1902

Considered 'one of the last romantic orientalists' (Ary Renan, *Gazette des Beaux-Arts*, vol. XI, January 1894, p. 51), Benjamin-Constant was born in Paris in 1845, but studied first at the Academy in Toulouse. In 1866 he travelled to Paris to complete his training and the following year entered the Ecole de la Rue Bonaparte under Cabanel (1823–1889). In 1870, when his career was interrupted by the Franco-Prussian War, he left for Spain, visiting Madrid, Toledo, Cordoba and Granada. From there, he travelled to North Africa in the suite of Charles Joseph Tissot, French plenipotentiary to Morocco, and returned to France in 1873 with a vast collection of Islamic artefacts. Throughout the 1870s and 1880s he regularly included Orientalist paintings among his exhibits at the Salon, his first submission being *Les Femmes du Riff* (Musée des Beaux-Arts, Carcassonne) in 1873. In the last two decades of his life, however, he devoted himself almost exclusively to portraiture and decorative painting. As a portraitist, Benjamin-Constant enjoyed great popularity with both British and American collectors, and could count among his patrons Princess Beatrice, the Marquis of Lorne, and the future Edward VII. In 1888 he executed a decorative cycle for the Sorbonne in Paris, the first of several schemes of the 1890s which included work at the Hôtel de Ville, the Capitole in Toulouse, and the Nouvel Opéra Comique in Paris.

4*

## Sketch for 'The Last Rebels'    c. 1880
*Les Derniers Rebelles*

99 × 133·3 cm
Signed bottom right: *B. Constant*
Forbes Magazine Collection, New York

In 1880 Benjamin-Constant exhibited at the Salon *Les Derniers Rebelles*, also known under the title *L'Exécution des Rebelles à Tanger*. This is probably a sketch for the final version, originally in the Musée du Luxembourg, but now lost.

Like that of many painters in the latter half of the nineteenth century, including Dehodencq, Rochegrosse and Renoir (*q.v.*), Constant's vision of the Near East reflected the profound artistic

4

impact of Delacroix's Orientalist oeuvre; *Le Harem: Maroc* (1878; present location unknown, ill. Archives du Musée d'Orsay) owes much to the compositional structure of Delacroix's *Noce juive* of 1839, and in this painting there is an unequivocal debt to the *Sultān of Morocco* (Cat. 17). However, the picture lacks the harmonious balance of the Delacroix prototype; both colour and incident distract the eye from the central theme of the picture, and dilute the expression of the solemnity of the occasion. In his 'Salon de 1876', Emile Zola noted the opposing forces in Constant's Orientalism, 'a good pupil of Cabanel, tormented by the long shadow of Delacroix' (*Mon Salon*, 1959, p. 179). In paintings such as his *Entrée de Mahomet II à Constantinople* (Musée des Augustins, Toulouse), exhibited that year, Constant very self-consciously sought to produce an Orientalist work in the 'Grand style', but in the profusion of exotic detail created an image suitable only as a 'tapestry design' (V. Cherbuliez, 'Salon de 1876', *Revue des Deux Mondes*, June 1870, p. 881). A similar excess of ambition is found in the finished version of this painting, where the disproportionate scale of the foreground rebels illustrates Constant's strong taste for the dramatic. By the 1880s, the curiosity value and picturesque qualities of the Orient had long lost their initial sensuous appeal, and were being regarded with a growing sense of déjà vu. In 1870, Henri Delaborde drew attention to the superficiality of the majority of Orientalist paintings, and complained of 'the ease by which one is seduced by the striking aspect of certain objects, or by the oddity of certain fittings' ('Salon de 1870', *Revue des Deux Mondes*, June 1870, p. 708). Painters, he felt, were blinded by the proliferation of empty, if colourful, detail, substituting 'impartial copying for selective imitation, the external features for the expression of the intimate life, the puppet for the moral being' (*ibid.* p. 708).

Constant's choice of Near Eastern subject-matter and exotic locations highlighted the continuing relevance of Orientalism for French artists in the late nineteenth century. The critics' lukewarm reception of his work, however, also reflected the contemporary need for a deeper awareness of the countries in question, and a reassessment of their artistic potentialities.  J.M.

PROVENANCE
The Fine Art Society, London; bought by the Forbes Magazine Collection, New York

EXHIBITION
1982, Rochester, New York, Memorial Art Gallery *Orientalism* (no. 15, fig. 88)

REFERENCES
J. Buisson, 'Le Salon de 1881', *Gazette des Beaux-Arts*, July 1881, pp. 52–53
J. Landrigan, 'The Forbes Magazine Collections at the Palais Mendoub, Tangier' *Antiques*, June 1982, p. 1387, ill. pl. VII

5

## 5
# Odalisque
### Odalisque

22 × 29·8 cm
Signed bottom right: *B. Constant*
The George A. Lucas Collection of the Maryland Institute, College of Art, on indefinite loan to The Baltimore Museum of Art (BMA L.1934.48.73)
[*repr. in colour on p. 102, plate 5*]

The odalisque, as the embodiment of the untold secrets of the harem, held a powerful and enduring fascination for French Orientalist painters from Delacroix and Ingres to Matisse. Benjamin-Constant took up this theme on several occasions, particularly in the late 1870s, beginning with the *Femmes du harem au Maroc*, exhibited at the Salon in 1875 (present location unknown), and including *Le Harem: Maroc* (1878; see Cat. 4) and *Le Soir sur les terrasses* (1879; Museum of Art, Montreal). Writers, too, were enchanted by the quiet but redolent sensuality of the Eastern woman. Baron Denon, in his seminal work of 1802 (see Cat. 20) was shocked by the extreme voluptuousness of the native women, and the explicit lasciviousness of the movements of their dance, which the more inhibited European mores *'ne permet que dans l'ombre du mystère'* (p. 59). Both Gérard de Nerval and Flaubert took a less morally exclusive stand, and the latter described in great detail his encounters with Kuchuk Hanem, his 'Pretty Little Princess', at Esna (Steegmuller, ed., 1979, pp. 113–16; see Cat. 31, 35). Access to Muslim households and harems was notoriously difficult throughout the century, and even in the 1880s Renoir complained of the difficulty of finding suitable models (see Cat. 86). In general, artists drew their subjects from the local Jewish population, with the notable exception of Delacroix, who was finally admitted to a Muslim household a few days before his return to Toulon in June 1832.

Though highly appealing, Constant's odalisque is hardly ethnographically true to life, but rather an artistic confection, representing the artist's attempt to interpret Eastern beauty according to Western ideals. In fact, she has more in common with the lusty Spanish gypsy in Henri Regnault's *Salomé* (1870; Metropolitan Museum of Art, New York) than with the melancholic interpretations of Chassériau, or the more classical vision of Ingres (see Cat. 56). Like Chassériau, Gérôme and Marilhat, Constant was a fanatical collector of the Oriental: his atelier in the Pigalle was draped with Persian and Turkish rugs, Eastern costumes, and objets d'art. Indeed, in this painting the 'orientalism' seems to lie in the exotic enrichments of decor and accessories rather than in the figure itself. Constant had established his reputation as a colourist in 1869 with *Hamlet et le Roi* (Musée d'Orsay, Paris), and subsequent Orientalist works allowed him to indulge this preference for strong colour. While his very painterly handling often weakened the impact of his large-scale didactic works, the broad, textural brushwork in this smaller painting enlivens the surface, and creates an image of great decorative beauty.  J.M.

PROVENANCE
Acquired from the artist by George A. Lucas; indefinite loan to The Baltimore Museum of Art

EXHIBITIONS
1965, Baltimore Museum of Art, *The George A. Lucas Collection of the Maryland Institute* (no. 64)
1969, Baltimore Museum of Art, *19th Century European Painting*
1982, Rochester, New York, Memorial Art Gallery, *Orientalism* (no. 85, ill.)

REFERENCES
Baltimore, *The George A. Lucas Collection of the Maryland Institute*, 1965, p. 30
L.M.C. Randall (ed.), *The Diary of George A. Lucas*, Princeton, 1979, I, fig. 53
Rochester, New York, Memorial Art Gallery, *Orientalism*, catalogue by D. Rosenthal, 1982, p. 85–88

# Bonnat, Joseph-Florentin-Léon  1833–1922

A native of Bayonne, Bonnat received his formative training
under Federico Madrazo in Madrid. Recalled to France by the
death of his father, he entered in 1854 the atelier of Léon Cogniet
(1794–1880), and spent three years in Italy from 1858 to 1861,
where he studied at the French Academy in Rome with Degas,
Jules Lefebvre, Jean-Jacques Henner and Gustave Moreau.

Bonnat made his first and only voyage to the Orient in 1868,
as one of a party headed by Jean-Léon Gérôme (q.v.), which
included the painter Paul Lenoir and the writer Edmond About.
They visited Egypt, Sinai, Palestine and parts of Turkey and
Greece, and in 1869 witnessed the opening of the Suez Canal.

Bonnat's prestigious career was marked by a number of official
honours: he became a member of the Institut de France and
President of the Société des Artistes Français in 1881, Chevalier
de la Légion d'Honneur in 1882, and was appointed Director of
the Ecole des Beaux-Arts in 1905. Apart from portraits of artistic
figures and political dignitaries of the Third Republic, biblical and
historical paintings formed the major part of his output, though
he also executed Italian genre scenes after his return from Rome,
as well as some landscapes in a fairly traditional style. Bonnat
received several important commissions to execute decorative
cycles for churches and public buildings in Paris, including work
at the Panthéon in 1886 with Puvis de Chavannes, Baudry and
Cabanel.

6

## 6

# An Egyptian Peasant Woman and her Child  1870

*Femme Fellah et son enfant*

186·7 × 105·4 cm
Signed bottom left: *L<sup>n</sup> Bonnat*
Metropolitan Museum of Art, New York

Bonnat is best known as a portraitist; his Orientalist work forms
a small, but significant part of his total oeuvre. *An Egyptian
Peasant Woman and her Child* is one of his first Orientalist
paintings, exhibited with *Une Rue à Jérusalem* at the Salon of
1870. Critics were far from unanimous in their praise of Bonnat's
new subject-matter, some considering the painting heavy, ugly
and beneath the artist's capabilities (Chaumelin, 1873, p. 431;
Ménard, July 1870, p. 39). With its thick impasto, severely
sculptural forms and dark tonalities, the painting technically
reflects little of the impact of Bonnat's eastern travels in 1868–69.
Instead, the handsome *fellāḥah* recalls the robust realism which
he so admired in Velasquez, and possesses the imposing stature
of a Michelangelo sibyl. Bonnat experimented only briefly with
bolder colours after 1869, most noticeably in the *Chieks d'Akabah*
(1872; present location unknown), where reds, yellows and
greens are set in bold opposition.

Gautier, for whom the Oriental woman personified the
romantic and melancholy mystery of the East, praised Bonnat's
portrayal of her Egyptian physiognomy, which was based on his
sketch of a peasant woman thought to have been made at the
ceremony of the opening of the Suez Canal (Musée Bonnat,
Bayonne, inv. no. 635). Bonnat may also have used photographs
since he is known to have found this medium helpful in achieving
a high degree of realism, particularly in his later portraits, which
are distinguished by a characteristic firmness of outline and
subdued tones.

The complex but graceful pose of the two figures echo that
of a Madonna and Child and refer back to his *Ascension de la
Vièrge*, painted in 1868 for St. André, Bayonne. One of Bonnat's
fellow travellers in fact drew attention to the similarities between
the *Egyptian Peasant Woman and her Child* and scenes painted by
Mattia Preti in the Chapel of St. Joan which they had visited in
Malta en route for Egypt (K. Bertrand, *L'Artiste*, June 1870,
p. 298).

The juxtaposition of biblical and exotic imagery in the present
painting looks forward to Gauguin's experiences in Tahiti at the
end of the century, and recalls in particular the pose of *La Orana
Maria* (1891; Metropolitan Museum of Art, New York).   J.M.

PROVENANCE
By 1879, John Wolfe, New York; 1882, 5–6 April, Leavitt's sale, New York (lot 95); 1882,
Catherine Lorillard Wolfe, New York; 1887, bequeathed by Catherine Lorillard Wolfe to
the Metropolitan Museum of Art

EXHIBITIONS
1870, Paris, Salon (no. 298)
1963, Claremont, California, Pomona College Gallery, *Muse or Ego, Salon and Independent
    Artists of the 1880s* (no. 8)

REFERENCES
K. Bertrand, 'Salon de 1870 – Peinture', *L'Artiste*, June 1870, p. 298
R. Ménard, 'Salon de 1870', *Gazette des Beaux-Arts*, 2<sup>e</sup> période, III, 1870, p. 39
M. Chaumelin, 'Salon de 1870', *L'Art contemporain*, Paris, 1873, p. 431
J. Castagnary, 'Salon de 1870', *Salons (1857–1870)*, I, Paris, 1892, p. 421
Ch. Sterling and M. Salinger, *French Paintings: A Catalogue of the Collection in the Metropolitan
    Museum*, New York, 1966, pp. 187–88

# Brangwyn, Sir Frank    1867–1956

The work of this astonishingly prolific and versatile artist is characterised by a love of brilliant colour and a Baroque exuberance of design. He was born in Bruges of Anglo-Welsh parentage. His father was an architect. Brangwyn began to study art after his family settled in London in 1875, and he made his Royal Academy debut in 1885. His early paintings are largely based on his experiences of travel on a cargo boat in the Mediterranean. In 1891 he went to Spain with Arthur Melville (*q.v.*) and in 1893 to Morocco. The 1890s saw the development of his distinctive painterly style, and with it his reputation, especially on the Continent. He began to paint large murals, for which he received commissions throughout his career, culminating in his *magnum opus*, the 'British Empire Panels'. Painted in 1925–33, these were intended for the House of Lords but were rejected and placed instead in the 'Brangwyn Hall', Swansea. He was made an Associate of the Royal Academy in 1904 and a full Academician in 1919. In 1936 he donated his art collection and many of his own works to become part of the collection of the William Morris Gallery in Walthamstow. In the same year he made another substantial gift of his work to his birthplace, Bruges, to form the Brangwyn Museum. The Royal Academy honoured him in 1952 with its first-ever retrospective exhibition devoted to a living artist.

## 7†

## A Trade on the Beach    1893

102 × 127 cm
Signed with initials and dated bottom left: *F.B. '93* [?]
Musée d'Orsay, Paris
[*repr. in colour on p. 103, plate 7*]

Brangwyn was a devotee of the exotic and travelled extensively throughout his life. The sea voyages he made as a young man took him to Constantinople and in 1891 he visited both Spain and South Africa. He was in Spain with Arthur Melville (*q.v.*), who exercised a considerable influence over his early work and may have been responsible for his decision to visit North Africa in 1893. In the spring of that year he spent several weeks in Tangier with his friend and fellow artist, Dudley Hardy. There he made sketches, mostly watercolours, which he worked up into larger-scale works after his return to England. The painting exhibited here shows the beach market at Tangier, and is the most important of these. When first exhibited in London it received mixed reviews. The *Athenaeum* pronounced it a failure but the *Saturday Review* was enthusiastic in its praise: 'The decorative quality and arrangement of this work are beyond criticism. The general buff and grey tone of the picture is set aglow with rich colours that fall upon it in well-placed patches balanced with rare art . . . The work is perfectly executed; the detail all subordinated to the decorative scheme – every little form and patch of colour as splendidly placed as in the best Japanese art. Above all, the artist has caught the spirit of the people as only genius can catch it' (quoted Brangwyn, 1978). It was widely admired when shown at the Salon the following year and, much to the enhancement of Brangwyn's prestige on both sides of the Channel, was bought by the French government.

Galloway's catalogue lists an untraced oil study painted in Tangier (no. 703).    M.W.

PROVENANCE
1895, acquired from the Salon des Champs-Elysées for the Musée du Luxembourg, Paris
EXHIBITIONS
1894–95, London, Insitute of Painters in Oil Colours (no. 7)
1895, Paris, Salon des Champs-Elysées (no. 281)
1952, London, Royal Academy, *Exhibition of Works by Sir Frank Brangwyn, R.A.* (no. 463)
REFERENCES
V. Galloway, *The Oils and Murals of Sir Frank Brangwyn, R.A., 1867–1956*, Leigh-on-Sea, 1962, p. 62, no. 702
R. Brangwyn, *Brangwyn*, London, 1978, pp. 68–69
A. Brejon de Lavergnée and D. Thiébaut, *Catalogue sommaire illustré des peintures du Musée du Louvre: II. Italie, Espagne, Allemagne, Grande-Bretagne et divers*, Paris, 1981, p. 80 (ill.)

7

# Chassériau, Théodore 1819–1856

Born in Santo Domingo (now Dominican Republic), Chassériau moved with his family to Paris in 1820. He entered the atelier of Ingres (q.v.), together with Amaury Duval and Ziegler, in 1830, and made his Salon debut in 1836 with two biblical subjects and two portraits in the classicising manner of his master. However, after a period of almost a year in Italy, from 1840 to 1841, Chassériau became disillusioned with his academic training, complaining of its lack of relevance to the modern-day painter: 'Ce n'est pas à Rome que nous pouvons voir la vie actuelle' (9 September 1840; quoted R. Escholier, 'L'Orientalisme de Chassériau', Gazette des Beaux-Arts, 5ᵉ période, III, 1921, p. 95). After this date the influence of Delacroix is revealed both in his iconography and in his freer, more assured technique.

Chassériau was attracted to Oriental subject-matter early in his career and drawings of Arabs and Mamlūks copied from popular prints and images d'Epinal date from as early as 1828. Possibly due to this youthful fascination, and his friendship with Dauzats (q.v.) and Marilhat (q.v.), Chassériau's brief stay in Algeria from May to July 1846 left a profound impression upon his work. The numerous detailed watercolours made during these two months continued to fire his imagination and provide material for work executed during the remaining ten years of his life.

In 1841, Chassériau received a commission to decorate the church of St.-Mérri, the first of a series of religious and allegorical paintings executed between 1844 and 1854 for public buildings. It was at the Cour des Comptes (1844–48; now destroyed) that Chassériau most firmly established himself as one of the leading decorative artists of the nineteenth century.

8

## 8

## 'Alī ibn Hāmid, Caliph of Constantine, followed by his Escort 1845

*'Alī-Ben-Hamed, Kalife de Constantine, suivi de son escorte*

320 × 261 cm
Signed and dated bottom left: *Théodore Chassériau 1845*
Musée National du Château de Versailles, Versailles
[repr. in colour on p. 61, plate 8]

The Salon of 1845, to which this portrait was sent, saw an interesting confrontation of Orientalist styles, with works exhibited by Decamps and Dauzats (see Cat. 11), four paintings by Delacroix (see Cat. 17) and Vernet's monumental *Prise de la Smala d'Abd-el-Kader* (Versailles). While the jury accepted this portrait of the Caliph of Constantine, they refused Chassériau's *Cléopâtre se donnant la mort*, subsequently destroyed by the artist in a fit of resentment. Critics inevitably drew comparisons between this portrait and Delacroix's equally grandiose portrayal of the Sultān of Morocco (see Cat. 17). Both Baudelaire ('Salon de 1845', p. 37) and Thoré ('Salon de 1845', p. 121) judged Chassériau's painting to be a weak emulation of the older master and reiterated accusations of copying which had been levelled at his lithographic illustrations to *Othello* in 1844. In fact the paintings differ in many respects: the scale of the figures in relation to the background, the degree of attention to detail, but above all, the mood. While Delacroix's painting is based on an actual event, albeit transformed through the artist's personal vision and memory, Chassériau's work pre-dates his journey to Algeria and, as Sandoz has suggested, may have been inspired by an evocative passage describing the pageantry of the Druse warriors in Lamartine's *Voyage en Orient* published in 1835 (Sandoz, 1974, p. 84). In its scale, and in the decorative effects created by the denial of perspectival illusionism, the painting recalls early Renaissance frescoes, and reflects the artist's contemporary involvement in mural decorations for the Cour des Comptes from 1844 to 1848, as well as his earlier work at St.-Mérri, regarded as his 'masterpiece in classicism' (A. Renan, 'Théodore Chassériau et les Peintures au Palais de la Cour de Comptes', *Gazette des Beaux-Arts*, 3ᵉ période, XIX, February 1898, p. 91). Whatever its relative merits, Chassériau successfully evokes the nobility and intellectual vigour of the Arab leader, who, from his introduction to French salon society in 1837, had charmed the Parisian *beau monde* and subsequently, after the capture and deportation of Abdal-Qādir in 1847, was promoted by the French as leader of Arab affairs in Algeria.

The source for the accurate view of Constantine in the distance may possibly be accredited to Dauzats, who had travelled there in 1839, and in 1840 painted *L'Intérieur de la tente du Kaïd Aly, chef ou kaïd des Arabes* (present location unknown), thought to be a representation of 'Alī ibn Hāmid (Bénédite, 1932, p. 236).   J.M.

PROVENANCE
1896, gift of M. Arthur Chassériau to the Musée National du Château de Versailles (inv. MV. 5407)

EXHIBITIONS
1845, Paris, Salon (no. 305)
1968–69, Paris, Petit Palais, *Le Centenaire de Baudelaire* (no. 125)

REFERENCES
C. Baudelaire, 'Salon de 1845', *Baudelaire Critique d'Art*, Paris, 1965, p. 37
Th. Thoré, 'Salon de 1845', *Salons de 1844 à 1848*, Paris, 1868 ed., p. 121
A. Bagnères, 'Théodore Chassériau', *Gazette des Beaux-Arts*, 2ᵉ période, XXXIII, March 1886, pp. 209–18
L. Bénédite, *Théodore Chassériau, sa vie et son oeuvre*, Paris, 1932, p. 235f.
M. Sandoz, *Théodore Chassériau 1819–1856*, Paris, 1974, pp. 84–85
P. Jullian, *The Orientalists, European Painters of Eastern Scenes*, Oxford, 1977, p. 50, ill. p. 51
Rochester, New York, Memorial Art Gallery, *Orientalism*, catalogue by D. Rosenthal, 1982, p. 57

# **Church**, Frederic Edwin  1826–1900

Church was the foremost American landscape painter of the mid-nineteenth century. A native of Hartford, Conn., he studied with the local artists Benjamin H. Coe and Alexander H. Emmons before becoming the first and most distinguished pupil of Thomas Cole (1801–1848) between 1844 and 1846.

A trip in 1850 to Maine, an area to which Church eventually returned on a dozen occasions, began a lifetime of extensive travel, the artistic equivalents of the scientific explorations of the period. Inspired by the writings of Alexander von Humboldt and the opening up of South America to European and American commerce, he journeyed to Columbia and Ecuador in 1853, returning there in 1857, and reaffirmed his interest in the tropics in 1865 with a stay in Jamaica. British and American arctic expeditions prompted a sojourn during 1859 in Labrador in search of icebergs. Between 1867 and 1869 he undertook his only tour of Europe and the Mediterranean, visiting Alexandria, Beirut, Jerusalem, Petra, Damascus, Baalbec, Constantinople and, in 1869, Athens, as well as London, Paris, Vienna, Berchtesgaden, Salzburg, Florence and Rome. During the winters of the last two decades of his life, he travelled to Mexico fifteen or sixteen times, largely for reasons of health.

Although his capabilities and reputation developed steadily from the mid-1840s, his fame as a creator of precisely detailed, New World landscapes on an epic scale, exemplifying the limitless horizons and unbounded energies of his homeland, was established by *Niagara Falls* (1857; Corcoran Gallery, Washington), *The Heart of the Andes* (1859; Metropolitan Museum of Art, New York) and *The Icebergs* (1861; Dallas Museum of Fine Arts), which were exhibited individually across the United States and in Europe. From 1868 onwards, he complemented his paintings of scenes in the Western hemisphere with a sequence of Mediterranean compositions, of which *Jerusalem* (1870; Cat. 9) and *El Khasné, Petra* (1874; Cat. 10) were among the most important. After 1870, he devoted much effort to the designing and building of his Persian-style mansion, Olana, commanding magnificent views overlooking the Hudson Valley. Deteriorating health and declining popularity curtailed his painting activities after 1882, although he continued to sketch in Mexico until 1898. He died in New York in 1900.   G.L.C.

ABBREVIATED REFERENCES
Huntington 1960 D.C. Huntington, 'Frederic Edwin Church, 1826–1900: Painter of the Adamic New York Myth', Ph.D. thesis, Yale University, 1960; Ann Arbor, London, University Microfilms, 1969
Huntington 1966 D.C. Huntington, *The Landscapes of Frederic Edwin Church*, New York, 1966

9

## 9*

## Jerusalem  1870

137·2 × 214·5 cm
Signed and dated bottom right: *F. E. CHURCH / 1870*
The Nelson-Atkins Museum of Art, Kansas City, Missouri
[*repr. in colour on p. 155, plate 126*]

A major purpose of Church's 1867–68 European and Mediterranean tour was to visit Jerusalem where, in late March 1868, he met Gérôme (*q.v.*). As he noted in a pocket diary, the overall 'appearance of newness' initially disappointed him. But walks within and outside the city, especially to the Mount of Olives, the presumed sites of the Transfiguration, the Tomb of Lazarus and the Crucifixion, changed his mind. After some initial difficulties with sketching he was able to 'secure the main thing – sketches of the city as seen from Olivet. I have all materials for an elaborate view of Jerusalem – and saw the city under some fine effects' (letter to William Osborn in New York, 11 April 1868; Olana Archives). The extant oil and pencil studies to which he referred are now in the Cooper-Hewitt Museum, New York, as is a spirited pencil sketch of *c.* 1870 for the camels and Arab attendants in the left foreground of the painting, while an oil compositional study of *c.* 1869 is in a private collection. Two photographs obtained by Church at the time, showing the city from viewpoints allied to that of the painting, are at Olana.

The finished picture, painted in New York in 1870, represents Jerusalem looking south-west from the Mount of Olives. What differentiates this depiction from numerous earlier representations (see Cat. 23, 61), taken from similar positions, are the afternoon lighting (rather than the morning aspect recommended by guide-books) and the wreath of low rain clouds parting to reveal a glistening architectural vision. The Mosque of Omar (Dome of the Rock) dominates the centre, with the Mosque of Aksa on the left and the Holy Sepulchre in the right central distance. Below, at the left, are the Jewish cemetery and Tomb of Absalom (marked by a conical structure), while at the right beyond gnarled, venerable olive trees are the Tomb of the Virgin and walled Garden of Gethsemene.

*Jerusalem* was Church's second major Near Eastern composition, succeeding a large canvas of *Damascus* (now destroyed) painted in Rome in 1869. Accompanied by an illustrated 'key' to the salient topographical features, *Jerusalem* was unveiled in a single-picture exhibition at a New York gallery in 1871. The exhibition opened a few weeks after the publication of the Palestine Exploration Fund's report by Wilson and Warren, *The Recovery of Jerusalem*, and anticipated the exhibitions in New York, in 1872 and 1873 respectively, of Gérôme's *Golgotha* (Salon 1868; present location unknown), and Selous's mammoth pair of paintings, *Jerusalem in her Grandeur* and *Jerusalem in her Fall* (each 304·8 × 426·7 cm; first exhibited 1860; present locations unknown).

Church's *Jerusalem* attracted extensive and generally very favourable comment in the contemporary press. Most thoughtful was the New York *Independent*, a weekly religious newspaper, whose reviewer recognised Church's recent subject-matter as evidence of a mature genius: the 'lavishness and splendour of youth', which characterised the artist's earlier works, had been supplanted by reflective contemplation tinged 'with the sighs and toils and sufferings . . . of every race / That tear-like trode [*sic*] the world's sad face.'

Extravagantly complimentary response to an 1872 exhibition of the painting in Hartford secured its reputation in Church's home town. After his death in 1900, the Hartford *Courant* recalled that he had considered *Jerusalem* to be his finest work. G.L.C.

PROVENANCE
1870, commissioned from the artist by Thomas M. Allyn, Hartford, Conn.; Mrs Harold Ransom, Hartford, Conn.; 1968–77, Priv. Coll.; 1977, Hirschl and Adler Galleries, New York; bought by the Nelson-Atkins Museum of Art, Kansas City, Missouri

EXHIBITIONS
1870, New York, Goupil's Gallery
1872, Hartford, Conn., Hartford Art Association (no. 1)
1966, Washington, National Collection of Fine Arts; Albany, N.Y., Institute of History and Art; New York, M. Knoedler and Co., *Frederic Edwin Church* (no. 137)
1977, New York, Hirschl and Adler Galleries, *A Gallery Collects* (no. 31)
1977–78, Kansas City, Missouri, Nelson-Atkins Museum of Art, *Kaleidoscope of American Painting* (no. 57)
1980, New York, Cooper-Hewitt Museum, *Close Observation: Selected Oil Sketches by Frederic E. Church*

REFERENCES
Huntington 1960, pp. 170–71, 198–99
Huntington 1966, pp. 97–101
New York *Evening Post*, 28 March 1871, 24 April 1871
New York *Evening Mail*, 31 March 1871
New York *Tribune*, 31 March 1871
New York *Times*, 2 April 1871
New York *World*, 2 April 1871
New York *Independent*, 20 April 1871
Hartford *Evening Post*, 6 June 1872
Hartford *Times*, 22 June 1872
Hartford *Courant*, 9 April 1900

## 10*

## El Khasné, Petra   1874

153·6 × 127·6 cm
Signed and dated bottom right: *F. E. Church / –74*
Olana State Historic Site, New York State Office of Parks and Recreation, Hudson, New York
[*repr. in colour on p. 156, plate 127*]

Thought to have been a temple, probably dating from the first century BC, El Khasné, 'The Treasury', is the most elaborate and best-preserved of the rock-cut buildings of Petra; it faces north-east towards the Siq, a narrow, towering two-mile-long rock defile which until the twentieth century provided the main entrance to the city. The edifice's striated salmon colouring and richly carved features contrast abruptly with adjoining dark grey stone surfaces and with the shadowed darkness of the Siq.

10

In Church's time, the monument embodied the mystery and melancholy of a ruined city popularly believed to have been the capital of Edom, a kingdom accursed in the Old Testament. Discovered by John Burckhardt in 1812, Petra thereafter was an alluring goal for travellers willing to brave an arduous journey through inhospitable terrain and to risk confrontation with local Bedouins, Burckhardt and later chroniclers, notably David Roberts (1839) and W. H. Bartlett (1845), concurred with De Laborde (1830) that 'a just impression' of El Khasné both defied visual representation, and called for an artist to attempt the feat.

Church's painting should be understood as an answer to such a challenge. His expedition to Petra in 1868, which took him through Hebron, the Yemen Valley and Mount Hor, had clearly been contemplated long in advance, and his detailed account of the trip in a pocket diary may have been intended for publication. The 'wild and picturesque' scenery of the region, exquisitely coloured rocks and 'tortuous' precipices of the Siq did not adequately prepare him for his first encounter on 24 February with the 'fairy temple blazing like sunlight among those savage black rocks'. Making several pencil sketches, while suspicious Bedouins lurked nearby, he added colour sketches to his portfolio the next day. Altogether, he spent two and a half days roaming the site. Most earlier illustrations, including two photographs purchased by Church (Olana) and his own oil sketch (Cooper-Hewitt Museum, New York), portrayed El Khasné at an angle, from the north. Church, however, following his pencil drawing (Cooper-Hewitt, inv. no. 1917–4–588) and the precedent of David Roberts's lithograph (D. Roberts, *The Holy Land, Syria, Idumea, Arabia, Egypt and Nubia*, 1842–49, vol. 3, pl. V) showed the temple seen almost frontally through the silhouetted Siq.

Exhibited at the National Academy of Design, New York, in the spring of 1874, the picture met with mixed reviews, but was enthusiastically received at Chicago's Academy of Design a year later. Church gave the painting to his wife and it was installed in the newly-completed sitting room of Olana by the end of 1875. The Near Eastern decor of this entire room emanates from the picture and its ornate frame. Appropriately enough, Church's major paintings of architectural subjects, *The Parthenon* (1871; Metropolitan Museum of Art, New York) and *El Khasné, Petra*, were exactly contemporary with his work as a practising designer of polychromatic architecture.   G.L.C.

PROVENANCE
1875, given by the artist to his wife; installed in the sitting room of Olana, Church's home

EXHIBITIONS
1874, New York, National Academy of Design (no. 320)
1874, New Haven, Conn., Yale College (no. 37)
1875, Chicago, Academy of Design (no. 1)
1900, New York, Metropolitan Museum of Art, *Paintings by Frederic E. Church, N.A.*
1966, Washington, National Collection of Fine Arts; Albany, N.Y., Institute of History and Art; New York, M. Knoedler and Co., *Frederic Edwin Church* (no. 138)
1984, Yonkers, New York, Hudson River Museum, *To Embrace the Universe: Drawings by Frederic Edwin Church* (no. 70)

REFERENCES
Huntington 1960, pp. 159–69, 203–06
Huntington 1966, pp. 93–96
New York *Times*, 6 April 1874; 13 April 1874
New York *Evening Post*, 8 April 1874
New York *Evening Mail*, 25 April 1874
New York *Tribune*, 25 April 1874
New York *World*, 27 April 1874
Chicago *Tribune*, 6 March 1875
Chicago *Sunday Times*, 7 March 1875

# Dauzats, Adrien   1804–1868

Born in Bordeaux in 1804, Dauzats worked first under Pierre Lacour in his home town and later, in 1821, became assistant to the scene painter Thomas Olivier (1772–1839), chief decorator at the Grand Théâtre in Bordeaux. In Paris he joined the atelier of Julien Michel Gué (1789–1843), and was recommended by him to the decorators of the Théâtre Italien – Mattis, Desroches and Blanchard.

Dauzats's association with Baron Taylor dated from 1827, when, together with J.-B. Isabey, Bonington, Villeneuve and Ebeniste Fragonard, he contributed designs for lithographs to the *Voyages pittoresques dans l'ancienne France* (1820–78). It was through Taylor that he made his first voyage to Egypt, Syria, Palestine and Turkey in 1830, as lithographer on a *mission civilisatrice*, the main purpose of which was to secure from Muḥammad 'Alī two obelisks from the ruins of Thebes.

In subsequent years Dauzats spent much time in Spain, Portugal and the French provinces, and in 1839 accompanied the Duc d'Orléans on the expedition to the Gates of Iron, an impressive fortress in the Djurdjura mountains in southern Algeria.

Throughout his career, Dauzats maintained an active interest in the recently established provincial art societies, and overcame a deteriorating asthmatic condition to serve on the 1862 selection committee for the London International Exhibition, and as a member of the jury at the Exposition Universelle of 1867.

## 11†

# Monastery of St. Catherine, Mount Sinai   1845

*Le Couvent de Ste. Catherine au Mont Sinaï*

130 × 104 cm
Signed bottom right: *A. Dauzats*
Musée du Louvre, Paris
[*repr. in colour on p. 92, plate 9*]

Having arrived in Alexandria on 20 April 1830, Dauzats's party spent several weeks in Cairo, before setting off at the beginning of July with guides from the Awlad Sa'īd tribe to cross the Sinai desert. After a rough and hazardous journey, lasting nearly three weeks, they reached the monastery of St. Catherine. The next four days, spent sketching and familiarising themselves with the environs, were, according to Dauzats, 'the most perfectly spent and happiest of my life' (A. Dauzats and Dumas [père], *Quinze jours au Sinaï*, 1841, p. 112). The monastery was frequently visited by artists and writers in the nineteenth century; both David Roberts (*q.v.*) and J.F. Lewis (*q.v.*) executed versions of the scene in 1842, and Alberto Pasini (*q.v.*) exhibited a view at the Salon of 1863. Access to the monastery was itself treacherous, and though the walled-up gateway was opened on the visit of the patriarch, the less-esteemed pilgrim was required to scale almost forty feet of sheer rockface to enter by chair lift through a skylight.

Dauzats's training in the theatre, with his ability to create the *pittoresque* within the confines of a stage set, is very apparent in this imposing image. The high horizon, deep shadow and dramatically illuminated cliffs form a backdrop to the monastery, 'suspended in space like the eyrie of an eagle' (P. Lenoir, *The*

*Fayoûm, or Artists in Egypt*, 1873, p. 213). The allusion to the insignificance of man in the face of the mighty forces of nature occurs too in Dauzats's earlier lithographic work, as in the evocative *Fontfroide, cloître de l'abbaye cistercienne, XIII siècle* (Priv. Coll., Toulouse). Contemporary writers were aware of the similarities between Gothic and Oriental architecture; as one observer noted, in providing the ogival arch as a point of departure, Oriental architecture might even be said to be 'the mother of our Gothic architecture' (N. L'Hôte, 'Egypte sous le point de vue pittoresque', *L'Artiste*, V, 1833, p. 244). For the English artist W.J. Müller (*q.v.*), Turkish costume brought to mind scenes from the Gothick novel *Vathek*, and Dauzats's later works, such as the *Portes de Fer* (1853: Musée des Beaux-Arts, Lille) and *Sinbad le marin* (1865; Musée des Beaux-Arts, Bordeaux) reveal his fascination with the emotive and picturesque qualities of the architecture, overlaid with its literary associations and fairy-tale allusions.

Oriental subject-matter provided scope for Dauzats's natural predilection for strong colour and powerful effects, which had in some cases been out of place in views of French buildings such as *Vue de l'abbaye de St. Denis* (1833).

Delacroix (*q.v.*) is known to have admired Dauzats's technical command as an architectural painter, and consulted him for the background of the *Deux Foscari* (B.710; 1855). For his part, Dauzats helped to promote local interest in Delacroix in Bordeaux, and for a time exercised a favourable influence on his behalf at the Orléans court.   J.M.

PROVENANCE
1845, acquired by the State from the Salon

EXHIBITIONS
1845, Paris, Salon (no. 45)
1968–69, Paris, Petit Palais, *Le Centenaire de Baudelaire* (no. 129, ill.)
1975, Marseille, Musée Cantini, *L'Orient en question* (no. 40)
1982, Rochester, New York, Memorial Art Gallery, *Orientalism* (no. 44)

REFERENCES
Thornton 1983, p. 30, ill.
W.J. Müller, 'Letters from Xanthus by W. Müller', *Art-Union*, VI, April 1844, p. 357
Ch. Baudelaire, 'Salon de 1845', *Le Centenaire de Baudelaire*, I, Paris, 1965, p. 64
Ph. Jullian, *The Orientalists. European Painters of Eastern Scenes*, Oxford, 1977, ill. p. 145

11

# Delacroix, Ferdinand Victor Eugène

## 1798–1863

Delacroix was born in Charenton-St-Maurice (Val de Marne), but moved to Paris in 1805 on the death of his father. At the age of seventeen, encouraged by his uncle, the painter Henri Riesener, he entered the private atelier of Pierre-Narcisse Guérin (1774–1833), and subsequently passed into his class at the Ecole des Beaux-Arts. Delacroix gained much of his formative training through his frequent visits to the Louvre, where, until 1815, he could study the Old Master paintings pillaged by Napoleon during his European campaigns.

In 1822, he made a remarkable, and controversial, Salon debut with *La Barque de Dante* (Louvre, Paris), and the emotional turbulence of his early works led him to be hailed as the Victor Hugo of painting and leader of the Romantic school.

Delacroix made his only voyage to North Africa in 1832, as a late replacement for the painter M. E. Isabey in the suite of the Comte de Mornay. Though the trip lasted only six months, its impact on his artistic career was both iconographically and technically profound. His vision of a living, sublime Antiquity in these countries enabled him to strike a balance between the romantic and classical elements in his work.

The year after his return from North Africa, Delacroix was asked to decorate the Salon du Roi (Palais Bourbon), the first of several large-scale works commissioned by the State. Subsequent cycles were executed for the Library (Palais Bourbon, 1833–47), the Library in the Palais du Luxembourg (1840–46), the ceiling of the Galérie d'Apollon in the Louvre (1850–51), decorations at the Salon de la Paix, Hôtel de Ville (1852–54, destroyed in 1871), and finally at the Chapelle des Anges, St. Sulpice (1853–61). Delacroix's repertoire was enormous. Though he frequently returned to themes later in his carer, they never dominated his œuvre to the exclusion of other genre, which included literary, mythological and allegorical subject-matter, battle-pieces, portraits, animal paintings and still-lifes.

ABBREVIATED REFERENCES

Robaut  A. Robaut and E. Chesneau, *l'Oeuvre complète de Eugène Delacroix, peintures, dessins, gravures, lithographies*, Paris, 1885
Journal  E. Delacroix, *Journal de Eugène Delacroix* (ed. A. Joubin), Paris, 1932, 3 vols.
Corr.  E. Delacroix, *Correspondance Générale de Eugène Delacroix* (ed. A. Joubin), Paris, 1936–38, 5 vols.
B.  L. Rossi Bortolatto, *L'Opera completa di Delacroix*, Classica dell'arte, Milan, 1972
J.  L. Johnson, *The Paintings of Eugène Delacroix. A critical catalogue 1816–1831*, Oxford, 1981, 2 vols.

12

12*

# Combat between the Giaour and the Pasha  1826

*Le Combat du Giaour et du Pasha*

59·6 × 73·4 cm
Signed bottom left: *Eug. Delacroix*
The Art Institute of Chicago

This painting is one of at least six versions of a theme inspired by Lord Byron's poem *The Giaour, a Fragment of a Turkish Tale* (1813), which were executed between 1824 and 1856. All vary considerably in composition and in their relative dependence upon the original poem. Like many nineteenth-century artists, Delacroix acquired a foretaste of the East through Romantic literature. He had become familiar with Byron's poetry through the translations of Amédée Pichot (1822–25) and in an entry in his journal of 11 May 1824, he referred to specific passages as potential sources of artistic inspiration: 'The poet is very rich, keep in mind forever certain passages of Byron to excite the imagination. They suit you well . . . the end of the *Bride of Abdyos*, the *Death of Selim*, his body tossed about by the waves . . . the *Death of Hassan* in the *Giaour* . . . the *Curses of Mazeppa* against those who have bound him to his steed' (Journal, I, pp. 99–100). As in other works inspired by such literary sources as Shakespeare, Dante, Scott and Milton, the original text of Byron's poem is not rigidly interpreted, but acts as a catalyst for Delacroix's powerful imagination. Here, the exoticism of the setting and violence of action are successfully combined with a nascent Orientalism; studies of Turkish weapons (J.27) and Greek costume (J.28) date from 1824, the year in which Delacroix is known to have made sketches of costumes and artefacts in the collection of the artist and traveller, M. Auguste (Journal, I, p. 117; 8 July 1824). As in the *Scène de la guerre actuelle entre les Turcs et les Grecs* (Salon 1824; J.115), the flamboyant dress and Oriental arms are not merely decorative additions but are subservient to the overall sense of the picture. The billowing cloaks of the combatants form a sweeping central diagonal, intensified by the horses' windswept manes, and the height of the dramatic conflict is held in suspension by the fiery glint of the armour, the poised weapons and the passionate gaze of the 'accursed Giaour'.

Rejected on two occasions by the Salon, this painting was exhibited at the Galerie Lebrun in September 1826 in aid of the Greek War of Independence, together with *L'Officier turc tué dans les montaignes* (1826; J.113) and *L'Exécution de Marino Faliero* (1826; J.112). As may be judged from *La Grèce sur les ruines de Missolonghi* (1826; J.98), Delacroix was fully aware of Byron's involvement in the Greek war, a sympathy he himself shared in the *Scènes des Massacres de Chios* (J.105), exhibited at the 1824 Salon. In these paintings, as in the *Combat between the Giaour and the Pasha*, Delacroix's ability to relate contemporary events to romantic verse served as a suitable prelude to his confrontation with the poetic actuality of life in North Africa.

There are six works relating to this painting: *Scène de la guerre actuelle entre les Turcs et les Grecs* (1827; B.168); *Un officier turc tué dans les montaignes* (1827; B.94); *Combat du Giaour et du Pasha* (1835; B.270); *Combat du Giaour et du Pasha* (1856; B.733); *Le Giaour poursuivant les ravisseurs de sa femme* (1849; B.541); *Giaour au bord de la mer* (1849/50; no B. no.).    J.M.

PROVENANCE
c.1827–May 1848, Alexandre Dumas, père; 1848, May, to at least 1885, Charles Mahler;
by 1889, Mr Potter Palmer, Chicago; 1902, Mrs Berthe Honore Palmer, his widow; 1918,
Mr Potter Palmer Jr.; 1943, Mrs Pauline Kohlsaat Potter Palmer, his widow; 1956, joint
ownership of her four heirs; 1962, 28 December, donated by them to the permanent
collection of the Art Institute of Chicago

EXHIBITIONS
1826, Paris, Galerie Lebrun (no. 44)
?1827, Paris Salon
1827, Douai (no. 94)
1829, Paris, Musée Colbert (no. 8)
1846, Paris, Galerie des Beaux-Arts, Suites du supplément (no. 98)
1860, Paris, Boulevard Italiens (supp. no. 345)
1864, Paris, Boulevard Italiens (no. 78)
1885, Paris, Ecole des Beaux-Arts, Exposition Eugène Delacroix (no. 135)
1889–1890, New York, American Art Association, Catalogue of the Works of Antoine-Louis
    Barye . . . for the benefit of the Barye Monument Fund (no. 613)
1910, Paris, Galeries Georges Petit, Exposition des chefs d'oeuvres de l'Ecole Française (no. 62)
1930, Chicago, Art Institute, Loan Exhibition of Paintings, Watercolors and Drawings by Eugène
    Delacroix (no. 3, ill.)
1930, Paris, Louvre, Exposition Eugène Delacroix. Centenaire du Romantisme (no. 40)
1938–1939 New York, Knoedler & Co. and Chicago, Art Institute, Gros, Géricault, Delacroix
    (no. 41, ill.)
1945, Washington, Phillips Memorial Art Gallery, Delacroix, A Loan Exhibition (no. 2)
1955, Paris, Musée de l'Orangerie, De David à Toulouse-Lautrec, Chefs d'oeuvres des collections
    américaines (no. 23, ill. pl. 13)
1974, London, Victoria and Albert Museum, Byron (no. 69. ill.)

REFERENCES
Robaut 202
Journal, I, pp. 99–100
Corr., I, p. 128
B. 130
J. 114
Th. Gautier, Les Beaux-Arts en Europe, Paris, 1855, pp. 184, 185
G. H. Hamilton, 'Eugène Delacroix and Lord Byron', Gazette des Beaux-Arts, 6ᵉ période, XXIII,
    1943, pp. 99–110

## 13

# Moroccan Military Exercises   1832

*Exercices militaires des Marocains*

59 × 73 cm
Signed and dated bottom centre: *Eug. Delacroix 1832*
Musée Fabre, Montpellier

During his stay in North Africa, particularly en route from
Tangier to Meknes, Delacroix witnessed several spirited 'powder
plays', or dramatic displays of horsemanship in mock battle. He
referred to a *course de poudre* at Alcassar-el-Kebir (Journal, I,
p. 131; 9 April 1832), and to a noisy reception at Souk el-Hadat
Rharbia (which he called Garbia), when his party was welcomed
by a riotous volley of crossfire (Corr., I, p. 321; 6 March 1832).

The *Moroccan Military Exercises* (also known as *Fantasia arabe*
and *Marocains courant le poudre*) is the first of five oil paintings
(*Fantasia arabe*, 1833, B.244; *Rencontre des cavaliers maures*, 1833,
B.245; *Rencontre des cavaliers maures*, 1847, Robaut 1268 bis;
*Exercises militaires des marocains*, 1847, no B. no.) and one
watercolour (Louvre, Paris; RF.3372) inspired by these events,
and executed between 1832 and 1847.

The almost contemporary *Fantasia arabe* of 1833 is similar to
the painting exhibited here, although the composition has been
reversed and is less dynamic, Delacroix having substituted a
seated Arab for the rearing horseman as a block to the furious
horizontal thrust of the group of riders. In *Moroccan Military
Exercises*, the landscape background all but disappears in the
gunsmoke and the dust raised by the horses' hooves. The
unremitting forward impulse is unchecked by the least detail of
costume and physiognomy, and only the headdress in the
foreground brings the fantasy earthbound.

Throughout his career, Delacroix was captivated by the horse,
both as a creature of untamed passions and as an animal of great
refinement and sensibility. In his work, the horse became 'almost

a human being: it is associated with the actions of his heroes,
and identified with their passions' (H. de la Madelène, *Eug.
Delacroix à l'Exposition du Boulevard des Italiens*, 1864, p. 18).
Letters and notes from the Moroccan period contain frequent
references to horses and Delacroix was particularly exhilarated
by the sight of two horses fighting in a stable, noting 'all the
furies of Gros and Rubens are tame by comparison' (Corr., I,
p. 311; 8 February 1832). In 1860, some twenty-eight years after
witnessing the scene, Delacroix recorded the battle in a painting
now in the Louvre, Paris (B.779). Significantly, the lyrical
*Chevaux sortant de la mer* (B.780) dates from the same year and,
though also based on his Algerian experiences, it differs entirely
in spirit and rhythm. In many respects Delacroix's representation
of the horse may be taken to symbolise the dualities which he
confronted in North Africa, and which are so prevalent in his
Orientalist work. Possessing both Rubensian fury and
Apollonian refinement, it captured in essence the unspoilt, vital
beauty of the country.    J.M.

PROVENANCE
Sold by Delacroix to Mr Wertheimer; 1861, acquired by Alfred Bruyas at Wertheimer sale;
1868, presented by Alfred Bruyas to the Musée Fabre, Montpellier

EXHIBITIONS
?1847, Paris, Salon (no. 460)
1864, Paris, Exposition des oeuvres de Delacroix (no. 300, as Charge des cavaliers arabes)
1900, Paris, Exposition centennale (no. 215)
1930, Paris, Petit Palais, Exposition du centenaire de la conquête de l'Algérie (no. 177)
1931, Paris, Exposition coloniale
19?, Bern, Kunsthalle, Meisterwerke des Museums in Montpellier (no. 32)
1936, Paris, Petit Palais, Gros, ses amis, ses élèves (no. 237)
1963, Paris, Louvre, Exposition du Centenaire de la mort d'Eugène Delacroix (no. 189)
1983, Tokyo, Yamaguchi, Osaka and Kamakura, Peintures des XVII, XVIII, XIXe siècles dans les
    collections françaises

REFERENCES
Robaut 408
B. 238
M. Sérullaz, 'Les Chefs d'Oeuvres du Musée de Montpellier', Chronique d'Art, April 1939,
    p. 243
L. Johnson, 'Delacroix's "Rencontre des Cavaliers maures"', Burlington Magazine, CIII,
    October 1961, pp. 417, 418 (fig. 14)

13

## 14

# Arab Chief visiting a Tribe    1837

*Le Kaïd, chef marocain*

98·3 × 125·7 cm
Signed and dated bottom right: *Eug. Delacroix 1837*
Musée des Beaux-Arts, Nantes
[*repr. in colour on p. 42, plate 12*]

Like the *Moroccan Military Exercises* (Cat. 13), and the *Sultān of Morocco* (Cat. 17), this painting was directly inspired by an incident which took place during Delacroix's travels through the North African countryside between Meknes and Tangier and is recorded in his notebooks on 9 April 1832. In the Salon *livret* of 1838 Delacroix explained the ceremony at Alcassar-el-Kebir: 'He [the Arab chief] is at the head of a troop of soldiers. The inhabitants of the village come to pay him homage on his way. A woman presents him with a bowl of milk into which he dips his fingers, and lifts it to his lips.' As in Delacroix's other Orientalist work, the realistic portrayal of the actual event is not the predominant concern. Instead, the portrayal of the incident is modified to meet specific pictorial demands; illumination is naturalistic but carefully directed to highlight the central group of figures; the lines of composition converge on the Qā'id through the turning movement of the woman who presents the milk and the horsemen approaching from the rear. These figures also draw the eye through the river valley into the distant landscape and enhance the pictorial unity, while a selective choice of colour relates the figures to the overall tonalities. As in *The Fanatics of Tangier* (Cat. 15), and in the earlier *La Liberté guidant le peuple* (1830; J.144), Delacroix uses the device of a flag to highlight key areas of the painting. Here, the generalised features of the Arab leader are framed above the horizon as he looks down towards the offering, thus drawing attention to the powerful but quiet gesture and hence to the very meaning of the ceremony. Exhibited in the same year as *The Fanatics of Tangier*, this calm pastoral scene dramatically differs in both spirit and composition. It evokes the innate grandeur and lyricism of the Arab people, which had immediately struck Delacroix on arrival in Tangier. In a famous letter to J. B. Pierret, he likened the dignified disposition and flowing *burnūs* of the natives to those of decorous Roman patricians: 'Imagine, my friend, what it is to see lying in the sun, walking about the streets, cobbling old

shoes, figures like Roman consuls, like Catos or Brutuses, with even that disdainful look which those rulers of the world must have worn' (Corr., I, p. 319; 29 February 1832). For Delacroix, the Antique was not to be found in the insipid copying of plaster casts, as recommended by academic training, but in the living realities of these exotic climes. In 1862 Delacroix painted a second version of this theme (B.794), in which the number and size of the figures have been reduced and their relationship with the landscape considerably altered.    J.M.

PROVENANCE
1839, acquired by the Musée des Beaux-Arts, Nantes, following the Salon des Artistes vivants
EXHIBITIONS
1838, Paris, Salon (no. 458)
1839, Nantes, Salon des Artistes vivants (no. 71)
1864, Paris, *Exposition des oeuvres de Delacroix* (no. 3, as *Chef marocain visitant un tribu*)
1930, Paris, Louvre, *Exposition Eugène Delacroix. Centenaire du Romantisme* (no. 84)
1933, Paris, Orangerie, *Voyage de Delacroix au Maroc* (no. 180)
1939, Zürich, Kunsthaus (no. 326)
1947–48, Brussels, Palais des Beaux-Arts, *De David à Cézanne* (no. 26)
1963, Paris, Louvre, *Exposition du centenaire de la mort d'Eugène Delacroix* (no. 261, ill.)
1963–64, Bern, Kunstmuseum, *Eugène Delacroix* (no. 42)
1973, Paris, Atelier Delacroix, *Delacroix et la peinture liberté*
1980, Nantes, Musée des Beaux-Arts, *Orients* (no. 4, ill.)
REFERENCES
Robaut 647
Journal, I, p. 148
B.296
M. Nicolle, *Catalogue, Musée des Beaux-Arts, Nantes*, 1913, no. 892

## 15

# The Fanatics of Tangier    1838

*Les Convulsionnaires de Tanger*

98 × 131 cm
Signed and dated bottom right centre: *Eug. Delacroix, 1838*
The Minneapolis Institute of Arts, bequest of Jerome Hill
[*repr. in colour on p. 43, plate 13*]

The 'Isāwiyyah *sufi* brotherhood was founded in Meknes by Sīdī Muḥammad ibn 'Isā (1452–1524) who had been a follower of the immense Shadhilī brotherhood. It spread throughout western Islamic lands. Its ceremonies were particularly strenuous involving jumping, leaping and other activities noted below and seemed particularly to have alarmed European observers, although as with all *sufis* they were controlled strictly by their

14

15

*shaykh.* Delacroix depicts in this work the fanaticism of their religious devotion, when, having been confined in the courtyard of a house, they burst forth into the streets of Tangier, screaming, gesticulating wildly and foaming at the mouth. Both the local populace and visiting foreigners found themselves spellbound by the spectacle with its throbbing musical accompaniment. In particular, it captured the romantic imagination of Théophile Gautier, who had witnessed the event during a voyage to North Africa: 'By means of prayer, the prolonged swaying of the upper body, the insistent rhythmical pounding of *tarboukas* and the odour of perfumes, perhaps mingled with that of hashish, these brothers reach a state of ecstasy or hallucination which enables them to roll on burning coals, eat scorpions, snakes or cactus leaves, lick red-hot irons and walk bare-footed on sword blades, apparently without noticing their injuries' (*L'Artiste*, 1870, p. 77).

Delacroix successfully evokes the frenzy of the occasion in the fervent colouring and convulsive gestures of the central group of fanatics and in places even the rhythmic staccato of the brushwork accentuates the ecstatic state of the participants. A note of sobriety is introduced in the stately bearing of the Arab chief and in the figures suspended over the balconies in curious wonderment. The sharp geometrical volumes of the architecture act as stabilisers to the emotional excess, as do the purer limpid blues and whites in the upper half of the picture. In the sharp contrast of action and passive observation, Delacroix, like Flaubert (see Cat. 41), clearly expresses the confrontation of a European rationality with a totally alien culture, steeped in mysticism and secret rites.

In 1857, Delacroix painted a second and much reduced variant of this theme, with a freedom of brushwork characteristic of his later style (B.743). In this later picture, far greater stress is placed on the violent gestures of the individual fanatics and the architectural framework becomes less defined and more atmospheric.   J.M.

PROVENANCE
Van Isacker; 1852, Jourdan; 1855, Melá; 1860, Boulevard des Italiens sale; 1863, acquired by Marquis de Lau; 1869, Edwards; 1881 Salensi (or Feder); 1885, Faure; 1888, George I. Seney, New York; 1895, James J. Hill; 1973, bequeathed by Jerome Hill to the Minneapolis Institute of Arts

EXHIBITIONS
1838, Paris, Salon (no. 457)
1855, Paris, *Exposition Universelle* (no. 2933)
1860, Paris, Boulevard des Italiens
1864, Paris, *L'Exposition du cercle de la Rue du Choiseul*
1878, Paris, Galerie Durand-Ruel (no. 145)
1930, Paris, Louvre, *Exposition Eugène Delacroix. Centenaire du Romantisme* (no. 85)
1941, Minneapolis, Institute of Arts, *Exhibition of Private Collectors*
1963, Paris, Louvre, *Exposition du centenaire de la mort d'Eugène Delacroix* (no. 259)

REFERENCES
Robaut 662
B. 293
Th. Gautier, 'Une Galerie romantique', *L'Artiste*, April 1870, p. 77
P. de Saint-Victor, 'L'Ecole moderne', *L'Artiste*, April 1870, pp. 81–82
E. Moreau Nelaton, *Eugène Delacroix raconté par lui-même*, Paris, 1916, pp. 163–64
J. Meier-Graefe, *Eugène Delacroix, Betruge und einer Analyse*, Munich, 1922, p. 128
R. Escholier, *Delacroix, peintre, graveur, écrivain*, II, Paris, 1927, p. 72

16*

# The Death of Sardanapalus   1844

*La Mort de Sardanaple*

74 × 93 cm
Henry McIlhenny Collection, Philadelphia

Painted in 1844, this is a smaller variant of the monumental *Death of Sardanapalus* (Salon 1827; J.125) now in the Louvre, Paris. The scene is partly inspired by Lord Byron's dramatic poem of 1821, itself ultimately drawn from a legend dating from the beginning of the fourth century BC. As in the *Combat between the Giaour and the Pasha* (Cat. 12), Delacroix took significant pictorial liberties and, while he followed the poet's characterisation of the dignified *ennui* of the king of Nineveh, he departed from the text in several details. In an exhaustive analysis of the picture, Lee Johnson has suggested a wide range of pictorial and literary sources, drawn from classical legend, pseudo-Etruscan reliefs, '"licentious paintings from Delhi"' and Romantic drama. He has also pointed to the spatial anomalies of the composition, in which the diagonal thrust of Rubens's *Descent from the Cross* is combined with the frieze-like disposition of the foreground figures (J., pp. 116–20). As an image of the Orient, *The Death of Sardanapalus* has provoked some controversial interpretations. Edward Said sees it as encapsulating and even encouraging the continuing desire by the West to dominate and oppress Eastern culture (*Orientalism*, New York, 1978, chap. 3). For Linda Nochlin, on the other hand, the erotic and sadistic elements in the painting powerfully suggest the 'ideology of male domination: the connection between sexual possession and murder as an assertion of absolute domination' (Nochlin, 1983, p. 125), with the Orientalist setting used to enchance 'an extreme state of psychic intensity '(*ibid.*, p. 124). However, Sardanapalus and the legendary slaughter of his retinue continued to fire his imagination. While this later version differs in its looser handling and less aggressive colouring, it remains similar in spirit and theme.

The ease with which very diverse sources are combined in this painting finds a parallel in the transformation of certain themes within Delacroix's work and is explained too by his belief that the imagination is 'the foremost quality of the artist' (Journal, III, p. 44; 25 January 1857). Thus, *La Liberté guidant le peuple* of 1830 (J.144) combines an allegory of a modern-day event, references to a classical 'Victory' pose, the gesture of the angel freeing St. Peter in Raphael's Vatican Stanze, and a character in Act III of Byron's *Sardanapalus*, without overwhelming the central theme

16

by the disparate nature of the sources. In the same way, Delacroix re-explores the format of the *Barque de Don Juan* (1847; B.351) in a series of pictures of Christ on Lake Gethsemane executed between 1853 and 1854.

Unlike artist-converts to Orientalism, such as Frère (*q.v.*), and, to a lesser extent, Guillaumet (*q.v.*) and Girardet (*q.v.*), Delacroix absorbed his experiences in Morocco both iconographically and technically into his wider artistic vocabulary. Literary, religious and mythological subject-matter was not rejected in the frantic desire to recapture the myriad picturesque facets of the East, but continued to occupy a considerable proportion of his output.    J.M.

PROVENANCE
Legrand; Crabbe, Brussels; Bellino; Paul Rosenberg, Paris; Henry McIlhenny

EXHIBITIONS
1944, New York, Wildenstein (no. 18)
1947, Philadelphia, Museum of Art (no. 4)
1949, Philadelphia, Museum of Art (loan)
1950–51, Philadelphia, Museum of Art (no. 52)
1962, San Francisco, California Palace of the Legion of Honour
1970, Philadelphia, Museum of Art (loan)
1977, Allentown, Penn., Allentown Art Museum, *French Masterpieces of the Nineteenth Century from the Henry P. McIlhenny Collection* (p. 30, ill, p. 31)
1982, Rochester, New York, Memorial Art Gallery, *Orientalism* (no. 27, ill.)

REFERENCES
Robaut 791
B.416
J., pp. 116–20
G. H. Hamilton, 'Delacroix and Lord Byron', *Gazette des Beaux-Arts*, 6ᵉ période, 23, February 1943, pp. 105–22
E. Porada, 'The Assyrians in the last hundred years', *Bulletin of the Metropolitan Museum of Art*, 1945, no. 4, p. 39, ill.
B. Farwell, 'Sources for Delacroix's "Death of Sardanapalus"', *Art Bulletin*, March 1958, pp. 66–71
J. J. Spector, *Delacroix: The Death of Sardanapalus*, London, 1974, pp. 43, 44, ill. p. 102
H. Toussaint, *La Liberté guidant le peuple de Delacroix*, Musées nationaux, Les Dossiers du département des peintures, 26, 1982
L. Nochlin, 'The Imaginary Orient', *Art in America*, 71, May 1983, pp. 119–31, 186–91

## 17*

## 'Abd al-Rahmān, Sultān of Morocco, leaving his Palace at Meknes, surrounded by his Guard and his Principal Officers    1845

*'Abd er-Rahman, Sultan du Maroc, sortant de son Palais de Mequinez entouré de sa garde et de ses principaux officiers*

384 × 343 cm
Signed and dated bottom left centre: *Eug. Delacroix 1845*
Musée des Augustins, Toulouse

Delacroix's party was officially received by the Sultān of Morocco, 'Abd al-Rahmān, on 22 March 1832, having been confined for several days in a house in Meknes. This painting, exhibited at the Salon of 1845, was intended to commemorate the signing of a treaty between the Moroccan leader and the French government, the principal aim of the diplomatic mission led by the Comte de Mornay in 1832, which in the event was never ratified. Subsequent diplomatic negotiations met with a similar lack of success. In 1844 relationships between the two countries reached a nadir when 'Abd al-Rahmān joined forces with 'Abd al-Qādir against the French and war nearly broke out in Spain after the murder of a consular agent, Victor Darmoni. With the support of a multinational fleet in the Mediterranean, the French navy bombarded the combined Moroccan forces at Mogador in the Battle of Isly on 13 August 1844 and the Sultān capitulated to the French. The French victory was reported in

*L'Illustration* of 21 September 1844. A compositional drawing in the Louvre, Paris (RF.9383) reveals Delacroix's initial intention to include members of the French diplomatic mission in the foreground, a solution rejected in the final version, possibly because it was considered inappropriate in the light of subsequent political developments.

The easy grace of the Sultān gives neither an indication of the turbulent events of the intervening years, nor any suggestion of his position as a defeated leader. The pose rivals in grandeur Chassériau's portrait of 'Alī ibn Hāmid (see Cat. 8), also exhibited in the Salon of 1845. In his account of the audience (Journal, I, 22 March 1832, p. 141), Delacroix remarked on the resemblance of the Sultān to King Louis-Philippe and noted the striking blue and white silks, as well as the effect of the parasol, so forcefully recreated in the painting. The pose itself possibly derives from a large etching of the Turkish Emperor Selim III in Antoine Melling's *Voyage pittoresque de Constantinople et des Rives de Bosphore* (1808–19). It is also similar to a wash drawing by Delacroix of 1831 for *Duqueslin au Château de Pontsoron* and to a copy by Thales Fielding after Richard Westall's *Wellington's Entry into Toulouse*. By using these sources, realism is characteristically sacrificed to pictorial considerations. Even the location of the ceremony is 'fictionalised', set outside the monumental Bāb Mansour gate on the outer wall of Meknes, and not in the inner courtyard, where the visitors were actually received.

The image is one of stability, created by the frame of the architecture and the *repoussoir* foreground figures, with only the very slightest movement in the billowing draperies of the figure who holds the Sultān's horse. The subtle, oblique lines of the soldiers' rifles and the long parasol handle, together with the turning movements of the figures on the extreme right and left, draw the eye gently but resolutely to the self-possessed figure of the Sultān. In contrast to the other lines in the composition, this central group is composed of a series of easy curves, the convex shape of the parasol echoed in the Sultān's hood and shoulders, and his right leg continuing the soft serpentine line formed by the poised head of his thoroughbred mount.

17

Baudelaire, in his review of the Salon of 1845, referred to the 'real and natural' effects of the composition, and to the harmonious and spiritual colouring of this *grande coquetterie musicale*: 'In spite of the splendour of its tones, this painting is so harmonious that it is grey – grey as in a summer's atmosphere, when the sun spreads out on each object an aura of trembling dust' (1965, I pp. 26–27).

Delacroix blends bright colours to create a luminosity which suggests not only the vibrant intensity of the light, but also the ferocious dry heat of the Orient. In this, and in the repetition of greens, blues and reds in the costumes and shadows, the painting conforms to Delacroix's concept of 'liaison', which he defined as 'this air, these reflections which make of the most disparately coloured objects a whole' (Journal, III, p. 14, 13 January 1857).    J.M.

PROVENANCE
Bought by the State; deposited by the State in the Musée des Augustins, Toulouse

EXHIBITION
1845, Paris, Salon (no. 438)

REFERENCES
Robaut 1744
Journal, I, p. 141
Corr., I, p. 323
B.423
J. Guiffrey, *Le Voyage de Eugène Delacroix au Maroc*, Paris, 1909, II, p. 7
E. Lambert, *Histoire d'un tableau. L'Abd-Er-Rahman, Sultan du Maroc de Delacroix*, Institut des Hautes Etudes Marocaines, No. XIV, Paris, 1953
C. Baudelaire, 'Salon de 1845', *Baudelaire Critique d'Art*, I, Paris, 1965, pp. 26–27
F. A. Trapp, *The Attainment of Delacroix*, Baltimore and London, 1971, p. 136
L. Johnson, 'Towards Delacroix's Oriental Sources', *Burlington Magazine*, CXX, 1978, pp. 144–51
L. Johnson, 'Delacroix's Road to the Sultan of Morocco', *Apollo*, CXV, 1982, pp. 186–89

## 18

# The Lion Hunt    1855

*La Chasse aux lions*

56·8 × 73·8 cm
Signed and dated bottom right centre: *Eug. Delacroix 1855*
Nationalmuseum, Stockholm
[*repr. in colour on p. 44, plate 16*]

Like Delacroix's images of the horse (see Cat. 13), his depictions of lion hunts were not exclusively inspired by recollections of North Africa, but were part of the development of a theme which had interested the artist early in his career. Following the

18

example of Géricault, Delacroix frequented the menageries at St.-Cloud from 1828, together with the sculptor Antoine Barye, and in 1829 produced two lithographs and one oil painting (J.55) which reveal his close anatomical study of these animals. Throughout the 1830s, he sustained an interest in lions and tigers and took up the theme with renewed enthusiasm in the 1840s. The present painting is one of a series of complex hunting scenes executed between 1854 and 1861. In each of these Delacroix is preoccupied less with the recording of a specific event than with the more general expression of the relationship between Man and Nature and with the technical solution to a purely artistic problem.

In terms of visual sources, *The Lion Hunt* is the most 'European' of all Delacroix's Orientalist works. As well as referring to contemporary albums and prints, such as Jules Gérard's *La Chasse aux Lions* (1854), Delacroix from *c*. 1830 is known to have been familiar with Rubens's hunting scenes, mainly through the engravings of Pieter Claesz. Soutman, but also through those of Bolswert and Suyderhoff. In his journal entry for 25 January 1847, he commented on the admirable execution of Rubens's *Lion Hunt* (Alte Pinakothek, Munich), and on the striking effect of 'the rearing horse, the shaggy manes and tails, a thousand props, unbuckled shields and tangled bridles.' However, he found 'the point of view confused: the eye does not know where to rest; one has the impression of fearful conflict, but it appears that art is not sufficiently in control to enhance through careful arrangement or selectivity the effect of so many brilliant inventions' (Journal, I, p. 168).

While it follows Rubens in spirit and composition, this painting, based on a highly coloured oil sketch (B.698) for the badly damaged *Chasse aux Lions* at Bordeaux (B.703), differs in the greater clarity of the groupings and the agitated, overtly constructive brushstrokes. Less abstract than its sketch, the Bordeaux picture with its jewel-like colouring was generally badly received by critics at the Exposition Universelle in 1855: 'The colour is very brilliant, but it vibrates, pulsates, and in this chaos of reds, greens, yellows and violets, all of the same tonal values, the *Lion Hunt* resembles a tapestry' (Petroz, *La Presse*, 5 April 1855; quoted Sérullaz, 1963, p. 154). Here, the picture space, while slightly deeper than in the Bordeaux painting, still forms a tightly-packed foreground running parallel to the picture plane, creating a strong, two-dimensional effect. Later versions at Boston (B.756) and Chicago (B.790) are formal variations on the theme, differing most obviously in their more open picture space, greater fluidity of composition and in the relationship of the figures to the landscape. Common to each is the subordination of anatomical and realistic detail to the expression of upheaval and the sense of the inherent struggle between Man and the forces of Nature.    J.M.

PROVENANCE
1876, Max Liebermann; Henri Huegel, Paris; A. F. Klaveness, Oslo; Professor Philip Sandblom; 1970, gift of Professor Sandblom to the Nationalmuseum

EXHIBITIONS
1935, Stockholm, Svensk-Franska Konstgalleriet, *Mästewerk i fransk 1800 – talskonst* (no. 10)
1941, Stockholm, *Mitt bästa Konstwerk* (no. 17)
1958, Stockholm, Nationalmuseum, *Fem sekler fransk konst* (no. 124)

REFERENCES
Robaut 1278
Journal, I, p. 111 n. 1, p. 168
B. 704
M. Sérullaz, *Memorial de l'Exposition du Centenaire de la mort d'Eugène Delacroix*, Paris, 1963, p. 144
F. A. Trapp, *The Attainment of Delacroix*, London, 1971, pp. 209–12
E. T. Kliman, 'Delacroix's lions and tigers: a link between man and nature', *Art Bulletin*, LXIV, September 1982, pp. 446–66

19*

## The Collection of Arab Taxes    1863

*La Perception de l'impôt arabe*

92·5 × 74·2 cm
Signed and dated bottom left of centre: *Eug. Delacroix 1863*
National Gallery of Art, Washington, Chester Dale Collection 1966
[repr. in colour on p. 45, plate 17]

Completed in the year of his death, this painting typifies Delacroix's later Orientalist work in which fantasy is given full reign and a mellowed recollection replaces any concern for realistic detail. Robaut catalogued this painting as *La Perception de l'impôt arabe* (1448), an interpretation upheld by Johnson, who has suggested that the subject was inspired by a conversation with Amin Bias, the Minister of Foreign Affairs in Morocco, who spoke of enforcing 'the imposition of taxes and arrest for sedition' (Journal, I, p. 137; Johnson, 1962, p. 60).

In the last years of his life, Delacroix became increasingly preoccupied with Man's relationship to his environment. This interest was reflected in his concern to integrate the subject and landscape settings of his pictures. The violent clashes between Man and Nature, in its wild and passionate state, find expression in the hunt scenes of the mid-1850s (see Cat. 18) and in several variations on the theme of Christ on Lake Gethsemane executed between 1853 and 1854, in which Delacroix explores the dramatic potential of waves and clouds to heighten the urgency of expression (B.651–60). These turbulent confrontations are balanced by the more serene landscapes executed during visits to Champrosay in the late 1840s and 1853 (B.672–79), as well as in the nostalgic, often melancholic reminiscences of his Moroccan trip. On several occasions, Delacroix returned to

themes from his early post-Moroccan period (see Cat. 13, 14, 15). The sharp contrast in mood is perhaps best stated in a comparison betweeen the vibrant colour and immediacy of the 1834 *Femmes d'Alger* (B.257; fig. 5) and its more subdued variant of 1849, now in the Musée Fabre, Montpellier (B.534). Although *The Collection of Arab Taxes* makes a tentative reference to the 1832 *Moroccan Military Exercises* (Cat. 13) in the figure with the rifle on the extreme right, its link with actual experience is far more tenuous and reveals a marked reduction in emotional intensity.

The potential violence of the theme is tempered by the lyrical movements of the Arab gunmen and the overall dream-like quality of the battle. Technically, the work is a good example of Delacroix's mature style. In the bold contrasts of reds and greens and the stage-set composition, it reflects the enormous influence of his mural decorations on his stylistic development. Working in poorly-lit buildings and difficult architectural settings, he was faced with the problem of relating the murals to their surroundings and sought a greater luminosity in the use of white underpainting and contrasts of pure colour. The rapid, almost dappled, brushstrokes in areas of the soil and vegetation recall Delacroix's mural decorations at the Chapelle des Anges, St. Sulpice (1853–61) where the *Lutte de Jacob et l'Ange* evokes the same poetic sense of suspended animation.    J.M.

PROVENANCE
1863, 12 April, sold by Delacroix to Tedesco, a Parisian dealer; by 1878 to c. 1890, Edouard André, Paris; A. Smit; by 1893, Durand-Ruel, Paris and New York; 1896, Matthew Challoner Durfee Borden; 1913, 14 February, American Art Association sale, New York (lot 77); acquired by Holst; by 1916, James J. Hill, St. Paul, Minnesota; by 1930, to his son, Louis W. Hill, St. Paul, Minnesota; by 1965, Jerome Hill, New York; 1966, bought by the National Gallery of Art, Washington

EXHIBITIONS
1878, Paris, Tuileries, *Exposition du Pavillon de Flore* (no. 77)
1885, Paris, Ecole des Beaux-Arts, *Exposition Eugène Delacroix* (no. 2398)
1930, Chicago, Art Institute, *Loan Exhibition of Paintings, Drawings, Prints by Eugène Delacroix* (no. 45)
1930, Paris, Musées nationaux, Louvre, *Centenaire du Romantisme. Exposition E. Delacroix* (no. 199a)
1940, New York, World's Fair (no. 249)
1958, Minneapolis, Institute of Arts, *The James J. Hill Collection* (no cat.)
1962–63, Toronto, Art Gallery; Ottawa, National Gallery of Canada, *Delacroix* (no. 25)
1963, Paris, Louvre, *Exposition du centenaire de la mort d'Eugène Delacroix* (no. 527, as *La Perception de l'impôt arabe*)
1965, Minnesota, St. Paul, *Jerome Hill: Film Maker, Collector* (no. 178, as *The Arab Tax*)
1979, Washington, National Gallery of Art, *French Romanticism*

REFERENCES
Robaut 1448
Journal, I, p. 137
Corr., IV, p. 372
B. 805
Toronto, Art Gallery of Ontario, *Eugène Delacroix 1798–1863*, catalogue by L. Johnson, 1962, p. 60
M. Sérullaz, *Mémorial de l'exposition Eugène Delacroix organisée au Musée du Louvre à l'occasion du centenaire de la mort de l'artiste*, Paris, 1963, p. 409, no. 532 (as *La Perception de l'impôt arabe*)

19

# Denon, Baron Vivant    1747–1825

Born in Burgundy, Denon had the good fortune to survive five changes of political régime in one of the most troubled eras of French history. At one time the engraving master to Madame de Pompadour, he later served as diplomatic attaché in St. Petersburg, Stockholm and Naples under Louis XVI, and became a member of the Comité du Salut Public during the Reign of Terror. In 1797 he was introduced to Napoleon by Talleyrand, and the following year was invited to join the French expedition to Egypt. He subsequently accompanied the army on campaigns to Austria, Spain and Poland, and in 1800 was appointed Director General of Museums, with the task of establishing the Musée des Monuments français, one of the first attempts systematically to classify a public collection of ancient monuments.

## 20*

### *Voyage dans la Basse et la Haute Egypte pendant les campagnes du Général Bonaparte*
### 1802

Paris, 2 vols., 141 plates
The Library of Congress, Washington

The two large volumes produced by Vivant Denon in 1802 occupied a crucial position in the awakening of European interest in Eastern culture, and was a stimulating source of reference for French Orientalist painters at the beginning of the nineteenth century.

Among the invading forces which landed in Alexandria in July 1798 was a distinguished group of scholars and artists, who accumulated a vast range of information on all aspects of the country. Scientific investigations in the fields of astronomy, zoology, geography and natural history were initiated and military and civilian hospitals were established. Napoleon himself led a party of scientists to investigate, and later survey, the ruins of the ancient Suez Canal, a project finally realised by de Lesseps in 1859. Within a month, Napoleon had established the Institut d'Egypte, still in existence today, and a report on the Rosetta Stone enabled Champollion to decipher Egyptian hieroglyphics, laying the foundation for modern Egyptology. One of the greatest technological benefits introduced to the country was the printing press. Though much of the equipment brought from France had been destroyed during the crossing, printing presses were soon improvised through the ingenuity of Conte, head of the balloon corps, and equipped to print in Arabic, Greek and French.

Denon was one of several artists and architects to record details of the country and its inhabitants, which as he himself acknowledged, was all but unknown to Europeans (vol. I, Preface). He accompanied the movements of the army under General Desaix and General Beliard, and Denon was present at many of the decisive battles of the campaign, including the Battle of Abū Qīr (see Cat. 50). Despite this, the *Voyage* is not purely a record of military events, but contains illustrations of towns and cities, architectural details and hieroglyphic tablets, views of ancient monuments, portraits of ethnic types and descriptions of religious customs, local costume, interiors, and even culinary practices. This comprehensive range of material was not always handled objectively by Baron Denon, whose position was very much that of the 'enlightened' European. While in some places he was blatantly anti-Jewish, in others he complained of the 'fantastic ignorance of the Arabs', which led them into idolatry and false worship (p. 59).

The *Voyage*, dedicated in the most laudatory terms to Napoleon, was the first of many investigative reports on the Near East and North Africa to be published in the course of the nineteenth century. By far the most ambitious of these was the *Description de l'Egypte*, published by the Institut d'Egypte between 1809 and 1829, though journals and periodicals such as the *Revue des Deux Mondes* and *L'Illustration* regularly carried articles on the political, social and economic conditions of North African countries, especially Algeria.

Growing knowledge of these countries was matched by a gradual erosion of native culture by the imposition of foreign ideas. By the mid-century it became fashionable to live, dress, and decorate one's palace 'à la française', so that, by the time of his voyage of 1849–51, Flaubert could complain of the 'deplorable' taste of Muḥammad 'Alī's tomb, 'rococo Canova, Europo-oriental, painted and festooned like cabarets' (Steegmuller, ed., 1979, p. 64). Whatever its long-term implications, the *Voyage* remained a valuable source for artists who sought authentically to portray the Near East. Baron Gros, who relied heavily on details from the volumes (see Cat. 48, 50) praised Denon's pioneering spirit, which had inspired him to 'cross burning deserts with the French army'. He was, Gros acknowledged, 'the first to teach us that it [Egypt] did not stop at the imposing aspect of the Ruins of Thebes' (1825, p. 2).    J.M.

REFERENCES
Baron A.-J. Gros, *Funérailles de M. le Baron Denon*, Institut Royal de France, Académie Royale des Beaux-Arts, Paris, 1825, pp. 1–3
A. France, *Notice Historique sur Vivant Denon*, Paris, 1890

# Deutsch, Ludwig    1855–1930

Though Austrian by birth, Deutsch worked mainly in France, where he achieved great popularity in the 1890s with his minutely detailed scenes of life in Egypt. He was born in Vienna and briefly attended the Vienna Academy but received most of his artistic training at the Ecole des Beaux-Arts in Paris under Jean-Paul Laurens. He exhibited his first picture at the Salon in 1879 and was a regular contributor for the rest of his life, winning a gold medal in 1892. He won a further gold medal at the Exposition Universelle in Paris in 1900 and was made Chevalier de la Légion d'Honneur by the French government. He derived the material for his pictures both from on-the-spot observation and from the large collection of Near Eastern artefacts, *mashrabiyyah* woodwork and painted tiles that decorated his studios in Paris and the South of France. His later work, from around 1909, tends to be more imposing in scale, theatrical in content and painterly in execution. Towards the end of his life he took French nationality.

21*

# The Scribe   1896

*Le Scribe*

Oil on panel: 53 × 38 cm
Signed and dated bottom left: *L.Deutsch PARIS 1896*
Private Collection, Houston, Texas
[*repr. in colour on p. 74, plate 19*]

Although from earliest times Islamic society stressed the
importance of literacy, the public scribe, well versed in subtleties
of style and officialese, and with an elegant script, was much in
demand by all classes. This was particularly true in cities, as here
in Cairo, especially as there was the complication of two
languages – Arabic, the language of the mass of the people, and
Turkish, the language of State (Cat. 100, 101). In this picture, a
scribe waits for custom in the street, perhaps at the doorway of
his own house. His upward gaze may indicate boredom but also
recalls the way writers have traditionally been represented in
European art, both in portraiture and religious subjects such as
St. John on Patmos, with their eyes fixed on heaven as if awaiting
divine inspiration. The loving care and attention Deutsch
devotes to the painting of exotic features such as the tiles, chair,
table and *gūzah* (pipe) clearly shows the influence of earlier Salon
Orientalists, above all Gérôme (*q.v.*).

Deutsch executed further versions of this subject. An almost
identical composition dated 1911 (sold 28 November 1980,
Christie's, London, lot 113), differs only in the model, the tiles
set around the doorway and the colour of the scribe's
costume.   M.W.

PROVENANCE
1906, 5 May, Christie's, London (lot 98); 1961, 23 June, Christie's, London (lot 114); 1976,
20 February, Christie's, London (lot 125); 1980, 20 June, Christie's, London (lot 146); P. and
V. Berko, Brussels; 1980, October, acquired by The Fine Art Society, London; 1981, June,
acquired by Kurt E. Schon Ltd, New Orleans; Priv. Coll., Houston, Texas

REFERENCES
H. Fuchs, *Die Österreichischen Maler des 19. Jahrhunderts*, Vienna, 1972, vol. I, fig. 84
P. and V. Berko, *Peinture Orientalistes*, Brussels, 1982, p. 115, ill.
Coral Petroleum, *A Near Eastern Adventure*, n.d., n.p., ill.

22*

# The Prayer at the Tomb   1898

*La Prière au tombeau*

Oil on panel: 68·5 × 59·5 cm
Signed and dated bottom left: *L. Deutsch Le Caire 1898*
Private Collection, Houston, Texas
[*repr. in colour on p. 68, plate 20*]

The setting of this painstakingly executed study of a wealthy
Muslim is identifiable as the tomb chamber of the Amīr Aqsunqur
in the Mosque of Aqsunqur (the 'Blue Mosque') in Cairo. The
tomb itself dates from the time the mosque was built in 1346,
but the impressive panels of provincial Ottoman tiles, which give
the mosque its alternative name, were installed during the
remodelling undertaken by Ibrahim Agha in 1652.   M.W.

PROVENANCE
1977, 3 November, Christie's, London (lot 115); 1978, The Fine Art Society, London; Priv.
Coll; 1980, June, acquired again by The Fine Art Society; acquired by Kurt E. Schon Ltd,
New Orleans; Priv. Coll., Houston, Texas

EXHIBITIONS
1898, Paris, Salon des Champs-Elysées (no. 666)
1978, London, The Fine Art Society, *Eastern Encounters* (no. 24)

REFERENCES
J. Harding, *Artistes Pompiers: French Academic Art in the 19th Century*, London, 1979, p. 78, ill.
Coral Petroleum, *A Near Eastern Adventure*, n.d., n.p., ill.

21

22

# Frère, Théodore   1814–1888

Brother of the popular realist painter Edouard Frère, Théodore was born in Paris in 1814, and studied first under Cogniet (1794–1880) and later under Roqueplan (1800–1855).

Frère began his career by painting interiors and views of the French countryside derived from his travels round Normandy, Alsace and the Auvergne. Following some months in Algeria, however, during which he witnessed the taking of Constantine, Frère devoted himself solely to Oriental subject-matter, exhibiting his first Orientalist work at the Salon of 1839.

In 1851 he undertook a second and longer voyage through Greece, Asia Minor, Constantinople (where he remained for eighteen months), Syria, Palestine and Egypt. This journey provided him with a wealth of material and impressions which he worked up in a series of paintings of the late 1850s. In the course of a final trip to the Near East in 1869, as part of the suite of Empress Eugénie, he produced a number of impressive watercolours, a medium which allowed him to capture the luminous, bleached tonalities of the landscape.

Frère also designed woodcuts and lithographs using Oriental subject-matter, such as his imaginary view of the Arab in Paris for Desnoyer's *Les Etrangers à Paris* (1846). His emotionless but picturesque views of architecture, ruins, bazaars, coffee-house interiors and landscapes proved immensely popular with collectors in Europe, notably the King of Würtemburg and Louis-Philippe, and from the early 1860s he was on intimate terms with the American art dealer George Lucas.

## 23

## Jerusalem, View from the Valley of Jehoshaphat   1881

*Jérusalem, Vue prise de la vallée de Josaphat*

74 × 110·5 cm
Signed bottom right: *TH.FRÈRE/JÉRUSALEM TERRE SAINTE*
Metropolitan Museum of Art, New York

Possibly exhibited at the 1881 Salon as *Jérusalem, Vue prise de la vallée de Josaphat*, (no. 925 bis.), it seems likely that the panorama was painted from the Mount of Olives to the north-east of the city, recommended to travellers in handbooks of the nineteenth century for its commanding vista.

Frère picked out the prominent features of the city: the Golden Gate, the Church of the Holy Sepulchre, the Hamra minaret, and the impressive parapets of the Turkish wall with its solid, square bastions, flanked to the south of the city by the Valley of Hinnem. Against the soft, opalescent mists of the distant mountains of Ammon and Moab, the foreground encampment of Arabs introduces a strong touch of local colour. The precise rendering of their costumes and tents gives the painting a highly finished quality, almost photographic in its insistence on realistic detail. In fact, from the 1850s, as the Near East became increasingly familiar through photographs, it was not uncommon for artists to refer to them as a visual reminder of scenes or locations viewed in these countries. Maxime du Camp recorded his impressions of landscapes and monuments in a series of photographs taken during his travels through Egypt and Nubia with Gustave Flaubert from 1849 to 1851, and the British artist Thomas Seddon (see Cat. 94) is known to have used photographic material in, for example, his *Jerusalem and the Valley*

*of Jehoshaphat from the Hill of Evil Counsel* (1854–55; Tate Gallery, London).

As access to the Holy Land grew easier in the latter half of the century, Jerusalem gradually assumed for the European traveller the popularity which Paris or Rome had enjoyed in the itinerary of the eighteenth-century gentleman, albeit of a religious, rather than purely cultural significance. French and British travellers from Chateaubriand onwards hastened to the City of David and, despite the filth and pestilence of the city itself, many were overwhelmed by the very sight of it: 'The scene was grand in its simplicity. . . . Now, indeed, for one brief moment, I knew that I was in Palestine; that I saw Mount Olivet and Mount Zion; and – I know not how it was – my sight grew weak, and all objects trembled and wavered in a watery film' (B. Taylor, *Pictures of Palestine, Asia Minor, Sicily and Spain or The Land of the Saracens*, 1855, p. 58).

Frère's view reflects the battered history of the city which, from the siege of Titus in AD 37 onwards, had continually changed hands between the Turks, the Saracens and the Christians. Inevitably, the Christian visitor was struck by the moral significance of the dominant position of the Omar and El Aska mosques among the mass of grey buildings, and saddened by the eternal theological dissentions which had plagued the city, the 'temple par excellence of peace and charity' (E. Melchior de Vogüé, 'Journées de voyage en Syrie, III', *Revue des Deux Mondes*, III, 1875, p. 552), ironically translated from the Hebrew as 'possession of peace'.   J.M.

PROVENANCE
1887, bequeathed by Catherine Lorillard Wolfe to the Metropolitan Museum of Art
EXHIBITION
1881, Paris, Salon (no. 925 bis)
REFERENCES
E. Montrosier, *Artistes Modernes*, II, Paris, 1896, pp. 9–11
Ch. Sterling and M. Salinger, *French Paintings: A Catalogue of the Collection in the Metropolitan Museum*, II, New York, 1966, p. 146
Rochester, New York, Memorial Art Gallery, *Orientalism*, catalogue by D. Rosenthal, 1982, fig. 104

23

# Fromentin, Eugène-Samuel-Auguste
## 1820–1876

Eugène Fromentin's birthplace, La Rochelle, is a port in western France where the flatness and dramatic skies recall Holland, an analogy lost neither on the artist nor on his subsequent critics. After passing his law exams in Paris, Fromentin persisted in his desire to be a painter. His father sent him to train under the classical landscapist Rémond, but Fromentin decided to study with the more naturalistic Cabat.

In 1846 Fromentin made a secret trip to Algeria with Charles Labbé, who also became an Orientalist painter. The following year Fromentin's first three submissions, two of which were Orientalist works, were accepted by the Salon. Their favourable reception encouraged him to pay a longer visit to Algeria after the Salon. His eleven Orientalist pictures in the Salon of 1850–51 established his reputation for such subject-matter. After his honeymoon in 1853 he made a final extended stay in Algeria that was to result not only in two books but also in a store of sketches and visual images upon which he was to draw throughout his career.

Fromentin's most successful Salon was that of 1859, when he gained conventional Second Empire kudos with a First Class medal and the Légion d'Honneur, as well as praise from more progressive critics like Baudelaire, and from the young Degas. He exhibited throughout the 1860s and 1870s before his sudden death in 1876.

Fromentin is remembered today more as a writer than a painter. After his travel books, *Un Été dans la Sahara* (1856) and *Une Année dans le Sahel* (1858), came his single celebrated novel *Dominique*, and in the year of his death he published his eloquent study of Dutch and Flemish art, *Les Maîtres d'autrefois*.

ABBREVIATED REFERENCE
Gonse 1881 Louis Gonse, *Eugène Fromentin: Peintre et Ecrivain*, Paris, 1881

24

## 24

# Arab Falconer  1863
*Fauconnier arabe*

108 × 73 cm
Signed bottom left: *Eug. Fromentin*
Chrysler Museum, Norfolk, Virginia, gift of Walter P. Chrysler Jr.
[*repr. in colour on p. 76, plate 22*]

The Arab cavalier is the central image in Fromentin's art. His first Oriental works divide fairly evenly between Arabs astride camels and those mounted on horseback, but in the last two decades of his life the balance shifted decisively towards the ancestor of Western thoroughbreds. This preference may well relate to a message of 1857 from Fromentin's dealer Beugniet, conveyed to the artist by Gustave Moreau, stating that pictures with horses were more saleable than those with camels (B. Wright and P. Moisey, *Gustave Moreau et Eugène Fromentin: documents inédits*, La Rochelle, 1972, p. 97).

In the Arab and his horse Fromentin found the 'accord of the two most intelligent and fully developed creatures that God has made', and he argued that the Greeks had invented a composite creature to represent this harmony, evoking the centaur as an analogue for the Arab's perfect communion with his animal (*Une Année dans le Sahel*, Paris, 1963 ed., p. 247).

The most obvious precedent for the central figure in this composition is one of the galloping trio in the 1861 Salon picture, *Courriers du pays de l'Ouled Nayls* (acquired by the State, Musée du Luxembourg). The horseman to the left in this horizontal composition, known only through engravings, reaches upward with his left hand, apparently to grasp some leaves from an overhanging tree. Two years later, in the *Arab Falconer*, Fromentin was to focus on a single figure, constructing a vertical composition around the diagonal sweep of his right arm holding a perch and leather traces that lead to an airborne falcon. The horse has both fore and rear legs extended in that conventional representation of the gallop, which two decades later was to be discredited by Muybridge and Degas.

Western images of the Arab were ordered according to Western cultural archetypes. In contrast to the industrialising West, he was seen as an unspoiled child of Nature. For many writers and artists, the Arab was a man from the Bible (see Warner, p. 32), while Delacroix saw him as a living Greek or Roman (see Cat. 14). Fromentin referred to all these archetypes, but clearly added a suggestion of the medieval *seigneur*; some scholars have claimed that falconry and chivalry came to the West from the East via the Crusades. The obvious association between the hunt and the battle, seen by Fromentin as a significant characteristic of Arab life, is implicit in this spirited image of a former foe.

On one level this picture can be read as a trophy, the image of a subdued enemy. Louis-Napoleon patronised what he called, in his only recorded remarks to the artist, Fromentin's 'pretty pictures'. Yet the falconer has genuine grandeur and can also be seen as a tribute, an elegy for a noble way of life fast disappearing. Fromentin often referred in his writing to the harmful effect the French were having upon their Algerian subjects and was most anxious to visit towns where the influence of his government had not yet been felt.

Fromentin sent three major works to the Salon of 1863, and the critical response was almost universally favourable. Théophile Thoré said he would rather have painted Fromentin's three contributions to the show than the three celebrated 'Venuses' of Cabanel, Baudry and Amaury-Duval. To Thoré, Fromentin's lightness of touch and execution was a positive quality. Gautier, like Mantz, doubted the durability of the thin paint, but he was full of praise for the conception. Fromentin, he felt, no longer copied Oriental types but had begun to create them. Such an imaginative approach was also noted by Maxime du Camp, who said that Fromentin would never be a realist, and what was most lovable in his paintings was not Nature but his manner of interpreting it. Emile Cantrell praised Fromentin as 'at once the truest, the most exact, the most picturesque of our Orientalists'. Finally, the most poetic appreciation of the picture came from Paul de Saint-Victor, who thought the falconer traversed the plain like a flash of lightening across the sky. Saint-Victor could hear the cry coming out of the mouth of the horseman, drunk with speed, the dust and the wind in his face. To him the fierce falconer looked like a magician from *The Arabian Nights*, setting off astride a griffon, with *jinns* and friendly demons, to fight some distant evil spell.

There are several studies related to this picture. The most outstanding are watercolours in the Cleveland Museum (CMA 73.7) and the collection of Fromentin's family. An exciting study of the horse was reproduced in a book containing drawings by Fromentin, Géricault and Gleyre. An attractive watercolour of a falcon in Rouen relates either to this picture or to another of Fromentin's entries in the same Salon, *La Curée* (Louvre, Paris), which has a predator similarly posed. The year after this picture Fromentin executed a variant (Metropolitan Museum of Art, New York), with the falconer coming from the opposite direction. It is a polished performance, a step perhaps in the direction of Horace Vernet, but it lacks the verve and power of the original.    J.T.

PROVENANCE
1877, Lepel-Cointet Coll., Paris; 1881, Lepel-Cointet sale, Paris; 1889, B. Wall Coll., Providence, Rhode Island; 1898, David V. Powers, New York; Durand-Ruel, New York; Samuel Untermeyer, New York; Baron Casil Von Doorn, New York; 1958, 16–17 May, Parke-Bernet, New York (lot 297); Mrs Paul B. Wertheimer Coll.; Walter P. Chrysler Jr. Coll.; presented by him to the Chrysler Museum, Norfolk

EXHIBITIONS
1863, Paris, *Salon* (no. 735)
1877, Paris, Ecole des Beaux-Arts, *Exposition posthume* (no. 32)
1893, Chicago, *Columbian Exposition*
1904, New York, *National Exhibition of Foreign Artists*

REFERENCES
Gonse 1881, p. 80, ill. opp. p. 180 (engr. by Leo Flameng)
E. Cantrel, 'Salon de 1863', *L'Artiste*, 1863, I, p. 200
M. du Camp, 'Salon de 1863', *Revue des Deux Mondes*, 15 June, 1863, p. 896
Th. Gautier, 'Salon de 1863', *Moniteur Universel*, 20 June 1863
P. Mantz, 'Salon de 1863', *Gazette des Beaux-Arts*, 1863, XIV, p. 496
P. de Saint-Victor, 'Salon de 1863', *La Presse*, 29 June 1863
Th. Thoré, 'Salon de 1863', in *Salons de W. Bürger: 1861 à 1868*, Paris 1870, II, p. 385
E. Strahan, *Art Treasures of America*, Philadelphia, 1879, III, p. 88
C. H. Stranahan, *A History of French Painting*, London, 1889, p. 305
E. Fromentin, *Correspondance* (ed. P. Blanchon), Paris, 1912, pp. 179, 184
Ch. Sterling and M. Salinger, *French Paintings: A Catalogue of the Collections of the Metropolitan Museum of Art, II*, New York, 1966, p. 157

25*

## Windstorm on the Esparto Plains of the Sahara    1864

*Coup de vent dans les plaines d'alfa (Sahara)*

116·5 × 152 cm
Signed bottom right: *Eug. Fromentin*
Dated bottom left: -1864-
Private Collection, Houston, Texas
[*repr. in colour on p. 78, plate 23*]

The essence of Fromentin's art, both literary and pictorial, is its descriptive subtlety, a subtlety through which both as writer and artist he sometimes succeeded in expressing the inexpressible. Thus Edmond de Goncourt credited Fromentin with the introduction of an auditory aspect to literature in his evocation of the silence of the desert (E. and J. de Goncourt, *Journal*, Paris, 1856 ed., III, p. 353). Similarly Gautier, in discussing one of Fromentin's entries for the Salon of 1859, *L'Isière d'Oasis pendant le Sirocco* (present location unknown), wrote: 'One would think that the wind could not be painted, being a colourless and formless thing, yet it blows visibly through M. Fromentin's picture' (Th. Gautier, 'Salon de 1859,' *Le Moniteur*, 28 May 1859).

*Windstorm on the Esparto Plains of the Sahara* represents the culmination of the artist's efforts to portray the existence of an invisible force through its physical effects. As early as 1857 Fromentin had attempted paintings of cavaliers caught in a windstorm. Though the whereabouts of these paintings are unknown, preliminary drawings exist in the Musée des Beaux-Arts in Ghent and in the collection of the Fromentin family. In *L'Isière d'Oasis pendant le Sirocco*, Fromentin widened his perspective to take in a sweeping landscape, in which the wind blows on the backs of a clump of flattened camels and against a small Bedouin woman struggling forwards; but the power of its blast is principally recorded in the straining fronds and slanted trunks of date palms and underlined by diagonal ridges of cloud, which register the storm like ripples on water.

In *Windstorm on the Esparto Plains of the Sahara* clouds and plants again have much to do with defining the force of the wind. The main measure of the wind's gust, however, is the group of five horsemen. Three of the four horses face into the wind. Only

25

one cavalier follows suit. The other Arabs, their *burnūses* billowing, turn away from the blast. They are exposed by the low horizon line and silhouetted against a bank of cottony cloud. A rock outcrop in the right distance provides a more solid, slightly ironic balancing bulwark.

Fromentin here demonstrates his mastery of values within a limited colour range, an approach partly inspired by Corot. 'Too knowledgeable in the greys', according to Henri Focillon's unfavourable judgement (H. Focillon, *La Peinture au XVIIIe siècle*, Paris, 1927, II, p. 219), Fromentin here puts that knowledge to good use, in a picture whose sombre palette suits its subject.

The painting has been much admired. Théophile Thoré, possibly the sanest critic of the century, picked it out of the Salon of 1864 as 'one of the best pictures in the whole exhibition'. Thoré was particularly struck by the figure of the grey horse, whose legs were like 'bars of steel' bracing it as firmly as the supports of the old harquebus rifles. Louis Gonze paired it with *L'Isière d'Oasis pendant le Sirocco*, which he considered Fromentin's greatest work. He found *Windstorm on the Esparto Plains of the Sahara* equally energetic as a conception and almost as beautiful in execution. Gonse referred to the wind as the '*khamsīn*', Victor Fournel as the '*simoun*'; both these hot desert winds, as well as the *sirocco*, have been used as titles for the painting. Echoing Gonse's sensitivity to the 'terrifying impression' made by the picture, Fournel spoke of the 'overwhelming and sinister effect' of the wind on a nature 'crushed and mute with horror'. Fournel also remarked that Fromentin's normally restrained palette was even more gloomy in this scene. Maxime du Camp did not like the painting on account of its 'harmony in grey minor', which to him suggested Normandy rather than North Africa. Léon Lagrange also doubted the truth of its colour but said it was nonetheless 'the most oriental painting in the Salon'.

There are at least two smaller versions of this painting, both about 45 × 60 cm, one on panel and the other on canvas. The latter, which is signed bottom left, was sold at Sotheby Parke Bernet in 1982. The former, autographed bottom right like this painting, is the only version in which the most prominent horse draws his muzzle back.    J.T.

PROVENANCE
Thoré claimed that the Salon painting was bought by an 'amateur from Manchester' (see References); David Sellar Coll.; 1918, Galerie Georges Petit, Paris, Sarlin sale (lot 46); Tanenbaum Coll., Toronto; Kurt E. Schon Ltd, New Orleans; Priv. Coll., Houston, Texas

EXHIBITION
1864, Paris, *Salon* (no. 758)

REFERENCES
Gonse 1881, pp. 79–80, ill. opp. p. 58 (engr. by M. Lalanne as *Le Simoon*)
M. du Camp, 'Salon de 1864', *Revue des Deux Mondes*, 1 June 1864, pp. 694, 695
L. Lagrange, 'Salon de 1864', *Gazette des Beaux-Arts*, 1864, XVII, p. 20
H. Roujon, *Fromentin*, Paris, 1912 (ill. pl. IV as *Le Sirocco à l'oasis*)
Th. Thoré, 'Salon de 1864' in *Salons de W. Burger: 1861–1868*, Paris, 1870, p. 87
V. Fournel, *Les Artistes français contemporains*, Tours, 1884, p. 388
P. Dorbec, *Eugène Fromentin*, Paris, 1926, p. 83 (ill. p. 67 as *Le Khamsin*)
H. Focillon, *La Peinture au XIXe siècle*, Paris, 1927, II, p. 219
La Rochelle, *Fromentin: le Peintre et l'Ecrivain*, 1970, p. 100, no. 63

## 26

# Land of Thirst    *c. 1869*

*Pays de Soif*

103 × 143 cm
Signed bottom left: *Eug. Fromentin*
Musée d'Orsay, Paris

Nineteenth-century Salons featured a succession of 'disaster pictures', which provided large-scale, eye-catching excitement for the general public. The godfather of the genre, one of the first and best, was Géricault's *Radeau de la Méduse* (1819; Louvre, Paris), and it is patently this picture from which Fromentin borrowed his composition. Both works feature a pyramid of dying figures culminating in an upraised arm, in the Géricault a gesture of hopeful entreaty, in the Fromentin of futility, or desperate defiance in the face of death. In both works men are dying of thirst, Fromentin's in a sea of sand, Géricault's in the South Atlantic.

The title of this painting is instantly recognisable to readers of Fromentin's travel books, for it is the phrase with which he concluded his book on the Sahara: 'I fear that I must soon go back to the North, and the day when I leave the gateway of the East never to return I will reside bitterly in that strange city and salute with profound regret this menacing horizon, so desolate that it is justly called: "Land of Thirst" ' (*Un Été dans le Sahara*, Paris, 1938 ed., p. 279). A page earlier he had given an account of a desert convoy disastrously decimated by a heat as sweltering as 'a shower of fire' which 'bore through your skull like a corkscrew', killing eight persons and most of their animals (*ibid.*, p. 278).

This picture is one of at least four works in the late 1860s where Fromentin returned to his own writings as a source of subject-matter, choosing those with the greatest dramatic potential. For the previous twenty years Fromentin had won solid Salon success as a purveyor of 'Orientalist genre' scenes, but the pictorial formulae of such works were going stale for both the artist and his critics. At a time when the nascent Impressionist movement was challenging the sacrosanct distinctions of subject-matter, Fromentin was moving in an opposite direction, aiming more at the by-gone glories of dramatic history painting. The ambition of this attempt exceeded his abilities, and he was unable to grasp the crude representation

26

of dramatic grandeur which established the pictorial credibility of a history painting. In a devastatingly accurate moment of self-analysis he once said, 'I see "pretty" and not "grand"' (E. Fromentin, *Lettres de Jeunesse*, P. Blanchon ed., Paris, 1909, p. 250).

Although never publicly exhibited in the artist's lifetime, this painting has not lacked admirers. Writing in 1877, the critic M. Proth said it 'nearly ranks as a masterpiece', while Fromentin's friend and biographer Louis Gonse was reminded of Berlioz's *Requiem* and remarked that the artist had never produced anything more powerful.

There is another major variant of this picture (1869; Musée des Beaux-Arts, Brussels), which includes a dead horse on the right (thus relating more closely to the written description) and lacks the upward gesture of the top figure. Various preliminary studies for the painting have passed through sale rooms this century; they reveal the almost classical care with which Fromentin found the contours for the figures which compose this major work.    J.T.

PROVENANCE
1876, posthumous sale, Paris (lot 5); 1879, Verdé-Delisle sale, Paris (lot 28); 1881, Lepel-Cointet sale, Paris; 1929, bequeathed by M. E. Martell to the Louvre, Paris (inv. no. RF 2671)

EXHIBITIONS
1877, Paris, École des Beaux-Arts, *Exposition posthume* (no. 20)
1970, La Rochelle, *Fromentin : Le Peintre et L'Ecrivain* (p. 85, no. 32)
1973, Paris, Musée des Arts Décoratifs, *Equivoques*

REFERENCES
Gonse 1881, p. 100
H. Houssaye, 'Eugène Fromentin', *Revue des Deux Mondes*, April 1877
P. Dorbec, *Eugène Fromentin*, Paris, 1926, p. 83
J. Alazard, *L'Orient et la peinture française au XIXe siècle, d'Eugène Delacroix à Auguste Renoir*, Paris, 1930, p. 281
Ch. Sterling, and H. Adhémar, *Musée Nationale du Louvre, Peintures : Ecole française, XIXe siècle*, 1959, p. 310, no. 885
M. Proth, 'Voyage au pays des peintres', *Salon de 1877*, quoted 1973, Paris, Musée des Arts Décoratifs, *Equivoques*
P. Jullian, *The Orientalists, European Painters of Eastern Scenes*, Oxford, 1977, p. 64
J. Marti, *On Art and Literature : Critical Writings*, edited with an introduction by Philip S. Foner, translated by Elinor Randall, New York, 1982, p. 85

## 27* 

## Dahabiyyah on the Nile at Luxor   1871
*Dahabieh sur le Nil à Luxor*

63 × 109·5 cm
Signed and dated bottom right : *Eug. Fromentin -71-*
The Art Institute of Chicago
[*repr. in colour on p. 79, plate 25*]

In 1869, as one of sixty select guests, Fromentin took a three-month trip to Egypt to witness the opening of the Suez Canal, travelling with a distinguished delegation of painters including Bonnat (*q.v.*), Belly (*q.v.*), Berchère and Gérôme (*q.v.*), as well as writers like Théophile Gautier. The inauguration of the canal marked a new era of colonial imperialism and at the same time represented the twilight of a certain type of pictorial Orientalism. Fromentin was not anxious to go; taking few artistic materials, he planned to write rather than draw, adding, 'moreover we have our photographers' (E. Fromentin, *Correspondance*, P. Blanchon ed., Paris, 1912, p. 223).

Although Orientalists like Horace Vernet had used photographs as artistic tools in their depiction of the East from the moment the process was made public, it is difficult to imagine Fromentin considering their extensive use earlier in his life. Later he explained what photographic documents of Egypt lacked : 'They will only give you quite an imperfect idea of the beauty of these things; you will see neither the incomparable quality of the light, nor the distances (all diminished), nor the colour, less varied than in the Sahara, but special and perhaps still more delicate' (*ibid.*, p. 227). In fact, Fromentin's main resource in recreating Egyptian views was to be his memory, and he even claimed to Edmond de Goncourt that he did not take any notes (an exaggeration) but often found that as much as a few years later he could recapture a precise perception of place (E. and J. de Goncourt, *Journal*, Paris, 1956, II, p. 1051). Fromentin began painting Egyptian scenes soon after his return, but he did not exhibit any in the Salon until the last year of his life. Critical reaction to these paintings in 1876 was unfavourable. Georges du Four excepted them from his general condemnation of the show, but Jules Castagnary was not so charitable. Resurrecting a pet theme he had propounded as early as 1872 on the end of Orientalism, he provided in his 1876 Salon review an abridged history of the movement. Castagnary nostalgically remembered 'the brilliant epoch of Fromentin' (p. 248), and his sparkling cavaliers, but found the Egyptian pictures unexciting and unconvincing : 'In this make-believe High Egypt, a chocolate Nile flows between chocolate banks, while women with chocolate complexions plunge chocolate vases into chocolate waves' (J. Castagnary, 'Salon de 1876' in *Salons 1872–79*, Paris, 1892, pp. 224, 249). Castagnary saw the end of Orientalism as parallel to the end of Fromentin as a painter. Perhaps aware of the artist's canvassing for a place as a writer in the Académie Française, he described Fromentin's dilemma : 'Powerless to renew himself, he appears to ask if the moment is not right to choose between painting and writing'.

This painting represents one of the Nile's large passenger boats, called a *dahabiyyah*. A striking feature of this boat was the enormous yard of the mainsail, which was tilted at an angle of forty-five degrees to the vertical when its lateen sail was unfurled. Fromentin often undercut the severe horizontality of the Egyptian landscape with diagonals drawn by these graceful rigs, whose great length he has here slightly exaggerated. The

27

traditional title, 'On the Nile, near Philae', is probably based on the ruins to the right, which are certainly not Philae, but most likely Luxor. Their location would indicate a view descending the Nile. Fromentin was most struck by the colour and character of the Egyptian sky and the waters of the Nile, which he found 'incomparably pure, and soft, and tender', and was impressed by the river's muddy thickness. He had never seen water denser nor richer in fertility, and anticipating Castagnary's criticism, he described the Nile as 'clear chocolate' (Gonse 1881, p. 266).

Perhaps the most interesting critique of Fromentin's Egyptian contribution to the 1876 Salon came from the artist himself. In an anonymously published review of the exhibition he also discussed Orientalism in general, reiterating views already given with reference to Delacroix in his book *Une Année dans le Sahel* (Paris, 1963 ed., pp. 208–09). To Fromentin the Orient's pictorial essence lay in its more general qualities. To be too particular was to produce 'ethnography and not art' (E. Fromentin, 'Salon de 1876: Chronique parisienne. Juin 1876', *Bibliothèque universelle et Revue suisse*, Lausanne, LVI, p. 355). The self-critical Fromentin thought he had succeeded in capturing 'the overwhelming melancholy of the flat and monotonous expanses' of Egypt. He also asked why the artist had to go so far in search of subjects rather than seeking them nearer to home, and perhaps here was a hint that in another attempt to break away from the Oriental genre mould, he might have again essayed the French landscape with which he began his studies under Cabat.

Gérôme and 'ethnographic orientalism' (Cat. 30, 36), was the wave of the future, and perhaps some of the sadness so many critics have seen in Fromentin's work comes from the end of an old Orient and an old Orientalism in the new age of camera and Canal.    J.T.

PROVENANCE
Chicago, Nickerson Coll.; the Art Institute of Chicago

EXHIBITIONS
1935, Providence, Rhode Island School of Design, *French Painting in Africa*
1942–43, Portland, Oregon, Museum of Art, *50th Anniversary Exhibition, 1892–1942* (no. 26)

REFERENCES
Gonse 1881, p. 313
*Yearbook*, Rhode Island School of Design, Providence, April 1934, p. 167
*Paintings in the Art Institute of Chicago: A Catalogue of the Picture Collections*, Chicago, 1961, pp. 166–67

# Gérôme, Jean-Léon    1824–1904

The leader of the 'Néo-grec' School of painting, an influential teacher at the Ecole des Beaux-Arts and son-in-law of the powerful Parisian art dealer and editor, Goupil, Jean-Léon Gérôme was born at Vesoul (Haute-Sâone). After studying between 1842 and 1845 under Delaroche (1797–1856) and from 1846 to 1847 with Gleyre (*q.v.*), he exhibited a classical genre painting, *Le Combat des coqs*, at the Paris Salon of 1847. Following excellent critical notices, Gérôme was launched on his career as a society portraitist and executor of large-scale State commissions. He visited Egypt for the first time in 1856; subsequent trips to the Near East took place in 1862, 1868, 1871, 1872 and 1874, together with two visits to Constantinople and Asia Minor in 1871 and 1875. Appointed Professor at the Ecole des Beaux-Arts in 1863 and elected to the Institut de France in 1865, Gérôme regularly exhibited at the Salon a brilliantly varied range of meticulously detailed classical history and genre paintings, costume pieces and scenes of the Near East. In 1878 he exhibited his first sculpture, an art form in which he worked increasingly during the later years of his life. Although he remained a lifelong friend of Degas, his position as an arch-opponent of Impressionism was sealed by his vociferous objection to the receipt by the State of the Caillebotte Bequest of Impressionist paintings, 1895–97.

ABBREVIATED REFERENCES
Galichon 1868   E. Galichon, 'M. Gérôme. Peintre ethnographe', *Gazette des Beaux-Arts*, I, 1868, pp. 147–251
Lenoir 1872   P. Lenoir, *Le Fayoum, Le Sinaï et Pétra*, Paris, 1872
Timbal 1876   C. Timbal, 'Les Artistes contemporains: Gérôme (étude biographique)', *Gazette des Beaux–Arts*, XIV, 1876, p. 218ff., p. 334ff.
Shinn Strahan   E. Shinn under the pseudonym of Edward Strahan, *Gérôme, a Collection of the Works of J-L Gérôme in One Hundred Photogravures*, 2 vols., New York, 1881–83

28

## 28

# The Plain of Thebes, Upper Egypt  1857

*La Plaine de Thèbes en Haute-Egypte*

76·8 × 131 cm
Signed and dated near the column in the foreground: *J. L. GÉRÔME
    MDCCCLVII*
Musée des Beaux-Arts, Nantes
[*repr. in colour on p. 80, plate 26*]

The Colossi of Memnon, standing some fifty-two feet high, lie on the west bank of the River Nile opposite the ancient city of Thebes and south-west of the Ramasseum which formed part of the Necropolis of Thebes. They represent Amenhotep III (*c.* 1417–1379 BC), and once fronted his immense mortuary chapel, now entirely despoiled. During the Roman occupation of Egypt, they were believed to be the statues of Memnon, the son of Eos and Tithounas, who slew Antilochus, son of Nestor, in the Trojan Wars and was himself slain by Achilles. The northern colossus had been famous in Roman times for the musical sounds it was said to have emitted. Given their prominent position overlooking the Nile, and deprived of their related temple, the two colossi were visible over a great distance from all sides. In the nineteenth century they were one of the most notable archaeological monuments of the area around Thebes and Luxor, outstripped in scale and grandeur only by the shattered colossus of 'Ozymandias' in the Ramasseum. The view looks south-west from the base of the Libyan Hills across the Nile towards Luxor.

Gérôme undertook his first trip to Egypt in 1856, financed by a commission of 20,000 francs, which he had received from the French Government the previous year for *Le Siècle d'Auguste : naissance de N.-S. Jésus Christ* (Musée d'Orsay, Paris). Possibly inspired by the earlier voyage to the Near East of his teacher, Gleyre (*q.v.*), and certainly fired with enthusiasm for distant places by his own trip down the Danube to Constantinople in 1854, Gérôme embarked with four friends to spend four months in Cairo, and a further four months on a boat or *qangah* sailing up the Nile. On his return to France, he exhibited six paintings at the Salon of 1857, five of which were based on his Egyptian trip: *Prayer in the House of an Arnavut Chief* (Cat. 30), *Egyptian Recruits Crossing the Desert* (Cat. 29), *Memnon et Sesostris, Chameaux à l'Abreuvoir* and the present painting.

This major monument of antiquity had been recorded many times by Western artists since at least 1785 and Gérôme's approach was not uninfluenced by traditional landscape conventions, as contemporary critics were quick to note. Timbal referred to 'the old Egypt, the debris of which is devoured every year by the sand' (1876, p. 335), and Théophile Gautier, in describing Gérôme's other painting of the colossi also exhibited in 1857, alerted the spectator to Gérôme's concern to record the collapse of empires and the passage of time: 'These two mountains carved in human form . . . which neither time, nor earthquakes, nor even the most terrible of conquerors were able to dislodge from their bases! They stand there, crushing their knees with their colossal hands, mishapen, monstrous, flesh reverting slowly to stone' (Gautier, p. 247). Furthermore, the caravan of camels in the middle distance serves as a stock means to highlight through the use of contrast the vast scale of the colossi themselves.

Yet, even in this early representation of an aspect of Egypt, Gérôme moved further than his predecessors in his desire to record with hyper-accuracy the contemporary appearance of specific scenes and sites. The harsh, stony terrain in the foreground and the winding column of camels hint at the presence of the expansive, implacable desert which lies behind the Necropolis of Thebes. The application of a thin film of light brushwork in the sky and the intense clarity in the rendering of the detail provide the technical means by which Gérôme translated that specific quality of overpowering heat and glaring light which prompted Gautier to remark on this painting's 'sky hazy with heat which is dispelled behind the luminous shimmer of the atmosphere' (p. 247).

The painting still hangs in its original frame. Designed to complement the ancient Egyptian subject, it received favourable comment from Gautier in the Salon of 1857 for the way it reinforced the painting's 'thoroughly Egyptian appearance' (p. 248).

There are two variants of this work, *Le Colosse de Memnon* (1857; with Joseph J. Dodge, Jacksonville, 1972) and *Memnon et Sesostris* (Salon of 1857; present location unknown, see Shinn-Strahan I, pl. XLIX). There is also a preliminary drawing, almost certainly executed on the spot (Musée des Beaux-Arts, Nantes; inv. 977.2.1.D).    M.A.S.

PROVENANCE
1858, bought from the Salon des Artistes vivants by the Musée des Beaux-Arts, Nantes
EXHIBITIONS
1857, Paris, Salon (no. 1160)
1858, Nantes, Salon des Artistes vivants (no. 182)
1975, Marseille, Musée Cantini, *L'Orient en question* (no. 88)
1982, Nantes, Musée des Beaux-Arts, *Les Orients* (no. 17)
REFERENCES
Timbal 1876, p. 335
Shinn-Strahan, II, pl. XCIX
Th. Gautier, 'Salon de 1857 (I)', *l'Artiste*, 14 June 1857, p. 191
Th. Gautier, 'Salon de 1857 (IV): MM. Gérôme, Mottez', *l'Artiste*, 5 July 1857, pp. 247–48

## 29*

# Egyptian Recruits Crossing the Desert  1857

*Les Recrues égyptiennes trasversant le désert*

61·9 × 106 cm
Signed and dated bottom right: *J. L. GEROME 1857*
Private Collection, Houston, Texas
[*repr. in colour on p. 80, plate 27*]

This is one of the five paintings derived from Gérôme's first visit to Egypt in 1856, which he exhibited at the Salon of 1857 (see Cat. 28, 30). It represents a scene, apparently common in Egypt during the nineteenth century, when young men from the villages were forcibly conscripted into the army of the pasha, a

29

process which dated back to the first attempt by Muḥammād ʿAlī (see Cat.102), to build up a regular army in 1824. The recruits trudge across the desert handcuffed and guarded by Arnavuts (see Cat. 30). Théophile Gautier was full of praise for this work when he reviewed the Salon of 1857, devoting an extensive part of his article on Gérôme to this painting. Possibly drawing upon his own experience of the desert, Gautier noted that Gérôme had succeeded in capturing three distinctive features of the Orient: the ethnic diversity, the typical range of Oriental responses, from the resignation of the recruits and the 'quiet and fatalistic contempt' (p. 247) of the Arnavut who leads the group, to the peculiar qualities of light and heat unique to the Egyptian desert. Gautier elaborated this latter point by arguing that, contrary to the current fashion for representing hot countries as torrid and highly coloured, Gérôme had observed that extreme light drains all colour from objects and renders the sky and land white: 'A white sand, like china clay, blown into ripples of water by the wind, bearing the stamp of the passing caravans, and rising up in opaque flurries; a sky veiled beneath a dusty mist and burnt up by the shafts of a sun baked white; in front, behind, to the right and to the left, above and below, a leaden, arid waste, pale, dry, overwhelmed and overwhelming, where no moisture falls but drops of sweat, where nothing breathes but the asphyxiating *khamsin* [desert wind]' (p. 247). Gautier's description of the effect of blinding light on the desert was confirmed in Lenoir's own account of the departure of Gérôme's caravan to cross the desert towards Sinai in 1868: 'In the afternoon, the full light of the sun turned all [the objects] an intense white, softened by some grey and gold tinges to create a most brilliant effect' (Lenoir 1872, p. 199). The problem of imposing a compositional structure on a flat, featureless landscape punctuated only by a group of figures was tackled by a number of artists (eg. Belly, Cat. 3) and the issue of translating into pictorial terms an alien, blinding light was confronted by Fromentin (Cat. 26) and Guillaumet (Cat. 51), among others. However, as Gautier perceived, in the handling of the composition, the recording of the reactions of individual figures, the role of the guards, the description of nature and the light, Gérôme contrived to imbue the subject with greater significance. The painting becomes the expression of the two universal characteristics of the Orient: *'L'implacabilité de la nature et l'implacabilité du despotisme'* (Gautier, p. 247).

The smaller version of this painting, which is now in the Tanenbaum Collection, Ottawa, was previously considered to be the one exhibited at the Salon of 1857. Professor Gerald Ackerman now holds that, on the grounds of its size and its relatively higher degree of finish, the larger painting exhibited here was the one accepted by the Salon of 1857.   MA.S.

PROVENANCE
Kurt E. Schon Ltd, New Orleans; Priv. Coll., Houston, Texas
EXHIBITION
1857, Paris, Salon (no. 1157)
REFERENCES
Galichon 1868, p. 149
Timbal 1876, p. 335
Shinn-Strahan, II, pl. XC
Th. Gautier, 'Salon de 1857 (I)', *L'Artiste*, 14 June 1857, p. 191
Th. Gautier, 'Salon de 1857 (IV): MM. Gérôme, Mottez', *L'Artiste*, 5 July 1857, p. 247
F. Field Hering, *Gérôme, His Life and Works*, New York, 1892, p. 65

## 30*
## Prayer in the House of an Arnavut Chief
### 1857
*Prière chez un chef arnaute*

63·7 × 91·9 cm
Signed and dated bottom right: *J. L. GÉRÔME MDCCCLVII*
Private Collection, Houston, Texas
[repr. in colour on p. 64, plate 28]

Arnavuts were Albanian soldiers favoured by Muḥammad ʿAlī, not least because he was one himself. He used them for his regular army to counter the resurgent power of the Bays and their Mamlūk retainers. This painting is one of the five Orientalist paintings which Gérôme exhibited at the Salon of 1857 (see Cat. 28, 29), the fruits of his first visit to Egypt in 1856.

The line of variously-clad and ethnically diverse soldiers at prayer, set in a discreet, domestic interior, rather than in a mosque, appears consciously to eschew all the picturesque possibilities of the subject. A mood of solemnity, which Lenoir certainly did not regard as an attribute of these military men, is cast over the scene. Indeed, Lenoir described the Arnavuts in Cairo as 'these sentries out of a comic opera' who have nothing

30

better to do than 'to take into custody the photographers who wish to favour them with their confidences . . . Their costume is artistically dishevelled, their costly weapons as glittering as they are inoffensive, their proud and disdainful poses, their slightest gestures, everything about them seems to have been studied in its effect' (Lenoir 1872, p. 27).

Whilst some critics attacked this painting for its stilted figures, rejection of the picturesque and total absence of any Oriental feeling (Clément de Ris, 1858), Théophile Gautier was particularly enthusiastic about the work, which he regarded as a masterpiece. He even judged it superior to Gérôme's popularly-acclaimed painting at the same Salon, *Le Duel des masqués* (three versions: Musée Condé, Chantilly; The Hermitage, Leningrad; The Walters Art Gallery, Baltimore). Gautier praised the painting for its calm air, its cool tonalities, the careful differentiation between racial types and the intense, deeply felt faith in Islam, where all classes and races are considered equal in the sight of Allah (see Cat. 34). From these characteristics, Gautier derived what for him were the most significant features of contemporary French painting: the pursuit of realism in the depiction of individual details such that their veracity could not be faulted, a concern with ethnography, and the accumulation of information about unknown peoples and landscapes which Gautier saw as the means of providing a more appropriate definition for the term 'exotic'.

Gérôme's interest in ethnographic subjects had been awakened on his trip down the Danube in 1854 and given visual expression in his first ethnographic painting exhibited at the Salon of 1855, *Musiciens russes* (present location unknown). It was on the strength of this painting together with *Prayer in the House of an Arnavut Chief* that his reputation as a *'peintre ethnographique'* was established. Throughout his subsequent career, Gérôme repeatedly depicted Arnavuts and meticulously recorded the myriad racial groups which populated the streets, bazaars and mosques of his Oriental world (see Cat. 34, 39). MA.S.

PROVENANCE
1860, Wertheimer sale, Paris; 1869, Poutalès sale, Paris; 1956, Charles Peltier Gallery, Rheims; Benedict Coll., New York; Kurt E. Schon, Ltd, New Orleans; Priv. Coll., Houston, Texas

EXHIBITIONS
1857, Paris, Salon (no. 1158)
1967, Vassar College Art Gallery, *Gérôme* (no. 1)

REFERENCES
Galichon 1868, p. 149
Timbal 1876, p. 335
Shinn-Strahan, II, pl. LXXIX
Th. Gautier, 'Salon de 1857 (I)', *L'Artiste*, 14 June 1857, p. 191
Th. Gautier, 'Salon de 1857 (IV): MM. Gérôme, Mottez', *L'Artiste*, 5 July 1857, pp. 246–47
Cte. L. Clément de Ris, 'Les Notabilités de l'art depuis dix ans-II', *L'Artiste*, 27 June 1858, p. 117

31

## 31

# Dance of the 'Ālmah 1863
*La Danse de l'almée*

Oil on panel: 50·2 × 81·3 cm
Signed and dated on the wall top left: *J. L. GEROME 1863*
The Dayton Art Institute, gift of Mr Robert Badenhop
[*repr. in colour on p. 101, plate 29*]

The name *'ālmah* (from the arabic *analeim*, learned women) was originally applied to professional female improvisers of songs and poems. It came to mean any female entertainer, and by 1850 referred to little more than dancing girls who were also prostitutes. In an attempt to clean up the morals of Cairo, Muḥammad 'Alī (Cat. 102) issued in 1834 an edict which banned female dancers and prostitutes in Cairo and ordered the deportation of all prostitutes to three cities: Qenā, Esnā and Aswān. Flaubert, deploring the absence of dancers and good brothels in Cairo (Steegmuller, ed., 1979, p. 83) visited all three of these cities in search of their illicit pleasures on his trip up the Nile.

The dances for which the *'ālmahs* were renowned were varied, ranging from the very static to the extremely energetic; the most famous and alluring was the *'bee'*, a striptease dance described by many European visitors to Egypt. Accompanied by a *darābukah* (clay drum), *kamangah* (two stringed cello) and a *zummarah* (double reed pipe), the dance would start slowly and accelerate with the music to an increasingly frenetic pitch, clothing being shed during this ultimate crescendo.

Gérôme's *Dance of the 'Ālmah* portrays many of the characteristics of *'ālmah* dances meticulously described by Flaubert (Steegmuller, ed., 1979, p. 121), though probably not in this case the *bee*. Accompanied by three musical instruments on the right, the *'ālmah* claps small castanettes as she twists her body towards the applauding audience of *bashibazuks*, identified by their elaborate headgear (see Cat. 36).

The subject of the *'ālmah* was as alluring to the nineteenth-century European as that of the harem, the baths or the slave market. Flaubert pointed out that a dance performed for his party at Esnā reminded him of a dance illustrated on an ancient Greek vase (Steegmuller, ed., 1979, p. 155), while Hector de Callias remarked that the *'ālmah's* dance is strictly of the Orient, having no connection whatsoever with those dances performed in the Paris Opéra or at the Bal de l'Opéra (p. 196). Preparatory evocations of such dancing girls and the promises which they held out to the European traveller were part of the anticipatory pleasure of a journey to the Orient. Lenoir described how his party had constructed a 'mirage' of these dancers while still in Paris (Lenoir 1872, p. 98), and when confronted with the reality, his vocabulary expressed the exoticism of this experience: 'strange', 'picturesque', 'erotic' (p. 106).

This painting attracted much controversy when it was exhibited at the Salon of 1864. It was a major success with the public and with certain critics such as Timbal and Hector de Callias, the latter noting the brilliance with which Gérôme captured this universal combination of the frenetic movement of the arms and the torso set upon the 'legs of marble' (p. 196). Yet the painting also provoked an intense and complex reaction which epitomises the contradictory responses of Europeans to the Near East. For example, Lagrange deplored the overt titillation of public sensibilities which the subject provoked, suggesting that it was too immoral to be placed in front of

Parisians, men and women alike. On the other hand, he measured the degree of realism in Gérôme's painting against his own voyeuristic experience of the dance ('*ce plaisir exotique*' [p. 529]) during his visit to Egypt. He deplored the lack of honest representation in the beauty of the dancer and pointed to Gérôme's failure to capture the shame which he felt he noted in her. It is here that Lagrange exhibits a possible double standard: he was quite prepared to observe the dance himself, but, by attributing to the performer the European concept of shame, he demonstrated his lack of real understanding of this particular cultural phenomenon.

In keeping with this Western fascination with the *'ālmah*, Gérôme executed a number of paintings based on this theme, for example *La Danse à l'épée* (Shinn-Strahan, I, pl. XVI) and *Almées jouant aux échecs* (Shinn-Strahan, II, pl. XLIII).

There are two related studies for this work, one for the *'ālmah*, and another for the seated *bashibazuk* (Dayton Art Institute, inv. nos. 83.4, 83.15)   MA.S.

PROVENANCE
By 1889, John Hoey, New York; Robert Badenhop, Newark, New Jersey; 1951, given by him to Dayton Art Institute, Ohio

EXHIBITIONS
1864, Paris, Salon (no. 794)
1867, Paris, *Exposition Universelle* (no. 297)
1958, Grand Rapids, Michigan, Art Gallery; Minneapolis, University of Minnesota Art Gallery, *Music and Art* (p. 8)
1972–73, Dayton, Art Institute; Minneapolis, Institute of Arts; Baltimore, The Walters Art Gallery, *Jean-Léon Gérôme (1824–1904)* (no. 14)
1982, Rochester, New York, Memorial Art Gallery, *Orientalism* (no. 39)

REFERENCES
Timbal 1876, p. 340
Shinn-Strahan, vol. II, pl. LXXXVII
E. About, *Salon de 1864*, Paris, 1864, p. 82
H. de Callias, 'Salon de 1864', *L'Artiste*, 1864, I, p. 196
H. de Callias, 'Salon de 1864 (VII): M. Gérôme', *L'Artiste*, 1864, I, p. 198
Th. Gautier, *Moniteur universel*, 4 June 1864
L. Lagrange, 'Le Salon de 1864', *Gazette des Beaux-Arts*, June 1864, XVI, pp. 529–30
E. Strahan, *The Art Treasures of America*, Philadelphia, 1879, II, p. 108, ill. p. 33
F. Field Hering, *Gérôme, His Life and Works*, New York, 1892, pp. 106–07
B. H. Evans, *Fifty Treasures of the Dayton Art Institute*, Dayton, 1969, p. 118
Rochester, New York, Memorial Art Gallery, *Orientalism*, catalogue by D. Rosenthal, 1982, p. 164, fig. 76

32

*32**

# General Bonaparte in Cairo   *c.*1863
## *Le Général Bonaparte au Caire*

Oil on panel: 35·5 × 25 cm
Signed bottom left: *J. L. GEROME*
The Art Museum, Princeton University, John Maclean Magie and Gertrude Magie Fund
[*repr. in colour on p. 87, plate 30*]

In this posthumous picture of Napoleon Bonaparte (1769–1821), Gérôme set the general in contemplative pose against a backdrop of the Mamlūk tombs in the Eastern Cemetery of Cairo. The pose was probably derived from the portraits of Napoleon's officers painted by André Dutertre which were exhibited at the Salons between 1804 and 1812 and hung in the Musée de Versailles. While the handling of the background is somewhat loose, the figure of Napoleon himself is solid and carefully painted, suggesting that it was almost certainly executed from a model in Gérôme's studio.

Napoleon Bonaparte arrived in Egypt in July 1798 on receipt of the supreme command of the French forces in the battle against the British. Determined to oust the British from the Mediterranean, Bonaparte occupied Malta and then landed at Alexandria with a substantial military and naval force, as well as 175 engineers and scholars (see Cat. 20). He defeated the Bays at the Battle of the Pyramids (21 July 1798) and entered Cairo three days later. While the attempt to establish French rule over Syria was thwarted at Jaffa and Acre (see Cat. 48–50), the French remained in control of Egypt until the Peace of Amiens, signed in March 1802.

This painting is one of four compositions depicting Napoleon on campaign in Egypt and Syria (*Le Général Bonaparte au Caire*, 1868, Shinn-Strahan, II, pl. XXV; *Le Général Bonaparte en Egypte*, Shinn-Strahan, II, pl. XLIV; *Oedipe: Bonaparte et le sphinx*, c.1886, Hearst Memorial Museum, St. Simeon, California). Together with such works as *La Mort du Maréchal Ney, le 7 décembre 1851, neuf heures du matin* (1868; City Art Gallery, Sheffield), these paintings reflect the enthusiasm for Napoleonic themes amongst artists during the second half of the nineteenth century. The declaration of the Second Empire in 1852 under Napoleon's nephew, Louis-Napoléon, fuelled renewed interest in the Consulate and the First Empire. In line with the new régime's determination to establish its own political legitimacy, Yvon, Doré and de Neuville provided important large-scale records of great French military battles for the walls of the Galeries des Batailles at Versailles. Meisonnier, Gérôme, Clairin and Detaille, who provided images of the military achievements of the Second Empire, also drew heavily upon this renewed enthusiasm for Napoleon I. The same interest was also reflected in contemporary literature, for example, A. Thiers, *Histoire du Consulat et de l'Empire* (1862). After the collapse of the Second Empire in 1870, the images of Napoleon became increasingly imbued with a sense of nostalgia. Gérôme's painting of '*le petit caporal*', with his glance directed away from the spectator and his hat casting a shadow over his face, would appear to convey a premonition of the imminent loss of Cairo. Thus the painting, despite its similarities in precise brushwork and in scale to the Napoleonic paintings by Meisonnier, forms an image which carries a meaning beyond that of mere anecdote.   MA.S.

PROVENANCE
1953, Van Doorn Estate sale; acquired by the Art Museum, University of Princeton

EXHIBITIONS
1972–73, Dayton, Art Institute; Minneapolis, Institute of Arts; Baltimore, The Walters Art Gallery, *Jean-Léon Gérôme (1824–1904)* (no. 16)
1982, Rochester, New York, Memorial Art Gallery, *Orientalism* (no. 40)

## 33

# The Moorish Bath   *c.* 1870

*Le Bain maure*

51 × 41 cm
Signed upper edge of partition: *J. L. GEROME*
Museum of Fine Arts, Boston, gift of Robert Jordan from the
Collection of Ebden D. Jordan
[*repr. in colour on p. 100, plate 31*]

The sunken fountain pool in the foreground with the two-colour
marble inlay, the silver water bowl with a Mamlūk blazon and
the Sudanese serving girl have suggested to R. Ettinghausen
(Dayton Art Institute, 1972, p. 20) that this picture does not
represent a Moorish bath but an Egyptian scene. Given the
pattern of Gérôme's travels in the Near East, it would seem that
a Cairene location is more likely. Gérôme visited at least two
baths while he was in the city in 1868: a very large bath, entered
through a 'mysterious' door which opened onto *'une salle immense
tout en marbre blanc'* (Lenoir 1872, p. 186), and the private bath
of the Persian ambassador, *'tout en faïence de perse, et les boiseries
peintes des plafonds furent particulièrement l'objet de notre admiration'*
(Lenoir 1872, p. 173).

To the Western visitor, the Turkish bath had both a real and
an imaginary significance. In the former sense, it represented a
luxurious and wholly un-European sensation. Lenoir likened the
experience to 'an opera in five, very distinct and regulated acts'
(p. 186). Flaubert, who gave a lengthy description of his own
visit to a Cairene bath, openly welcomed the cultural dislocation
engendered by these baths: 'I was alone in the hot room,
watching the daylight fade through the great circles of glass in
the dome . . . It is very voluptuous and sweetly melancholy to
take a bath like that, quite alone, lost in those dim rooms where
the slightest noise resounds like a canon shot' (Steegmuller, ed.,
1979, p. 85). Gérôme's painting attempts to capture elements of
both Lenoir's and Flaubert's experiences. The Persian tiles could
have been inspired by the Persian ambassador's private bath. The
high vaulted room and the dim light are depicted by Gérôme,
who lays special emphasis on the half-light of the dim interior,
in contrast to the shafts of intense light filtering through the
dome beyond the top of the picture, touching the wall in the
background, the Sudanese woman's turban, the bowl of water
and, more diffused, the *nargīlah*.

In the realm of the imagination, Gérôme's *Moorish Bath*
belongs to an iconographic tradition which goes back to
eighteenth-century engravings and to descriptions of the baths
in Montesquieu's *Lettres persanes* (1721). Typically, such
iconography involved one or more partially nude, fair-skinned
women attended by darker-skinned serving women. By the
middle of the nineteenth century, this iconography had become
an accepted format in the hands of Ingres and Chassériau (eg.
*Le Bain mauresque*, Musée des Beaux-Arts, Strasbourg), which
fulfilled two related aesthetic intentions. At its most simple, the
juxtaposition of white nude and dark semi-nude highlights the
former's perfection in Western eyes (L. Nochlin, 1983, p. 126, ill.
p. 131). Yet this perfection was obviously not set within the
Western tradition of the classical ideal of Beauty. Hence *The
Moorish Bath*, as in Ingres's *Odalisque and Slave* (Cat. 56), with
its combination of exotic setting and pure classical beauty,
permitted the integration of Eastern motifs with Western artistic
principles, yet without denying their inherent exotic overtones.
In this painting not only could the white nude sit as comfortably
as in one of the artist's 'Néo-grec' paintings, but by placing her

beyond the pool he invites the spectator to become a voyeur.

Some critics felt that this marriage between Eastern exotic and
eternal Western beauty was inappropriate. Paul Mantz upbraided
Gérôme with regard to two of his Turkish bath paintings, *Femmes
au bain* and *Bain turc*: 'A little frisson of voluptuousness
would perhaps animate the oriental pictures of the *Femmes au
bain* and the *Bain turc*, if these women were not made of ivory:
they are all just as moving as billiard balls' ('L'exposition
universelle: la peinture française', *Gazette des Beaux-Arts*, 1878,
XVIII, p. 437). Gérôme executed several paintings on the theme
of the Turkish bath, some more explicit in their reference to
harem settings, for example, *Le Bain* (Memorial Art Museum, San
Francisco) and *Dans le harem* (The Hermitage,
Leningrad).   MA.S.

PROVENANCE
1870, presented to H. J. Turner, London; 1903, 4 April, Christie's London (lot 138); Arthur
Tooth, London and New York; Ebden D. Jordan; Robert Jordan; 1924, gift of Robert Jordan
to the Museum of Fine Arts, Boston (24.217)

EXHIBITIONS
1873, Vienna, *Welt Ausstellung* (no. 276)
1895, London, Guildhall, *Loan Collection of Pictures* (no. 51)
1898, London, Guildhall, *Pictures of the French School* (no. 123)
1979–81, Atlanta, The High Museum of Art; Tokyo, Seibu Museum; Nagoya, City
    Museum; Kyoto, National Museum of Modern Art; Denver, Art Museum; Boston,
    Museum of Fine Arts (at Faneuil Hall), *Corot to Bargue* (no. 27)

REFERENCES
Shinn, Strahan, I, pl. IV
Dayton, Art Institute, 'Jean-Léon Gérôme as a Painter of Near Eastern Subjects', R.
    Ettinghausen, in *Jean-Léon Gérôme (1824–1904)*, 1972, p. 20
L. Nochlin, 'The Imaginary Orient', *Art in America*, May 1983, p. 126, ill. p. 131

33

34

# Prayer in the Mosque of 'Amr   c.1872

*Prière à la mosquée d'Amron*

88·9 × 74·9 cm
Signed top right on the beam: J. L. GEROME
Metropolitan Museum of Art, New York
[*repr. in colour on p. 65, plate 32*]

The precision of detail in this painting suggests that it must be based upon careful sketches of the Mosque of 'Amr made during Gérôme's visit to Egypt in the company of Paul Lenoir in 1868. Furthermore, the sharp linear style and tight handling of paint place the execution of this painting in the early years of the 1870s.

The picture shows one of the five prayer hours of the day. A diverse group of Muslims celebrate the moment in the sanctuary of the Mosque of 'Amr. Standing to the south-west corner of Cairo amongst the ruins of the city of Fustāt, which it had once dominated, this mosque was the first on the continent of Africa. It was erected by 'Amr ibn al-'As, who conquered Egypt for the Khalif 'Umar in AD 640. Despite partial destruction by earthquakes and fires, the mosque, according to Lenoir, still retained in 1868 its vast square courtyard flanked on two sides by colonnades of 230 columns with, in the centre, a fountain sheltered by a palm tree. The sanctuary, with its *minbar* (pulpit) and *miḥrāb* (sacred niche) set in the wall turned towards Mecca, was composed of six rows of columns whose Corinthian capitals had been removed from classical or coptic buildings elsewhere in Cairo.

Gérôme's painting discloses a number of typical European responses to Islamic architecture and religious practices in the nineteenth century. The careful delineation of the Corinthian capitals, the serried ranks of deeply plunging columns, the simple polychromy of the Arab arches and the patterned tiles on the floor form a visual counterpart to Lenoir's awe-struck response

to the Mosque of 'Amr, where 'the naivety and character of Arabian architecture is at its most primitive, its most simple and consequently its most beautiful' (Lenoir 1872, p. 43). The deliberate alignment of the praying figures and the columns, turned south-east towards the *miḥrāb* and to Mecca, integrate the figures and the architecture into a solemn religious statement. The differentiation between rich and poor, Egyptian and Arnavut, serves to underline that equality of all Muslims in front of Allah which was so much admired by the West and commented upon, for example, by Lady Duff Gordon, Renoir and Lenoir.

Yet Gérôme's painting studiously avoids reference to two notable features of the Mosque of 'Amr. By 1868 the mosque had already fallen into decay (Lenoir 1872, p. 44). Second, the mosque was noted in popular folklore for three objects: a holy stone, a pair of columns and a single column miraculously transported from Mecca. The tales surrounding these objects were confirmation to many Westerners that Islam was a superstitious, barbaric and pagan religion (Steegmuller, ed., 1979, p. 71; Galichon 1868, p. 150). Thus, whilst avoiding reference to these features of the mosque, Gérôme may have jeopardised the veracity of this image. He may also have succeeded in evoking a favourable response on the part of the Western spectator to the power of Islam by conveying the standing of the mosque as the oldest in Egypt, hence the symbolic and actual cradle of Islam in that country.   M.A.S.

PROVENANCE
Catherine Lorillard Woolfe, New York; 1887, bequest of Catherine Lorillard Woolfe to the Metropolitan Museum of Art, New York

REFERENCES
Shinn-Strahan, II, pl. LVIII
E. Strahan, *Art Treasures of America*, Philadelphia, 1879, I, p. 126
F. Field Hering, *Gérôme, His Life and Works*, New York, 1892, p. 126
G. Haller, *Nos grands peintres*, Paris, 1899, p. 101
A. Hoeber, *The Treasures of the Metropolitan Museum of Art*, 1900, p. 80
Ch. Sterling and M. Salinger, *French Paintings: Catalogue of the Metropolitan Museum of Art*, II, XIX Century, New York, 1966, p. 171
Dayton, Art Institute, 'Jean-Léon Gérôme as a Painter of Near Eastern Subjects', R. Ettinghausen, in *Jean-Léon Gérôme (1824–1904)*, 1972, p. 22

34

35*

# Harem in the Kiosk   c. 1875–80

*L'Harem à la kiosque*

76·2 × 115 cm
Signed bottom right on parapet: J. L. GEROME
Private Collection, Houston, Texas
[*repr. in colour on p. 98, plate 33*]

The schematic yet instantly recognisable silhouette of the Golden Horn in the background sets this harem scene in Constantinople rather than Egypt. Gérôme had visited the capital of the Ottoman Empire on his first foreign tour in 1854, which had taken him, in the company of his friend, the actor Got, down the Danube, through Greece to Constantinople. He visited the capital in 1871 and again in 1875 as the guest of the court painter, Abdullah Sirez, who provided him with aide-mémoire photographs of the major sights and buildings of Constantinople. The architectural background, the tight handling of the paint and the fact that the work was with Gérôme's father-in-law, the dealer Goupil, by 1881, suggest a date for the painting of c. 1875–80.

The only description which we have of Gérôme at the entrance to a harem comes from his visit to the Persian ambassador's residence in Cairo in 1868. Lenoir, who accompanied him, had two observations to make about harems. They were a luxury, not a common social institution, and the number of their women and guards was an expression of the owner's worldly wealth. Second, for the West the harem was accessible only to women and hence was prey to 'the imagination of some writers . . . to give the most unbelievable and false descriptions' (Lenoir 1872, p. 173–4).

Despite Shinn-Strahan's conviction that this painting is 'absolutely free from this most inartistic sin of moralising', the *Harem in the Kiosk* plays to the Western myth surrounding harems as morally reprehensible but appealingly erotic institutions. By setting the scene in Constantinople, Gérôme evaded his own Cairene experience, whilst exciting the Western imagination through reference to the fabled luxury of the Sultān's harem already captured in the eighteenth-century 'turqueries' of van Loo and Montesquieu's *Lettres persanes*. Indeed, the play of light and shade, the separation of the pampered women from the immediate gaze of the spectator, the emphasis on surface texture and the richness of the colour reinforce this interpretation.

Certain nineteenth-century writers recognised the gap between the Western myth and the reality of harems in the Near East. Gautier, for example, stressed the nobility of the relationship between the Muslim and his wives. Lady Duff Gordon reported that harems were not a licence for debauched living but rather the source of heavy responsibilities, both financial and moral (*Letters from Egypt*, 1893 ed., pp. 73, 79). Yet the West continued to demand the myth of the inaccessible woman aptly captured by Gérard de Nerval in his description of Smyrna (*Voyage en Orient*, 1856, I, p. 160). Gautier attacked the subject more ironically: 'The first question that one addresses to every traveller who returns from the Orient is this: "and the women?" Nothing decorates better a voyage to the east than an old woman who, at the turning of a deserted alleyway, makes a sign for you to follow her and leads you by a secret door into an apartment decked with all the most sought-after objects of Asian luxury, where awaiting you, seated on squares of brocade, is a Sultana shimmering in gold and precious stones' (*Constantinople*, 1853, p. 88).    MA.S.

PROVENANCE
1881, Goupil and Co., Paris; Jay Gould, New York: 1968, Parke Bernet, New York, Knox Coll. sale; Bernard K. Crawford, Montclair, New Jersey; The Fine Art Society, London; Kurt E. Schon Ltd, New Orleans; Priv. Coll., Houston, Texas
EXHIBITIONS
1972–73, Dayton, Art Institute; Minneapolis, Institute of Arts; Baltimore, The Walters Art Gallery, *Jean-Léon Gérôme (1824–1904)* (no. 22)
1978, London, The Fine Art Society, *Eastern Encounters: Orientalist Painters of the Nineteenth Century* (no. 4)
REFERENCES
Shinn-Strahan, I, pl. XXXVII
F. Field Hering, *Gérôme, His Life and His Works*, New York, 1892, p. 241

## 36*

## A Bashibazuk   *c.*1878

*Un Bashi-Bazouk*

81 × 66 cm
Signed centre left: *J. L. GEROME*
Anonymous loan to the Museum of Fine Arts, Boston
[*repr. in colour on p. 90, plate 34*]

A *bashibazuk* was a mercenary soldier belonging to the irregular troops of the Turkish army. Racially diverse, they were unpaid but supported themselves by living off permitted plunder. They were also notorious for their lawlessness and savage brutality.

Gérôme's persistent interest in ethnographic types, awakened during his trip down the Danube in 1854 (see Cat. 30), was frequently remarked upon by contemporary critics. Gautier, for example, praised Gérôme for his 'ethnographic veracity', believing that his paintings, such as the *bashibazuk*, not only provided information sufficiently reliable for them to be consulted by scholars – 'M. Serres, the anthropologist, would be able to consult with absolute certainty these specimens of unrecorded races' ('Salon de 1857 IV', *l'Artiste*, 5 July 1857, p. 246) – but also fulfilled a current thirst for precise and reliable information about the human race: 'M. Gérôme satisfies one of the most demanding instincts of the age: the desire which people have to know more about each other than that which is revealed in imaginary portraits. He has everything which is needed in order to fulfill this important mission' (*loc.cit.*).

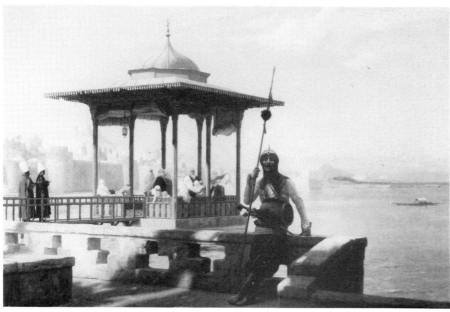

35

The attention to exact detail in this painting would fully support Gautier's claim. Set against a sombre, grey background, the head is turned in profile to reveal the distinctive physiognomy of the sitter. The characteristic cut of the pink coat with its grey braiding and the organisation of the complex head-dress with its overlapping reds, dull yellows, greens and patterned areas are handled with brushstrokes which are deceptive in their looseness. The figure is lit by a careful pool of light. The overall effect is statuesque, yet, in character with such works as *The Return from the Hunt* (Cat. 37) and *The Moorish Bath* (Cat. 33), the palette is carefully limited and, by highlighting the creases and the cut of the pink jacket, the individual parts of the painting are all given equal weight within the composition as a whole. The quiet monumentality of the image belies the ferocious reputation of the sitter and, as in the *Prayer in the House of an Arnavut Chief* (Cat. 30), creates an icon which is more sympathetic than the popular view of *bashibazuks* held by the West. While Galichon maintained that this superb finish and attention to individual detail lay at the base of Gérôme's contemporary popularity among connoisseurs (1868, pp. 150–51), Timbal and Paul Mantz ('Salon de 1867', *Gazette des Beaux-Arts*, vol. 22, 1867) expressed a certain unease about the technical facility of such highly polished paintings. Timbal, for example, felt that the perfection threatened to impose a certain monotony on his paintings, which he could however overcome through diversification of his subject-matter (1876, p. 338). Mantz was more scathing. Noting the transformation of Gérôme from a painter of classical anecdotal scenes to Orientalist subjects, he stated: 'With all his talent of execution, with the rare dexterity of his subtle paintbrush, this Greek has become like a Dutch painter of the Decadent Period' (p. 531).

*Bashibazuks* are incorporated in many of Gérôme's paintings: *Dance of the 'Ālmah* (Cat. 31), *Le Coulage de balles des Bashi-Bazouks* (Metropolitan Museum of Art, New York) *Bashi-Bazuks chantant* (The Walters Art Gallery, Baltimore), *Bashi-Bazuks dansant* (present location unknown, Shinn-Strahan II, pl. LIX).     MA.S.

PROVENANCE
1981, 23 June, Sotheby's, London (lot 29); bought by present owner

## 37*
## The Return from the Hunt   *c.* 1878
*Le Retour de la chasse*

73·6 × 58·4 cm
Signed bottom centre on fountain base: *J. L. GEROME*
Private Collection, Houston, Texas
[*repr. in colour on p. 75, plate 35*]

Circassians, noted for their noble beauty and pale skin, came from the Caucasus Mountains and provided the Ottoman Empire with excellent horsemen and much sought-after women for their harems. Characteristically depicted on horseback, this figure of a Caucasian is one of numerous compositions of individuals or groups which record the ethnic types noted by Gérôme during his visits to the Near East (see Cat. 36). However, the colcasia plant, the doe, the fountain and the niche, albeit Orientalised, occur in paintings by Gérôme as early as the 1850s (eg. *L'Idylle*, 1852, Musée Massey, Tarbes), and thus suggest that this painting was executed in Paris, the pink jacket and rifle being familiar studio props.

Despite its modest dimensions, *The Return from the Hunt* demonstrates several characteristics of Gérôme's oeuvre. In keeping with Timbal's analysis of the nature of realism in Gérôme's work (1876), the painting maintains a subtle balance between the intense detail of different textured surfaces – the satin jacket, the stone, the plants, the architectural decoration – and the overall unity of the composition. The resulting image is one in which the figure of the Circassian and his horse exist within, rather than dominate, the assemblage of compositional elements.

The absence of an explicit message in this work casts it within the mould of genre paintings whose primary function was to entertain the eye rather than to instruct the mind. Some critics, notably Paul Mantz, took Gérôme to task for this negation of the moral power of painting, accusing him of 'small mindedness' (*Gazette des Beaux-Arts*, XXIII, 1867, p. 531). Others, such as Galichon, however, considered that Gérôme's intense

36

37

understanding of the Near East enabled him to convert a genre scene into a picture which encapsulated the very spirit of Orientalism (1868, p. 150). The fact that a debate over the acceptability of genre painting could be provoked by works such as *The Return from the Hunt* points to the links which existed in mid-nineteenth-century French painting between realism and anecdotal, or genre, works. Contemporary critical opinion demanded of Orientalist paintings both sound information and aesthetic pleasure. To achieve these ends, the genre scenes of everyday Orientalist life, executed by artists such as Girardet (see Cat. 45) and Gérôme, could seek out simultaneously intense veracity and rely for composition and effect upon, as Paul Mantz noted, Dutch seventeenth-century precedents. In this light, both the atmosphere and intense finish in Gérôme's painting suggest parallels with Metsu and Terborch.    MA.S.

PROVENANCE
Priv. Coll., New York; Kurt E. Schon, Ltd, New Orleans; Priv. Coll., Houston, Texas
EXHIBITION
Paris, *Exposition Universelle*, 1878 (no. 365)
REFERENCES
Shinn-Strahan, II, pl. LXVIII
F. Field Hering, *Gérôme, His Life and Works*, New York, 1892, pl. 193

38

38\*

# The Mu'adhdin's Call to Prayer    *c.*1879–80
*L'Appel du muezzin à la prière*

90·5 × 65·4 cm
Private Collection, Houston, Texas
[repr. in colour on p. 62, plate 36]

In *The Mu'adhdin's Call to Prayer*, as with his interior views of mosques (see Cat. 34, 40), Gérôme exactly describes the exterior dome, minaret and *mu'adhdin* in order to provide careful information about specific manifestations of the Islamic faith. The dome, or cupola, covers the chamber in which the tomb of the mosque's founder is placed (see Cat. 34). The minaret, described by Lenoir (1872, p. 164) as the '*clocher*' or belfry, is the most elevated place of the mosque, and the point from which the *mu'adhdin* calls the faithful to prayer five times a day. By intoning a '*psalmodie languoreuse*' (Lenoir 1872, p. 164), the *mu'adhdin* reminds the Muslim faithful of the need to cease all work and pray: 'Allah is great; I testify that there is no god but Allah, and Muḥammad is the prophet of Allah; come to prayer; come to prosperity; Allah is greatest, there is no god but Allah.' The five Calls to Prayer also serve as the divisions of the day and as in the mosque, where architecture and liturgy are integrated, so the Call to Prayer regulates the actions of daily life by a constant reminder of the need for religious observance.

The vertiginous view in this painting, a detail of the dome of the mosque of Amir Khayrbak over a *capriccio* of the city of Cairo, is taken from the old walls of the city, looking north-west towards the mosque of Sultān Hassan with the Mosque of Amir Khayrbak in the middle ground. It recalls a view enjoyed by Flaubert during a visit to an unidentified Cairo mosque in 1849: 'We climb the minaret; the stones are worn, chipped. On the steps near the top, debris of birds come here to die, the highest they could come, almost in the air. From there I have Cairo beneath me; to the right the desert with camels gliding over it and their shadows beside them as escorts; opposite beyond the plains and the Nile, the Pyramids . . . The sky is completely blue, hawks wheel above us; below, far down, men are small, moving noiselessly. The liquid light seems to penetrate the surface of things and enter into them' (Steegmuller, ed., 1979, pp. 46–47).

The translucent effect of the light together with the characteristically meticulous detail and the cut-off cupola on the left suggest that Gérôme may have derived the composition of this painting from a photograph rather than from a sketch. By the time of Gérôme's first visit to Egypt in 1856, photography had become an accepted method of recording scenes of contemporary life and the remains of antiquity. For example, Maxime du Camp, who had accompanied Flaubert, undertook an exhaustive photographic record during their trip to Egypt in 1849–51, and Horace Vernet used the daguerreotype on his Egyptian visit of 1839. Indeed, Gautier, reviewing the character of French painting exhibited at the Salon of 1857, remarked on the replacement of the idealised human figure by a vastly increased range of geographic and ethnic subjects, including Oriental ones, which he attributed to the commendable and extensive use of the daguerreotype ('Salon de 1857 (I)', *L'Artiste*, 14 June 1857, pp. 189–90).    MA.S.

PROVENANCE
J. W. Drexel, Philadelphia; San Francisco Art Association; Oakland Art Museum (on long loan); 1979, 18 June, Sotheby Parke Bernet, Los Angeles (lot 46); Mr and Mrs Joseph M. Tanenbaum, Toronto; Kurt E. Schon Ltd, New Orleans; Priv. Coll., Houston, Texas
REFERENCE
Shinn-Strahan, II, pl. LXXXI

## 39

# The Carpet Merchant   *c.1887*

*Le Marchand de tapis au Caire*

83·5 × 64·7 cm
Signed bottom right: *J. L. GEROME*
Minneapolis Institute of Arts, The William Hood Dunwoody Fund
[*repr. in colour on p. 69, plate 37*]

In 1902, Baedeker's guide described the extensive bazaar of Cairo as 'inferior to those of Damascus and Constantinople' yet able to 'present to the European visitor many novel features and many interesting traits of Oriental character' (p. 38). Previously Lenoir had identified these 'oriental traits' in his evocative description of the courtyard of the carpet merchant's house, based on a visit to Cairo in 1868. Beyond the glittering clutter of jewellery, fabrics, harness and weapons, Lenoir, in the company of Gérôme, Edmond About and Frédéric Masson, stumbled into a courtyard whose architecture equalled the beauty of the magnificent Persian carpets piled high on its floor. As an artist himself, Lenoir noted the particular quality of light which filtered through the opening in the roof, fell on the merchandise on the floor and increased the '*tons éclatants*' of the carpets. He concluded that the courtyard and the carpets created '*un des interieurs les plus pittoresques que nous ayons rencontrés au Caire*' (Lenoir 1872, p. 161). Very often on his travels through Egypt, prompted perhaps by Gérôme, Lenoir identified subjects which he considered were admirably suited to paintings for a Western audience. In *The Carpet Merchant* Gérôme has confirmed, like Lewis (Cat. 68, 74) and W. J. Müller (Cat. 81), Lenoir's choice of a 'picturesque' subject: the colourful pile of carpets in the foreground, the careful detailing of architectural decoration and the characteristically varied group of merchants and clients. Although there are no Europeans in the painting, Lenoir reported that all his party bought rugs with great enthusiasm, ordering their purchases to be crated and sent ahead of them to France.

By 1880 Gérôme had begun to execute polychrome sculpture in keeping with the realisation that classical Greek sculpture had itself been coloured. It has been suggested by Gerald Ackerman (Dayton Art Institute, 1972, no. 39) that the donkey in this painting on the right had 'escaped' from two earlier groups of sculpture by Gérôme, *Le Christ entrant dans Jérusalem* and *La Fuite en Egypte*.   MA.S.

PROVENANCE
William Shaus, New York; Crocker family, San Francisco; Sloan and Roman Inc., New York; Institute of Arts, Minneapolis
EXHIBITIONS
1969, University of California at Davis, *Pre-Impressionism*
1972–73, Dayton, Art Institute; Minneapolis, Institute of Arts; Baltimore, The Walters Art Gallery, *Jean-Léon Gérôme (1824–1904)* (no. 39)
REFERENCES
F. Field Hering, *Gérôme, His Life and Works*, New York, 1892, p. 225
J. C. van Dyke, *Modern French Masters*, New York, 1896, ill. opp. p. 36

## 40*

# Prayer at the Mosque of Qāyt-bāy   *c.1895*

*La Prière dans la mosquée de Caïd Bay*

77·5 × 101·6 cm
Signed bottom left on the wall: *J. L. GEROME*
Private Collection, Houston, Texas
[*repr. in colour on p. 67, plate 38*]

This scene of private prayer is set in the prayer hall of the *madrasah* (religious school) and tomb of the Mamlūk sultān, Qāyt-bāy (1468–1496) in Cairo. The mosque was erected in the Eastern Cemetery of Cairo and was completed by one of the most graceful minarets in the city. Unlike the columnar hall of the Mosque of 'Amr (see Cat. 34), the interior is a simple, open hall, the decorative stress being laid upon the rich detailing of the *qiblā* wall, facing Mecca, with its marble *miḥrāb* (niche), the focal point of prayer, and its *minbar* (pulpit), embellished with intricate wooden carving, from which the Friday sermon is delivered. The predominant colours of green and red highlight the arabesques on the frieze and determine the rhythm of the individual architectural features. The carved inscriptions on panels set above the arches are painted in gold and blue against a blue-green ground.

Gérôme and Lenoir certainly visited this mosque during their

39

40

trip to Egypt in 1868, when Lenoir noted that its interior was characteristic of many of Cairo's 400 mosques. Given the freer handling of the paint and the sophistication of the composition, this painting, however, appears to have been executed *c.* 1895, some twenty years after Gérôme's last visit to Cairo. It has been suggested, therefore, that Gérôme must have relied upon stock poses taken from his sketchbooks for the figures and upon photographs for the architectural setting (G. Ackerman, Ottawa, National Gallery of Canada, 1978, p. 118). Despite the lapse of time, Gérôme had nonetheless retained a remarkable recollection of the intense light peculiar to Egypt. The shaft of light coming through the window at the top right of the picture both obliterates all colour and creates a dominant white 'dust' or haze. This drains the detail of the carved inscriptions and, at the same time, intensifies the colours of the figures standing in the shade. Timbal (1876) had earlier commented upon Gérôme's fascination with light, especially its effect when falling on buildings and figures. In his view, however, this did not make Gérôme a 'colourist', since he did not use colour with the eye of the imagination but rather in keeping with his concern for realism as *'un homme scrupuleux'* (p. 342).

As in *Prayer in the Mosque of 'Amr* (Cat. 34), the artist has both accentuated the distinct architectural characteristics of the Mosque of Qāyt-bāy and underlined its function as *'le rendez-vous de la prière'* (Lenoir 1872, p. 164). Indeed, the variety of poses, the expanse of grey marble in the foreground and the direct confrontation with the *qiblā* suggest that the artist sought in this painting to convey to Western spectators that 'impression which dominates in a visit to the mosques . . . that exclusively religious and almost poetic character of these monuments' (Lenoir, 1872, pp. 164, 167). MA.S.

PROVENANCE
Mr and Mrs Joseph M. Tanenbaum Coll., Toronto; Kurt E. Schon, Ltd, New Orleans; Priv. Coll., Houston, Texas
EXHIBITION
1978, Ottawa, The National Gallery of Canada, *The Other Nineteenth Century: Paintings and Sculpture in the Collection of Mr and Mrs Joseph M. Tanenbaum* (no. 38)
REFERENCE
Dayton Art Institute, 'Jean-Léon Gérôme as a Painter of Near Eastern subjects', R. Ettinghausen, in *Jean-Léon Gérôme 1824–1904*, 1972, p. 23

41*

# The Whirling Dervishes  *c.*1895

*Les Derviches tourneurs*

70·4 × 91·3 cm
Signed bottom right: *J. L. GEROME*
Private Collection, Houston, Texas
[*repr. in colour on p. 63, plate 39*]

Since monasticism is expressly forbidden in Islam, those for whom the prescribed religious observances were not enough became itinerants, receiving the Persian name, *dervish*. They devoted themselves to the mystical life whereby the soul journeys through a series of stages, ultimately entering into an ecstatic dialogue with Allah. From these beginnings various great *sufi* brotherhoods developed and the terms *dervish* and *sufi* became virtually synonymous. The *dhikr* (remembrance), a ceremony common to all the brotherhoods, was a means of encouraging the attainment of a heightened state of mystical awareness, in various forms, which alarmed innocent European observers, who described the dervishes variously as whirling,

shouting and howling, as well as eating glowing embers, live serpents, scorpions and glass, or passing needles through their bodies and spikes through their eyes.

The *dhikr* which is depicted in Gérôme's painting is almost certainly set in the mosque of Ma'bad al-Riffā'ī in the Eastern Cemetery of Cairo. Many dervishes belonged to more than one brotherhood and occasionally they held joint ceremonies, as seems to be case here. Framed by a line of *Bayūmmiyyah* (howling dervishes), the *Malawiyyah* (whirling dervish), has cast off his *khirka* (black coat), the symbol of death; he still wears his *sikke* (hat), the symbol of the tomb, retained during the ceremony. Rotating on his right foot, his increasingly frenzied dance is accompanied by a small ensemble of instruments on the left: reed flute, tambourines, rebeck and drum. It is suggested that the founder of the whirling dervishes, Jalāl al-Dīn Rumī (d. Konya, 1273), adopted this ritual as a means of attaining an ecstatic communion with Allah because of the tradition for dance in his native Asia Minor.

Western visitors to the Near East eagerly sought out the dervishes' *dhikrs*. Their reaction was one of fascination and disbelief. Gautier, Lamartine, Maxime du Camp and Flaubert all attended such ceremonies. For Flaubert, who witnessed in Cairo both the *dūsah* (trampling) of the dervishes and what would appear to have been a howling *dhikr*, the latter event provoked a curiously sober response. He saw the tradition of Western rationalism challenged by an intense, enthralling emotionalism: 'we saw one [dervish] fall into convulsions from shouting "Allah!" These are very fine sights, which would have brought many a good laugh from M. de Voltaire (*sic*). Imagine his remarks about the poor old human mind! About fanaticism! Superstition! None of it made me laugh in the slightest, and it is all too absorbing to be appalling' (Steegmuller, ed., 1979, pp. 93, 94). Gautier and Lamartine visited Pera specifically to see whirling dervishes, which prompted Gautier to draw upon the full range of exotic, Orientalist imagery in an intensely poetic description of the ecstatic state of the dancers, their 'eyes fixed, contemplating the splendours of Allah' (*Constantinople*, Paris, 1863, p. 88). MA.S.

PROVENANCE
Bessonneau d'Angers Coll.; Mr Willian Schauss, New York; Mr T. H. Burchell; John Levey Galleries, New York; Mr Francis R. Welch; 1938, Parke Bernet, New York (lot 512); 1939, Parke Bernet, New York (lot 413); 1954, 23 July, Hôtel Drouot, Paris; Schickman, New York; Kurt E. Schon, Ltd, New Orleans; Priv. Coll., Houston, Texas

41

## 41a

# An 'Ālmah   1882

*Une Almée (L'Orientale)*

46·3 × 38·4 cm
Signed and dated top left: *J. L. GEROME 1882*
David E. Rust, Washington

E. W. Lane, writing in 1836, stated that 'there are female professional singers of an inferior class who sometimes dance in the harem; hence travellers have often misapplied the name *Almeh* (sic) to the common dancing girl' (quoted Shinn-Strahan, II, pl. IXLIII). However, by 1850, the term *'ālmah* had come to be applied to professional female entertainers who were also prostitutes (see Cat. 31).

   This picture of an *'ālmah* is one of a series of ethnographic portraits in which Gérôme depicted the characteristic physiognomy, costume and occupation of his Oriental sitters. The crisp outline, sumptuous colour and texture, and the concern for meticulous detail relates this painting to such works as the *Bashibazuk* (Cat. 36) and *The Return from the Hunt* (Cat. 37). MA.S.

PROVENANCE
Mme. Boussod-Gérôme, Paris; 1965, Durlacher Brothers; David E. Rust

EXHIBITIONS
1934, Paris, Galerie Gazette des Beaux-Arts, *Le Salon entre 1880 et 1890* (no. 80)
1972–73, Dayton, Art Institute; Minneapolis, Institute of Arts; Baltimore, Walters Art Gallery, *Jean-Léon Gérôme (1824–1904)* (no. 31)

REFERENCES
R. Cogniat, *Le Salon entre 1800 et 1900*, Paris, 1934, no. 80
G. Ackerman, 'Gérôme, the academic realist', *Art News Annual*, XXXIII, 1967, pp. 275–76

# Gifford, Sanford Robinson   1823–1880

'He was born in Saratoga County. As an artist, he was born in the Catskill Mountains.' That is how Gifford's friend, the landscape painter Worthington Whittredge, summarised the facts of Gifford's early life (*Gifford Memorial Meeting of The Century*, p. 43). Born in Greenfield, Saratoga County, New York, he was brought up in comfortable and cultivated surroundings in Hudson on the east bank of the Hudson River, overlooked by the Catskill Mountains. He attended Brown University for two years and, with the aim of being a figure painter, studied drawing in New York City with John Rubens Smith. But it was the experience of nature that determined his vocation as a landscape painter, and the direct study of nature was probably his chief education in art. In 1847, just a year after dedicating himself to landscape painting, he began to exhibit professionally at the National Academy of Design and the American Art-Union, and in 1854 was elected to the National Academy of Design.

   Despite his lifelong attraction to the Catskills, Gifford's professional home was New York City, where he worked in one of the centres of New York's artistic life, the Studio Building on Tenth Street. He also travelled widely. He made two trips to Europe, the first from 1855 to 1857, the second from 1868 to 1869 – during which he visited Egypt and the Near East – and two trips to the American West, in 1870 when he joined the Hayden surveying expedition, and in 1874. He died in New York City in 1880.

ABBREVIATED REFERENCES
Weir 1881         J. F. Weir, Address, *Memorial Catalogue of the Paintings of Sanford Robinson Gifford, N.A.*, New York, 1881
Cikovsky Jr. 1970   N. Cikovsky, Jr., *Sanford Robinson Gifford 1823–1880*, exhibition catalogue, University of Texas at Austin, Texas, 1970
Weiss 1977        I. J. Weiss, *Sanford Robinson Gifford (1823–1880)*, New York, 1977
Letters MS.       S. Robinson Gifford, 'European Letters', 3 vols, Archives of American Art, Smithsonian Institute

41a

## 42*

# On the Nile   1872

43·2 × 78·7 cm
Signed and dated bottom right: *S. R. Gifford 1872*
Mr and Mrs Eugene B. Sydnor, Jr
*[repr. in colour on p. 154, plate 125]*

Gifford arrived in Egypt in January 1869. He was prepared for his experience, to the extent at least of being reminded of 'Jerome' [Gérôme] in Alexandria, and also, perhaps, by a

42

sensibility for warmth and sunlight that some of his critics thought to be Oriental. But like many other visitors, Gifford evidently went to Egypt largely for the climate – in his first letter from Egypt he complained of the recurrence of an old illness, saying, 'I had hoped that a warmer climate might prevent its return' (Letters MS., III, 8 January 1869) – and as a tourist. 'You are very much mistaken', he wrote later to a friend, 'if you think I brought back anything corresponding with the beautiful pictures, which glow in your Oriental brain, or did anything that I ought to have done – for I didn't. During nearly three months I sailed magnificently on the Nile, and whacked my donkey among temples and tombs, and under the broken nose of the Sphinx, and through the color-lighted streets of Cairo, and scarcely a line records it' (Weiss 1977, pp. 319–20).

For an artist who was in general an avid sketcher in pencil and oil, Gifford sketched relatively little in Egypt. Nevertheless, the experience of Egypt obviously impressed him deeply. In his letters he described Egyptian life and the landscape (much more than its monuments) with extraordinary feeling and precision. Indeed, his verbal descriptions have such colour and graphic detail that they actually took the place of sketches.

Gifford's major Egyptian paintings were executed several years after his visit – *On the Nile*, for instance, was painted in New York in 1872 – but it is not clear if they were made from sketches done in Egypt. In an 1869 letter from Egypt Gifford wrote of 'the golden light and delicate purple shadows of the Arabian and Lybian mountains . . . the little caravans of camels, donkeys, women and children . . . the river crafts with their beautiful sails, which look like the wings of birds' (*New York Evening Post*, 26 April 1869). In both its principal motif and its details *On the Nile* depicts a scene so like the one described in that verbal sketch that it could easily and plausibly have served as the painting's source.

Gifford's style is characterised by its sensitive depiction of coloured light and atmosphere, 'when the air is charged with an effulgence of irruptive and glowing light' (Weir 1881, p. 9). Some of his critics believed that characteristic found its happiest realisation in his Egyptian subjects. *On the Nile* is a case in point, showing how Gifford's 'love for certain effects of light can develop new force in him when it has undeniable conditions of nature to work upon. His former pictures were never completely satisfactory because he could not find their justification in the American Scenery from which they professed to be taken. But here on the Nile the artist has found an atmosphere that suits his talent' (Weiss 1977, p. 320).   N.C.

PROVENANCE
J. I. Nesmith, Brooklyn, New York; Vose Galleries, Boston, Massachusetts; Douglas Collins, Longmeadow, Massachusetts; Vose Galleries, Boston, Massachusetts; bought by the present owner

EXHIBITIONS
1872, Brooklyn Art Association (no. 225)
1876, Philadelphia Centennial Exhibition (no. 24)
1881, New York, Metropolitan Museum of Art, Memorial Exhibition (no. 580)
1970, Texas, Austin, University of Texas Art Museum, *Sanford Robinson Gifford* (no. 50)
1980, Washington National Gallery of Art, *American Light* (unnumbered)

REFERENCES
Cikovsky, Jr. 1970, no. 50, p. 29
'Fine Arts. The Association Exhibition. Third Notice', *Brooklyn Eagle*, 14 December 1872
'Art. The Brooklyn Association. 25th Exhibition of Pictures', *New York Daily Tribune*, 14 December 1872
L. Fellows Andrus, 'Design and Measurement in Luminist Art', *American Light*, p. 46

## 43*

## The Desert at Siout    1874

53·3 × 101·6 cm
Signed and dated bottom right: *S. R. Gifford 1874*
Mr Jerald Dillon Fessenden
[repr. in colour on p. 154, plate 124]

As the capital of Upper Egypt, Siout was a regular stop on Nile voyages. An English traveller who visited Siout at about the same time as Gifford said it 'possesses very respectable bazaars; but beyond this, has small claims for admiration, so wretched, dirty, and dilapidated is its general appearance' (A. C. Smith, *The Nile and its Banks*, London, 1868, p. 191). But in Gifford's painting, as it was described when exhibited in Brooklyn in 1879, Siout is transformed into 'a magnificent little bit of Eastern scenery, full of sunlight and remarkable perspective' (*Brooklyn Eagle*, 26 April 1879).

After visiting the 'wild, strange scenery, so desolate and so savage', of the desert near Aswān (Letters MS. III, 16 February 1869), Gifford arrived at Siout on 4 March 1869. A week later, he noted: 'Made oil sketch of Asyout . . . to show Miss Scott [the daughter of Gifford's travelling companions, Mr and Mrs Leonard Scott of New York] the process of painting in oil' (Letters MS. III, 11 March 1869). Perhaps this was either *A Sketch near Siout, Egypt*, dated 4 March 1869, or *A Sketch on the Nile*, dated 7 March 1869 (nos. 525 and 526 in the 1881 Memorial Exhibition Catalogue), and perhaps he used either or both of these sketches in making his large painting five years later. But a 'sketch' Gifford wrote in a letter from Egypt of a late afternoon at Siout, precisely and evocatively describing figures, landscape and conditions of light, colour and atmosphere, fits the painting with such exactness that it must have been its primary source: 'Looking westward, the town with its domes and minarets lay between us and the sun, bathed in a rich and beautiful atmosphere. Behind, on the right, were the yellow cliffs of the Lybian mts., running back into the tender grades of distance. Between us and the town were fields of grain, golden green with the transparent light. On the right was a tent with sheep and beautiful horses, the sunlight sparkling on a splendid white stallion. On the left the road ran in, with a fountain and figures of men and women and camels. The whole glowing and gleaming under the low sun' (III, 4 March 1869).

PROVENANCE
Vose Galleries, Boston, Massachusetts; Douglas Collins, Longmeadow, Massachusetts; Vose Galleries, Boston, Massachusetts; bought by the present owner

EXHIBITIONS
1879, Brooklyn Art Association (no. 342 as *Siout, Egypt*)
1881, New York, Metropolitan Museum of Art, Memorial Exhibition (no. 620 as *Siout, Egypt*)
1970, Austin, University of Texas Art Museum, *Sanford Robinson Gifford* (no. 52 as *Siout, Egypt*)
1980, Washington D.C., National Gallery of Art, *American Light* (unnumbered)

REFERENCES
Cikovsky, Jr. 1970, no. 52, p. 29
Pictures. Notes on the Works in the Academy', *Brooklyn Eagle*, 26 April 1879
L. Fellows Andrus, 'Design and Measurement in Luminist Art', *American Light*, p. 46

43

# Girardet, Eugène    1853–1907

Eugène Girardet was the eldest son of a third generation of Swiss artists. He began his artistic training under his father, Paul Girardet (1821–1893), and later became a pupil of Gérôme (*q.v.*) at the Ecole des Beaux-Arts, Paris. Fired with his master's enthusiasm for the East, and perhaps inspired, too, by the voyages of his uncle Karl Girardet (1813–1871), he travelled to Spain and Morocco in 1874, and in 1879 visited Algeria for the first time. In all Girardet made eight trips to this country, and, like Guillaumet, preferred the southern towns of Biskra, Boghara, El-Kantara and Bou-Saada. It was in Bou-Saada that Girardet met the writer and painter A. E. Dinet (1861–1929), one of the most committed Orientalists, who accepted the Islamic faith in 1913. Later, he also visited Egypt, Turkey and Palestine, where he is believed to have contracted a painful and disfiguring illness.

Girardet exhibited Orientalist genre scenes and landscapes of Normandy and Calvados from 1874, and from the mid-1880s his work was exhibited frequently in Geneva, Zürich, London, and at the Glasgow Institute of Fine Arts. In the last decades of his life, Girardet was beset by ill-health, and died in Paris in 1907.

The uniformly blond tonalities and unbroken surfaces of the desert would seem to offer little scope for the artist. In a scientific analysis of the Sahara desert, Charles Martins examined the various soils, climates and vegetation, from the coastal plains to the beautiful cedars of the Djurdjura and Teniet-el-Had mountain ranges in the south, characterising the general aspect of the desert as, 'vast, denuded surfaces, interspersed with salt lakes or *chotts*, devoid of arborescent vegetation, and overrun in summer by immense flocks of sheep which strip the plants down to their very roots' ('Le Sahara et la végétation du désert', *Revue des Deux Mondes*, July–August 1864, p. 304). Only the bare mountains relieved the severe horizontality of the skyline; even the alfalfa, one of the few grasses to withstand the arid conditions, conformed to the overall silvery whiteness. Girardet captures the neutral tonalities caused by the ferocity of the heat and sun. By the addition of a strip of vegetation in the middle distance and the pinks and violets of the distant mountains, he successfully alleviates the potential monotony of the scene, without detracting from the sensation of the caravan's laborious journey.    J.M.

PROVENANCE
Priv. Coll., Paris; Kurt E. Schon Ltd, New Orleans; Priv. Coll., Houston, Texas

## 44*

## Salt Caravans in the Desert

*Caravanes de sel dans le désert*

48·5 × 99 cm
Signed bottom left: *Eugène Girardet*
Private Collection, Houston, Texas
[*repr. in colour on p. 81, plate 40*]

Salt was by no means a rare commodity in Algeria, but because of transportation difficulties usually served only local requirements. This was the case at Tellout, one of the major sources of salt located some twenty miles east of Tlemcen, and in the lakes in the southern part of the district of Constantine. Only the salt mines at Bou-Zian and Arzew in the Oran region were fully exploited, the latter being highly esteemed for the purity of the mineral.

In the course of his eight visits to the southern part of Algeria, Girardet experienced native customs and life at first hand, and came to specialise in the depiction of nomadic tribes and desert views. This painting highlights the sheer physical effort required in moving the salt from its sources across wide expanses of desert by setting the few, scattered figures in a vast, inhospitable landscape.

## 45*

## The Tailor's House in an Arab Town

*La Maison du tailleur dans une ville arabe*

48·3 × 72 cm
Signed bottom right: *Eugène Girardet*
Private Collection, Houston, Texas
[*repr. in colour on p. 84, plate 41*]

Though regarded as primarily an Orientalist painter (Bénédite, 1908, p. 10), Girardet continued throughout his career to execute both landscape paintings and genre scenes from the environs of Houlgate (Calvados) where he spent his summers. He made his Salon debut in 1874 with a genre scene *La Faim fait sortir le loup du bois* (present location unknown), and in many respects his representations of life in Algeria were coloured by the same

44

45

# Color Plates

WORKS BY AMERICAN ORIENTALISTS AND KANDINSKY

124  Gifford *The Desert at Siout*

125  Gifford *On the Nile*

126 Church *Jerusalem*

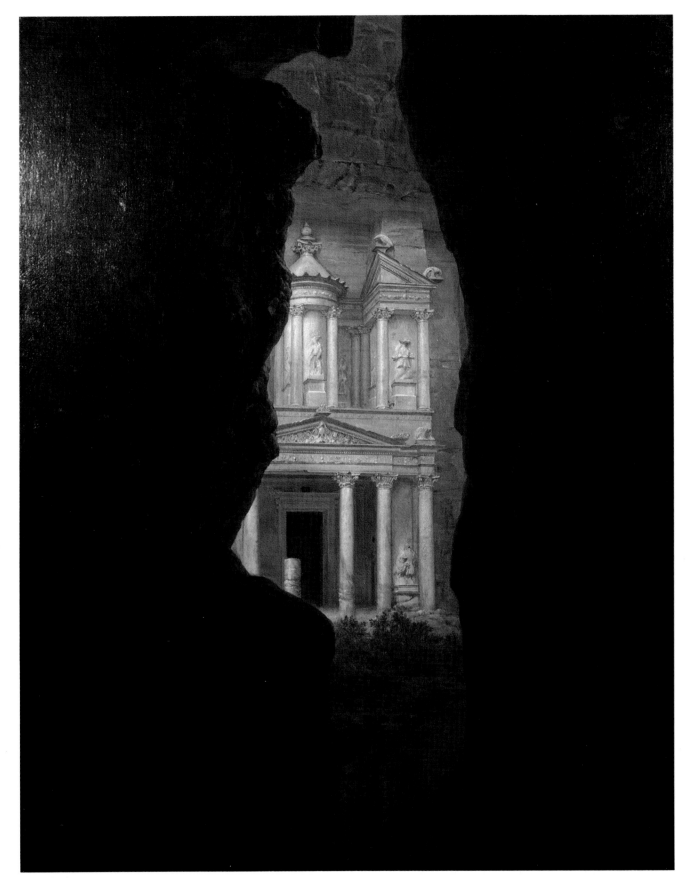

127 Church *El Khasné, Petra*

128 Vedder *The Questioner of the Sphinx*

129 Kandinsky *Improvisation 6*

130  Kandinsky *Oriental*

anecdotal approach. Léonce Bénédite has pointed to the artist's predominantly painterly preoccupations, noting that 'his canvases are far from being mere remembrances of his travels or ethnographical descriptions, but true portraits done by an artist who sees them with a painter's eye' (*op. cit.*, p. 9). On a purely technical level, *The Tailor's House in an Arab Town* reveals Girardet's attempt to come to terms with the almost overwhelming intensity of sunlight. Fromentin, in *Une Année dans le Sahel* (1859), stressed the total reversal of traditional formulae for the illumination of certain areas of the picture. In Europe, he wrote, 'paintings are composed in shadow, with a dark centre and corners of light', and to comprehend the effects of light in the Orient, the artist should imagine himself as, 'a sort of Rembrandt in reverse' (*op. cit.*, 1898 ed., p. 228). Girardet shows an understanding of the distinctive quality of the light in the application of pure white paint to the areas exposed to the full brilliance of the sun. Only in the shadows do colours attain their fullest value: in the bold oppositions of reds and greens in the tailor's material, and in the range of atmospheric colours overlaid in brisk brushstrokes across the foreground.

The group of figures in the doorway become the focal point of attention in the painting with their expressive physiognomies, lively gestures and animated discussion. Girardet's views of Arab villages and desert landscapes are rarely unpopulated, and, like Guillaumet, he treated the theme of peasant labour with sympathy. Nevertheless it was the curiosity value and pictorial priorities rather than the documentary element which predominated in his genre work. A similar concentration on narrative detail occurs to a lesser extent in *Camels in the Dunes at Bou-Saada* (Cat. 46), and very clearly in the *Caravane passant un gué* (1877–78; Priv. Coll., Houston, Texas), where even the animals are made to exude an affable charm.

There are at least two related works: *Le Tailleur sur le pas de sa porte à Bou-Saâda* (n.d.; Atelier sale, 1908; present location unknown), and *Le Tailleur d'El-Kantara* (n.d.; Musée des Beaux-Arts, Saintes).    J.M.

PROVENANCE
1977, Hôtel Drouot; Priv. Coll., New York; Kurt E. Schon Ltd., New Orleans; Priv. Coll., Houston, Texas

REFERENCES
Thornton 1983, ill. pp. 183–84
L. Bénédite, *Catalogue des tableaux provenant de l'atelier Eugène Girardet*, 1908, pp. 5–10

foot leads the ass carrying the kitchen utensils and the women act as faggot bearers, while the men, on camels, oversee the entire procession. It was precisely to be exposed to the social realities of native existence that artists such as Girardet, Guillaumet and Dinet chose to live in the southern extremities of Algeria, where French influence was yet to impinge on the indigenous culture. Nevertheless, from the 1870s these regions were of increasing economic interest to the French government who sought to re-establish commercial links with the Sudan through the oases of the Sahara. French domination of tribes in the Sahara was largely assured by the permanent occupation of Géryville, El-Agouat, Biskra and Touggourt; expeditions which hoped to penetrate as far as Ghadmes and In-Salah were dependent on the goodwill and protection of the Touareg tribe. Girardet, in his depiction of all aspects of native life, was clearly very conscious of the imposition of colonialism in these regions and of the resulting eradication of native customs. A similar awareness consituted the very *raison d'être* of the Société des Peintres Orientalistes Français, founded in 1893. According to Bénédite, the Orientalist painter had more than a purely artistic role to fulfill; he held the responsibility of retaining from 'all this Oriental fantasy . . . at least the image, all that still remains of its colour, poetry, strangeness and seductive charm' (1899, I, p. 240).

As a result of the close observation of the effects of light and atmosphere made during his stays in the Orient, Girardet's palette brightened considerably and his brushstroke became more rapid. Here he effectively conveys the vibrant luminosity of the scene in the greens and blues of the deep shadows, which contrast boldly with the touches of ochre, orange, beiges and greys in the rock face.

The painting remains in its original ornate frame of decorative arabesques.    J.M.

PROVENANCE
Acquired by 'an amateur' (probably David) following the exhibition at Nantes in 1898; given by David to the Musée des Beaux-Arts, Nantes

EXHIBITIONS
1898, Nantes, *Exposition de la Société des Amis des Arts de Nantes* (no. 107)
1908, Paris, Salon des Peintres Orientalistes Français (no. 30)
1980, Nantes, Musée des Beaux-Arts, *Orients* (no. 37)

REFERENCES
L. Bénédite, 'Les Peintres orientalistes français', *Gazette des Beaux-Arts*, March 1899, I, p. 240
R. Burnard, *L'Étonnante Histoire des Girardet, artistes suisses*, 1944, p. 261

## 46

## Camels in the Dunes at Bou-Saada
*Chameaux dans les dunes à Bou-Saâda*

67·7 × 108·7 cm
Signed bottom right: *Eugène Girardet*
Musée des Beaux-Arts, Nantes
[*repr. in colour on p. 81, plate 42*]

First exhibited in Nantes in 1898, this scene depicts a tribe of nomads emerging from the Saharan Atlas mountains in southern Algerian. From each of his 'Algeria campaigns' (quoted R. Burnard, 1944, p. 261), Girardet brought back numerous studies of the inhabitants and the landscape as an aide-mémoire of ethnographical details. In this picture he accurately records not only costumes, animals and accoutrements, but also the functions fulfilled by different members of the caravan: the little girl on

46

## Goodall, Frederick    1822–1904

Son of an artist, Goodall made his precocious debut at the Royal
Academy exhibition in 1837 with four watercolours. His first
essays in oil were genre pictures and landscapes, but later he
turned to subjects from British history. In 1852 he became an
Associate of the Royal Academy. He went to the Near East for
the first time at the age of thirty-six and from then onwards made
a speciality of genre scenes and biblical subjects based on his
first-hand experience of life in Egypt. Armed with letters of
introduction from David Roberts, he arrived in Cairo in the
autumn of 1858 and was based there until April the following
year. By chance he met Carl Haag (1820–1915) and the two men
sketched and travelled together, making expeditions to the
pyramids at Gizah and to Suez. From the sketches and examples
of Arab dress he brought back, Goodall painted *Early Morning
in the Wilderness of Shur*. Exhibited at the Royal Academy in
1860, this work attracted the admiration of Roberts, Landseer,
Clarkson Stanfield and many others, and established his
reputation. He was elected a full Royal Academician in 1864.
From 1868 until his death, his London home was in Avenue
Road, near Regent's Park, where his studio was full of
*mashrabiyyah* woodwork and other Egyptian artefacts.

47

## The Subsiding of the Nile    1873

76 × 152 cm
Signed with monogram and dated bottom left: *FG 1873*
Guildhall Art Gallery, Corporation of London

Goodall made his second and last visit to Egypt in 1870–71.
Basing himself at Saqarah, he spent several months, as before,
making sketches of Egyptian places and people to be used as the
raw material for future paintings. In 1872 he began working up
some of these as a large composition and the result was *The
Subsiding of the Nile*, exhibited at the Royal Academy in 1873
(no. 292). The work was conceived as a pendant to *The Rising
of the Nile* (1865; present location unknown), a scene of people
escaping from an inundated village. The reduced version of *The
Subsiding of the Nile* exhibited here is a quarter of the size of the
original. The view is of Gizah from the south-east, with the Great
Pyramid on the right, the Second Pyramid on the left and the
Sphinx just visible in the centre. The sheep in the foreground
were painted from the flock the artist bought in Egypt and sent
back to England to be used as models for pictures. 'I used my
Egyptian sheep for this picture and all the studies I had made
for it in the immediate locality, especially the ancient causeway
supposed to have been built for transporting the stones of which
the Pyramids are built,' he noted in his autobiography. 'The
enormous quarries are on the other side of the Nile, some eight
miles away. The most beautiful time of the whole year is when
the Nile overflows almost to the foot of the Pyramids. As it
subsides, there almost immediately springs up on the higher
portions of the land the vegetation which affords without any
cultivation an immense quantity of food for the Bedouin flocks'
(*The Reminiscences of Frederick Goodall, R.A.*, London, 1902,
pp. 383–84). Goodall generally saw Egypt in biblical terms but
here the emphasis is more on the classical aspects of the scene.
The feeling of order and clarity in the composition, along with
elements such as the blocky architectural features, the road
winding off into the distance, the glassy reflections in the water
and the figure partially hidden behind a bank of earth, recall
Poussin. Under the circumstances, it is tempting to see the old
man being led along the road by a child as Goodall's Egyptian
version of the blind Homer. M.W.

PROVENANCE
Probably commissioned from Goodall by the dealers Pilgeram and Lefevre; 1873, 4 April,
acquired from them by Agnew's; 1873, 17 June, acquired by Charles Gassiot; 1902,
bequeathed by him to the Guildhall Art Gallery, London

47

# Gros, Baron Jean-Antoine   1771–1835

Gros received his initial training from his parents, both of whom were painters of miniatures, and later from the portraitist Mme Vigée-Lebrun (1755–1842). In 1785 he entered the atelier of Jacques-Louis David (1748–1825) and, with his support, left for Italy in 1793 at the beginning of the Reign of Terror. There he painted portraits of French society in Naples, Florence and Genoa, where in 1796 he was recommended to the Emperor by his consort Josephine. As a result of this meeting, Napoleon not only granted Gros a rare sitting but made him a member of the commission set up to select plunder from Italian museums and art galleries for the Musée Napoléon in the Louvre.

Though never asked to accompany the army to Egypt, Gros became the official chronicler of the campaigns fought between 1798 and 1800. While Vivant Denon in his *Voyage dans la Basse et la Haute Egypte* (1802; Cat. 20), and the encyclopaedic *Description de l'Egypte* (1809–29) provided scholarly and accurate accounts of every aspect of Egyptian life, Gros's turbulent and romantic battle scenes contributed far more effectively to the propagation of the Napoleonic legend.

Gros proved very resilient to political change in early nineteenth-century France; in 1814 he was made official painter to Louis XVIII and created Baron by Charles X in 1824. His relaxation of the severity of Davidian classicism made his atelier an attractive environment for young artists and during the last twenty years of his life, it became the training ground for over one hundred painters, including Lami, Roqueplan, Delestre, Delaroche, Riesener and Charlet.

His return to historical and mythological subject-matter from *c.* 1815 aroused the hostility of contemporary critics, who found paintings such as *Hercule et Diomède* (1835; Musée des Augustins, Toulouse) empty, dry and lacking the style of his earlier Orientalist work. Depressed by this obvious lack of success, Gros is thought to have drowned himself in the River Seine near Bas-Meudon on 26 July 1835.

48*

## The Battle of Nazareth   1801
*Le Combat de Nazareth*

134·4 × 195·5 cm
Signed and dated bottom right: *GROS AN IX*
Musée des Beaux-Arts, Nantes
[*repr. in colour on p. 58, plate 64*]

In its freedom of handling, brilliant colouring and dynamic composition, *The Battle of Nazareth* marked a radical break with the restrained rhetoric of the traditional battle scene and was of seminal importance for the next generation of Orientalist painters. Both Auguste and Géricault made copies of the work and the latter is known also to have owned a copy by P.-F. Lehoux.

The scene depicts an episode during the campaigns in Egypt organised under the Directoire. Ostensibly to free the people from the Mamlūk oppression, these campaigns were also intended to establish a strategic and commercial foothold in North Africa and the Near East, a possibility diplomats had investigated as early as 1777.

The Battle of Nazareth took place on the plains near Loubia, twelve miles from Nazareth itself, on 19 Germinal an VII (8 April 1799). Gros records the remarkable victory of the 500-strong French army over 6000 Turks and Arabs, focussing on the gallantry of its leader, General Junot, who holds together the various incidents of the painting in the sweep of his right arm. Napoleon was quick to recognise the political expediency of representing one of the few successes of the expedition and on 25 April, barely two weeks after the event, announced a competition for the commission of the picture. Many leading artists of the day were attracted by the subject and the competition soon degenerated into a polemic between the partisans of Gros and those of Hennequin, who felt their candidate presented a more heroic version of Junot's actions. Whether out of jealousy, or simply to avoid any reference to the campaigns which were engendering increasing public hostility, Napoleon forbade Gros's completion of the painting, and ordered him to proceed instead with *The Pesthouse at Jaffa* (Cat. 49).

48

Gros, who had never travelled further south than Italy, made every effort to reconstruct accurately the details of the engagement: its location, the local colour and even the specific angle of the sun at the time of battle. He used a battle plan drawn up by General Junot himself, and copied details of Oriental costume and physiognomy from Vivant Denon's *Voyage dans la Basse et la Haute Egypte*. Despite this fastidiousness in the recording of detail, the image which Gros evokes of the Orient is almost overwhelmed by *'un sentiment d'exaltation guerrière'* (Anon., 1835, p. 265) in the warrior-like poses of the French officers, and in the bolder, less defined treatment of the frenzied battle scene.    J.M.

PROVENANCE
Acquired from the artist by Bizet; 1828, 21–22 May, Bizet sale, acquired by M. de Vaucourbon; M. Jazet; Urvoy de Saint-Bedan; 1854, presented by Urvoy de Saint-Bedan to the Musée des Beaux-Arts, Nantes
EXHIBITIONS
1826, Paris, Galerie Lebrun, *Ouvrages de peinture exposés au profit des Grecs* (no. 99)
1900, Paris, *Exposition Universelle* (no. 399)
1936, Paris, Petit Palais, *Gros, ses amis, ses élèves* (no. 3)
1959, London, Tate Gallery, *The Romantic Movement* (no. 199)
1974–75, Paris, Grand Palais, *De David à Delacroix* (no. 88; with exhaustive references)
1982, Nantes, Musée des Beaux-Arts, *Orients* (no. 1)
REFERENCES
Anon., 'M. Gros', *L'Artiste*, 1835, v, p. 265
Anon., 'Vente des tableaux, dessins et esquisses de M. Gros', *L'Artiste*, 1836, x, pp. 209–10
E. Chesneau, *Les Chefs d'école*, Paris, 1862, pp. 80–82
M. Nicolle, *Catalogue du Musée des Beaux-Arts, Nantes*, 1913, no. 1005
Rochester, New York, Memorial Art Gallery, *Orientalism*, catalogue by D. Rosenthal, 1982, fig. 9

## 49*

## The Pesthouse at Jaffa    1804

*Les Pestiférés à Jaffa*

117·5 × 165 cm
Museum of Fine Arts, Boston
[repr. in colour on p. 59, plate 65]

With the exception of minor alterations in the architecture in the background, this painting is almost identical to the full-scale version now in the Louvre which was executed in less than six months and rapturously received at the Salon of 1804. The

incident of Napoleon visiting the pesthouse took place on 11 March 1799, after plague had broken out in the city of Jaffa occupied by the French. In a poem written in honour of the painting, the artist Girodet recaptured the emotion of the scene:

*Aussitôt tout s'émeut, tout accourrent le voir
Et dans leurs yeux mourants brille un rayon d'espoir,
Frappé de cécité, dans sa marche hâtive,
L'un d'eux prête à son chef une oreille attentive;
Sans garde, sans bâton, empresse d'accourir,
Si le héros lui parle, il est sûr de guérir.*
(quoted J.B. Delestre, 1867, p. 93)

*(All at once the men stirred with a note of surprise,
A glimmer of hope in their faint dying eyes,
From among them, a blind man, desperate to hear
The words of his leader, hastes to draw near,
Without guide, without stick, he tries to advance;
The hero can cure with a word or a glance.)*

Napoleon's visit to the pesthouse and the capture of Jaffa itself, were, in fact, highly contentious events. British accounts of the episode pointed to the brutal slaughter of more than 3000 Turkish prisoners, and to Napoleon's ruthless abandonment of plague-ridden men whose condition threatened to impede his own retreat. Even on the French side doubts were expressed as to Napoleon's supposed benevolence. One eye witness, Bourienne, refers to Napoleon lightly kicking the infested men with the sole of his boot (quoted P. Lelièvre, 1936, p. 293) and Captain Etienne-Louis Mâlus, himself a plague victim, while commenting less on the Emperor's activities in the pesthouse, speaks strongly of the atrocities committed elsewhere in Jaffa (E. L. Mâlus, 1892, pp. 130–37). Gros's interpretation of the events gives no hint of this controversy. Following the report of the surgeon Desgettnes, he chose to portray Napoleon's great compassion as he willingly exposed himself to the plague in order to bring comfort to his men.

The development towards the final pictorial solution may be traced in a preliminary drawing (Louvre, R.F.2015), and in an oil sketch (Priv. Coll., Paris), in each of which Napoleon is shown supporting one of the stricken men. Initially set inside the lazaret,

49

the scene is opened out to give Napoleon greater prominence against a composite view of Jaffa, based on an original plan by Tarachemy. In the final version, Napoleon's gesture becomes less naturalistic, but gains a supreme eloquence through its allusion to the healing of Christ. It is thus his position as moral and spiritual leader of the French people and not his military role which is most clearly stressed in this unequivocally propagandist image. As such, Gros realises his function as an official painter: 'Just as Charles le Brun painted the former Alexander, I should paint the new one' (quoted E. Chesneau, 1862, p. 79).

In his depiction of events in the Egyptian campaign, Gros inevitably recalled his own close participation in the chaotic Italian Wars, and particularly the two harrowing months of the Siege of Genoa in 1799. Here he clearly sympathises with the suffering of the common soldier, and introduces that element of pathos which was to colour other artists' and writers' interpretations of the Near East, notably Delacroix, Chassériau and Gautier.    J.M.

PROVENANCE
?Commissioned by Marshal Mortier; 1st Duc de Trévise; Priv. Coll., England; 1934, Duc de Trévise; bought from him by the Museum of Fine Arts, Boston

EXHIBITIONS
1936, Paris, Petit Palais, *Gros, ses amis, ses élèves* (no. 29)
1938, New York, Knoedler and Co., *Gros, Géricault, Delacroix* (no. 3, ill.)
1938, Paris, Musée de l'Orangerie, *Bonaparte en Egypte* (no. 78)
1939, Springfield, Mass., *The Romantic Revolt* (no. 1)
1939, San Francisco, Museum of Art, *French Romantic Artists* (no. 3)
1955–56, New York, Jacques Seligman and Co.; Minneapolis, Institute of Arts; Cleveland Museum of Art, *Baron Antoine-Jean Gros (1771–1835), Painter of Battles. The First Romantic Painter* (no. 14)

REFERENCES
E. Chesneau, *Les Chefs d'école*, Paris, 1862, p. 79f.
J.B. Delestre, *Gros, sa vie, ses ouvrages*, Paris, 1867, pp. 90–96
E.L. Mâlus (ed. Général Thoumas), *L'Agenda de Mâlus, Souvenirs de l'expédition d'Egypte 1798–1801*, Paris, 1892, pp. 130–37
P. Lelièvre, 'Gros, peintre d'histoire', *Gazette des Beaux-Arts*, May 1936, pp. 292–93
W. Friedlaender, 'Napoleon as "Roi Thaumaturge"', *Journal of the Warburg and Courtauld Institutes*, 1940–41, IV, pp. 139–41
N. Schlenoff, 'Baron Gros and Napoleon's Egyptian Campaign', *Essays in Honour of Walter Friedlaender*, New York, 1965, pp. 157–60

## 50*

## Sketch for 'The Cavalry Charge under General Murat at the Battle of Abū Qīr, Egypt: 25 July 1799'    1806

*Charge de cavalrie, executée par le général Murat à la bataille d'Aboukir en Egypte: 25 juillet 1799*

87 × 140 cm
Detroit Institute of Fine Arts

On 1 August 1798, at the Battle of the Nile in Abū Qīr Bay, Nelson destroyed the French fleet which had conveyed Napoleon to Egypt, thereby securing for Britain naval supremacy in the Mediterranean, and effectively sealing the fate of the French campaign in Syria. The news of the brilliant French land action also at Abū Qīr, and the victory over the Ottoman army under Mustafa Serasker helped to disguise the almost total annihilation of 55,000 troops in an apparently profitless expedition. Recognising the successful formula for propaganda established by Gros in his representations of the Battle of Nazareth and the events in Jaffa (see Cat. 48 and 49), Murat commissioned the artist to record the action at Abū Qīr almost immediately after the Salon of 1804.

This painting is the sketch for the final version now at Versailles, and was submitted to military officials for confirmation of the accuracy of details of the fighting. As in the case of *The Battle of Nazareth* (Cat. 48), Gros based his representation on the report of a friend, in this instance General Berthier. He illustrates the culmination of the battle when Murat, seizing the initiative, charged the enemy ranks and finally confronted Mustafa (the figure at centre left turning away from Murat) and cut off two of his fingers. The Ottomans retreated to the fort in the background but were eventually defeated and Mustafa captured. One combatant who escaped was the leader of the Albanian contingent Muḥammad 'Alī. The dense composition combines a shallow picture plane, reminiscent of a classical bas-relief, with a wealth of action, sweeping from left to right across the canvas. Gros was careful to distinguish between the various physiognomies of the combatants, and to describe accurately the action, without distracting the eye by a proliferation of detail.

In an article in the *Revue des Deux Mondes* of 1848, Delacroix referred to the striking realism of Gros's battle scenes and praised his ability to evoke the frenzied heights of the conflict: 'He can paint the sweat which drenches his horses' manes in the heat of battle, and even the fiery breath from their nostrils. He shows you the glint of the sabre at the very moment when it strikes the enemy's throat' (1923, III, p. 179).

Contemporary critics drew analogies between Gros's glorification of this incident from the Egyptian campaigns and the heroism of Homeric legend. Indeed, by idealising contemporary subject-matter, through reference to classical prototypes, Gros established the vocabulary for modern-day history painting on an epic scale.    J.M.

PROVENANCE
1828, 21 May, Paris, rue de Clery (former Salle Lebrun) unsold; M. Dicot (until 3 March 1847); Duc de Cambacères, Paris (until end of 1935); Duc de Trévise, Paris; Mr. Edgar B. Whitcomb Coll., Detroit, Michigan; given by Mr. and Mrs. Edgar B. Whitcomb to the Detroit Institute of Arts

EXHIBITIONS
1936, Paris, Petit Palais, *Gros, ses amis, ses élèves* (no. 33)
1938, Paris, Musée de l'Orangerie, *Bonaparte en Egypte* (no. 95)
1938, New York, Knoedler and Co., *Gros, Géricault and Delacroix* (no. 5)
1939, San Francisco, Museum of Art, *French Romantic Artists* (no. 4)
1940, New York World Fair (no. 230)
1952, Seattle, Art Museum, *Nineteenth Century Paintings and Sculpture*
1952, Hartford, Wadsworth Atheneum, *The Romantic Circle* (no. 4)
1954, Detroit, Institute of Arts, *Paintings and Sculptures given by Mr. and Mrs. Edgar B. Whitcomb* (p. 83)
1955, Rome and Milan (no. 55)
1955–56, New York, Jacques Seligmann and Co. Inc.; Minneapolis, Institute of Art; Cleveland, Museum of Art, *Baron Antoine-Jean Gros (1771–1835), Painter of Battles. The First Romantic Painter* (no. 13)

REFERENCES
J. Tripier Le Franc, *Histoire de la vie et de la mort du Baron Gros*, Paris, 1880, p. 130
E. Delacroix, 'Le Baron Gros', *Oeuvres Littéraires*, III, Paris, 1923, pp. 173–74
N. Schlenoff, 'Baron Gros and Napoleon's Egyptian Campaigns', *Essays in Honour of Walter Friedlaender*, New York, 1965, pp. 162, 163

50

# Guillaumet, Gustave    1840–1887

Son of a manufacturer in Puteaux (Seine et Oise), Guillaumet studied under Picot (1786–1868) and Barrias (1822–1907) and in 1857 entered the Ecole des Beaux-Arts as a pupil of Abel de Pujol (1785–1861). From 1861 he exhibited regularly at the Salon. The following year he set out to study in Rome but changed route on impulse, embarking at Marseille for North Africa. In spite of recurring bouts of malaria, this decisive voyage was to be the first of ten trips to Algeria and Morocco. At the Salon of 1863 he exhibited the *Prière du soir dans le Sahara* (ill. fig. 15; Musée d'Orsay, Paris), which attracted much favourable attention and was bought by the State for 4000 francs. This marked the beginning of a highly successful career and Guillaumet went on to win medals at the Salons of 1865, 1867 and 1872, and in 1878 he was made Chevalier de la Légion d'Honneur.

Guillaumet was immediately attracted to the southern extremities of Algeria around Biskra and the Hodna region south of Bou-Saada, where ethnic customs and lifestyles were still untainted by the presence of Europeans in the coastal towns. He spent much of his time among the people of the oases' *quṣūrs* or hamlets, depicting the inhabitants, their dwellings and their labours with a force and sympathy that led him to be regarded as the Orientalist counterpart to Millet.

From 1882 Guillaumet exhibited pastels at the Société des Pastellistes, a medium which, with its soft nuances of colour, was particularly suited to his sensitive observations. In 1883–84 he travelled for the last time to Algeria and in 1886 completed the journey to Italy he had begun twenty-four years earlier, where he was much impressed by Michelangelo.

Guillaumet died in Paris in 1887.

ABBREVIATED REFERENCE
*Nouvelle Revue* 1879  G. Guillaumet, 'Tableaux algériens', *Nouvelle Revue*, 1879, I, no. 1, pp. 144–58 (later published as part of *Tableaux algériens*, Paris, 1888)

## 51

## The Desert (The Sahara)    1867
*Le Désert (Le Sahara)*

110 × 200 cm
Signed and dated bottom right: *G. Guillaumet 1867*
Musée d'Orsay, Paris
[*repr. in colour on p. 83, plate 67*]

This powerful painting has been subject to much interpretation since its original showing at the Salon of 1868 and has been described as anything from '*un peu exagéré*' (Renan 1887, p. 408) to 'surrealist' (Rosenthal, 1982, p. 89). It belongs to Guillaumet's early, rather melodramatic work and very clearly illustrates the artist's technical and emotional quandry when confronted with the strangeness of an unfamiliar culture and climate. In *Famine en Algérie* (Musée des Beaux-Arts, Algiers), exhibited at the Salon of 1869, Guillaumet attempted to overcome this problem by referring to the examples of Géricault and Delacroix in the extreme pathos of the figures. In the work exhibited here, the artist is faced with the particular formal problem of a broad, fairly featureless terrain quite alien to European landscape traditions. The desolate, parched land is accentuated by the severe horizontality of the brushwork in the desert and sky, relieved only by the distant mirage and the haunting skeleton of the camel. The intense heat and light contribute to the infinite stillness of the image, so that the only movement is the 'almost imperceptible vibrating of the air above the scorched earth' (*Nouvelle Revue* 1879, p. 145). The sight of the noble camel, an animal passionately admired by Guillaumet, fallen prey to the vermin of the desert, is one which had also impressed Flaubert while on the shore of the Dead Sea in 1850: 'The hide, dried and stretched out by the sun, is intact, but has been gnawed from within until it is no thicker than an onion-skin' (Steegmuller, ed. 1979, p. 184).

51

Guillaumet's concern in this painting, however, goes beyond straightforward realism. The camel, *'cet être abîmé dans le mouvement de transformation universelle'* (Renan, 1887, pp. 419–20), could be read as a symbol of the struggle between Man and Nature, victim of the abstract destructive forces of the desert. The re-naming of the painting from its more specific original title, *Le Sahara*, perhaps confirms this reading of the image.    J.M.

PROVENANCE
1888, gift of the artist's family to the State

EXHIBITIONS
1868, Paris, Salon (no. 1178)
1968, Berlin, Academie der Kunst, *Le Musée imaginaire* (no. 60)
1973, Paris, Musée des Arts Décoratifs, *Equivoques*
1975, Marseille, Musée Cantini, *L'Orient en Question* (no. 91)
1982, Rochester, New York, Memorial Art Gallery, *Orientalism* (no. 50)

REFERENCES
Ch. Sterling and H. Adhémar, *Musée Nationale du Louvre. Peintures: École français, XIXᵉ siècle*, Paris, 1958–61, 4 vols., no. 1026, ill.
A. Renan, 'Gustave Guillaumet', *Gazette des Beaux-Arts*, 1887, 2ᵉ période, 35, pp. 404–22
Paris, Musée du Louvre, *Catalogue des peintures I. École Française*, 1972, p. 195
Ph. Jullian, *The Orientalists, European Painters of Eastern Scenes*, Oxford, 1977, p. 68, ill. 69

## 52

## The 'Seguia', Biskra   1884

*La Séguia, près de Biskra*

100 × 155 cm
Signed and dated bottom right: *G. Guillaumet 1884*
Musée d'Orsay, Paris
[repr. in colour on p. 94, plate 68]

Originally the Roman town of Ad Piscinam, Biskra was the capital of a wide district in western Algeria known to the Arabs as Aïn Salahin. After some years under Turkish sovereignty, it was captured in May 1846 by the Duc d'Aumâle, and named after a commandant killed in the Zaatcha insurrection of 1849.

The present painting is very different both in tonality and tempo from Guillaumet's earlier imagery, a transition which first occurs in *Le Labour à la frontière du Maroc*, exhibited at the 1869 Salon. As in *The Desert*, the landscape is used to enhance the mood of the scene. The figures are sharply accentuated against the barren rock and unwelcoming architectural features and, together with the intensity of light and the depth of shadow,

they stress the harshness of life in this desert settlement. The apparent ease and spontaneity of the composition, which depicts an everyday task in the life of the *fellāḥah*, belie the numerous close preparatory studies for the landscape and figures. While Guillaumet's contemporaries in France had already begun to look at the fleeting, transitional qualities of nature, the climate in North Africa invited a very different interpretation: Guillaumet achieves a harmonious colouring through a precise understanding of the effects of the intense light and its consolidation of form, rather than a disintegration of the figure. Light fascinated Guillaumet not only as an artistic problem but also as a determining force on the very lives of the people of the *ksours*. In *'Un jour au soleil'* (*Nouvelle Revue* 1879, p. 144), he discussed the harmony created by violent oppositions of colour echoed in the harmony of the cycle of life, pointing to the oneness between Man and Nature. Here, this theme is taken up with a tenderness of observation characteristic of Guillaumet's representation of the *fellāḥah*, most particularly in *Les Femmes de douar à la rivière* (1872; Musée des Beaux-Arts, Algiers) and in *Les Fileuses de laine à Bou-Saâda* (1885; Musée d'Orsay). The heroic and timeless aspect of the rural population, a society untainted by the materialistic preoccupations of Western civilisation, invoked for Guillaumet, as for many of his contemporaries including Flaubert, Vernet (see Cat. 99) and Holman Hunt, images from the Bible. In these agricultural and pastoral scenes, he wrote: 'One could believe oneself transported to the bosom of those partriarchal families whose poetry characterises the first pages of Hebrew history' (*Nouvelle Revue* 1879, p. 150).    J.M.

PROVENANCE
1885, acquired by the State

EXHIBITION
1885, Paris. Salon des Champs-Elysées (no. 1186)

REFERENCE
Ph. Jullian, *The Orientalists. European Painters of Eastern Scenes*, Oxford, 1977, p. 131, ill.

52

# Hunt, William Holman   1827–1910

A founder member of the Pre-Raphaelite Brotherhood, William Holman Hunt was the son of a London warehouse manager. He entered the Royal Academy schools at the third attempt in 1844, and made his exhibition debut the following year in Manchester. Hunt was dissatisfied with current academic teaching, and his search for an original style and iconography was influenced by his discovery of Ruskin's *Modern Painters* and the poetry of Keats, the innovative technique of David Wilkie, and his discussions with John Everett Millais, whom he met *c*. 1844. Hunt's 1848 Royal Academy exhibit, *The Eve of St. Agnes* (Guildhall Art Gallery, London), based upon Keats's poem, led to his friendship with Dante Gabriel Rossetti and thence to the foundation of the Pre-Raphaelite Brotherhood in September of that year. Hunt's first major figure painting with a landscape background painted from nature, *Rienzi* (1848–49; Priv. Coll., England), was followed by *A Converted British Family* (Ashmolean Museum, Oxford), exhibited at the Royal Academy in 1850 and sold that autumn to Thomas Combe, who became a major patron. Works such as *The Hireling Shepherd* (1851–52; Manchester City Art Gallery) and *Claudio and Isabella* (1850–53; Tate Gallery, London) helped to establish Hunt's reputation, but in January 1854 he left England to join Seddon (*q.v.*) in Egypt, thus turning his back on a most promising career. *The Light of the World* (1851–53; Keble College, Oxford) and *The Awakening Conscience* (1853–54; Tate Gallery, London) were shown at the Royal Academy in 1854.

Following his return to England, Hunt exhibited in 1856 *The Scapegoat* (Lady Lever Art Gallery, Port Sunlight), painted at the Dead Sea and in Jerusalem between 1854 and 1855. *The Finding of the Saviour in the Temple* (1854–60; Birmingham City Art Gallery, see fig. 10), exhibited privately, established Hunt's reputation as the founder of a new style of religious painting based on accurate archaeological reconstructions of biblical scenes. Its success was followed by that of *The Shadow of Death* (Manchester City Art Gallery, see fig 12), the outcome of Hunt's second trip to the Holy Land, 1869–72, and *The Triumph of the Innocents* (Walker Art Gallery, Liverpool), begun on his third visit, 1875–78. Hunt's painstaking methods precluded a large production of paintings in oil.

He was never elected to the Royal Academy, an institution which he bitterly attacked, but rather allied himself to alternative exhibiting bodies, such as the Grosvenor Gallery, and favoured one-picture exhibitions for his major works. He was awarded the Order of Merit in 1905 and died in London on 7 September 1910.

ABBREVIATED REFERENCE
Hunt 1905 W. Holman Hunt, *Pre-Raphaelitism and the Pre-Raphaelite Brotherhood*, London, 1905, 2 vols.

Note: All transcriptions of Hunt are transcribed literally

## 53*

## The Afterglow in Egypt   1854/63

Arched top: 185·4 × 86·3 cm
Monogrammed, inscribed and dated bottom left: *Whh/Memphis 54–63*
Southampton Art Gallery
[*repr. in colour on p. 97, plate 77*]

Hunt began working on this picture at the pyramids of Gizah shortly before 26 April 1854. At this point the canvas was approximately half its present size, and the artist concentrated on painting the head of the *fellāḥah* and the view across the eastern side of the Nile towards the mountain range of the Gebel Mokattum. The difficulties of securing a reliable model (Hunt 1905) and the desert winds, which were once again hindering Hunt's progress, led him to inform his patron, Thomas Combe, on 27 April, that this work was 'in danger of being abandoned'. In fact the artist did not leave Gizah until 6 May, when the picture had been 'brought into a condition to be finished' (Hunt 1905).

One advantage of painting a *fellāḥah* was that the model could be persuaded to pose unveiled. The costume and jewellery may well have been worked up with the aid of Lane's *Account of the Manners and Customs of the Modern Egyptians*, and it is possible that an illustration in this book (1846 ed., I, p. 79) was the source for portraying the girl balancing a wheat sheaf on her head. Similarly the woman in the lithograph *Entrance of the Temple of Amun, Thebes*, published in David Roberts's *The Holy Land, Syria, Idumea, Arabia, Egypt and Nubia*, 1842–49, may, as Kenneth Bendiner has suggested, have influenced the figure's pose and the way in which the water pot is balanced in her right palm.

53

Hunt informed William Bell Scott in a letter of 11 February 1860 that he intended finishing this picture and *A Street Scene in Cairo: The Lantern-maker's Courtship* (City of Birmingham Museum and Art Gallery) once *The Finding of the Saviour in the Temple* (ibid.) was completed: 'I cannot believe that Art should let such beautiful things pass as are in this age passing for good in the East without exertion to chronicle them for the future.' The canvas was extended *c.* 1860–61 and completed in late November 1863.

The title alerts the spectator to the fact that *The Afterglow in Egypt* is not a simple ethnographic study, and in 1886 Hunt explained that it was intended 'to express nothing but that the light is not that of the sun, and that although the meridian glory of ancient Egypt has passed away, there is still a poetic reflection of this in the aspect of life there' (Hunt 1886). The frame, designed by the artist, incorporates pomegranate motifs, an allusion to Demeter, the Greek goddess of corn, whose other attributes include poppies and sheaves of wheat.    J.E.B.

PROVENANCE
*c.* 1862–64, acquired from the artist by Ernest Gambart; by 1867, acquired by Charles P. Matthews; 1891, 6 June, Christie's, London (lot 60) bought by McLean; by 1905, acquired by Thomas Clarke; 1920, 27 February, Christie's, London (lot 149) bought in; 1926, 29 January, Christie's, London (lot 40) bought by H.H. Clarke; 1946, 26 April, Christie's, London (lot 151) bought in; 1946, presented by Dr H.H. Clarke to Southampton Art Gallery

EXHIBITIONS
1864 and 1865, London, The New Gallery, Works by William Holman Hunt and Robert Braithwaite Martineau
1867, Paris, *Exposition Universelle*, British Section, Oils (no. 53)
1877, London, Grosvenor Gallery, First Summer Exhibition (no. 46)
1969, Liverpool, Walker Art Gallery; London, Victoria and Albert Museum, *William Holman Hunt* (no. 29)
1972, Coral Gables, Florida, University of Miami, Lowe Art Museum, *The Revolt of the Pre-Raphaelites* (no. 59)
1973–74, Baden-Baden, Staatliche Kunsthalle, *Präraffaeliten* (no. 44)
1983, Brighton, Museum and Art Gallery; Manchester City Art Gallery, *The Inspiration of Egypt: Its Influence on British Artists, Travellers and Designers, 1700–1900* (no. 331)
1984, London, Tate Gallery, *The Pre-Raphaelites* (no. 87)

REFERENCES
Hunt 1905, I, pp. 382–83
W. Holman Hunt, 'The Pre-Raphaelite Brotherhood: A Fight for Art', *Contemporary Review*, XLIX, 1886, p. 828
K. P. Bendiner, 'The Portrayal of the Middle East in British Painting 1835–1860', Columbia University, Ph.D. thesis, 1979, p. 109
W. Holman Hunt letter to Thomas Combe, Plains of Memphis, 26–27 April 1854, MS. Arizona State University Library, Tempe
W. Holman Hunt letter to William Bell Scott, Kensington, 11 February 1860, MS. Princeton University Library, Troxell Coll.
G. Holman-Hunt, 'History of the Pre-Raphaelite Movement', MS. Priv. Coll., n.d., pp. 505–06

54

## 54†
# The Afterglow in Egypt    1860/63

82 × 38 cm
Monogrammed bottom left: *Whh*
The Visitors of the Ashmolean Museum
[*repr. in colour on p. 96, plate 78*]

This painting, started in 1860, was initially intended as a compositional study for the full-length Southampton version of *The Afterglow in Egypt* (Cat. 53; Hunt 1886 and 1905). On 11 February 1861 Hunt offered the picture to T.E. Plint: 'The Egyptian girl, which is 32 × 14¼ inches will with frame be 300 Guineas. it is as you know, the sketch of a larger picture 6 feet in height. in three or four months it will probably be ready.' Hunt was over-optimistic about the date of completion and Plint decided instead to purchase *The Finding of the Saviour in the Temple* (City of Birmingham Museum and Art Gallery) and five of Hunt's Eastern watercolours, including *The Plain of Rephaim from Zion* (Whitworth Art Gallery, University of Manchester), from Gambart's 1861 German Gallery exhibition.

Originally the girl in the Ashmolean version was set in the centre of the composition, in keeping with its conception purely as a study for the larger painting. However, by late 1861 Hunt had decided to vary the treatment and was adding a brown and white calf lent to him by Maria Pattle Jackson. He wrote to a pupil, Miss E. Tuckett, on 13 November, that 'whenever I am interrupted by torrents of rain or storms of wind I have to change my work with the unconsoling reflection that my live model is growing out of all likeness to the outlines already done – and far too large for the space I have spare for him in my picture.' Problems of overcrowding led to the canvas being extended by about half an inch down the right-hand side. Hunt then added the boy, partly based on the figure in a red turban and blue loincloth in *The Great Pyramid* (Priv. Coll.) and the white calf, derived from sketches of cattle on the Nile (Mrs Elisabeth Burt Coll.).

On 19 August 1863 Hunt wrote to Mrs Pattle Jackson: 'If by chance . . . you have a little calf again at Hendon I shall ask you to let me come over for a day and finish the one in the little Egyptian which requires a few hours work to complete it'. The picture was probably finished in November 1863 and sold to Thomas Combe soon afterwards.

The linear pattern on the frame designed by the artist is similar to that of *The Plain of Rephaim from Zion*. The abstract tracery of the roundels is particularly suited to an Arab subject.    J.E.B.

PROVENANCE
*c.* 1863–64, acquired by Thomas Combe; 1893, bequeathed by Mrs Thomas Combe to the Ashmolean Museum

EXHIBITIONS
1886, London, The Fine Art Society, *The Pictures of Mr. Holman Hunt* (no. 8)
1969, Liverpool, Walker Art Gallery; London, Victoria and Albert Museum, *William Holman Hunt* (no. 30)

REFERENCES
Hunt 1905, vol. II, p.203
W. Holman Hunt, 'The Pre-Raphaelite Brotherhood: A Fight for Art', *Contemporary Review*, XLIX, 1886, p. 828
W. Holman Hunt letter to T.E. Plint, Kensington, 11 February 1861, MS. Yale Center for British Art, New Haven
W. Holman Hunt letter to Miss E. Tuckett, Kensington, 13 November 1861, MS. J.S. Maas
W. Holman Hunt letter to Maria Pattle Jackson, Newnham Paddox, 19 August 1863, MS. Berg Coll., New York Public Library
W. Holman Hunt letter to Thomas Combe, 29 November 1863, Bodleian Library, Oxford, MS.Eng.lett.c.296
W. Holman Hunt letter to Thomas Combe, Kensington, 2 February 1864, MS. Priv. Coll.

55†

# Portrait of the Artist   1867/75

103·5 × 73 cm
Monogrammed and dated bottom left: *18 Whh 75*
Gallerie degli Uffizi, Florence

This painting was begun in London in 1867 as a pendant to the posthumous portrait of Hunt's late wife Fanny (Toledo Museum of Art), so that their son 'might have both father and mother to look at when another generation has found all of our places empty' (Landow, 1982). Although the 1907 catalogue of Hunt's Liverpool retrospective exhibition states that 'the artist has depicted himself in the dress in common use in Syria, and constantly worn by him in his painting room', the cross-over gown of striped Oriental cloth was almost certainly made up to the artist's specifications for ease of movement while working, and bears little relationship to the specifically Arab dress of David Roberts (Cat. 95).

Hunt would have been aware that painting himself in Oriental costume was a means of asserting his place in an historical tradition: he had, for instance, seen Van Dyck's portrait of the Earl of Denbigh in a striped Eastern jacket (Cecilia, Countess of Denbigh, *Royalist Father and Roundhead Son*, 1915, ill. facing p. 78) during his visit to Newnham Paddox in August 1863. Moreover, the architectural setting and works of art on the right in the background reflect the artist's interest in the Renaissance, stimulated by his year-long stay in Florence, from where Seymour Kirkup wrote to William Michael Rossetti on 23 March 1867: 'They tell me he [Holman Hunt] is going to change his style & give up preraphaelism & in fact he talks to me more of Titian than of the Beato [Fra Angelico]' (MS. University of British Columbia, Angeli-Dennis Coll.). This new style can be seen in *Portrait of the Artist*, which, as W. M. Rossetti noted in his diary of 11 February 1868, was 'painted with brushes of great length, so that he stands a good way off the canvas, and finds he can thus give features better as a general whole' (Rossetti, 1903).

The decision to paint himself in Oriental dress reflects Hunt's own assessment of his reputation as resting primarily on the works he painted in the Near East, and projects an image of the artist as intrepid explorer. The importance of this pioneering role for Pre-Raphaelite artists had been set forth in a letter that Hunt wrote to W. M. Rossetti on 12 August 1855 (Landow, 1982), and his continuing adherence to the original Pre-Raphaelite ideal of 'truth to nature' is underlined by his wearing of the gold intaglio signet ring (Mrs Elisabeth Burt Coll.) given to him by Millais in 1853 as a pledge of affection and solidarity with the Brotherhood.   J.E.B.

PROVENANCE
1907, presented by the artist to the Gallerie degli Uffizi

EXHIBITIONS
1875, Liverpool, *Fifth Autumn Exhibition* (no. 763)
1876, Philadelphia, *International Exhibition*, British Section, Department IV, Class 410 (no. 79)
1906, London, Leicester Galleries, *An Exhibition of the Collected Works of W. Holman Hunt, O.M., D.C.L.* (no. 12)
1906-07, Manchester City Art Gallery, *The Collected Works of W. Holman Hunt, O.M., D.C.L.* (no. 25)
1907, Liverpool, Walker Art Gallery, *Collective Exhibition of the Art of W. Holman Hunt, O.M., D.C.L.* (no. 28)
1907, Glasgow, Kelvingrove Art Gallery, *Exhibition of Pictures and Drawings by W. Holman Hunt, O.M., D.C.L.* (no. 17)
1971, Florence, Pitti Palace, *Firenze e l'Inghilterra: Rapporti artistici e culturali dal XVI al XX secolo* (no. 82)

REFERENCES
W.M. Rossetti, *Rossetti Papers: 1862 to 1870: A Compilation*, London, 1903, p. 298
Liverpool, Walker Art Gallery, *Collective Exhibition of the Art of W. Holman Hunt, O.M., D.C.L.*, 1907, p. 28
G.P. Landow, 'William Holman Hunt's "Oriental Mania" and his Uffizi *Self-Portrait*', *Art Bulletin*, LXIV, December 1982, p. 646 (Hunt letter to John Lucas Tupper, Bayswater, 19 November 1867, MS. Henry E. Huntington Library, San Marino), p. 653 (Hunt to W.M. Rossetti, Jerusalem, MS. *ibid.*)

[The compiler would like to thank Dr Aileen Ribeiro for information relating to Hunt's costume in this portrait.]

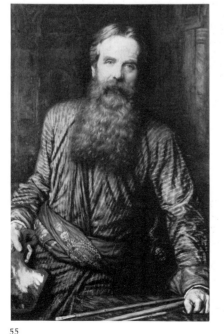

55

# Ingres, Jean-Auguste-Dominique   1780–1867

A highly successful establishment painter, Ingres was born in Montauban (Tarn et Garonne) in 1780, and became the accredited opponent of the emergent 'Romantic' school. He studied initially at the Toulouse Academy under Roques (1754–1847) and Vignan (d. 1829), before moving to Paris in 1797, where he entered the studio of Jacques-Louis David (1748–1825). In 1801 he won the Prix de Rome with his *Ambassadeurs d'Agamemnon* (Ecole des Beaux-Arts, Paris), but delayed his departure for Italy until 1806, where he remained until 1824, spending the last four years of this period in Florence.

On his return to Paris, Ingres received the Croix de la Légion d'Honneur, and was elected to the Institut de France. In 1825 he opened an atelier which was immediately popular and attended by young artists such as Amaury-Duval, Flandrin, Ziegler and Chassériau (*q.v.*). During each of his stays in Italy (the second from 1835 to 1840 as Director of the Villa Medici in Rome), Ingres executed numerous portraits and his popularity in official circles earned him several commissions for large-scale decorative work as well as smaller literary and historical genre scenes.

Like Gros (*q.v.*), Ingres travelled only within Europe, but by choosing overtly unclassical and exotic themes he sought to widen the range of subject-matter which could legitimately be included within the classical traditions of Western art.

ABBREVIATED REFERENCE
Momméja 1906 Jules Momméja, 'Le "Bain Turc" d'Ingres', *Gazette des Beaux-Arts*, September 1906, pp. 177–98

## 56

# Odalisque and Slave   1842
*L'Odalisque et l'esclave*

76 × 105·4 cm
Signed and dated bottom left: *J. Ingres, 1842*
Walters Art Gallery, Baltimore
[*repr. in colour on p. 41, plate 80*]

The theme of the odalisque follows a distinct pattern of development within Ingres's oeuvre, from the *Baigneuse* (1807; Musée Bonnat, Bayonne) to the famous *Bain turc* (Louvre, Paris; fig. 3), executed for Prince Napoleon in 1862. The present odalisque possibly refers back to the lost *Dormeuse* of 1808 painted for Queen Caroline of Naples (to which the *Grande Odalisque* [1814; Louvre] was intended as the pendant) and also to the 1828 *Baigneuse, Intérieur d'un harem* (Momméja 1906, p. 24).

This painting is a later variant of a subject first painted in 1839 (Fogg Art Museum, Cambridge, Mass.), differing only in slight formal refinements, such as the moderation of some of the patterned surfaces, the heavier necklace which more clearly accentuates the curve of the stomach, and in the addition of the landscaped courtyard, which allows some air to penetrate into the claustrophobic oppression of the earlier painting. With no first-hand experience upon which to draw for his representation of an odalisque, Ingres sought documentary authenticity in eighteenth-century travellers' accounts, and in particular the letters of Mary Wortley Montague describing the interior of the baths at Adrianopolis. He also referred to Persian miniatures, using Feriol's *Receuil de cent estampes représentant différentes nations du Levant* (1714), a publication owned by Delacroix.

56

The cross-reference between the bather and the odalisque suggests Ingres's desire to Westernise an Oriental theme. A pencil drawing at the Musée Ingres, Montauban (inv. no. 867.2030), thought to be an initial sketch for the lost *Dormeuse*, bears the inscription *Mariucca, blonde belle via Margutta 106*, thus confirming the European origins of the odalisque prototype. This is further substantiated in a letter from Ingres to M. Marcotte, for whom the original version of 1839 was painted, in which Ingres stated his intention to paint 'a rather beautiful body, of generous proportions, and as baroque as possible (it is after all a Turk!)' (H. Delaborde, *Ingres, sa vie, ses travaux, sa doctrine*, 1870, p. 237).

Nevertheless, the odalisques were criticised for their lack of perspective and archaicising gothic qualities (*Journal de Paris*, 1819, quoted Thoré, 'Salon de 1845', p. 249), a criticism first levelled at his portraits of the Rivière family of 1805 (Louvre). In the *Odalisque and Slave*, the perspectival discrepancies in the scale of the figures and the uniform treatment of local colours against the warmer flesh tones flatten the picture into a formal surface arabesque. Although partially disguised through its references to the Renaissance nude, the painting represents a significant step towards the depiction of nudity in a modern context, albeit distanced in space and, to some extent, time. Not all critics were blind to the erotic element in the *Odalisque and Slave* and, as Thoré observed in his review of the Salon of 1845, 'the face and the eyes clearly reveal the nonchalance and voluptuousness of a courtesan coming out of the bath' (*op. cit.*, p. 250–51). In general, however, the classical overtones in Ingres's representation of the nude left him morally irreproachable and more than compensated for any potential lack of taste. He thus avoided the extreme controversy provoked by Manet's more uncompromising *Olympia* (Musée d'Orsay, Galerie du Jeu de Paume, Paris), painted over twenty years later.    J.M.

PROVENANCE
Painted for King Wilhelm I of Würtemburg; Delessert Coll.; Baron Gustave de Rothschild; Sir Philip Sassoon Coll.; Wildenstein and Co.; 1925, acquired by Henry Walters, Baltimore; bequeathed to the Walters Art Gallery

EXHIBITIONS
1844, Paris, M. Léopold, Boulevard Italien
1950, New York, Paul Rosenberg Gallery, *The Nineteenth Century Heritage* (no. 11.)
1951, Baltimore, Museum of Art, *From Ingres to Gauguin* (no. 6)
1951, Philadelphia, Museum of Art, *Masterpieces of Painting* (no. 51)
1952, Fort Worth Art Center, *Inaugural Exhibition* (no. 42)
1953–54, New Orleans, Isaac Delgado Museum, *Masterpieces of French Painting* (no. 53)
1954, Manitoba, Winnipeg, Art Gallery Association, *French Pre-Impressionist Painters* (no. 10)
1955, Paris, Musée de l'Orangerie, *De David à Toulouse-Lautrec, chefs d'oeuvre des collections américaines* (no. 37)
1960, Berkeley, University of California, *Art from Ingres to Pollock*
1961, New York, Paul Rosenberg Gallery, *Ingres in American Collections* (no. 52)
1965, Indianapolis, Herron Museum of Art, *The Romantic Era* (no. 29)
1967, Montauban, Musée Ingres, *Ingres et son temps. Exposition organisée pour le centenaire de la mort d'Ingres* (no. 114)
1967, New York, Wildenstein and Co., *An Exhibition of Treasures of the Walters Art Gallery* (no. 44)
1967–68, Paris, Petit Palais, *Ingres* (no. 198)

REFERENCES
Ch. Blanc, 'Ingres, sa vie et son oeuvre', *Gazette des Beaux-Arts*, January 1968, ill. opp. p. 18
Th. Thoré, *Salons de 1844–1848*, Paris, 1868, pp. 250–51
H. Lapauze, *Ingres, sa vie et son oeuvre*, Paris, 1911, p. 352
E. S. King, 'Ingres as a classicist', *Journal of the Walters Art Gallery*, 1942, p. 79–80
G. Wildenstein, *Ingres*, London, 1954, no. 237, pl. 83
Walters Art Gallery, Baltimore, *Catalogue*, 1982 (no. 6)

## John, Augustus    1878–1961

Son of a solicitor, John was born and brought up in Wales. He attended the Slade School of Art in London from 1894 to 1898, gaining a reputation for flamboyant behaviour, wild love affairs and bohemianism. From 1901 to 1904 he taught painting at Liverpool University, also acting as co-principal with William Orpen of the Chelsea Art School. In 1903 he became a member of the New English Art Club. On a visit to Paris in 1907 he saw an exhibition of drawings by Puvis de Chavannes and met Picasso. Both experiences left their influence on his work, which for a while kept abreast of European avant-garde painting. John became an Associate of the Royal Academy in 1921 and a full Academician in 1928. His later work failed to live up to the promise of his youth.

57

## Portrait of Colonel T. E. Lawrence    1919

80 × 59 cm
The Trustees of the Tate Gallery

Thomas Edward Lawrence, 'Lawrence of Arabia' (1888–1935), became fascinated with the desert and the Arabs after studying archaeology and taking part in excavations in the Near East. He worked for military intelligence as liaison officer with Emir Feisal and was the inspiration behind Arab hostilities against the Turks during the First World War, later describing his experiences in *Seven Pillars of Wisdom* (1926). From 1922 he served in the Royal Air Force under the name of 'T. E. Shaw'. He was killed in a motorcycle accident in 1935. Lawrence and Augustus John first met at the Versailles Peace Conference in 1919, during which this work was painted. Through Lord Beaverbrook, John had obtained a commission as official artist in Canadian War Records and it was in this capacity that he attended the conference, with a view to making portraits of its main participants. Lawrence was there as a member of the British Foreign Office delegation, interpreter to Emir Feisal and supporter of Arab interests. The two men struck up a friendship that lasted until Lawrence's death. 'He sat for me frequently in Paris and later in England,' John wrote. 'Lawrence actually enjoyed being painted and always seemed vastly tickled by the results' (*Chiaroscuro. Fragments of Autobiography: First Series*, London, 1952, p. 238). Three portraits in oil came out of their first meeting, and several drawings, though none relating directly to the present work (for an example, see *op. cit.*, ill. facing p. 240). Later portraits by John of Lawrence as 'Aircraftman Shaw' can be seen at the Ashmolean Museum, Oxford and the National Gallery of Canada. He also made a portrait of Emir Feisal at the conference, with whom Lawrence would converse in Arabic during sittings. This portrait shows Lawrence in the Arab dress he wore for the occasion and wearing the ornamental dagger presented to him by Feisal as a token of gratitude. Lawrence lent this to John, presumably in connection with the portrait. He mentioned it in a letter to the artist of 1 March 1920, after which John notes: 'I returned the dagger T.E. had confided to my care' (*ibid.*, p. 247). It was perhaps this feature, along with the tough expression, that prompted Lawrence to refer to the work in letters to John as 'the rebellious one', as opposed to 'the goody-goody one' and 'a third (called by you a dud)', when the three portraits of 1919 were exhibited at the Alpine Club Gallery in 1920. 'O.C. gallery tells me that you told him the other one (called the rebellious one) was mine: and I wanted to ask you about it', he wrote. 'I have told you I wanted it and I think it's wonderful . . . but the value of it beats me at present and so I can't offer' (ibid., p. 245). In spite of wanting the work for himself, Lawrence was greatly amused when it was bought by the Duke of Westminster. 'Really I'm hotter stuff than I thought: the wrathful portrait went off at top speed for a thousand to a *Duke!*' he exlaimed in a letter to John of 19 March 1920. 'Of course I know you will naturally think the glory is yours – but I believe it's due to the exceeding beauty of my face' (ibid., p. 246).    M.W.

PROVENANCE
1920, acquired from the artist by the Duke of Westminster at the Alpine Club Gallery exhibition; 1920, presented by him to the Tate Gallery

EXHIBITIONS
1920, London, Alpine Club Gallery, *War and Peace Conference Portraits by Augustus John* (no. 8)
1930, Bradford, *Jubilee Exhibition* (no. 123)
1936, Caernarvon, *Eisteddfod, Arts and Crafts Section*
1939, British Council: Warsaw, Helsinki, Stockholm, *Contemporary British Art* (no. 44, ill.)
1946, Leeds, Temple Newsam, *Augustus John* (no. 35)
1955–57, Cardiff, National Museum of Wales (long loan)

REFERENCE
A. John, *Chiaroscuro. Fragments of Autobiography: First Series*, London, 1952, pp. 238, 245–46

57

# Kandinsky, Wassily    1866–1944

Born in Moscow, Kandinsky seemed destined for a distinguished academic career. Only at the late age of thirty did he decide to become an artist, travelling to Munich at the end of 1896 and enrolling in the private painting class of Anton Azbé; he later studied at the Munich Academy under the noted Secessionist artist, Franz von Stuck. In 1901 Kandinsky was one of the founder members of the artists' association 'Phalanx'. Between 1904 and 1908 he travelled extensively throughout Europe, and to North Africa and Russia, in the company of his mistress Gabriele Münter; they returned to Munich in the summer of 1908. In 1909 he became President of the newly-formed Neue Künstler-Vereinigung München (New Artists' Association of Munich). Together with Franz Marc he edited the *Blaue Reiter Almanac*, a conspectus or yearbook of primitive and contemporary art, which appeared in May 1912; Kandinsky and Marc also resigned from the NKVM to organise the two exhibitions of the 'Editors of the *Blaue Reiter*', held in Munich in December 1911 and spring 1912.

At the outbreak of the First World War, Kandinsky, as an enemy alien, was obliged to leave Germany and return to Russia where, in the wake of the 1917 Revolution, he was active for a time in reorganising art education and museums. In 1922 he accepted an invitation from Gropius to join the staff of the Weimar Bauhaus, and remained at the Bauhaus throughout the years in Dessau and Berlin, leaving Germany only after the Nazis came to power in 1933. His last years were spent in Paris, where he died in December 1944.

Apart from his contribution to the development of abstract painting, Kandinsky is remembered as one of the most important teachers and theorists of this century, whose two books, *On the Spiritual in Art* (Munich, 1911) and *Point and Line to Plane* (Munich, 1926), exerted a considerable influence on subsequent generations of painters.

ABBREVIATED REFERENCES
Grohmann 1958    W. Grohmann, *Wassily Kandinsky, Leben und Werk*, Cologne, 1958
Roethel 1970    H.K. Roethel, *Kandinsky, Das Graphische Werk*, Cologne, 1970
Gollek 1974    R. Gollek, *Der Blaue Reiter im Lenbachhaus München*, Munich, 1974
Hanfstaengl 1974    E. Hanfstaengl, *Wassily Kandinsky, Zeichnungen und Aquarelle. Katalog der Sammlung in der Städtischen Galerie München*, Munich, 1974
Roethel and Benjamin 1982    H.K. Roethel and J.K. Benjamin, *Kandinsky. Catalogue Raisonné of the Oil Paintings. Volume One 1900–1915*, London, 1982
Lindsay and Vergo 1982    *Kandinsky. Complete Writings on Art*, K.C. Lindsay and P. Vergo eds., Boston and London, 1982

58*

## Improvisation 6 (African)    1909
*Improvisation 6 (Afrikanisches)*

107 × 95·5 cm
Signed and dated bottom left: *KANDINSKY 1909*
Städtische Galerie im Lenbachhaus, Munich
[*repr. in colour on p. 158, plate 129*]

Between 1900 and 1914 Kandinsky visited North Africa only once, in 1904–05. He travelled to Bizerta by way of Marseille, arriving on Christmas Day, 1904, in Tunis, where he stayed until April 1905. He recorded his impressions of the North African countryside, and of towns like Carthage, in a series of landscapes and small oil studies, many done in front of the motif.

Intermittently over the next five or six years, he continued to paint pictures with titles such as *Arabs*. While *African* was not Kandinsky's original title for the present painting (see Roethel and Benjamin 1982, p. 272), so too the date of the painting is problematic. *Improvisation 6* is signed and dated *Kandinsky 1909*, whereas the artist entered the work in his own 'house catalogue' of paintings under 1910; the earlier date inscribed on the canvas has been followed here.

In his treatise *On the Spiritual in Art*, published in December 1911, Kandinsky distinguished between three types of paintings which currently occupied the greater part of his attention: 'Compositions', 'Improvisations' and 'Impressions', describing 'Improvisations' as 'chiefly unconscious, for the most part suddenly arising expressions of events of an inner character, hence impressions of "internal nature"'.

The iconography of the present painting has been linked with the Easter Day subject of Mary and Mary Magdalen at the Tomb, a hypothesis made more plausible by the relationship between *Improvisation 6* and Kandinsky's 1909 painting *Arabs I (Cemetery)* (Roethel and Benjamin 1982, no. 283).    P.V.

PROVENANCE
Estate of Gabriele Münter; acquired by the Städtische Galerie im Lenbachhaus, Munich
EXHIBITIONS
1910, London, Albert Hall, *Allied Artists Exhibtion* (no. 962)
1910–11, Odessa, Salon Izdebsky, *2nd International Art Exhibition* (no. 213)
1912, Berlin, *Der Sturm, Kandinsky Kollektiv-Ausstellung* (no. 62)
1963, New York; Paris; The Hague, Basel, *Retrospective Exhibition* (no. 16)
1976, Munich, Haus der Kunst, *Wassily Kandinsky 1866–1944* (no. 24)
1982, New York, Solomon R. Guggenheim Museum, *Kandinsky in Munich 1896–1914* (no. 261)
1982, Munich, Städtische Galerie im Lenbachhaus, *Kandinsky und München, Begegnungen und Wandlungen 1896–1914* (no. 305)

REFERENCES
Grohmann 1958, p. 331
Gollek 1974, p. 81
Hanfstaengl 1974, p. 165
Roethel and Benjamin 1982, p. 272, no. 287

59*

# Oriental
*Orientalisches*

Oil on cardboard: 69·5 × 96·5 cm
Städtische Galerie im Lenbachhaus, Munich
[*repr. in colour on p. 159, plate 130*]

Neither the title nor the date of this painting can be established with complete certainty. It is not listed in Kandinsky's 'house catalogue', and the inscription *Orientalisches* on the back of the picture is in Gabriele Münter's hand, not the artist's. It has usually been ascribed to 1909 on the basis of its similarity to other, securely datable paintings. However, if this date is correct, it makes *Oriental* one of the most advanced paintings of that year: figurative motifs are schematised to a high degree, and the work as a whole creates a distinctly 'abstract' impression. A related drawing contained in a sketchbook in use during 1909–10 (Städtische Galerie im Lenbachhaus, Munich; GMS 345) may well have been executed after the painting, having the character of a rapidly sketched aide mémoire. Kandinsky also translated the work in highly literal fashion into the medium of colour woodcut as one of the illustrations for his poetry and prints album *Klänge* (Sounds), published in Munich late in 1912 (Roethel 1970, no. 106). The album as a whole served as a pictorial resumé in graphic form of some of the artist's most important paintings of the preceding two or three years. A watercolour, also in Munich, which again shows the same composition (Hanfstaengl 1974, no. 158) is a preparatory study for the woodcut rather than for the painting.    P.V.

PROVENANCE
Estate of Gabriele Münter; acquired by the Städtische Galerie im Lenbachhaus, Munich
EXHIBITIONS
1961, London, Marlborough Fine Art, *Kandinsky, The Road to Abstraction* (no. 30)
1972, Charleroi, Palais des Beaux-Arts, *Kandinsky* (no. 5)
1976, Munich, Haus der Kunst, *Wassily Kandinsky 1866–1944* (no. 23)

REFERENCES
Grohmann 1958, p. 400
Roethel 1970, cat. no. 106
Gollek 1974, p. 81
Hanfstaengl 1974, p. 165
Roethel and Benjamin 1982, p. 280, no. 294

58

59

# Lear, Edward  1812–1888

In an age when many undertook long and arduous journeys to uncharted territories, Lear, who once called himself a 'Painter of Poetical Topography', was an unusually intrepid traveller. He lived for several years in Italy at the beginning and end of his career, and also in Greece, which he hoped to illustrate in its entirety. He toured many parts of Europe, Egypt, Palestine and Syria, and at the age of sixty travelled the length and breadth of India and Ceylon. He sketched all these places assiduously and at the same time wrote copious descriptions in his diaries and long, amusing letters to his sister and friends. He also composed his famous nonsense rhymes and stories, and published several illustrated travel accounts; but he did not succeed in his aspiration to be recognised as a serious landscape painter. When nearly forty years old, he attended the Royal Academy schools, sought advice from William Holman Hunt (*q.v.*) and exhibited at the Royal Academy and the British Institution. But his two most ambitious works, *Masada* (present location unknown) and *The Cedars of Lebanon* (present location unknown, see Cat. 62), were failures and, although he continued to paint small oils for patrons, from the late 1860s he aimed merely 'to topographize all the journeyings of my life' (letter to Lady Waldegrave, Cannes, 9 January 1868, LLEL, 1911, p. 91).

ABBREVIATED REFERENCES
LEL 1907      Lady Strachey, ed., *Letters of Edward Lear*, London, 1907
LLEL 1911    Lady Strachey, ed., *Later Letters of Edward Lear*, London, 1911
Noakes 1979  V. Noakes, *Edward Lear: The Life of a Wanderer*, London, rev. ed. 1979
MS. Journal  E. Lear, MS. Journal, The Houghton Library, Harvard University
MS. Letters (Ann)  E. Lear, MS. Letters to Ann, transcription in Priv. Coll.

[The compiler wishes to thank Vivien Noakes for her invaluable assistance in the cataloguing of the following works.]

## 60

# Philae on the Nile  1855

34 × 53·5 cm
Signed and dated bottom right: *E. Lear 1855*
Inscribed on a label *verso* at top of frame: *Philae on the Nile Edward Lear 1855*
The Brooklyn Museum, gift of David Nash
[*repr. in colour on p. 57, plate 82*]

The Island of Philae, just above the first cataract of the Nile, was for many nineteenth-century visitors the most attractive of Egypt's ancient sites. Lear was one of many who eulogised its beauty. On his first visit in February 1854 he camped there for ten days, writing to his sister Ann: 'It is impossible to describe the place to you any further than by saying it is more like a real *fairy island* than anything else I can compare it to. The Nile is divided here into several channels by other rocky islands, beyond you see the desert and the great granite hills of Assouan. The great T. of Isis, on the terrace of which I am now writing, is so extremely wonderful that no words can give the least idea of it' (letter to Ann, 7 February 1854; quoted Noakes 1979, p. 122).

Lear well appreciated the pictorial value of the scene: finding the Ptolemaic temples on the island the easiest of all the Nile antiquities to represent, he made twenty-five drawings from several different viewpoints (MS. Letters [Ann], 15 February 1854).

During the five years following his return, he used these sketches for about a dozen oil paintings. The present example is a view from the rocky bank of the Nile to the south-east of the island with the Kiosk of Trajan and to its left the first pylon

at the southern end of the Temple of Isis. Of the eleven paintings of Philae listed by Lady Strachey as sold by Lear between 1855 and 1858 (LEL 1907, pp. 314–15), the present exhibit could be either no. 116, acquired by William Nevill, or no. 118, acquired by Henry F. Walter. Another possibility is *The Island of Philae, above the first cataract on the Nile, from the south – afternoon*, one of the two Philae subjects exhibited at the Royal Academy in 1856 (no. 625).

Lear was no less enthusiastic on his last visit to Philae in 1867, finding it 'more beautiful than ever' (MS. Journal, 30 January 1867; quoted Noakes 1979, p. 220); this resulted in yet more watercolour and oil paintings.

The painting exhibited here, with its strong colours and emphasis on natural phenomena, such as the rocks and palm trees in the foreground, is characteristic of Lear; hence it is a more poetic rendering of the scene than that of David Roberts (Cat. 90).      B.L.

PROVENANCE
Dr. Myer H. Salaman; 1970, 17 June, Sotheby's, London (lot 134) bought by J. Maas; bought from Maas by William Dally; 1980, 6 October, Sotheby's Belgravia, London (lot 10); Mr David Nash; 1980, presented by him to the Brooklyn Museum, New York

EXHIBITION
1865, Royal Academy, Summer Exhibition (no. 625, as *The Island of Philae, above the first cataract on the Nile, from the south – afternoon*)

60

## 61*

## Jerusalem from the Mount of Olives, Sunrise   1859

40 × 60·3 cm
Signed with initials and dated bottom left: *EL 1859*
Signed, inscribed and dated on label *verso* and on the stretcher:
*Jerusalem from the Mount of Olives, Sunrise From Drawings made by me in April/*
*May 1858 Painted for Sir James Reid – Edward Lear 1858/9*
Private Collection
[*repr. in colour on p. 57, plate 83*]

Lear's original intention of visiting the Holy Land with William Holman Hunt in 1854 did not materialise; instead he travelled there from Corfu four years later. He arrived in Jerusalem on 27 March 1858 and the next day, Palm Sunday, explored the country immediately outside the walls. After visiting Petra, he returned to the city on 20 April and spent a week encamped on the Mount of Olives making drawings for a painting of Jerusalem at sunset which Lady Waldegrave had commissioned (MS. Letters [Ann], 23, 28 April, 2 May 1858; 1977, 29 July, Christie's, London, lot 107, 174; Priv. Coll., England).

The present exhibit shows Jerusalem from an almost identical viewpoint, but at sunrise. In a letter to his patroness, he described 'an oblique North-East view', which included 'the site of the temple & the two domes, – and it shews the ravine of the valley of Jehoshaphat, over which the city looks: – and Absalom's pillar (if so be it is his pillar), the village of Siloam, part of Aceldama, & Gethsemane are all included in the landscape . . . add to all of which there is an unlimited foreground of figs, olives & pomegranates, not to speak of goats, sheep, & huming [*sic*] beings' (letter to Lady Waldegrave, Damascus, 27 May 1858; Taunton Records Office, Somerset). As well as the many drawings he accumulated, he also obtained photographs, and believed that the picture would be among his best.

Sir James Reid, for whom *Jerusalem from the Mount of Olives, Sunrise* was painted, had been Supreme Judge in the Ionian Islands when Lear was living in Corfu before his visit to the Holy Land. Reid had first suggested a painting of Jerusalem in February 1858 but for Sir Moses Montefiore rather than for himself (letter to Fortescue, Corfu, 27 February 1858, LEL 1907, p. 88). A year later Lear wrote to Ann that several of his paintings from his Holy Land trip were well advanced, including Lady Reid's Jerusalem (MS. Letters [Ann], Rome, 3 February 1859).

In the painting exhibited here, Lear appears to emulate some of the methods of his Pre-Raphaelite mentor, William Holman Hunt (*q.v.*), notably in the high viewpoint, the diagonal of the hillside, which is more strongly emphasised in the painting than in the drawings (eg. one signed, inscribed and dated 1858, sold Sotheby's, London, 13 March 1969, lot 138), and the detailed treatment of the plants among the rocks in the foreground.

The Mount of Olives had strong biblical associations, and although Lear's reasons for his choice of this viewpoint seem to have been purely pictorial, he was as much aware of the associations of the Holy City and its surroundings as were the many other visitors during the nineteenth century (see Warner p. 32, Bugler p. 28).   B.L.

PROVENANCE
1859, painted for Sir James Reid; 1980, 29 February, Christie's, London (lot 14)

EXHIBITIONS
1980, London, The Fine Art Society, *Travellers Beyond the Grand Tour* (no. 3; ill. p. 12)
1983, London, The Fine Art Society, *The Travels of Edward Lear* (no. 89; ill. p. 41)

REFERENCES
LEL 1907, pp. 88, 315, no. 148
MS. Letters (Ann), Rome, 3 February 1859

## 62

## The Cedars of Lebanon   *c.* 1862

68 × 113·5 cm
H. Fritz-Denneville Fine Arts Ltd
[*repr. in colour on p. 56, plate 84*]

After leaving Jerusalem (see Cat. 61), Lear sailed from Jaffa to Beirut to visit the Lebanon in May 1858. He spent only a few days exploring the interior of the country because, although he found it 'wonderfully fine: – a kind of Orientalized Swiss scenery', the extreme cold of the mountains made him unwell and he had to return to the coast; but he did manage to make a 'drawing of the Cedars as a sign of my Lebanon visit' (letter to Lady Waldegrave, Damascus, 27 May 1858; LEL 1907, p. 109).

Two on-the-spot sketches are known: one inscribed and dated *The Cedars Lebanon 21.May 1858* (Victoria and Albert Museum, London; P.4-1930), the other inscribed and dated *The Cedars. Lebanon 20.21.May 1858* (Priv. Coll., London). The latter is similar in composition to a more finished watercolour, signed and inscribed *Edward Lear Lebanon 1858* (exhibited Norwich Castle Museum, 1957, no. 44), and also to the present exhibit.

Lear is known to have painted the cedars in oil at least four times (LEL 1907, pp. 316–18, and Arts Council of Great Britain, *Edward Lear 1812–1888*, London, 1958, no. 6). The first (present location unknown) was one of two huge paintings with which he hoped to establish his reputation in England, and in September 1860 he went to Oatlands Park Hotel at Walton-on-Thames to paint from the ancient cedars in the grounds (Noakes 1979, pp. 177–79). The oil was finished in May 1861, the first for which he had received no help from William Holman Hunt, and

61

62

later that year it was exhibited in Liverpool where it was favourably received. The following year, however, when it was exhibited in London at the International Exhibition, it was badly hung and was slated by *The Times*'s critic; nor did it sell until 1867. Severely depressed by this blow, Lear became increasingly disillusioned and isolated.

Lear's second version of *The Cedars of Lebanon* (the present exhibit) was painted by 1862 and purchased by Charles Roundell. Some years later Roundell was described by Lear as 'a great friend of mine' and as owning four of his pictures (letter to Fortescue, Turin, 31 July 1870; LLEL 1911, p. 123).　B.L.

PROVENANCE
Charles S. Roundell, MP for Grantham and Skipton, and thence by descent; 1980, 6 June, Christie's, London (lot 118)
REFERENCES
LEL 1907, p. 317, no. 226
LLEL 1911, p. 123

## 63

## The Pyramids Road, Gizah　1873

52·1 × 103·2 cm
Signed with monogram and dated bottom left: *EL 1873*
Inscribed on an old label *verso: A View of the Pyramids Road at Gizeh, with the avenue of Trees planted in 1868 by the Empress Eugenie, at the opening of the SUEZ CANAL*
The Fine Art Society, London
[*repr. in colour on p. 56, plate 85*]

Before his first trip to Egypt in 1849, Lear foresaw that 'the contemplation of Egypt must fill the mind, the artistic mind I mean, with great food for the rumination of long years' (letter to Fortescue, Rome, 12 February 1848; LEL 1907, p. 8). Egypt was indeed a potent source of inspiration for his art: he visited the country on five occasions, in 1849, 1853–54, 1858, 1866–67 and 1872, and painted at least forty-six Egyptian subjects in oils as well as many watercolours and on-the-spot sketches.

The present exhibit resulted from his last visit in October 1872, when he spent a few days in Cairo on his way to Suez to pick up a boat for Bombay. Lord Northbrook, his friend and patron, who had invited him to India, had already asked him to paint 'two pictures of the Pirrybids' (letter to Fortescue, San Remo, 28 February 1872; LLEL 1911, p. 145), and now commissioned a drawing of Cairo from him (Noakes 1979, p. 263). In his journal Lear commented on how much the neighbourhood of Cairo had changed since his last visit five years earlier, especially in the area around the Pyramids: 'Nothing in all life is so amazingly interesting as this new road & avenue – literally all the way to the Pyramids!!! – I could really hardly believe my own senses remembering the plain in 1867' (MS. Journal, 13 October 1872). He sketched there on 13 and 14 October: 'I drew again at the head of the great Acacia avenue – but flies made the work *impossible*' (MS. Journal, 14 October 1872). A compositional thumbnail sketch for the present exhibit is included in this journal entry.

Later that year he finished a watercolour of the Pyramids Road (F. H. Sasse Coll.; exhibited The Fine Art Society, London, 1983, no. 78) and in 1873 he repeated the composition (the present exhibit) apparently for Lord Northbrook. Another view of the Pyramids of the same size was painted in the same year, also apparently for Lord Northbrook (1980, Christie's, London, lot 25; Priv. Coll.). The two pictures may be the 'Pirrybids' in Lady Strachey's list (LEL 1907, p. 318, nos. 272, 273).　B.L.

PROVENANCE
?The Earl of Northbrook; The Fine Art Society, London
EXHIBITION
1983, The Fine Art Society, London, *The Travels of Edward Lear* (no. 80; ill. pp. 44–45)

## Lecomte-du-Nouÿ, Jules-Jean-Antoine
1842–1929

The descendant of a noble Piedmontese family, Lecomte-du-Nouÿ was born in Paris in 1842. He entered the Ecole des Beaux-Arts in 1861 where he studied under Gleyre (*q.v.*) and Signol, and in 1864 became a pupil of Gérôme (*q.v.*). Like his fellow students Paul Lenoir and Albert Aublet, he was strongly influenced by the polished realism of the 'Néo-grec' School, and executed a number of meticulously detailed scenes drawn from antiquity. Though he exhibited historical genre, religious paintings and portraits from the Salon of 1863 onwards, official recognition came only in 1869, when one of his works was acquired by the State. In 1872, Lecomte-du-Nouÿ turned his attention to the Orient, and set out for Greece, Egypt, Turkey and Asia Minor, returning to France with a large store of very exact documentary information.

From the mid-1870s he received commissions for the decoration of the churches of St. Nicholas and Ste. Trinité (Chapelle de St-Vincent-de Paul) in Paris, and later executed religious cycles for churches in Rumania.

In 1895 he exhibited his first sculpture, and obtained an honourable mention for his *Mort de Gavroche* at the Salon of 1901.

63

64

## The Guard of the Seraglio: Souvenir of Cairo 1876

*La Poste du Sérail: souvenir du Caire*

74 × 130 cm
Signed and dated bottom left: *LECOMTE-DU-NOUŸ/1876*
Pierre Bergé Collection, Paris
[*repr. in colour on p. 99, plate 86*]

This painting, perhaps Lecomte-du-Nouÿ's most direct reference to his travels in 1872, typifies the languid opulence of the artist's vision of the East. His choice of dramatic themes of despotism, violence and eroticism was affected partly by his readings of early romantic interpretations of the Orient; the *Porteur de mauvaises nouvelles* (1872; Musée du Luxembourg) and the *Ramsès dans son harem* (1885; with The Fine Art Society, London, 1978) are both drawn from Gautier's *Roman de la momie* (1800), and in 1885 he exhibited a painting based on Victor Hugo's *Orientales* (1829) as part of a polyptych dedicated to the poet.

Nominally inspired by Cairo, *The Guard of the Seraglio* reveals the fantastic architectural confections of which the Khedival royal family were so fond, with 'fairy-tale grounds' as reported by Emile Lott. The site is the Harem Pavilion of the Gazirah Palace on the island of the same name looking north-east across the Nile to Bulāq. Half a mile away the Mosque of Sinān Pasha can be seen although the artist has judiciously rearranged the surrounding minarets. The gleaming, lithe bodies of the black eunuchs and the indolent luxuriance of the chief guard, set against the dark entrance to the harem introduce an element of the voyeur, undoubtedly designed to titillate European sensibilities with its erotic overtones. Significantly, the painting had already found a purchaser by the time it was exhibited in 1877.

In the precise rendering of rich surface textures and vivid colouring, the painting risks becoming oppressively claustrophobic, but for its exterior location and the cool tones of the architecture in the subdued light of dawn. In both his Orientalist painting and his other work, Lecomte-du-Nouÿ made frequent use of the eerie qualities of half-light to dramatic or melancholic effect. In *L'Heure du prière* (c. 1872; National Gallery of Jordan) an evocative half-light suggests the strange impression left by the religious ceremony, and in *La lune de miel; Venise au XVIe siècle* (Salon, 1875; present location unknown) a cool, reflected moonlight evokes the historic past of this romantic city. The exotic contemporary location of the present painting, however, could not conceal the essential '*caractère antique*' of the figures (Houssaye, 1877, p. 844) and many critics were of the opinion that the artist's new Oriental subject-matter was unsuited to the archaeological precision of his earlier 'Néo-grec' style. As early as 1865, Maxime du Camp had recognised the inquiring spirit behind Lecomte-du-Nouÿ's *Sentinelle grec* (present location unknown) but had warned against the emptiness of including detail for detail's sake, and an excessive preoccupation with 'le bric-à-brac' (1867, p. 157).

For many academic and 'Néo-grec' painters, Orientalist detail served more to expand a repertoire of authentically and dispassionately observed facts than to enhance the specific meaning of a painting.   J.M.

PROVENANCE
By 1877, Comte Daupias Coll., Paris; 1892, 16–17 May, Galerie Georges Petit, Paris (lot 143); 1977, November, Christie's, London (lot 8); 1977, Pierre Bergé Coll., Paris

EXHIBITION
1877, Paris, Salon (no. 1267)

REFERENCES
Thornton 1983, ill. pp. 188–89
M. du Camp, 'Le Salon de 1865', *Les Beaux-Arts à l'Exposition Universelle et aux Salons de 1863, 1864, 1865, 1866 et 1867*, Paris, 1867, p. 157
A. Houssaye, 'Le Salon de 1877 – II', *Revue des Deux Mondes*, June 1877, p. 844
L-E. Duranty, 'Réflections d'un bourgeois sur le Salon', *Gazette des Beaux-Arts*, July 1877, pp. 79–80, ill. p. 81
Paris, *Catalogue des Tableaux anciens et modernes composant l'importante collection de M. le Comte Daupias*, 1892, pp. 116–17, ill. p. 117

64

# Lord Leighton, Frederic    1830–1896

Born in Scarborough, the son of a doctor, Leighton spent long periods of his childhood on the Continent, where his parents lived for the benefit of his mother's health. He received his first training at the Städelsches Kunstinstitut in Frankfurt in 1846–48 and 1850–52, latterly under the Nazarene painter Edward von Steinle. He was in Rome from 1852 to 1855 and there painted his *Cimabue's Madonna* (Royal Coll.), which attracted much attention at the Royal Academy in London in 1855. Based in Paris from 1855 to 1858, he came under the influence of the French neo-classicists. In 1859, after another short stay in Italy, he finally settled in London. With *Helen of Troy* (Priv. Coll.), exhibited in 1865, he began to paint the dreamy, sensuous pictures with classical themes and impassively beautiful female figures that make up the bulk of his mature work. His major large-scale essays in this vein are *The Syracusan Bride* (1865–66; Priv. Coll.), *The Daphnephoria* (1874–76; Lady Lever Art Gallery, Port Sunlight) and *Captive Andromache* (*c.* 1888; Manchester City Art Gallery). He painted a pair of large frescoes at the Victoria and Albert Museum, London, in 1870–73 and in the 1870s played an important role in the development of the 'New Sculpture'. Leighton became an Associate of the Royal Academy in 1864, a full Academician in 1870 and President in 1878. He was a respected public figure and entertained on a lavish scale at his home in Holland Park (now Leighton House).

ABBREVIATED REFERENCE
Ormond 1975  R. and L. Ormond, *Lord Leighton*, New Haven and London, 1975

65

## 65*

## Old Damascus: Jews' Quarter    1873–74

129·5 × 104·1 cm
Private Collection

Leighton travelled to North Africa and the Near East five times: in 1857 to Algiers, in 1867 to Constantinople and other parts of Asia Minor, in 1868 to Egypt, where Ismail Pasha provided him with a steamer, a French chef and an Italian waiter for his journey up the Nile to Aswān, in 1873 to Damascus and in 1882, fleetingly, to Egypt again (for a fuller account of his journeys, see Ormond 1975, chap. XI, pp. 95–101). Arriving at Damascus in the autumn of 1873, he was more impressed by the distant prospect of the city than its interior but did enjoy the old houses 'of which some few are standing, though grey and perishing, and which are still lovely to enchantment' (Ormond 1975, p. 98). He had hoped to see Richard Burton (see Cat. 95), whom he had known since being introduced to him by his friend Mrs Sartoris in 1869, but was disappointed to find he was no longer British Consul there, having been transferred, against his will, to Trieste. Nevertheless, he did make an oil sketch of the house in which Burton and his wife had lived (Ormond 1975, no. 222). His well-known portrait of Burton, now in the National Portrait Gallery, London, was made in 1875. Leighton did much sketching in Damascus with a view to working up 'one or two pot-boilers', as he called them, on his return home. The main 'pot-boilers' to result were *Old Damascus: Jews' Quarter* and *Portions of the Interior of the Grand Mosque of Damascus* (Cat. 66). In both cases, the architectural details are plausible but Leighton made little effort to achieve any kind of authenticity with the figures, obviously using the same models as he used for other, non-Oriental subjects. There are also figure-compositions that reflect his experience of the Near East in their accessories, for instance, the *Study: at a Reading Desk* (Holt Bequest, Sudley) and the *Music Lesson* (Guildhall Art Gallery, London), both exhibited at the Royal Academy in 1877, but again the models are clearly European. Another result of the Damascus trip was the 'Arab Hall' Leighton added to his house in 1877–79. A fanciful imitation of an Islamic interior, this contains tiles, stained glass and woodwork brought back from Damascus, augmented by modern British furnishings designed in a matching style.

A study for *Old Damascus: Jews' Quarter* is at the Ashmolean Museum, Oxford.    M.W.

PROVENANCE
By 1907, Lord Mildmay; Taxation Publishing Company Ltd; 1983, 25 November, their sale, Christie's, London (lot 66); acquired by Christopher Wood for the present owner

EXHIBITIONS
1874, London, Royal Academy, Summer Exhibition (no. 303)
1907, London, Royal Academy, Winter Exhibition (no. 163)

REFERENCES
Ormond 1975, pp. 98, 162, no. 218
E. Rhys, *Frederic, Lord Leighton, P.R.A.*, revised ed., London, 1900, pp. 29, 33
A. Corkran, *Frederic Leighton*, London, 1904, p. 101
Mrs Russell Barrington, *Life, Letters and Work of Frederic Leighton*, London, 1906, II, p. 205
E. Staley, *Lord Leighton of Stretton, P.R.A.*, London, 1906, p. 95
A. L. Baldry, *Leighton* (Masterpieces in Colour series), London, 1908, ill. opp. p. 24 (as *Gathering Citrons*)

## 66†

## Portions of the Interior of the Grand Mosque of Damascus 1873–75

158 × 120 cm
Harris Museum and Art Gallery, Preston, Lancs.
[repr. in colour on p. 66, plate 88]

The 'Great Mosque', as it is now usually known, was built on the site of the Basilica of the Head of John the Baptist during the Caliphate of Walid I (705–15). Leighton's picture is based on a small oil sketch made on the spot during his 1873 visit to Damascus (Ormond 1975, no. 217), studies of the *minbar*, hanging lamp and other details in one of his notebooks now at the Royal Academy (vol. IX), and possibly photographs (see Barrington, 1906, II, p. 208). Although the architecture is accurately recorded, the figures are implausible: the two Muslim men would not be praying in different directions, the faces of the girls on the left would be covered, and as females they would never be walking around on the mosque's main floor.    M.W.

PROVENANCE
By 1897, Lord Armstrong; 1910, 24 June, his sale Christie's, London (lot 73) acquired by the Harris Museum and Art Gallery, Preston, Lancs.

EXHIBITIONS
1875, London, Royal Academy, Summer Exhibition (no. 215)
1897, London, Royal Academy, *Exhibition of Works by the late Lord Leighton of Stretton* (no. 71)
1906, London, Royal Academy, Winter Exhibition (no. 134)
1980, Royal Institute of British Architects, *George Aitcheson*

REFERENCES
Ormond 1975, pp. 98, 162, no. 216, ill. pl. 138
E. Rhys, *Frederic, Lord Leighton*, revised ed., London, 1900, pp. 29, 33, 111, ill. opp. p. 28
Mrs Russell Barrington, *Life, Letters and Works of Frederic Leighton*, London, 1906, II, p. 206
E. Staley, *Lord Leighton of Stretton, P.R.A.*, London, 1906, pp. 97–98
*Preston Guardian*, 2 July, 1910

66

## Lewis, John Frederick    1805–1876

Born in London, J. F. Lewis seems to have received little art education beyond that offered by his father, an engraver. By the age of twenty-one, he had decided to concentrate upon painting in watercolour, a medium particularly suited to his abilities, and in which he was to achieve his fame. Lewis spent most of his middle years abroad. He stayed for almost two years in Spain and Morocco from 1832 to 1834, and in 1837 he left England and spent the next fourteen years travelling through Italy, Greece and the Levant before finally setting up house in Cairo in 1841. Tantalisingly little is known about Lewis's decade in Egypt, although the last chapter of Thackeray's *Notes of a Journey from Cornhill to Grand Cairo* (London, 1846) gives a vivid account of the author's visit to the artist in 1844, when Thackeray found Lewis living in great style in a large Mamlūk house in the Ezbekiya quarter of Cairo, 'going about with a great beard and dressed up like an odious Turk' (p. 290).

The watercolours of Egypt that Lewis exhibited in the years following his return to England in 1851 earned him great critical acclaim, but, disheartened by the lack of financial reward, he turned to oil painting in the late 1850s. Thenceforth, Lewis was a regular contributor to the Royal Academy, but retained an habitual aloofness from the London art scene at his house in Walton-on-Thames.

ABBREVIATED REFERENCE
Lewis 1978 Major-General Michael Lewis, CBE, *John Frederick Lewis, R.A., 1805–1876*, Leigh-on-Sea, 1978

## 67*

## A Frank Encampment in the Desert of Mount Sinai, 1842 – The Convent of St. Catherine in the distance    1856

Watercolour and bodycolour: 64·8 × 134·3 cm
Signed and dated bottom right: *J.F. Lewis 1856*
The Yale Center for British Art, Paul Mellon Collection
[repr. in colour on p. 51, plate 89]

When this painting was first exhibited at the Old Water-Colour Society it drew volumes of praise from Ruskin, who wrote, 'I have no hesitation in ranking it among the most *wonderful* pictures in the world; nor do I believe that since the death of Veronese anything has been painted comparable to it in its own way.' What caught the critic's imagination was the extraordinary combination of microscopic detail and compositional unity and breadth, and the painting still ranks as Lewis's most outstanding achievement.

The Englishman in the picture is Lord Castlereagh, whose Near Eastern journey is recorded in his *Diary of a Journey to Damascus*, 1847. Castlereagh and his retinue, which included Count von Pahlen, A. Schranz (his hired artist), Mr Tardew (his physician), Shaykh Hussein (his guide) and Mahmoud (his dragoman), set off from Cairo to Damascus across the Sinai desert in mid-May, 1842, and spent five days encamped at Mount Sinai at the end of the month. In a letter to Lewis he commissioned the artist, for the generous fee of 200 guineas, to paint his portrait with his companions before he left Cairo, and the artist was free to decide upon the setting (quoted *Country*

*Life,* 21 June 1979). Lewis had already sketched some members of the party before they went, but it is not certain if he actually observed the group *in situ.* He may simply have drawn upon his sketches of the Sinai desert and of the monastery of St. Catherine made on another, undated, trip. The painting does not seem to have been finished until fourteen years after the original commission, despite Castlereagh's plea for an early completion date.

As Ruskin was quick to note, the picture is far from being a straightforward portrait. It represents a meeting between East and West, with Shaykh Hussein, whose homeland was Mount Sinai, standing on the left with the camels, and Castlereagh, dressed in Eastern clothes, recumbent amidst the Western refinements of books, furniture, a newspaper, a map and a bottle of 'Harvey's' on the right. The dead game represents the outcome of a day's shooting, a popular pastime among Western tourists. In the background is the monastery of St. Catherine (see Cat. 11), whose monks frequently extended their hospitality to travellers; the Christian shrines of the Chapel of the Burning Bush and the Tomb of St. Catherine were housed in the monastery, which stood alongside a mosque.

An oil replica of the painting (present location unknown) was exhibited at the Royal Academy in 1863.   C.B.

PROVENANCE
1860, sold by G. R. Burnett; G. W. Moss; 1919, sold by C. D. Rudd; Mrs. Fiona Campbell-Blair; 1968, 4 April, Sotheby's, London (lot 76); R. T. Laughton; 1976, 14 April, Sotheby's, London (lot 68) bought by the Fine Art Society; 1977, gift of Paul Mellon to the Yale Center for British Art

EXHIBITIONS
1856, London, Old Water-Colour Society (no. 134)
1868, Leeds Art Gallery, *Exhibition of Works of Art*
1886, Liverpool, Walker Art Gallery, *Grand Loan Exhibition of Pictures* (no. 982)
1887, Manchester, *Royal Jubilee Exhibition*
1892, Southport, *Centenary Exhibition*
1970, Scarborough Art Gallery, *Paintings from the Collection of R. T. Laughton Esq.* (no. 50)
1971, Newcastle, Laing Art Gallery, *J. F. Lewis* (no. 74)
1981, New Haven, Yale Center for British Art, *Works of Splendor and Imagination* (no. 80)

REFERENCES
Lewis 1978, pp. 28, 40 (no. 564), fig. 47
J. Ruskin, *Academy Notes on some of the Principal Pictures,* 1856, reprinted in Cook and Wedderburn, *The Works of John Ruskin,* London, 1903–12, XIV, pp. 73–78
J. L. Roget, *A History of the Old Water-Colour Society,* London, 1891, II, pp. 145–46
R. Davies, 'John Frederick Lewis R.A. 1805–76', London, *Old Water-Colour Society's Club,* 1926, III, pp. 35–36, 39–40, ill. pl. VI
Major-General Michael Lewis, letter in *Country Life,* 21 June 1979
R. Searight, 'An Anonymous Traveller Rediscovered', *Country Life,* 4 May, 1979
K. Bendiner, 'The Portrayal of the Middle-East in British Painting, 1835–1860', Ph.D. thesis, Columbia University, 1979, p. 213 ff.

## 68

# In the Bezestein, El Khan Khalil, Cairo   1860
## (The Carpet Seller)

Oil on panel: 58·5 × 45·7 cm
Signed and dated bottom left: *J. F. Lewis 1860*
Private Collection
[*repr. in colour on p. 46, plate 90*]

This picture was exhibited at the Royal Academy in 1861 as *In the Bezestein, El Khan Khalil, Cairo,* and it is closely related in setting to the later *The Bezestein Bazaar* (Cat. 74), which seems to represent a longer view of the same street, including the same arch at the centre of the composition. Lewis frequently painted the two main Cairo bazaars, the Khān al-Khalīlī (of which the Bezestein is a part) and the Ghawriyyah. The Khān al-Khalīlī, built in medieval times, specialised in the sale of swords, slippers, embroidered goods, silks and fabrics from Constantinople. The old gentleman in this picture is resplendent in Turkish dress, complete with sword.

68

67

The painting was done soon after Lewis took the decision to abandon watercolours in favour of oils, and his consequent resignation from the Presidency of the Old Water-Colour Society in 1858. Although he had achieved fame with the exquisite watercolours exhibited on his return from Egypt, such as *The Hhareem* (1850; ? destroyed) and *A Frank Encampment* (1856; Cat. 67), he soon tired both of the labour that they cost him and of the fact that working in this medium was so 'thoro'ly unremunerative . . . no rest and such little pay' (Lewis 1978). But this painting, with its small, precise, touch and beautifully-observed detail, is very much closer in approach to the watercolours than the later oils, where the handling is broader and sketchy passages may be seen. It was Lewis's avowed intention, at the outset of his experiment with oils, to finish his paintings with as smooth a surface as possible. Holman Hunt recorded a meeting between Millais and Lewis in which the latter berated the Pre-Raphaelites for their lack of delicacy in oils, and in which he declared that he felt oils should not be more 'piled up' than watercolours. In other respects, Lewis admired the work of the Pre-Raphaelites, thinking that they represented the most promising development in English art, but his own approach to painting, though similar, was arrived at independently.   C.B.

PROVENANCE
Sir Thomas Devitt, Bart; 1924, 16 May, Christie's, London (lot 119); acquired by Leggatt; 1976, 24 November, Sotheby's, London (lot 303)

EXHIBITIONS
1861, London, Royal Academy, Summer Exhibition (no. 266)
1978, London, The Fine Art Society, *Eastern Encounters* (no. 45; ill. p. 46)

REFERENCES
Lewis 1978, no. 582
P. and V. Berko, *La Peinture Orientaliste*, Brussels, 1982, ill. p. 80

## 69†

# Edfou, Upper Egypt   1860

Oil on panel: 30 × 76 cm
Signed and dated bottom left: *J. F. Lewis 1860*
The Trustees of the Tate Gallery
[*repr. in colour on p. 51, plate 91*]

The temple of Edfou, a Ptolemaic structure of later construction than many of the temples along the Nile, resembles Dendarah (see Cat. 88) in date, plan and mythology, and, like that temple, bears many well-preserved inscriptions. In the nineteenth century Edfou was considered one of the most beautiful monuments on the Nile, but the subject was unusual for Lewis, who painted few strictly topographical views while in Egypt. It seems likely that he had been stung by Ruskin's review of *Waiting for the Ferry* (present location unknown), exhibited at the Royal Academy in 1859, in which the critic had lamented Lewis's restricted subject-matter and constant dwelling upon Arabs and camels, and urged him to paint the 'Sphinx, and the temples, and the hieroglyphics, and the mirage and the simoun, and everything that we want to know about' (*Academy Notes*, reprinted in E.T. Cook and A. Wedderburn, *The Works of John Ruskin*, 1903–12, vol. XIV, pp. 218–99). Lewis accordingly included a temple in this work, shown the following year, although the painting received no comment from Ruskin, who wrote no *Academy Notes* in 1860.

The painting is far from being a conventionalised, topographical work, however, in that the architecture is subservient to the anecdote of the Bedouin encampment in the foreground. A preliminary sketch of Edfou drawn from the same viewpoint (H. Stokes, 'John Frederick Lewis, R.A. (1805–1876)', *Walker's Quarterly*, no. 28, 1929, ill. facing p. 19) seems to indicate that Lewis moved the minaret to the right in order to accommodate the tent in the finished painting, and so include elements of the ancient (the temple), medieval (the mosque) and modern (the tent). The juxtaposition of modern Egyptian life and ancient Egyptian civilisation is one that frequently occurs in the work of other artists (eg. David Roberts, *q.v.*), often implying some criticism of contemporary Egyptians who failed to live up to the ideals established by their illustrious ancestors. But there is no such moralising intention in Lewis's canvas. In pictorial terms, the painting represents no radical departure; the camel is identical to one that had appeared in the watercolour *A Halt in the Desert* (1855; Victoria and Albert Museum, London) some five years previously, and the recumbent Arab in the foreground is highly reminiscent of a figure in *Waiting for the Ferry*.

There is a watercolour version of the right side of the picture in a private collection and a similar, but smaller watercolour of the whole composition was sold at Christie's in 1981.   C.B.

PROVENANCE
1894, 6 February, bought from H. Roberts by Agnew's, London; 1894, 22 February, purchased by the Tate Gallery (Clarke Fund)

EXHIBITION
1860, London, Royal Academy, Summer Exhibition (no. 350)

REFERENCES
Lewis 1978, p. 40 (no. 584), fig. 60
K. Bendiner, 'The Portrayal of the Middle-East in British Painting, 1835–1860', Ph.D thesis, Columbia University, 1979, p. 234

69

## 70

### The Hósh (Courtyard) of the House of the Coptic Patriarch, Cairo; the patriarch is dictating to his secretary despatches to a convent in the desert, to be conveyed by the Arabs in waiting    1864

81 × 109 cm
Signed bottom left: *J. F. Lewis*
Private Collection
*[repr. in colour on p. 48, plate 92]*

The juxtaposition of one race or creed with another is a theme in several paintings by Lewis. In this example the group of Copts around their patriarch face the Bedouin messengers waiting beside their camels; to the right, a venerable *ḥājj* (identified by his green turban) sits in front of a young Nubian slave; in the left foreground a boy and an unveiled girl, probably Copts, feed the animals. The impression of variety and abundance in this crowded scene reflects the heterogeneity to be found outside in the streets of Cairo. Lewis was probably also aware of William Holman Hunt's *Afterglow in Egypt* (Cat. 53) representing a young Egyptian girl surrounded by pigeons which, although not exhibited until 1864, had been published seven years earlier as an etching entitled *The Abundance of Egypt*.

By placing the animals so prominently in the foreground of his composition, Lewis deliberately displays his virtuosity in rendering texture and pattern. Other decorative elements such as the reflections in the water, the brightly coloured costumes and rugs, the architecture and the foliage of the tree are also carefully rendered, but some of the figures, notably the faces of the girl and of *ḥājj*, are clumsily executed, and appear unfinished.

The scene is almost exactly described by Thackeray who visited Lewis in Cairo in 1844: 'First we came to a broad open court with a covered gallery running along one side of it. A camel was reclining on the grass there; near him there was a gazelle to glad J. with his dark blue eye . . . On the opposite side

to the covered gallery rose up the walls of his long, queer, many-windowed, many-galleried house. There were wooden lattices to those arched windows through the diamonds of which I saw two of the most beautiful, enormous ogling black eyes in the world, looking down upon the interesting strangers. Pigeons were flapping and hopping and fluttering, and cooing about. Happy pigeons you are, no doubt, fed with the crumbs from the henna-tipped fingers of Zuleikah' (*Notes on a Journey from Cornhill to Grand Cairo*, London, 1845, pp. 284–85).

The painting shown here does indeed depict the courtyard of Lewis's house. This is confirmed by a drawing reliably entitled *Courtyard of the Painter's House, Cairo* (Victoria and Albert Museum, London, E. 5680–1910). The house was built in Mamlūk style, one of many houses still standing in Lewis's day (Lane 1836, I, pp. 6–24) and was almost certainaly situated in the Esbekiya district of Cairo (see Artist's sale, 1877, lot 176, *Interior of Upper Room in a House, Esbekieh, Cairo, occupied by J. F. Lewis, R.A.*). This area underwent much reconstruction later in the century and it is unlikely that the house still exists.

Since Lewis was generally accurate in his representation of Cairo scenes, the title he gave to his picture for the 1864 Royal Academy exhibition is puzzling. It is possible that his house was owned by the Coptic Patriarch. It may have been the same house as that which was later occupied by another British resident in Cairo, a Mr Lockwood, and which was visited and drawn by Thomas Seddon in 1854 (J. P. Seddon, *Memoir and Letters of the late Thomas Seddon*, London, 1858, p. 38; Seddon's *Interior of a Deewan, formerly belonging to Copt Patriarch, near the Esbekeeyah, Cairo* [present location unknown], exhibited 1856, Royal Academy, no. 895).

A large unfinished watercolour version of this painting (City Museums and Art Gallery, Birmingham, no. 44/48) was mistitled before 1948 as *House of the Sheikh Amin-al-Suhaimi, Barb-al-Asfar, Cairo*. This house is another characteristic Mamlūk dwelling which has survived, but it is in a different part of the old city (J. Revault and B. Maury, *Palais et Maisons du Caire du XIV<sup>e</sup> au XVIII<sup>e</sup> siècle*, Cairo, I, 1975, pl. LVI, fig. 27; see also a drawing

70

by James Wild, 1842, Victoria and Albert Museum, London, E.3766–1938).

A small oil version also exists (Tate Gallery, London, no. 1688) which although more evenly executed is apparently a finished study for the exhibited painting (see Leverhulme sale, 1926, lot 171, ill. as 110·5 × 106·7 cm). The top of the painting shown here has been cut. The same courtyard, viewed from the *maq'ad* (gallery), also appears in a late oil, *The Mid-Day Meal, Cairo* (1875; Owen Edgar Gallery, London).  B.L.

PROVENANCE
1875, William Leaf; Ralph Brocklebank; 1893, L. Huth; 1909, Holbrook Gaskell; 1924, Sir Thomas Devitt; 1926, 1st Viscount Leverhulme; 1926, 18 February, his sale, Anderson Galleries, New York (lot 171); Brooklyn Paramount Theatre, New York; 1976, 24 November, Sotheby's, London (lot 307); acquired by the present owner

EXHIBITIONS
1864, London, Royal Academy, Summer Exhibition (lot 110)
1878, Paris, *Exposition Universelle*
1901, London, Royal Academy, *Exhibition of Works by British Artists deceased since 1850* (no. 33)
1901, Glasgow, *International Exhibition* (no. 13)

REFERENCES
Lewis 1978, no. 590
*Athenaeum*, 7 May 1864, p. 651
*Art Journal*, 1864, pp. 157, 166

71*

# A Turkish School in the Vicinity of Cairo   1865

Oil on panel: 66 × 118 cm
Signed and dated bottom left: *J. F. LEWIS 1865*
Private Collection, Houston, Texas
[*repr. in colour on p. 49, plate 93*]

Painted fifteen years after Lewis's return from Egypt, this picture is based on an earlier watercolour of 1853 which is far simpler in conception, with plain glass windows in place of the elaborate *mashrabiyyahs* and no ornamentation on the chest upon which the scribe leans. In the oil painting, Lewis was unable to resist his customary portrayal of the delicate play of light through the lattice work and the patterns it forms on the carpet. The setting is similar to many other paintings by Lewis, and was probably assembled from elements in the artist's own home in Cairo. The figure of the scribe is related to a drawing Lewis had made in Broussa (present location unknown) and he also reappears in Lewis's *The Commentator on the Qur'ān* (1869; Priv. Coll.).

The children are probably the sons and daughters of the Turkish middle classes in Cairo, their wholesome appearance contrasting strongly with contemporary descriptions of Egyptian children, who were often left unwashed and disease-ridden in order to avert the evil eye. Mid-nineteenth-century accounts of education in Egypt stress that reading and writing were unusual accomplishments for girls, and female illiteracy is referred to in paintings of the period (see Cat. 73, 100). However, Edward Lane conceded that some privileged girls were occasionally taught with boys in a public school, although they were generally veiled and had little to do with the opposite sex (Lane, 1835, I, pp. 57–70). Islamic education consisted of memorising and reciting passages of the *Qur'ān* and certain prayers. Accordingly, there is a *Qur'ānic* inscription on the wall behind the schoolmaster that reads, 'There is no God but God, and Muḥammad is his prophet. In the name of God, the compassionate, the merciful, and praise be to God, the Lord of the faithful.' A government certificate on the wall probably proclaims the proficiency of the teacher.

Cats and birds frequently appear in Lewis's work (Cat. 70), but here the placing of the drowsy cat perilously near the pigeons forms an amusing analogy with the children under the watchful eyes of the schoolmaster and his stick.

There is an undated and virtually identical watercolour in the Victoria and Albert Museum, London.   C.B.

PROVENANCE
C. P. Matthews; 1891, 6 June, Christie's, London, acquired by Mr Vokins; Stephen G. Holland; 1908, 25 June, Christie's, London (lot 68), acquired by the Rt. Hon. Lord Joicey; 1955, 13 May, Christie's, London, acquired by The Fine Art Society; F. C. Stringer; Priv. Coll., Houston, Texas

EXHIBITIONS
1865, London, Royal Academy, Summer Exhibition (no. 121)
1895, London, The Guildhall (no. 49)
1901, London, Royal Academy, Winter Exhibition (no. 26)
1971, Newcastle, Laing Art Gallery, *J. F. Lewis R.A.* (no. 80)

REFERENCE
Lewis 1978, pp. 53, 95, 96 (no. 595)

71

## 72

# A Mamlūk Bay, Egypt    1868

Oil on panel: 35·4 × 24·9 cm
Signed and dated bottom left: *J. F. Lewis 1868*
Inscribed on the *verso*: *A Mimlook*
Private Collection
[*repr. in colour on p. 91, plate 94*]

When this painting was first shown at the Royal Academy in
1869, it bore the title *A Memlook Bey, Egypt*. 'Memlooks', or
Mamlūks, were a people of Turkish origin who had originally
been brought to Egypt as slaves. They gradually rose above their
humble station in the social hierarchy to become the virtual rulers
of Cairo by the end of the eighteenth century, a development
that was halted by Muḥammad 'Alī during the early nineteenth
century. When Lewis was resident in Egypt in the 1840s there
were still a number of Mamlūks holding positions of distinction
in the army or administration; the title of 'Bay' was conferred
on some of those who achieved this eminence.

 Mamlūks were traditionally fair-skinned, but this sitter, like so
many of Lewis's models, has a rather British air about him.
Almost two decades after his return from Egypt, Lewis was
undoubtedly relying upon British models as well as his Egyptian
sketches to furnish material for his oil paintings. The Mamlūk
also bears more than a passing resemblance to the seated Pasha
in *The Hhareem* (1850; Victoria and Albert Museum, London),
providing another example of how Lewis constantly re-used the
same figures in his work. The Mamlūk's costume is a mixture of
authentic detail and artistic licence, and is probably based upon
one of the many costumes that Lewis brought back from Egypt
(some of which he wore to fancy-dress parties). The scimitar is
of Ottoman origin and the cloak a plausible garment, but the
paisley turban is somewhat unlikely.   C.B.

PROVENANCE
1973, 15 June, Christie's, London (lot 52) bought by Colnaghi; Priv. Coll.
EXHIBITIONS
1869, London, Royal Academy, Summer Exhibition (no. 876)
1973, London, Colnaghi, *English Drawings, Watercolours and Paintings* (ill. XLV)
REFERENCE
Lewis 1978 (no. 601)

## 73*

# An Intercepted Correspondence, Cairo    1869

Oil on panel: 74·3 × 87·3 cm
Signed bottom left: *J. F. Lewis R.A.*
Private Collection, Houston, Texas
[*repr. in colour on p. 50, plate 95*]

*An Intercepted Correspondence, Cairo* is one of many paintings by
Lewis that depict harem life, but unlike most other harem
pictures, it presents a narrative. A woman of the harem has just
been discovered in possession of an illicit love-message in the
form of a bunch of flowers, but the identity of the intended
recipient remains something of a mystery. When the painting
was first reviewed in the *Athenaeum* (1869), it was suggested that
the girl in green in the centre of the painting, discovered with
the flowers by the woman grasping her wrist, had merely been
acting as an intermediary; the message was destined for the
woman seated on the floor, shielding her eyes with her hand, a
gesture which was interpreted as one of shame. However, her
jovial expression, and the fact that she may simply be protecting
her eyes from the sun filtering through the lattice work,
somewhat undermine this interpretation; the girl in green may
herself be the guilty party.

 The picture revolves around the notion that flowers were the
love-letters of the illiterate in Near Eastern countries, and this
would have been understood by Lewis's public. A number of
popular books on the subject were published in mid-Victorian
England, for example, *The Language of Flowers* published in 1869
by *The Young Ladies' Journal*, whose preface proclaimed that this
form of communication originated in the East and had been
popularised in England by Lady Mary Wortley Montague. The
book's glossary could lead to the following interpretation of the
flowers in the bouquet. The pansy, or heart's ease, exhorts the
receiver to think of the giver, the anenome signifies that the giver
feels forsaken, the *hibiscus syriacum* pays homage to the woman's
delicate beauty and the roses probably symbolise love. In the
vase beside the master of the harem stand larkspur (haughtiness),
a rose (love) and a scarlet dahlia (instability), suitable attributes
for an outraged husband.

72

73

The mood of this painting is gently humorous, reminiscent of the amusing tales related by writers such as Gérard de Nerval and Lady Mary Wortley Montague of amorous escapades conducted by ladies of the harem who were able to reach their rendezvous undetected because of their veils. Certainly, the picture gives no hint of the drastic punishments of divorce, and sometimes death, that actually accompanied the discovery of a woman's adultery. Lewis's attitude towards Near Eastern women, and his pictorial treatment of such themes, is far closer to that of his French contemporaries who delighted in the colourful and erotic possibilities inherent in the depiction of harem life (see Cat. 56), than that of his fellow English artists, many of whom were appalled by the oppressive nature of this social institution.

The left side of the picture is very similar, but not identical, to the watercolour of *The Hhareem* (1850; Victoria and Albert Museum, London).   C.B.

PROVENANCE
Bought from the artist by Charles P. Matthews; 1891, 6 June, Christie's, London (lot 71), acquired by Agnew's; William Kenrick and thence by descent to Hugh Kenrick; 1979, 25 May, Christie's, London (lot 259); Priv. Coll., Houston, Texas

EXHIBITIONS
1869, London, Royal Academy, Summer Exhibition (no. 157)
1906, London, Royal Academy, (no. 109)
1920, Birmingham, City Museum and Art Gallery, on loan
1953, Birmingham, City Museum and Art Gallery, *Works of Art from Midland Homes* (no. 48)
1968, Sheffield, Mappin Art Gallery, *Victorian Paintings* (no. 71)
1971, Newcastle, Laing Art Gallery, *J. F. Lewis R.A.* (no. 83)

REFERENCES
Lewis 1978 (no. 602)
*Athenaeum*, 1869, p. 674
*Art Journal*, 1869, p. 167
K. Bendiner, 'The Portrayal of the Middle-East in British Painting 1830–1860', Ph.D. thesis, Columbia University, 1979, pp. 200 ff.

74

## 74

# The Bezestein Bazaar of El Khan Khalil, Cairo 1872

Oil on panel: 113 × 85 cm
Signed and dated bottom left: *J. F. Lewis 1872*
Private Collection
[*repr. in colour on p. 47, plate 96*]

This crowded composition, in which the brilliant reds and blues of the costumes stand out against the sombre background of the covered bazaar, matches Gérard de Nerval's description of the Bezestein bazaar given in *Voyage en Orient*, in which he likens the streets to those of *The Arabian Nights* with their 'narrow dark passages, overhung with cage-like windows, like our own streets from the middle-ages. The freshness of these almost subterranean ways is a refuge from the heat of the Egyptian sun' (Paris, 1958 ed., I, p. 173).

When the picture was first exhibited, its departure from Lewis's usual approach was noted. The reviewer for the *Art Journal* commented, 'We have been so long accustomed to discourse with Mr Lewis over his small pieces of microscopic finish, that anything larger brings with it a surprise for which there has been no preparation' (1874). Most reviewers spoke favourably of the animation of the composition, although others found the colours strident. The greatest accolade came from a Scottish collector who saw the work at the Royal Academy's private view. Thomas Woolner recalled the episode in a letter to Lewis: 'Old Mr Graham of Glasgow, who has the most wonderful picture Turner ever painted, and also the beautiful Gainsborough of *Two Ladies* which cost him last year nearly £7,000 – he asked me to point out to him any remarkable work, and on enquiring I found that he had not seen your Cairo picture. I took him to it and pointed out with a great deal of satisfaction what struck me as its most prominent characteristics and beauties . . . I told him a work so entirely unique and original, and of such quality in art could not be valued in money, however large the sum . . . He looked at it much longer and asked me if I thought he could get it for £10,000, for he would willingly give it if it were possible to buy it' (Woolner MS., Major-General J. M. H. Lewis Coll.). Graham's attempt to purchase the painting was frustrated by the fact that the owner, David Price, refused to part with it. Woolner's anecdote both delighted and amazed Lewis, who was by 1874 an invalid recluse, suffering from serious doubts that all he had accomplished had been futile.

A similar, but smaller, watercolour is in the Cecil Higgins Art Gallery, Bedford.   C.B.

PROVENANCE
1872, David Price; 1892, Thomas Woolner, R.A.; 1895, C. D. Rudd; 1920, Lord Leverhulme; 1925, David Grieg; acquired by the present owner

EXHIBITIONS
1874, London, Royal Academy, Summer Exhibition (no. 332)
1887, Manchester, Jubilee Exhibition (no. 873)
1893, London, Burlington House, Winter Exhibition (no. 45)
1910, London, Shepherds Bush–White City, Great Japan British Exhibition
1971, Newcastle, Laing Art Gallery, *J. F. Lewis R.A.* (no. 87)
1980, London, The Fine Art Society, *Travellers Beyond the Grand Tour* (no. 20)

REFERENCE
Lewis 1978, p. 98, ill. pl. 65

# Marilhat, Prosper-Georges-Antoine
1811–1847

Born in Vertaizon (Auvergne), Marilhat was a pupil of Roqueplan and made his debut at the Salon of 1831 with a landscape of the Auvergne. In this year he joined the scientific expedition of Baron Karl von Hügel, travelling to Greece, Syria, the Lebanon, Palestine and Egypt, where the two men parted company; von Hügel continued his journey as far as India, while Marilhat remained in the Near East for a further twenty-two months.

The ten albums of sketches and drawings made during this, his only trip to the Orient, provided inspiration and material for his subsequent work, and although he specialised in landscapes and architectural paintings he also executed several portraits, including those of Muḥammad ʿAlī, and his friend Chassériau (1834; Louvre), as well as two decorative schemes for the theatre in Alexandria.

From 1840 to 1844, Marilhat drew most intensely from his experiences in Egypt and won great critical acclaim at the Salon of 1844 with his *Souvenir des bords du Nil* (present location unknown), and *Arabes syriens en voyage* (Musée Condé, Chantilly). He did not, however, devote himself entirely to Orientalist paintings, but continued to exhibit landscapes of Provence and his native Auvergne, particularly from 1846 onwards.

Though he died young, at the age of thirty-six, Marilhat was greatly admired by the next generation of Orientalist landscape painters and exercised a profound influence on the early work of Fromentin and Pissarro.

75

## Ruins of the al-Hākim Mosque, Cairo    1840
*Ruines de la mosquée du Kalife Hakem au Caire*

84·5 × 130·7 cm
Signed bottom left: *Marilhat*
Musée du Louvre, Paris

The Fātimid Mosque of al-Hākim (built 990–1013) lies inside the north wall of Cairo between the two great gates, the Bāb al-Futūh (Gate of Conquest) and the Bāb al-Nasr (Gate of Victory) to the east. Although much dilapidated and almost completely abandoned by the nineteenth century, it continued to attract artists and writers with its echoes of the grandeur of bygone civilisations. The artist, Lenoir, visited the mosque on a tour of Egypt and the Sinai in 1868–69, and Gérard de Nerval wrote at great length on Caliph al-Hākim in *Druses et Maronites* (1847).

This painting, exhibited at the Salon of 1840 as *Ruines d'une ancienne mosquée dans la ville des tombeaux au Caire*, captures both the monumentality of the ruins and the romanticism of the location. A preliminary drawing (Musée Fabre, Montpellier; inv. no. 876-3-120) shows Marilhat's initial concern accurately to record details of the architecture and topography. At a later stage, figures were added, the buildings originally visible in the background were transformed into misty ruins, and the shading became more expressive, thus enhancing the atmospheric effects of the scene. Théophile Gautier was deeply impressed by the evocative power of Marilhat's Near Eastern landscapes and recalled the effect of his *Place de l'Esbekieh au Caire* (present location unknown), exhibited at the Salon the year after his

return to France: 'On seeing this painting I became sick at heart, and yearned for an Orient in which I had not yet set foot' (July 1848, pp. 56–57). The freshness of the delicate pearl-grey tonalities so keenly observed by Gautier were characteristic of Marilhat's work of this period and were largely attributable to his preparation of the ground using bitumen, Cassel red, and broad touches of lacquer.

Marilhat's oeuvre falls into at least three different stylistic periods. The fairly traditional treatment of the early landscapes and portraits gives way to the luminosity and elegant draughtsmanship of his Orientalist work, while after 1838, under the influence of Cabat and his friend d'Augny, his work became somewhat mannered. In mythological works, such as *Paysage pastoral de la Grèce* (Salon, 1837; Musée Tessé, Le Mans) or the *Nymphes dans une clairière* (Salon, 1839; Musée Bargoin, Clermont-Ferrand), which were badly received by critics, Marilhat sought more self-consciously to achieve a grand manner reminiscent of Poussin. Towards the end of his life, as he retreated into a state of insanity, his colouristic preoccupations predominated and his style became more abstract.    J.M.

PROVENANCE
1877, 23 April, acquired at the Oppenheim sale by the Louvre

EXHIBITIONS
1840, Paris, Salon (no. 1148)
1928, Cairo, *Exposition d'Art français, 1827–1927* (no. 65)
1930, Paris, *Centenaire de l'Algérie*
1931, Paris, Musée des Colonies, *Exposition coloniale*
1947, Paris, Musée de la France d'Outre-Mer, *Histoire de l'exotisme*
1949, Paris, Musée des Arts Décoratifs, *France-Egypte*
1955, Paris, Bibliothèque Nationale, *Gérard de Nerval* (no. 186)
1955, Nantes, Musée des Beaux-Arts
1955, Caen, Musée des Beaux-Arts
1960, Brest, Musée des Beaux-Arts
1971–72, Paris, *Quelques Aspects du Paysage Français du XXe siècle*
1973, Clermont-Ferrand, Musée Bargoin, *Marilhat* (no. 8, ill.)
1975, Marseille, Musée Cantini, *L'Orient en question* (no. 108, ill.)
1982, Rochester, New York, Memorial Art Gallery, *Orientalism* (no. 31)

REFERENCES
Thornton 1983, ill. pp. 34–35
Th. Gautier, 'Marilhat', *Revue des Deux Mondes*, July 1848, pp. 56–75
E. Feydeau, 'Voyages à travers les collections particulières de Paris', *L'Artiste*, 1858, III, pp. 269–71
H. Gomot, *Marilhat et son oeuvre*, Clermont-Ferrand, 1884, pp. 87, 99
J.M. Carré, *Voyageurs et écrivains français en Egypte*, Cairo, 1932, I, pp. 209–10
D. Menu, 'Prosper Marilhat (1811–1847) Essai de Catalogue', Université de Dijon, U.E.R. de Sciences Humaines, 1972, p. 84, no. 228
P. Miquel, *Le Paysage français au XIXe siècle 1824–74. L'Ecole de nature*, Paris, 1975, pp. 346–59

75

# Matisse, Henri   1869–1954

Born at Le Cateau-Cambressis (Nord), Matisse moved to Paris in 1887 to study law. He began painting in 1890, and the following year he enrolled as a student of Bouguereau at the Académie Julian, Paris. In 1982 he transferred to the atelier of Gustave Moreau at the Ecole des Beaux-Arts, where he met the future Fauve painters, Marquet and Manguin. He made his debut at the Salon du Champs de Mars in 1896 with four paintings, and three years later met Derain, and then Vlaminck in 1901. Having spent most of 1898 in the south, Matisse acquired a taste for this region, working from 1904 at Collioure and St. Tropez with Signac and Derain, and then regularly at other places along the Riviera. Matisse visited Morocco briefly in 1906, and returned for two further visits during 1912. From 1901 he exhibited at the Salon des Indépendants and from 1903 at the Salon d'Automne. His work was collected by German, Russian and American patrons and included easel paintings, sculpture, ceramics and large-scale decorative works.

ABBREVIATED REFERENCES
Barr 1951 H. Barr, *The Art of Henri Matisse*, New York, 1951
Luzi 1971 M. Luzi, *L'Opera di Matisse: rivolta 'fauve' all' intimisme*, Milan, 1971

76*

## The Blue Nude – Souvenir of Biskra   1907
*Le Nu bleu – souvenir de Biskra*

92·1 × 121·6 cm
Signed bottom right: *Henri Matisse*   *c.* 1927 at the request of Claribal Cone via Michael Stein (see Cone Archives, Correspondence, Michael Stein to Etta Cone, 8 December 1926)
The Baltimore Museum of Art: The Cone Collection, formed by Dr. Claribel Cone and Miss Etta Cone of Baltimore, Maryland (BMA 1950.228)
[*repr. in colour on p. 108, plate 98*]

Matisse was already an established member of the Fauve group when he visited North Africa for the first time in 1906. He spent two brief weeks in Biskra and Algiers. His stated intention for the trip was 'to see the desert' (quoted Barr 1951, p. 83, n.5). In effect, the immediate impact of the encounter with the Orient was the execution of a few sketches (eg. *Alger, paysage*, 1906, Statens Museum fur Kunst, Copenhagen) and the purchase of contemporary pottery and textiles which he introduced into a series of still-lifes executed on his return to Collioure (eg., *Le Tapis rouge*, 1906, Musée de Peinture et de Sculpture, Grenoble).

One year later, in early spring, he executed *The Blue Nude – Souvenir of Biskra*. Apart from the palm fronds in the background, there is little in this painting to demonstrate the direct impact of North Africa. Painted in Collioure, it was linked to two recent technical innovations in Matisse's work: the execution in 1906 of three, harshly primitivising linoleum prints, which were exhibited together with *The Blue Nude – Souvenir of Biskra* at the Salon des Indépendants, 1907, and a group of fifteen to twenty sculptures created between 1905 and 1907. The pose of the nude in the painting is in part based upon one of these sculptures, *Reclining Nude*, which Matisse was modelling in clay in early 1907 before starting on this painting. The accidental partial destruction of this piece unintentionally turned *The Blue Nude – Souvenir of Biskra* into a painting which was both based upon a sculpture and became in turn the study for the reconstruction of the original damaged work.

76

The colour of this nude is said to have been determined by a friendly competition with his fellow Fauve artist, Derain, as to who could paint the best figure in blue. When Derain saw *The Blue Nude – Souvenir of Biskra*, he apparently destroyed his own canvas (H. Purrmann, quoted Barr 1951, p. 94, n.3). The essential factors in the painting are the emphasis upon an unnaturalistic colour for the contour of the nude, rather than an overt use of flesh tones, and the uncompromising pose of the model. Although the latter found its genesis in Matisse's recent Fauve paintings, such as the figure drinking coffee in *Luxe, Calme, Volupté* (1904–05, Priv. Coll., Paris) and in the reclining woman centre right in *Bonheur de vivre* (1905–06, Barnes Foundation, Merion, Penn.), a comparison between *The Blue Nude – Souvenir of Biskra* and these earlier works reveals a rejection of the decorative properties of colour in favour of the constructive use of colour, through the bold, blue swinging line and the blocks of pigment which form the figure. This anti-decorative handling of colour links the painting back to Matisse's pre-Fauve works, such as *Homme nu* (*c.* 1900, Priv. Coll., New York). In addition, Matisse has virtually rid himself of any sense of three dimensionality in this work by distorting and flattening the figure, which thus seems to adhere to the flat picture surface.   MA.S.

PROVENANCE
Until *c.*1913, Leo Stein, Paris; Paris dealer; Alphonse Kahn, Paris; Georges de Zayas, Paris; Marius de Zayas, Paris; 1920, December, bought by John Quinn, New York; 1926, October, Hôtel Drouot, Paris, Quinn Estate (lot 61); bought through Michael Stein by Dr. Claribel and Miss Etta Cone, Baltimore; 1949, given by them to the Baltimore Museum of Art

EXHIBITIONS
1913, New York, Armory of the Sixty-ninth Infantry, *International Exhibition of Modern Art* (no. 411)
1913, Chicago, Art Institute (no. 248)
1913, Boston, Copley Hall (no. 129)
1920, New York, M. de Zayas Gallery, *Paintings by Matisse*
1924, New York, Brummer Gallery, *Exhibition of Works by Matisse* (no. 2)
1926, New York, *Memorial Exhibition of Representative Works. Selected from the John Quinn Collection* (no. 36)
1931, Basle, Kunsthalle, *Matisse*
1931, Paris, Galerie Georges Petit, *Matisse*
1948, Philadelphia, Museum of Art, *Henri Matisse: Retrospective Exhibition*
1951, New Haven, Yale University Art Gallery; Baltimore, Museum of Art, *Pictures for a picture of Gertrude Stein as a Collector and Writer on Art and Artists* (no. 18)
1952, New York, Museum of Modern Art; Cleveland, Museum of Art; San Francisco, Museum of Art; Chicago, Art Institute, *Matisse Retrospective*
1955, Richmond, Virginia Museum of Fine Arts, *The Cone Collection*
1956, Minneapolis, Walker Art Center, *Expressionism*
1970, Paris, Grand Palais, *Henri Matisse: Exposition du Centenaire* (no. 84)

REFERENCES
Barr 1951, pp. 49, 58, 83, 84, 94-95, 96, 99, 100, 150, 180, 199, 201, 208, 218, 262, ill. p. 336
Luzi 1971, no. 97
Ozenfant et Jeanneret, *La Peinture moderne*, Paris, n.d, n.p.
G. Stein, *The Autobiography of Alice B. Toklas*, New York, 1934, p. 21
J. Selz, *Henri Matisse*, New York, 1964
B. L. Reid, *The Man from New York . . . John Quinn and His Friends*, New York, 1968
L. Gowing, *Henri Matisse: 64 Paintings*, New York (Museum of Modern Art), 1966, p. 27, ill
Baltimore, Museum of Art, *Handbook of the Cone Collection*, 1967 (revised ed.), no. 40, ill. in colour, p. 24
J. D. Flam, *Matisse on Art*, London, 1973, pp. 4, 12, 24, 49, ill. fig. 18
J. Elderfield, *Fauvism; The "Wild Beasts" and its Affinities*. New York (Museum of Modern Art), 1976, p. 118, ill. p. 117

**77a**

# Moroccan Landscape    spring 1912
*Paysage marocain*

115 × 80 cm
Signed bottom left: *Henri Matisse*
Moderna Museet, Stockholm
[*repr. in colour on p. 112, plate 99a*]

**77b***

# Moroccan Garden    autumn 1912
*Le Jardin marocain*

117 × 81 cm
Signed bottom right: *Henri Matisse*
Private Collection
[*repr. in colour on p. 110, plate 99b*]

**77c**

# The Palm Leaf, Tangier    autumn 1912
*La Palme, Tanger*

117·5 × 81·9 cm
Signed bottom right: *Henri Matisse*
National Gallery of Art, Washington, Chester Dale Fund 1978
[*repr. in colour on p. 111, plate 99c*]

Despite their differences in tonality, these three paintings, representing the garden of the Villa Bronx, Tangier, Morocco, were intended to form a decorative triptych. The combination of one dominantly blue panel and two predominantly red ones is accounted for by the fact that *Moroccan Landscape* (Cat. 77a) was executed during the spring of 1912, when the vegetation in the garden had burst into luxuriant growth following the wet season, whereas the other two landscapes date from autumn 1912, when the garden had been scorched by the hot, dry summer season.

The pictures were executed during two separate visits to Morocco undertaken by Matisse in the course of 1912. Matisse returned to North Africa after a gap of six years (see Cat. 76) at the end of January 1912. He remained until the spring, returning again in October 1912 for a more extensive visit which was to last probably until February 1913. Basing himself at Tangier, he became enraptured with the light and the landscape and determined to integrate these elements into his work.

The reasons underlying Matisse's decision to return to North Africa on both occasions in 1912 are not clear. Prior to the first visit, Matisse had seen the 1910 exhibition of Islamic art at Munich and later that same year, had travelled to Spain where he had been particularly impressed by the Moorish cities of Cordoba, Grenada and Seville. He might also, by 1912, have wished to escape the apparent domination by Cubism of the Paris avant-garde. In search of a viable alternative for his art he may have concluded that a visit to a land which encapsulated his new-found interest in Muslim art, the innovative force of southern light (already experienced at Collioure and St. Tropez between 1904 and 1906) and his established admiration of African art, was an essential move. It has been suggested that the visit might have occurred earlier than 1912 had Matisse not been delayed by the unsettled political situation in North Africa, which was not resolved until the Franco-German treaty of November 1911.

The decision to return to Morocco in autumn 1912 was probably motivated by two factors: Matisse's disappointment at the drabness of northern France, when compared to the scintillating colours which he had recently discovered in North Africa, and a continued unease with the pre-eminence of the Cubists and the Futurists in Paris.

*Moroccan Landscape* (Cat. 77a), executed towards the end of Matisse's first visit in 1912, is in large measure structured by the juxtaposed areas of dense tonalities – greens, blues and pink-mauves – suggestive of a thick, burgeoning plant life. These tonalities occur in other works completed during this same visit, for example, *La Fenêtre ouverte sur Tanger* (Museum of Western Art, Moscow) and *La Porte du Casbah* (Museum of Western Art, Moscow). Intending to work further on this painting, Matisse took it back with him to Tangier when he returned in October 1912. Shocked by the parched appearance of the private garden in which he had executed the painting, he embarked on the other two pictures which complete the triptych, *The Palm Leaf, Tangier* (Cat. 77c) and *Moroccan Garden* (Cat. 77b). In contrast to *Moroccan Landscape*, the paint in both of these later pictures is sparingly applied and the colours are provocative in their reds, oranges, browns and thin greens, all characteristic of the scorched landscape which Matisse wished to evoke. However, all three paintings display bold use of black outline. Rather than serving a descriptive purpose, these lines both create an intense patterning across the surface of the landscapes and provide a strong tonal contrast, in keeping with Matisse's view that black was not a medium for delineating the forms of objects, but should be seen as yet another colour available to the artist.

Apart from this decorative triptych, there are at least two other groups of paintings which Matisse viewed as similar forms: one consisting solely of three figures (*Fatma, la Mulatresse*, Josef Müller Estate, Switzerland, *Amido, le marocain*, The Hermitage, Leningrad, *Zorah, La Marocaine*, Museum of Western Art, Moscow), the other of a figure and two townscapes (*La Porte du Casbah, La Fenêtre ouverte sur Tanger, Zorah sur la terrasse*, all Museum of Western Art, Moscow).

An intended visit to Tangier in the autumn of 1913 never materialised. However the impact of these two intense periods of activity, 1912–13, on Matisse's subsequent work can be seen in the sparsely-handled, rigorously-decorative paintings, *Le Café arabe* (1913; The Hermitage, Leningrad) and *Les Marocains* (1916; Museum of Modern Art, New York), as well as in the more superficial references to Oriental elements which persisted in his costume pieces (see Cat. 78) and still-lifes executed during the two succeeding decades.    MA.S.

**77a**

PROVENANCE
1917, given by Mr Walther Halvorsen, Paris, to the Moderna Museet, Stockholm

EXHIBITIONS
1934, Copenhagen, Ny Carlsberg Glyptothek, *Henri Matisse*
1949, Lucerne, *Henri Matisse*
1950, Nice, Musée des Beaux-Arts, *Henri Matisse*
1951–52, New York, Museum of Modern Art; Chicago, Art Institute; San Francisco, Museum of Art, *Henri Matisse*
1970, Copenhagen, Statens Museum fur Kunst, *Henri Matisse*
1970, Paris, Grand Palais, *Henri Matisse, Exposition du Centenaire* (no. 113)
1982, Zurich, Kunsthaus; Dusseldorf, Kunsthalle, *Henri Matisse*

REFERENCES
Barr 1951, pp. 144, 145, 154, 155, ill. p. 380
Luzi 1971, no. 182
J. D. Flam, 'Matisse in Morocco', *Connoisseur*, August 1982, pp. 80, 82, ill. p. 85

**77b**

PROVENANCE
M. Knoedler and Co., New York; Marx Coll., Chicago; Priv. Coll., New York

REFERENCES
Barr 1951, pp. 145, 154, ill. p. 380
Luzi 1971, no. 166
J. D. Flam, 'Matisse in Morocco', *Connoisseur*, August 1982, pp. 80, 82, ill. p. 84

**77c**

PROVENANCE
By 1914, Prof. Oskar and Mrs Greta Moll, Breslau; ?1932, Galerie Tannhauser, Berlin (Justin K. Tannhauser); early 1940s, Weyhe Galleries, New York; by 1957, Mr and Mrs Alfred H. Barr, Jr.; 1978, purchased by the National Gallery of Art, Washington

EXHIBITIONS
1952, Montreal, Museum of Fine Art; Berlin, Nationalgalerie, *Six Centuries of Landscape* (no. 64)
1956, Paris, Musée National d'Art moderne, *Henri Matisse, exposition retrospective* (no. 32)
1970, Paris, Grand Palais, *Henri Matisse, Exposition du Centenaire* (no. 114)
1982–83, Zurich, Kunsthaus; Dusseldorf, Kunsthalle, *Matisse*

REFERENCES
Barr 1951, pp. 145, 154, ill. p. 381
Luzi 1971, no. 167
S. and D. Salvmann, *Oskar Moll, Leben und Werk*, Munich, 1975, p. 63
J. D. Flam, 'Matisse in Morocco', *Connoisseur*, August 1982, p. 82, ill. p. 84

77a

77b

77c

78

# Odalisque in Red Trousers    1921

*Odalisque à la culotte rouge*

65 × 90 cm
Signed bottom right: *Henri Matisse*
Musée National d'Art moderne, Centre Georges Pompidou
[*repr. in colour on p. 109, plate 100*]

Executed nine years after his final trip to Morocco, this painting belongs to a series of Oriental costume pieces in which Matisse reworked Oriental, decorative motives around Western models (eg. *Les Trois Soeurs*, triptych, 1916/ second half 1917, Barnes Foundation, Merion, Penn.). Despite the brilliant explosion of colour and the use of patterned tiles in the background, this is, in many ways, a conventional image of an odalisque. In contrast to the uncompromisingly two-dimensional paintings of the previous decade (eg. *l'Atelier rouge*, 1911, Museum of Modern Art, New York; *La Leçon du piano*, 1917, Guggenheim Museum, New York), this model sits firmly within an illusion of three-dimensional space, created by the diagonal of the sofa on which she lies. Both in this respect and in her pose – arms behind her head and the somewhat provocative gaze – she both looks back to such nineteenth-century odalisques as Renoir's *Femme d'Alger* (Cat. 84) and forward to the more classical figure paintings of the 1920s (eg. *Nu à la chaise bleue*, 1934, Priv. Coll., Los Angeles; *Odalisque aux magnolies*, 1924, Marx Coll., New York). The picture was bought by a somewhat nervous Musée du Luxembourg in 1921, as Matisse's first painting in a French public collection.

The *Odalisque with Red Trousers* retains an important position within Matisse's work inspired by the Orient. First, the odalisque was an excuse for Matisse to paint nudes. In 1929, Matisse stated that he was unwilling to paint an odalisque which was 'artificial' and so he went to Morocco where he knew that such figures

existed ('Entretien avec Tériade', 1929, reprinted in H. Matisse, *Ecrits et propos*, Paris, 1972, p. 99). Second, the decorative patterning of the tiles in the background prefigures the large decorative panels of later years, such as the *Grande decoration avec masques* (1953, National Gallery of Art, Washington).    MA.S.

PROVENANCE
Galerie Bernheim-Jeune, Paris; 1922, bought by the State (Musée du Luxembourg)
EXHIBITION
See I. Monod-Fontaine, 1979, p. 48
REFERENCE
For full references see I. Monod-Fontaine, *Matisse* (catalogue raisonné des collections au Musée National d'Art moderne), Paris 1979, p. 48, no. 13

78

# Melville, Arthur    1855–1904

Born at Loanhead of Guthrie, Melville started his working life as a grocer's apprentice, walking miles to attend evening classes at Edinburgh. In 1878 he travelled to Paris to study at the Académie Julian, and during his stay encountered the work of the Impressionists and began to paint in watercolours. A new interest in painting out-of-doors led to a prolonged visit to Grez-sur-Loing in 1879. The following year, Melville went to Egypt where he spent the next two years, living in Cairo but making occasional excursions to places such as Luxor, where he met Sir Flinders Petrie. In 1882 he continued his travels and embarked on a ship bound for India where he spent only a few days. An original plan to come back through Persia with a friend was abandoned, and Melville rode back alone across Asia Minor from Baghdad to the Black Sea.

On his return to England, Melville started to exhibit his Oriental watercolours in London and Edinburgh, where their innovative approach met with a mixed critical reception. While he was living in Edinburgh from 1882 to 1889, he befriended some of the Scottish artists of the Glasgow School, but in 1889 he moved back to London, where he was to be based for the rest of his life. Melville made several trips to Spain and Algeria during the 1890s.

## 79†

## Awaiting an Audience with the Pasha    1882/1887

Watercolour and bodycolour on paper: 66·6 × 100·3 cm
Inscribed bottom right: *Awaiting an Audience with the Pasha, Arthur Melville 1887*
Mr and Mrs Tim Rice
[*repr. in colour on p. 99, plate 101*]

This painting was executed in 1882 and exhibited in London in the following year. Given that it is clearly dated 1887, it is assumed to have been further worked on by the artist between 1883 and 1887. In 1888, it was again exhibited in London, when it may well have still been in the artist's possession.

This watercolour is probably based on a scene witnessed during Melville's first trip to the Near East undertaken in 1882. While riding through Asia Minor, he was twice attacked by bandits. On the second occasion he was robbed and left for dead in the middle of the desert near Mosul in present-day Iraq. The Arabs of the nearest village sheltered him and dressed his wounds, but the local pasha, though kind and hospitable, detained him for three weeks on suspicion of spying before allowing him to continue on his journey to Constantinople. During this time, Melville would presumably have had the opportunity to observe such scenes as this where local people have come to seek an audience with the pasha to obtain justice, give presents, or denounce their enemies. Certainly the building in the picture, with its wooden columns and rolled-up blind above the doorway, is closer to the architecture of Iraq than to that of Egypt.

Melville's use of watercolour at this stage in his career is reminiscent, in certain areas of detail, of the work of J. F. Lewis (*q.v.*). In this picture the lattice work and the pattern on the Turkish carpet are clearly delineated, but in later paintings Melville was to abandon this minute approach for a much freer method of working, where superfluous details were sponged out in the interest of a broader effect. The extraordinary luminosity of this picture was achieved by Melville's practice of painting onto paper which had been repeatedly saturated with Chinese white, first of all putting in the background using umber, and then filling in the patches of brilliant colour when the background was dry.    C.B.

PROVENANCE
Until 1888, with the artist; Priv. Coll., Canada; 1982, acquired by The Fine Art Society, London; sold by them to Mr and Mrs Tim Rice

EXHIBITIONS
1883, London, Dudley Gallery, *Spring Exhibition*
1888, London, Royal Society of Painters in Water Colours (no. 199)
1983, Edinburgh, The Fine Art Society, *Tenth Anniversary Exhibition*

REFERENCE
A. E. Mackay, *Arthur Melville, Scottish Impressionist 1855–1904*, Leigh-on-Sea, 1951, pp. 70, 147 (no. 335)

79

# Müller, Leopold Carl   1835–1892

The leading Viennese Orientalist painter, Müller was born in Dresden, the son of a lithographer, and trained at the Vienna Academy under its director, Christian Ruben. His first career was as an illustrator on the city's satirical newspaper *Figaro*, but after a visit to Paris in 1867, when he saw and admired the work of Fromentin (*q.v.*) amongst others, he reverted to painting as his main occupation. From 1870 onwards he made frequent visits to Italy, and in 1873–74 travelled to Constantinople, Smyrna and Cairo. Fascinated by the quality of the light, he began to paint the Egyptian genre subjects for which he is best known. He visited Egypt nine times between 1873 and 1886. In 1875–76 he went in the company of Hans Makart and other artist friends, living and working with them in the Musāfir-Khānah in Cairo. He sold much of his work to British collectors through contacts made in the city. This was a field of patronage that he was particularly well equipped to cultivate after becoming friendly with the Prince of Wales. He was appointed to a Professorship at the Vienna Academy in 1877, and was artistic supervisor and a major contributor to Georg Ebers's *Ägypten in Bild und Wort*, published in 1879–80. He died at Weidlingen, near Vienna, in 1892.

For a fuller discussion of Müller as the central figure in Viennese Orientalism, see G. Frodl, 'Wiener Orientmalerei im 19. Jahrhundert', *Alte und Moderne Kunst*, no. 178–79, 26, 1981, pp. 19–25.

## 80*

# Encampment in the Desert at Gizah   1874
*Rast in der Wüste bei Gizeh*

109 × 210 cm
Signed and dated bottom left: *Leopold Carl Müller/1874*
Private Collection, Houston, Texas
[*repr. in colour on p. 85, plate 102*]

This picture shows the halt of a caravan, with the Great Pyramid and Second Pyramid in the background. Gizah was an obvious attraction for Orientalist painters: compare, for example, the view from a different angle in Frederick Goodall's *The Subsiding of the Nile* (Cat. 47). *Encampment in the Desert at Gizah* resulted from Müller's first visit to Egypt in 1873–74, and according to Boetticher (1898) was completed at the end of 1874 in a studio that he shared with Makart in Vienna. It is similar in size to the work of 1878 generally considered to be his masterpiece, the *Markt in Cairo* (Österreichische Galerie, Vienna), which may have been intended as a pendant, the pair together representing urban and desert gatherings of Arabs. Like *Markt in Cairo*, this painting depicts an animated crowd intended to show off to best advantage Müller's observation of different racial types, their characteristic gestures and poses.

Gerbert Frodl has pointed out (*loc. cit.*, Frodl, 1981) that there was less demand for Orientalist painting in Austria than in Britain and France, perhaps because of its relative lack of political involvement in the Near East. As a result, the number of Orientalists based in Vienna was small: apart from Müller, the only noteworthy painters to make a speciality of Oriental subjects were his students, Charles Wilda (1854–1907), Rudolf Swoboda (1859–1914) and Franz Kosler (1864–1905), and they all depended on foreign, mostly British, patrons.   M.W.

PROVENANCE
1893, 2–4 March, the artist's sale, Künstlerhaus, Vienna; 1898, G. Reichert; George McCulloch; 1913, 23 May, his sale, Christie's, London (lot 37); acquired by W. W. Sampson; 1980, June, acquired from The Fine Art Society, London, by Kurt E. Schon Ltd, New Orleans; Priv. Coll., Houston, Texas

EXHIBITIONS
1875, Vienna Künstlerhaus
1898, Vienna, Künstlerhaus, *Funfzig Jahre Österreichischer Malerei* (no. 650)

REFERENCES
G. Ebers, *Ägypten in Bild und Wort*, Stuttgart and Leipzig, 1879–80, I, ill. p. 189
F. von Boetticher, *Malerwerke des 19. Jahrhunderts*, Dresden, 1891–1901, II, part 1, p. 103, no. 22
A. F. Seligmann, *Karl Leopold Müller*, Vienna, 1922, p. 58

80

# Müller, William James  1812–1845

Müller was one of the earliest British artists to set out to paint realistically the rich and varied world of the Orient. Born in Bristol, he soon gained a reputation for his ability to sketch with rapidity and assurance. In 1834–35 he travelled through Europe to Italy. In 1838, attracted by the more exotic subject-matter of the Near East, he travelled via Greece to Alexandria, arriving at Cairo in mid-November. After two weeks sketching in the bazaars, he ascended the Nile to Luxor where he drew the ruins and scenery on both sides of the river before returning to Cairo in mid-January.

On his return to London in 1839 he painted several Egyptian subjects in oils, exhibiting at the Royal Academy, the British Institution and the Royal Society of Arts; he also went on sketching trips to Wales and France.

In 1843, on the invitation of the archaeologist Charles Fellows, Müller and his young pupil Harry Johnson travelled to south-west Turkey. Sailing from Smyrna (now Izmir) via Rhodes they joined the Fellows expedition in Lycia at the end of October. For three months Müller sketched both the rugged scenery surrounding the ruins of Xanthus, Pinara and Tlos, and the local nomadic tribes. Returning to Rhodes from the Lycian port of Telmessus (now Fethiye), the two artists sailed for England. Much of the remaining year of his life was spent working on and exhibiting his Lycian watercolours, as well as a few oil paintings.

He died in Bristol in September 1845.

81

# The Carpet Bazaar at Cairo  1843

Oil on board: 62·2 × 74·9 cm
Signed and dated bottom left: *W. Müller Cairo 1843*
The City of Bristol Museum and Art Gallery
[*repr. in colour on p. 71, plate 103*]

In Egypt from 1838 to 1839, Müller, like many other visitors, was amazed by the picturesque variety of the people in the streets: 'like humanity put into a kaleidoscope', he wrote (W. Müller, 'An Artist's Tour in Egypt', *Art-Union*, September 1839, p. 131). The subjects of his numerous sketches (listed in N. N. Solly, *Memoir of the Life of William James Müller*, London, 1875, pp. 83–84), reveal the range and extent of his interest in all that he saw and experienced.

On his return to England he exhibited paintings of the Egyptian temples, but more popular with his patrons were his lively and colourful street and market scenes. Whereas views of Cairo by David Roberts (see Cat. 91) are composed around the forms of the lofty minarets and ornate doorways of Cairo's Islamic buildings, Müller sought to evoke the city's atmosphere, particularly through the use of strong colour. In 1843, the date of this painting, he wrote in a letter from Bristol of his delight on seeing an Eastern bazaar for the first time. The scenes reminded him of pictures by Rembrandt: 'The sun streams through a little opening in the wall and falls on the figures, lighting them up with all but a supernatural brilliancy; reflection plays its part and bit by bit the whole is revealed; and as figure after figure pass by, some in the richest dresses and superb stuffs, while others, such as the pipe-cleaners, walk on shouting their avocations, and literally clothed in rags, you have a constantly changing picture before you' (quoted James Dafforne, 'William John [sic] Müller', *Art Journal*, October 1864, pp. 293–94). On that occasion Müller was referring to another bazaar picture, 'an Opium Shop at Monfaloot', but the scene described also resembles the present painting. There is also a description in Solly of a view which corresponds to this work (*op. cit.*, p. 65).

Müller's observation of the patterns formed by bright sunlight, filtering through the awnings on to the bazaar below, anticipates J. F. Lewis's more sophisticated rendering of similar effects (see Cat. 68, 74).  B.L.

PROVENANCE
1896, Alfred East; 1918, presented by Mrs S. Lloyd in memory of her husband Alderman Samuel Lloyd, J. P., to the City of Bristol Museum and Art Gallery

EXHIBITIONS
1896, Birmingham, City Museum and Art Gallery, *Loan collection of paintings in oils and watercolours by W. J. Müller* (no. 21)
1925, Wembley Palace of Arts (W.28)
1928–30, Leamington Spa, Public Library and Museum
1955, London, Arts Council of Great Britain, *Narrative Painting* (no. 28)
1962, Bristol City Art Gallery, *William James Müller 1812–1845* (no. 23)
1969, London, Wildenstein and Co., *Pictures from Bristol* (no. 31)
1983, Brighton, Museum and Art Gallery; Manchester, City Art Gallery, *The Inspiration of Egypt* (no. 290)

REFERENCES
C. G. E. Bunt, *The Life and Art of William James Müller 1812–1845*, Leigh-on-Sea, 1948, pp. 69, 74, 92, ill. pl. 43
Bristol City Art Gallery, *Catalogue of Paintings*, 1970, K509, ill. p. 81

81

# Pasini, Alberto 1826–1899

Pasini was born in Busseto and attended the Academy at Parma. From 1851 to 1853 he studied under Eugène Cicéri (1803–1886) in Paris, where he completed his training in the atelier of M.E. Isabey (1813–1890). He made his Salon debut in 1853. From his first visit to Persia in 1855, as part of the suite of the French legation to the Persian Gulf and Tehran, Pasini specialised in views of remote corners of Turkey and Persia. He travelled to Constantinople between 1868 and 1869 and to Asia Minor and Syria in 1873. Pasini was also a seasoned traveller within Europe and from 1878 visited Venice on several occasions, and made a journey to Spain with Gérôme from 1879 to 1883.

Principally a landscape and architectural painter, Pasini came under the influence of Théodore Rousseau and Fromentin in the late 1850s, though his later style reveals affinities with the 'Néo-grec' School of painters. Apart from his Orientalist work, he painted some genre scenes and subjects taken from Turkish history and was also known for his lithographic work.

After the Franco-Prussian War (1870–71), Pasini returned to Italy, but continued to exhibit at the Salon until his death in 1899.

82*

# Entrance to the Yeni-Cami Mosque in Constantinople 1870

*Porte de la mosquée Yeni-Djami, à Constantinople*

156·8 × 115·5 cm
Signed and dated bottom left: *A. Pasini 1870*
Musée des Beaux-Arts, Nantes

The Yeni-Cami (New Mosque) was the product of the plans of the two *Valide Sultāns* (Queen Mothers). It was begun in 1597 by the Venetian Sophia Baffo, mother of Mehemed III, but suffered long delays in construction until its completion in 1663 by Tarkhan, mother of Sultān Mehmed IV. An extremely elegant building in both external and internal detail and with a remarkable sixty-six cupolas, the mosque was much frequented by European travellers, particularly after the Crimean War when restrictions on Christians visiting Muslim places of worship were relaxed. Pasini himself was greatly attracted to this building and in 1873 exhibited a scene of the 'Egyptian Bazaar', located on the south side of the mosque.

In this painting, Pasini shows the mosque not so much as a place of worship, but as the meeting place of a cross-section of male Turkish society. Like the beggar and the solitary dervish, the woman, on the right of the picture, is excluded from the general discussion to indicate her subordinate role, and her exclusion from public religious affairs. The older men in their traditional robes and turbans, and the *sarvels* (full trousers), embroidered waistcoats and white tunics of the younger men, are rendered with a precision typical of Pasini's keen observation; the wide range of colours harmonise with the overall grey tonalities of the architecture. The touches of local colour and various animated gestures of the figures to some extent recall Decamps, although they are observed with an impartiality which transforms the scene from the anecdotal to the documentary.

The tightness of handling and the concentration on the high finish of the brushwork place the painting firmly within the European Beaux-Arts tradition. Pasini clearly delighted in the defined geometrical lines of Oriental architecture and in the texture of the marble, which he transcribes in the unbroken smoothness of the paint surface. Castagnary, champion of the *'école naturaliste'*, though vehemently opposed to the whole concept of Orientalist painting, was much impressed by this picture when it was first exhibited at the Salon of 1870: 'The harmony is so accurate, the drawing so fine, and the animated figures on the steps form such a natural scene, that, on seeing it, I wholly forgot my former detestation of orientalism' (*Salons*, 1892, p. 410). J.M.

PROVENANCE
1873, January, acquired by the Commission du Musée for the Musée des Beaux-Arts, Nantes

EXHIBITIONS
1870, Paris, Salon (no. 2182)
1872, Nantes, Salon des Artistes vivant (no. 579)
1931, Paris, *L'Exposition coloniale* (p. 35)
1980, Nantes, Musée des Beaux-Arts, *Orients* (no. 25)
1983, Pau, Dunkirk and Douai, Musées des Beaux-Arts, *Les Orientalistes de 1850 à 1914*

REFERENCES
C. Lemonnier, *Salon de Paris*, 1870, pp. 125f.
J.A. Castagnary, *Salons, I, 1857–1870*, Paris, 1892, p. 410
Nantes, Musée des Beaux-Arts, *Catalogue*, 1913, pp. 433–34, no. 1123

82

# **Phillips**, Thomas   1770–1845

Born in Dudley, Thomas Phillips had an early training as a craftsman through his apprenticeship to a japanner and glass painter. His career in painting began when he entered Benjamin West's studio and attended drawing classes at the Royal Academy schools. During the 1790s he gradually built up a reputation as a portrait painter, which led to his election as Associate of the Royal Academy in 1804, and full Academician in 1808. Although his early works were mainly confined to portraits of men of science, Phillips soon widened his repertoire to include lawyers, clerics and surgeons. His contact with such patrons as Lord Egremont and the publisher John Murray also resulted in commissions to paint the portraits of several members of the aristocracy as well, and literary figures, including Byron, Scott, Southey, Crabbe, Campbell and Coleridge.

## 83

## Portrait of Lord Byron   after 1835

76·5 × 63·9 cm
Signed with monogram bottom left: *TP*
National Portrait Gallery, London
[*repr. in colour on p. 89, plate 105*]

During the summer of 1813 and the spring of 1814, Byron gave a number of sittings to Thomas Phillips, from which two types of portrait emerged. The first, of which there are four known versions, shows Byron in a black cloak, the second, of which there are at least three versions, shows the poet in Albanian dress. The National Portrait Gallery painting is a smaller and later replica of the upper part of the picture exhibited at the Royal Academy in 1814 as *Portrait of a Nobleman in the dress of an Albanian* (British Embassy, Athens), in which Byron stands in front of a romanticised Greek landscape complete with swirling mists and ruins. According to the artist's son (letter in the National Portrait Gallery Archives), it was painted some time after 1835, following the return of the original work to the artist's studio. There is a similar version in the possession of the publishers, John Murray.

The original portrait was painted when Byron was in his mid-twenties, at the height of his fame as a poet. 1812 had seen the publication of the first two cantos of *Childe Harold*, which were followed by *The Giaour* and *The Bride of Abydos* in 1813, and *The Corsair* and *Lara* in 1814. Byron himself obviously approved of the picture, which complemented the Oriental settings of his poems and affirmed his own image as a romantic adventurer. Contemporary opinion as to whether it was a good likeness varied: John Cam Hobhouse thought it did not look anything like the poet (*Diary*, 19 March 1814), and Hazlitt considered the face too smooth, although the picture conveyed something of 'the softness and wildness of character of the popular poet of the East' (*Morning Chronicle*, 3 May 1814).

The costume, which is that of an Arnavut (an Albanian tribesman), was one that Byron had obtained during his tour of the Continent from 1809 to 1811, when he became an ardent Hellenophile. He bought it in Epirus, and enthused about it in a letter to his mother dated 12 November 1809: 'I have some very "magnifiques" Albanian dresses, the only expensive articles in this country. They cost fifty guineas each, and have so much gold, they would cost in England two hundred' (*Byron's Letters and Journals*, L. A. Marchant ed., London, 1973–76, I, p. 223). When the portrait was finished, Byron offered the costume to Lady Elphinstone to wear to masquerades, and it can now be seen at Bowood House, Wiltshire.   C.B.

PROVENANCE
1862, acquired from Henry W. Phillips, the artist's son, by the National Portrait Gallery

EXHIBITIONS
1969, London, Victoria and Albert Museum, *Berlioz and the Romantic Imagination* (no. 99)
1974, London, Victoria and Albert Museum, *Byron* (no. H8)
1979–80, Munich, Haus der Kunst, *British Painting and Munich 1680–1880* (no. 344)
1981, Hamburg, Kunsthalle, *Goya – The Age of Revolutions* (no. 532)
1982, Manchester, Whitworth Art Gallery, *Richard Payne Knight: The Arrogant Connoisseur* (no. 193)

REFERENCES
D. Parker, *Byron and his World*, London, 1968, ill. p. 29
L. Marchand, *Byron's Letters and Journals*, London, 1973–76, I, p. 233; III, pp. 60; IV, pp. 112–13
R. Walker, forthcoming catalogue raisonné of Regency Portraits in the National Portrait Gallery, to be published 1984

83

# Renoir, Auguste    1841–1919

Born in Limoges (Haute-Vienne), Renoir moved with his family to Paris in 1844. He received his initial artistic training at the atelier of the painters of porcelain, Frères Levy. In 1860, he began copying in the Louvre and two years later entered the atelier of Gleyre (*q.v.*), where he met the future founders of Impressionism, Bazille, Monet and Sisley, and began to paint modern figure subjects and scenes drawn from contemporary life. Despite acceptance at the Salon of 1864, the next fourteen years saw only intermittent success with that establishment, encouraging Renoir, together with Monet, Pissarro, Sisley and Degas, to found an independent exhibiting body. Renoir's doubts about the artistic objectives of Impressionism had significant repercussions on his art during the 1880s, for which he sought a more timeless quality through classicising nudes and monumental figure subjects. At the same time he travelled to Italy, the South of France and twice to Algeria (1881, 1882) in search of new subjects and fresh artistic stimulus. He declined to exhibit at the eighth and final Impressionist exhibition (1886), preferring to show at the Salon and in one-man and small group exhibitions at the galleries of Georges Petit and Durand-Ruel. In 1892, the State purchased his *Jeunes Filles au piano* and from the following year he began to spend his winters in the South of France, to which he moved permanently in 1902. He died in 1919 at Cagnes (Alpes-Maritimes).

ABBREVIATED REFERENCE
D.  F. Daulte, *Auguste Renoir, catalogue raisonné de l'oeuvre peint*, vol. I, *Figures 1860–1890*, Lausanne, 1971

## 84*

## Woman of Algiers or Odalisque    1870
*Femme d'Alger ou Odalisque*

69·2 × 122·6 cm
Signed and dated bottom left: *A. Renoir 70*
National Gallery of Art, Washington, Chester Dale Collection, 1962
[*repr. in colour on p. 104, plate 106*]

Executed in the winter of 1869–70 in Renoir's studio, this painting of his model Lise in Oriental costume owes nothing to his first-hand experience of North Africa, which Renoir was not to visit for another eleven years. The picture was accepted at the Official Salon of 1870, together with *Baigneuse au Griffon* (Museo de Arte, Sao Paulo), which also used Lise as a model. Whereas this latter painting revealed debts to Courbet and Corot, the *Woman of Algiers* declared Renoir's admiration for two other formative influences on the evolution of Impressionism, Manet and Delacroix.

The sultry, defiant gaze of the model, her horizontal pose propped up against a pillow, with the carefully-placed still-life on the left, and the relatively shallow picture-space recall Manet's nude courtesan, *Olympia* (1863; Musée d'Orsay, Paris), exhibited at the Salon of 1865. Manet's painting was itself dependent upon Titian's *Venus of Urbino* and it is possible that Renoir intended *Woman of Algiers* to be read as the North African equivalent of a contemporary nude, as well as an image of timeless, classical beauty.

Significantly, however, Renoir's odalisque is fully clothed, in contrast to the more usual nineteenth-century representations of odalisques (eg. Ingres [Cat. 56], Chassériau, Gérôme [Cat. 33]). In this respect and for many of its other compositional elements – the confined space, the tiled walls, the costume and the exotic trappings – Renoir's painting looks to Delacroix's picture of a harem interior, *Femmes d'Alger* (1834; Louvre, Paris; fig. 5). Delacroix's influence can also be seen in the scintillating colours and loose brushwork which Renoir derived from the older artist's Orientalist works and from his late and technically brilliant works, such as the murals in the Chapelle des Anges (St. Sulpice, Paris, 1853–61).

Arsène Houssaye, in a letter addressed to the reviewer of the 1870 Salon for the journal, *L'Artiste*, confirms this affinity between Delacroix and Renoir: 'One can study the proud, painterly temperament which appears with such brilliance in *Woman of Algiers* that Delacroix could have signed it' (1 June 1870, quoted J. Rewald, 1973, p. 246). Houssaye in the same letter also links Renoir's name with Monet as 'the two great masters . . . who . . . say "nature for nature's sake"'. While the studio setting and the references to visual prototypes show no immediate concern to paint directly from nature, the looseness of certain passages of brushwork might owe something to Renoir's and Monet's shared experience at La Grenouillère, on the River Seine in September 1869. Here, they evolved the Impressionist technique of the rapid, comma-like brushstroke of pure colour laid onto light grounds as the means of capturing the transitory moments of nature.

Renoir painted one further overtly Orientalist picture in 1870, *Portrait of Mme. Stora ou L'Algérienne* (D. 47). Two years later, he executed another harem scene, *Parisiennes en costume algérienne* (D.73), which was rejected by the Salon jury of 1872. Apart from his copy of *The Jewish Wedding*, by Delacroix (see Cat. 85); and the *Girl with a Falcon* (Cat. 86), he produced no other Orientalist-inspired paintings until his first visit to Algiers in 1881.
MA.S.

PROVENANCE
Before 1914, an officer, rue de Téhéran, Paris; Priv. Coll., Germany; Dr G. F. Reber, Basle; Paul Rosenberg, Paris; *c.* 1928, Hugo Perls, Berlin and New York; 1933, Mr and Mrs Chester Dale, New York; 1962, given to the National Gallery of Art

EXHIBITIONS
1870, Paris, Salon (no. 2406)
1904, St. Louis, Universal Exposition (French Section) (no. 463a)
1913, Munich, *L'Art français du XIXᵉ siècle*, ill. pl. 160
?1931, Paris, Grand Palais, *Exposition coloniale internationale*

REFERENCES
D. 48
J. Rewald, *The History of Impressionism*, London, 1973, pp. 243, 246, ill. p. 239
K. .S. Champa, *Studies in Early Impressionism*, New Haven and London, 1973, pp. 49, 90, ill. fig. 88

84

85

# The Jewish Wedding (after Delacroix) 1875

*La Noce juive (d'après Delacroix)*

108 × 144 cm
Signed bottom left: *Renoir d'après E. Delacroix*
The Worcester Art Museum, Worcester, Mass.
*[repr. in colour on p. 106, plate 107]*

This painting is a copy by Renoir after Delacroix's *La Noce juive* (105 × 140·5 cm; exhibited in the Salon of 1841; Louvre, Paris). It was commissioned by Jean Dollfus, an industrialist from Alsace, who was forming a collection of Impressionist paintings for his homes in Mulhouse and Paris. He made Renoir's acquaintance in 1875, and shared with him a deep admiration for Delacroix. The painting is related to the *Portrait de M. Choquet* (1876, D. 176), where the sitter's enthusiasm for Delacroix led him to ask Renoir to include behind his head the sketch for *Numa et Egerie*, one of the pendentives in Delacroix's decorative cycle executed in the Library of the Palais Bourbon, Paris (1840-46).

Renoir has provided a faithful transcription of the subject of Delacroix's painting. The image derives from a ceremony which Delacroix himself witnessed at Tangier on 21 February 1832 and belongs to a group of works executed in the years immediately following his brief visit to North Africa (Cat. 13, 14, 15). Delacroix took copious notes of the event (*Journal*, A. Joubin ed., Paris, 1933, I, pp. 127–30) and elaborated on the nuptial rites in an article for the *Magazin pittoresque* in 1842 (*Oeuvres littéraires*, I, Paris, 1923, p. 103 ff.). The ceremony took place in the house of the bride's parents and access was permitted to the public, who looked on as musicians played a stream of music to which only the women, singly, would perform. Delacroix placed great emphasis on this scene, referring to it in a letter to Moreau, where he stated, 'It is imperative that I set about reproducing, while the memories are still fresh, the things which impressed me during my trip (in Morocco)' (*Eugène Delacroix, Lettres intimes*, A. Dupont ed., Paris, 1954, p. 198).

Renoir's acceptance of this commission indicates that, unlike his fellow Impressionists, Monet, Degas and Pissarro, who studied another 'primitive' art in the Japanese print, the sources of his technique were the scintillating colours and exotic scenes of Delacroix's Orientalist works. This painting was executed six years after Renoir's technical innovations at La Grenouillère (see Cat. 84) and it reveals the fluent handling of his own Impressionist technique. The rear wall is constructed of feathery brushstrokes which cascade down the surface. The back of the man, seated in the right foreground, is a network of red, blue, yellow, purple, orange and green, whereas the counterpart in Delacroix is handled as blue-black. In sum, the shorter, more fluid brushwork throughout Renoir's picture brings action to Delacroix's more static, monumental work.

As in the *Woman of Algiers*, the balance between Delacroix's and Renoir's own technique in this painting is still uncertain. It was only later, when Renoir visited North Africa to view these scenes at first-hand, that he at last saw a way out of Impressionism by fusing colour with light, and technique with exotic subject-matter (see Cat. 87). MA.S.

PROVENANCE
1875, Jean Dollfus, Paris; 1911, Durand-Ruel, Paris; James J. Hill, St. Paul, Minnesota; Gertrude Hill Gavin; Knoedler and Co. Inc., New York, from whom it was bought by the Worcester Art Museum

EXHIBITIONS
1940, Los Angeles, Los Angeles Museum, *The Development of Impressionism* (no. 64)
1948, Paul Rosenberg and Co., *Masterpieces by Delacroix and Renoir* (no. 30)
1955, Los Angeles, County Museum; San Francisco, Museum of Art, *Pierre Auguste Renoir* (no. 16)
1963, Bordeaux, Galerie des Beaux-Arts, *Delacroix, ses maîtres, ses amis et ses élèves* (no. 374)
1969, New York, Wildenstein and Co., *Loan Exhibition in Commemoration of the Fiftieth Anniversary of Renoir's Death* (no. 17)
1982, Rochester, New York, Memorial Art Gallery, *Orientalism* (no. 68)

REFERENCES
D. 139
Worcester Art Museum, *News Bulletin*, VIII, no. 8 (Supplement), May 1943, ill.
Worcester Art Museum, *Annual Report*, 1943, pp. 9, 14
Worcester Art Museum, *Art Through Fifty Centuries*, 1948, p. 83, fig. 114
Rochester, New York, Memorial Art Gallery, *Orientalism*, catalogue by D. Rosenthal, 1982, p. 145, fig. 144
Worcester Art Museum, *Catalogue of Paintings*, pp. 276–77, no. 1943.1

85

86

# Girl with a Falcon    1880

*Jeune Fille au Faucon*

126·8 × 78 cm
Signed and dated bottom right: *Renoir 80*
Sterling and Francine Clark Art Institute, Williamstown, Mass.
*[repr. in colour on p. 105, plate 108]*

In contrast to his earlier Orientalist paintings, for example, *Parisiennes en costume algérienne* (D.73), the compositional sophistication and technical brilliance of this picture could invite the suggestion that 1880 may not be its correct date. Might it have been executed either during or after one of Renoir's two brief visits to Algeria in 1881 and 1882? Whilst some of the painting's impact springs from the evolution of Renoir's Impressionist technique during the 1870s, the vivid colours of the girl's dress especially the richness of the belt and headdress, and the blue-white background on the left set off against the blue-green of the right background, all point towards Renoir's hotter palette of the early 1880s. Similarly, the dense, impastoed paint applied to the thick, white ground of the figure relates less

to the thin glazes of Renoir's work *c.* 1877–80, than to the denser, more heavily-worked surfaces of the early 1880s. Furthermore, the picture's blond tonality could result from Renoir's discovery of the role of intense white light during his first Algerian visit of 1881. Finally, the first extant record of the painting is probably the sale, together with two other Algerian works, to Durand-Ruel on 22 May 1882 of a work entitled *Jeune Fille à l'oiseau*, almost certainly *Girl with a Falcon*.

Despite these mainly stylistic considerations, there are good reasons for leaving the execution of the painting in 1880. First, Daulte (D. 349) suggests that the model for the girl was Mlle. Fleury, a Parisian whom Renoir used *c.* 1880, which would place the picture in the sequence of Algerian costume pieces executed in Paris during the 1870s (see Cat. 85). This is reinforced by the fact that the model holds what appears to be a cuckoo, rather than a falcon, and the bird sits on her right hand, contrary to falconry practice. Second, during his Algerian visit of 1882, Renoir wrote to Durand-Ruel, his dealer, that he had already seen some very picturesque children and intended 'this time to bring you back figure paintings, which I was unable to do on my last journey [i.e. 1881]' (*Renoir en Italie et Algérie*, introduction by Georges Besson, Paris 1955, n.p.). While it is not entirely correct that Renoir executed no figure pictures during his first visit to Algeria (eg. D. 367–70), none of the 1881 studies was as monumental or as finished as *Girl with a Falcon*, and the use of thin glazes, which are particularly evident in the top left and right of the painting, rules out Renoir's second visit to Algeria in 1882 as a possible date for the painting. Finally, there is no evidence to suggest that Renoir ever deliberately mis-dated his paintings.

Therefore, it could be suggested that the painting was executed in 1880, prior to Renoir's first journey to North Africa, and that Durand-Ruel bought the picture from Renoir in May 1882, with a view to making a ready sale on the lively contemporary market for Orientalist subjects. The dealer may also, by *c.* 1884, have converted 'the bird' into a falcon, to meet popular expectations of Orientalist imagery. As a transitional work between the 1870s and the 1880s, the picture was sufficiently similar to the works that resulted from the Algerian trips to be in accord with both of the Algerian paintings purchased by Durand-Ruel on 22 May 1882, and with a further one purchased the following day.    MA.S.

PROVENANCE
1882, 22 May, bought from the artist by Durand-Ruel; 1884, 30 December, sold to David; 1884–88, sold to Charles Leroux, Paris; 1888, 27–28, February, Vente Charles Leroux, Paris (lot 72); Durand-Ruel; 1909, Miss Anna Thompson, New York; 1928, bought from her by Durand-Ruel; 1937, 6 May, Robert Sterling Clark, New York; 1955, Sterling and Francine Clark Art Institute

EXHIBITIONS
1883, Paris, Durand-Ruel, *Renoir* (no. 3, as *Jeune Fille à l'oiseau*)
1929, New York, Durand-Ruel, *Paintings by the Master Impressionists* (no. 15)
1930, Paris, Petit Palais, *Centenaire de la Conquête de l'Algérie* (hors catalogue)
1932, New York, Durand-Ruel, *Masterpieces by Renoir* (no. 2)
1933, Paris, Orangerie, *Renoir* (no. 9)
1934, Chicago, Art Institute, *Exhibition of Paintings and Sculpture* (no. 234)
1967, New York, Wildenstein and Co., *Treasures from the Sterling and Francine Clark Institute* (no. 33)
1973, Chicago, Art Institute, *Renoir Paintings and Drawings* (no. 32)

REFERENCES
D.349
A. Boime, *Thomas Couture and the Eclectic Vision*, New Haven, 1980, p. 111, ill. fig. v. 24

[The compiler is indebted to John House for information on the provenance of this painting and to Peter Stocks for identifying the bird]

86

87

# Arab Festival, Algiers. The Casbah    1881
*Fête Arabe à Alger. La Casbah*

73·5 × 92 cm
Signed and dated bottom right: *Renoir 81*
Musee d'Orsay, Galerie du Jeu de Paume, Paris
[*repr. in colour on p. 107, plate 109*]

This painting is almost certainly a record of a religious celebration witnessed by Renoir in the Casbah of Algiers. It is one of six pictures he painted during his first trip to Algeria, March–April 1881.

By the end of the 1870s, Renoir had become increasingly uneasy with Impressionism, as a mark of which he returned to exhibiting at the official Salon of 1878 and disassociated himself from the Fifth Impressionist Exhibition of the following year. His technique and subject-matter also became more diversified, with the introduction of greater finish in his paintings (see Cat. 86), the exploration of pure colour in a group of flower pieces (*c.* 1880) and the execution of large, 'official' figure groups and portraits (eg. *Mme. Charpentier et ses enfants*, 1878, D. 266). Impressionism, at this time, even came under attack from its most devoted supporter, Emile Zola. In two articles published in *Le Voltaire* (18 and 22 June 1880, 'Le Naturalisme au Salon'), he regrets the inability of the Impressionists to produce masterpieces that could withstand the test of time. The opening years of the 1880s saw Renoir, as well as Monet and Pissarro, searching for the means by which the ephemeral images of Impressionism might be stabilised through a reassessment of subject-matter, artistic antecedents and colour. Renoir's two brief visits to Algeria in 1881 and 1882 provided much important and stimulating material for him. His decision to visit Algeria was prompted by his admiration for Delacroix (see Cat. 84, 85) and by his desire to see '*le pays du soleil*' (letter to Théodore Duret [1881], quoted D., p. 45). Apart from echoing Delacroix's wonder at the luxuriance of the North African vegetation (letter to Mme.

Charpentier, dated March 1881, quoted *Renoir en Italie et en Algérie*, 1955, n.p.; letter to Théodore Duret [1881], quoted D., p. 45), Renoir was also deeply impressed by the nobility and the biblical character of the people, the mysterious women, and the light.

Jean Renoir reports that his father declared of Algeria: '"Everything is white: the burnūses they wear, the walls, the minarets, the road . . . And against it the green of the orange trees and the grey of the figs"' (J. Renoir, *Renoir*, Paris, 1962, p. 228). The *Arab Festival* concentrates on this whiteness in the Algerian light, yet the flashes of intense colour, especially in the foreground, are evidence of Renoir's understanding of the equally significant presence of rich colour, which he expressed more overtly in such Algerian landscapes as *Champ des bananiers* (Jeu de Paume, Paris) and *Ravin de la femme sauvage* (Jeu de Paumes, Paris).

The formal structure of *Arab Festival* is less stable than in the paintings of his second visit to Algeria such as *La Mosquée à Algers* (1882, Priv. Coll.). The successful introduction of stability as a new formal ingredient into his work awaited Renoir's trip to Italy (autumn 1881–January 1882), and his stay with Cézanne at L'Estaque (January–March 1882). The impact of Renoir's discovery of the light and luxuriance of North Africa during his first visit can however be found in works executed immediately on his return to Paris in April 1881, notably *Le Déjeuner des cannotiers* (1881, D. 379).    MA.S.

PROVENANCE
1888, 8 December, on deposit with Durand-Ruel from the artist; 1892, 3 February, bought from the artist by Durand-Ruel; from 1900, 31 January, Claude Monet; 1936, Wildenstein and Co.; 1955, Mrs. Margaret Biddle; 1957, Gift of the Biddle Foundation, in memory of Mrs. Margaret Biddle, to the State

EXHIBITIONS
1906, Marseille, *Exposition Nationale coloniale: Exposition retrospective des Orientalistes* (no. 53, as *Fête au camp*)
1965, Lisbon, Palais de la F.I.L., *Un Seculo de pintura francesca, 1850–1950* (no. 120)
1967–68, Paris, Orangerie, *Vingt ans d'aquisitions au Musée du Louvre: 1947–1967* (no. 423)
1975, Recklinghausen, Museen der Stadt, *Der Einzelne und die Masse* (no. 203)

REFERENCES
Musée du Louvre, *Catalogue des peintures, I, Ecole française*, Paris, 1972, p. 322
H. Adhemar and A. Dayez, *Musée du Louvre, Musée de l'Impressionnisme, Jeu de Paumé*, Paris, 1973, p. 155
J. Rewald, *History of Impressionism*. London, 1973, p. 454, ill. p. 462

87

# Roberts, David    1796–1864

Born in Stockbridge, near Edinburgh, the son of a cobbler, David Roberts received no formal art education. He started his career as a painter of theatrical scenery, panoramas and dioramas, doing studio work in his spare time. In 1830, spurred on by success at the Royal Academy, he became a full-time artist. Roberts travelled extensively in search of pictorial material, visiting Spain in 1832–33, Belgium in 1845, 1849, 1850 and 1851, France in 1822, 1832 and 1843, and Italy in 1851 and 1853. He also returned to his native Scotland every year. One of the first independent British artists to make the journey to the Near East, he spent eleven months in 1838–39 going up the Nile, seeing Cairo, the Sinai desert, Syria, Palestine and Lebanon, sketching virtually every monument of note on the way, many from several viewpoints. The sketches were reproduced as lithographs in the six volumes of *The Holy Land, Syria, Idumea, Arabia, Egypt and Nubia* published in the years following his return to England, and many of Roberts's oil paintings are based upon these compositions.

Robert's work was highly acclaimed during his own lifetime, but he trained no assistants and left no obvious successors.

ABBREVIATED REFERENCES
Ballantine 1866 J. Ballantine, *The Life of David Roberts R.A.*, Edinburgh, 1866
*The Holy Land . . . and Nubia*, 1842–49
       D. Roberts, *The Holy Land, Syria, Idumea, Arabia, Egypt and Nubia*,
       London, 1842–49, 6 vols

## 88

## The Temple of Dendereh    1841

119 × 212 cm
Signed and dated bottom left: *David Roberts 1841*
The City of Bristol Museum and Art Gallery
[*repr. in colour on p. 54, plate 110*]

One of the last temples to be built on the Nile, Dendarah was begun in the time of the Ptolemys and added to by successive Roman emperors. It was dedicated to the cow-goddess Hathor, here married to Horus Behdeti of Edfou (Cat. 69). Although the temple is still in a good state of preservation, it suffered defacement at the hands of the fanatical early Christians who tried to obliterate the heads of the pagan goddess that graced the tops of the columns. When David Roberts first saw it in 1838, Dendarah was still only partially exavated, with sand reaching the roof in some places. The original zodiacal ceiling had been removed in 1821 and installed in the Louvre.

All travellers, including Roberts, were impressed by the beauty of the elaborate carvings which showed processions in honour of Hathor. Many found the sheer scale of the structure, which stood alone in a plain two miles from the river, to be awe-inspiring. Roberts was aware of the contrast between the temple's former splendour and its present state. His journal entry for 19 October 1838, as transcribed by Ballantine, records his emotions on first seeing Dendarah: 'I felt sad and solitary – not a soul but myself and my black guide within miles . . . and I reached my boat overcome with melancholy reflections on the mutabilility of human greatness and the perishable nature of even the most enduring works of human genius.'

It was not until he came back up the Nile ten weeks later that he made the sketch of the temple on which this painting is based. There is no trace of his gloomy ponderings in the broad theatrical sweep of the composition, which reminds one of Roberts's early training as a scene painter. The picture is related to plate 161 in volume IV of *The Holy Land . . . and Nubia*, 1842–49.    C.B.

PROVENANCE
1841 David Barclay M.P.; 1910, 5 March, Christie's, London, anon. sale (lot 51); 1910 presented by Lord Winterstoke to The City of Bristol Museum and Art Gallery

EXHIBITIONS
1841, London, Royal Academy, Summer Exhibition (no. 223)
1975, Bristol, City Museum and Art Gallery; Swansea, Glynn Vivian Art Gallery, *Anthology of Victorian and Edwardian Paintings* (p. 4)
1981–82, Scottish Arts Council Touring Exhibition, *Artist Adventurer David Roberts 1796–1864*, (no. 18)

REFERENCES
Ballantine, 1866, pp. 88–89, 99, 175
D. Roberts, 'Eastern Journal', 2 vols., MS., National Library of Scotland, Edinburgh

88

## 89

# The Gateway to the Great Temple at Baalbec  1841

74·9 × 62·2 cm
Unsigned
The Royal Academy of Arts, London
[*repr. in colour on p. 55, plate 111*]

Interest in Baalbec in the Lebanon dated from the eighteenth century, when visits were first made by explorers such as Maundrell and Pococke in the 1730s, and Wood and Dawkins in the 1750s. By the time Roberts went there in 1839, Baalbec was becoming a more common destination for those tourists brave enough to risk the journey through the troubled surrounding countryside. However, Roberts saw himself as following in the tradition of the earlier explorers. Accordingly, he paid homage to some of the first visitors to Baalbec by including their names in this painting. Just visible inside the doorway on the right are the names of Irby and Mangles (naval officers who had made detailed measurements of the site in 1816), Wood and Dawkins (Wood published *The Ruins of Baalbec* in 1757) and Shaykh Ibrim (the pseudonym adopted by J. L. Burckhardt who visited Baalbec in September 1810).

Roberts arrived at Baalbec and set up camp on 2 May 1839, but unfavourable weather conditions – the rain drenched him and his bedding and brought on a fever – caused him to seek refuge in a nearby Greek monastery. He was, however, greatly revived by the splendour of the ruins and the richness of their ornament. He spent the next few days making a number of studies of the three temples from various angles, many of which were later used as the basis for oil paintings and lithographs. This picture shows the gateway to the Temple of Bacchus, a building which, at various stages in its history had been a Greek temple, a Christian church and a Muslim fortress. Here Roberts takes the opportunity to depict the elaborate carvings of acanthus leaves

and wreaths of vines. The famous dropped keystone, subsequently restored to its original position, hangs suspended over a group of apparently unconcerned men. Their presence in front of the temple acts both as an indication of the vast size of the doorway and as an implied criticism of the negligent attitude displayed by contemporary Arabs in allowing their architectural heritage to fall into decay. The letterpress to the lithograph based on this composition, and published in *The Holy Land . . . and Nubia*, 1842–49 (II, pl. 81), reinforces this point: 'These beautiful structures, though replete with interest and delight, carry with them a mingled feeling of humiliation at the transitory greatness of all human conceptions, and regret that such proud relics of genius should be in the hands of a people incapable of appreciating their merits and consequently heedless of their complete destruction.'   C.B.

PROVENANCE
1841, Diploma work deposited by the artist at the Royal Academy on his election to
     membership

EXHIBITIONS
1843, London, Royal Academy, Summer Exhibition (no. 219)
1866, London, British Institution (no. 177)
1868, Leeds Art Gallery, *Works of Art Exhibition* (no. 1173)
1901, London, Royal Academy, Winter Exhibition (no. 111)
1951–52, London, Royal Academy, *The First Hundred Years Exhibition* (no. 357a)
1961, Arts Council Touring Exhibition, *Diploma and Other Pictures from the Collections of the
     Royal Academy, 1798–1851* (no. 34)
1967, London, Guildhall Art Gallery, *David Roberts and Clarkson Stanfield* (no. 21)
1976, Edinburgh, Royal Scottish Academy *150th Anniversary Exhibition* (no. 4)
1981–82, Scottish Arts Council Touring Exhibition, *David Roberts, Artist Adventurer: 1796–
     1864* (no. 20)

REFERENCES
Ballantine 1866, pp. 137–39, 250
J. Maas, *Victorian Painters*, London, 1969, ill. p. 95
H. Guiterman, *David Roberts R.A. 1796–1864*, London, 1978, p. 17
K. Bendiner, *The Portrayal of the Middle East in British Painting (1835–1860)*, Ph.D thesis,
     Columbia University, 1979, pp. 101, 128

## 90

# The Island of Philae, Nubia  1843

76·5 × 152·9 cm
Signed and dated bottom right: *DAVID ROBERTS. RA 1843*
Private Collection
[*repr. in colour on p. 52, plate 112*]

The Island of Philae stood just past the first cataract, at the entrance to Nubia. It presented a particularly welcome sight to the nineteenth-century traveller ascending the river, who had just navigated the turmoil of the previous stretch of water. One of the best-known landmarks in the whole of Egypt, it was sketched and described by everyone who visited the area (see Cat. 60), but the modern tourist is deprived of the view that greeted Roberts and his contemporaries, as the island was submerged following the construction of the Aswān Dam and the monuments were moved to a neighbouring island.

Many commented on the romantic and serene appearance of Philae, an impression no doubt heightened by the knowledge that the island had been one of the most sacred places in Egypt during the period of Greek and Roman rule. At that time, the neighbouring Bigah Island was sacred to Osiris, burial site of his legs and a place of pilgrimage. Roberts thought Philae 'a paradise in the midst of desolation,' the high barren rocks of the surroundings reminding him of Scotland and the setting of the Island of Roslin, which also possessed religious ruins in the form of its chapel. In order to show the number of temples on the island, the artist chose to present a panorama of Philae viewed from Bigah. The painting shows from right to left, the pylon;

89

the birthplace of Horus; the Hypaethral temple or 'Bed of Pharaoh', built under the Emperor Trajan; and the Ptolemaic main temple dedicated to Isis. The whole view is bathed in a rosy glow suggestive of dawn or dusk. The general treatment of the subject reminds one of the commercial panoramas that David Roberts would have worked on at the outset of his artistic career.

The painting was engraved by L. Haghe in *The Holy Land . . . and Nubia*, 1842–49, I, as pl. 26.    C.B.

PROVENANCE
1843, Mr Pell; Mr Dialus; 1852, 27 February, Christie's, London (lot 132) bought by Gambart; 1858, 20 February, Christie's, London (lot 132) sold by Charles Morgan, bought by Mr Butler; 1937, 19 February, Christie's, London (lot 156), sold by Capt. Butler, bought by Barber; 1983, 18 March, Christie's, London (lot 77), bought by The Fine Art Society; 1983, bought by the present owner

EXHIBITION
1843, London, Royal Academy, Summer Exhibition (no. 53)

REFERENCE
Ballantine 1866, pp. 92–93, 250

## 91*

## A Street in Cairo    1846

76·1 × 63·4 cm
Inscribed bottom right: *David Roberts RA 1846*
Royal Holloway College, London University
[*repr. in colour on p. 53, plate 113*]

Towards the end of December 1838, Roberts arrived back in Cairo after his three-month trip up the Nile. He rented a house, intending to spend some time drawing the monuments of the city, notably a few of its 400 mosques. He set about his task with an enthusiasm that was soon dampened by the practical problems he encountered. The artist complained in a letter to his daughter Christine that 'narrow, crowded streets render it very difficult to make drawings, for in addition to the curiosity of the Arabs, you run the risk of being squeezed to a mummy by the loaded camels, who, although they are picturesque in appearance, are ugly customers to jostle' (Ballantine 1866, p. 106). Nonetheless, Roberts left Cairo a month later with a large number of drawings that were later engraved by Louis Haghe for *The Holy Land . . . and Nubia*, 1842–49.

The view depicted here is based on a drawing made by the artist on 1 January 1839 (City Museum and Art Gallery,

Nottingham), and it focusses upon the minaret of the Mosque of al-Ghamri (since destroyed). The letterpress that accompanied the lithograph of the work in *The Holy Land . . . and Nubia*, 1842–49 (III, pl. 13) gives the following description of the subject: 'This mosque is situated in the main line of the street leading to the Bab el Nasr. There are great beauty and symmetry in its minaret . . . It is surmounted by a bronze crescent, and the props, often decayed and unsafe, from which lamps are suspended during the feast of Rhamadan . . . The narrow streets, thus overhung by the houses on either side, are darkened but cooled by the exclusion of the sun's rays, yet those objects of beauty, the minarets of the mosques, frequently burst upon the observer as they rise above the buildings, and strikingly characterise the architecture of Cairo.'

The painting, executed seven years after Roberts's return from Cairo, differs from the lithograph in a way that suggests that accuracy was not Roberts's prime concern. Despite his frequently declared aim to increase the knowledge of Near Eastern architecture in England, Roberts felt free to alter certain details of the buildings on either side of the mosque, adding and subtracting elements at will. Striving rather for an overall effect, Roberts emphasises the dramatic contrast between the dark passage below and the light that falls diagonally across the street to illuminate the upper storeys of the building on the right and the minaret.    C.B.

PROVENANCE
1846, Elhanan Bicknell; 1863, 25 April, Christie's, London, Elhanan Bicknell sale (lot 75) bought by Agnew's; 1863, 6 May, sold by them to Duncan Fletcher; 1865, 20 May, Christie's, London, Duncan Fletcher sale (lot 31), bought by Flatow; F. T. Turner; 1878, 4 May, Christie's, London, F. T. Turner sale (lot 47), bought by Thomas Taylor of Aston Rowant Gallery, Oxfordshire; 1883, 28 April, Thomas Taylor sale (lot 64), bought by Thomas Holloway under the pseudonym of Martin

EXHIBITIONS
1846, London, Royal Academy, Summer Exhibition (no. 91)
1951–52, London, Royal Academy, *The First Hundred Years of the Royal Academy 1769–1868* (no. 335)
1981–2, Scottish Arts Council Touring Exhibition, 'David Roberts, Artist Adventurer, 1796–1864' (no. 22)

REFERENCES
Ballantine 1866, pp. 163, 250 (no. 141)
J. Chapel, *Victorian Taste: The Complete Catalogue of Paintings at the Royal Holloway College*, London, 1982, pp. 131–32, ill. pl. 22

90

91

# Schreyer, Adolf    1828–1899

This painter of swashbuckling Arab warriors was born in Germany but made his reputation in Paris. He was trained at the Städelsches Kunstinstitut in Frankfurt, then at the Düsseldorf Academy. From 1849 he was based in Vienna, initially specialising in landscapes and military subjects. He travelled in Turkey, Wallachia and southern Russia with Prince von Thurn und Taxis and accompanied the Prince's regiment as a war artist during the Crimean War (1854–57). In 1861 he went to Algeria, and the sketches he made there formed the foundation for his subsequent work. He lived and exhibited in Paris from 1862 to 1870, returning to Germany during the Franco-Prussian War.

## 92*

## Arab Horsemen

87 × 120 cm
Signed bottom right: *Ad. Schreyer*
Denver Art Museum, gift from the Lawrence C. Phipps Foundation
[*repr. in colour on p. 77, plate 114*]

The restless, angry-looking figures of the Arabs, the amorphous landscape setting and the loose, rapid brushwork make this a completely typical work of Schreyer. In both subject-matter and style, he was clearly influenced by Fromentin (*q.v.*). The horsemen in the foreground appear to be chiefs discussing the progress of the battle visible on the horizon to the left, their troops waiting watchfully behind them. There are no clues as to exactly where and when the scene is intended to be set, or whom the Arabs might be fighting against. But the obvious interpretation, surprising in view of Schreyer's French connections, is that they are engaged in resistance against the French in Algeria. This came to a head in 1871 when 100,000 tribesmen waged war on the occupying forces under the banner of Islam and nationalism.    M.W.

PROVENANCE
1958, presented by the Lawrence C. Phipps Foundation to the Denver Art Museum

# Scott Lauder, Robert    1803–1869

Born in 1803, Lauder was unwilling to join his father's tannery business in Edinburgh, and enrolled instead at the Trustees' Academy. After a further period of study in London, during which he drew assiduously from the Elgin Marbles, Lauder started his painting career as a portraitist, depicting his family and friends. He gradually expanded his work to include history paintings, and subjects drawn from the writings of Sir Walter Scott and the Bible. Although it is said that Lauder's initial inspiration to become an artist came from seeing a beautifully illustrated edition of *The Arabian Nights*, he never went to the Near East. Instead, he spent five years in Rome from 1833 to 1838, earning a living from portraiture. On his return, Lauder settled in London, and concentrated his efforts on trying to achieve success at the Royal Academy. However, the prize of membership eluded him, and by 1848 he had ceased to exhibit there. He went back to Edinburgh in 1852 to take up the Directorship of the Trustees' Academy, a position in which he was to prove very influential upon a young generation of Scottish artists that included W. Quiller Orchardson, John Pettie, William McTaggart and John Herdman.

92

93

## 93
## David Roberts Esq. in the Dress he wore in Palestine   1840

133 × 101·5 cm
Scottish National Portrait Gallery, Edinburgh
[repr. in colour on p. 88, plate 115]

Robert Scott Lauder was an old friend of David Roberts; the two had met as young men in Edinburgh, and Roberts frequently acted as mentor and creditor to the younger artist. The picture was commissioned by a mutual friend, David Ramsay Hay, and later passed into the Roberts family. It was painted the year after Roberts's return from his eleven-month tour of Egypt and the Holy Land in 1839, and shows him in the clothes he bought while on his travels.

The convention of painting Westerners in Turkish costume had been popularised in the eighteenth century by artists such as J. E. Liotard and the genre took on a new lease of life in the early nineteenth century as souvenirs of voyages when explorers, scholars and writers began to travel in greater numbers to the Near East. Lauder's picture is firmly rooted in the traditions of romantic portraiture. This is particularly noticeable in the stance of the subject, his rather distant gaze and the indeterminate cloudy background which lacks the recognisable topographical features of pyramids or ruins that are usually found in such paintings of travellers. Roberts was evidently pleased with this vision of himself; in a letter to David Hay he praised the broad and dashing handling of paint and claimed that it was thought to be a good likeness (letter to D. R. Hay, quoted 1983, Edinburgh, p. 58). Nevertheless, it is obvious that Lauder romanticised his sitter's features, and the painting can hardly be considered a faithful rendering of Roberts's face. Comparison with a photograph of the artist by D. O. Hill (Scottish National Portrait Gallery, Edinburgh) taken four years after this portrait was painted shows him to have coarser, blunter features than this picture would suggest.   C.B.

PROVENANCE
1840, David Ramsay Hay; Henry Sandford Bicknell (Roberts's son-in-law); 1881, 9 April, Christie's, London (lot 436); acquired by Lady Selfe (Roberts's granddaughter); by descent to John Stanton (Roberts's great-great-grandson); 1979, 7 November, Christie's, London (lot 261); 1980, acquired by The Fine Art Society; Scottish National Portrait Gallery, Edinburgh

EXHIBITIONS
1840, London, Royal Academy, Summer Exhibition (no. 169)
1980, London, The Fine Art Society, Travellers Beyond the Grand Tour (no. 63; ill. frontispiece)
1983, Edinburgh, National Gallery of Scotland and Aberdeen Art Gallery, Masterclass: Robert Scott Lauder and his Pupils (no. 21; ill. frontispiece)

94

## Seddon, Thomas   1821–1856

A member of the Pre-Raphaelite circle of artists, a friend of Ford Madox Brown, the Rossettis and William Holman Hunt, Seddon was acclaimed by Ruskin as 'the purest Pre-Raphaelite landscape painter'. He was born in the City of London, the son of a cabinet-maker. At sixteen he entered his father's business as a designer. In 1841 he visited Paris to study ornamental art and in 1848 won a silver medal from the Society of Arts for a design for a sideboard. Hoping to become a painter, he took drawing lessons from Charles Lucy at his school in Camden Town and attended life classes at the Artists' Society in Clipstone Street. He painted landscapes in North Wales in 1849 and at Barbizon in France in 1850. In the latter year he set up his own art school in Camden Town for the instruction of working men, the North London School of Design. He suffered a near-fatal attack of rheumatic fever in 1850–51, after which he became a devout Christian. He went to Egypt in 1853 and on to the Holy Land with Holman Hunt in 1854. The main result of this first Near Eastern trip, which lasted just over a year, was The Valley of the Jehoshaphat, now in the Tate Gallery, London. Seddon returned to Egypt in 1856 but died of dysentery in Cairo on 23 November. A memorial exhibition of his work was held at the Society of Arts in May 1857.

ABBREVIATED REFERENCE
Seddon 1858   J. P. Seddon, Memoir and Letters of the late Thomas Seddon, Artist, London, 1858

## 94*
## Dromedary and Arabs at the City of the Dead, Cairo, with the Tomb of Sultān El Barkook in the background   1853/56

Top corners rounded: 30·5 × 41·9 cm
Signed [initials in monogram] and dated bottom right: TSeddon 1856
Private Collection, Houston, Texas
[repr. in colour on p. 85, plate 116]

The buildings referred to in the artist's title as 'the tomb of Sultān El Barkook' are the early fifteenth-century madrasah of Sultān Farag and Tomb of Barqūq in the Eastern Cemetery at Cairo, here seen from the south-east. This may be one of the first pictures Seddon began in Cairo in 1853 (see below), or possibly the replica commissioned from him in 1855 (see Seddon 1858, pp. 141, 146). Shortly after his arrival in Cairo on 6 December he met Edward Lear, who took a friendly, encouraging interest in his work. 'I have been very glad of Lear's arrival,' he wrote to his fiancée Emmeline Bulford on 30 December, 'both because his advice as an experienced traveller has been very useful, and also because I have been able to consult him about the pictures I think of painting. He says that I have become accustomed to the language and habits of the people, and have settled down to work, in much shorter time than most persons, so my conscience is at ease. I have already painted a camel and Bedouin on a small canvas, 14 inches by 10 inches, which is finished, except the desert for a background' (Seddon 1858, p. 32). The reference is clearly to the original version of Dromedary and Arabs at the City of the Dead, Cairo. It would be difficult to point to any specific influence of Lear in the work exhibited here. The combination of ancient Islamic architecture and idle Arabs is reminiscent of David Roberts, whose Near Eastern views Seddon would certainly have known. But the most remarkable feature of

Seddon's picture, his meticulous, documentary approach to the landscape, came out of his commitment to the principles of Pre-Raphaelitism, which won him the praise of Ruskin. 'Mr Seddon's works are the first which represent a truly historic landscape art,' the critic wrote, 'that is to say, they are the first landscapes uniting perfect artistical skill with topographical accuracy, being directed with stern self-restraint to no other purpose than that of giving to persons who cannot travel trustworthy knowledge of the scenes which ought to be most interesting to them. Whatever degrees of truth may have been attained or attempted by previous artists have been more or less subordinate to pictorial and dramatic effect. In Mr Seddon's works the primal object is to place the spectator, as far as art can do, in the scene represented, and to give him the perfect sensation of its reality, wholly unmodified by the artist's execution' (Seddon 1858, p. 171). 'Before I saw these,' he declared after visting Seddon's private exhibition in 1855, 'I never thought it possible to attain such an effect of sun and light without sacrificing truth of colour' (*ibid.*, p. 137). M.W.

PROVENANCE
1855, if the original version, acquired from the artist by Lord Grosvenor; 1974, 18 October, Christie's, London (lot 85); 1978, March, acquired by The Fine Art Society, London; Priv. Coll.; 1981, November, acquired again by The Fine Art Society, from whom acquired by Kurt E. Schon Ltd, New Orleans; Priv. Coll., Houston, Texas

EXHIBITIONS
?1855, London, the artist's room, 14 Berners Street
?1856, London, Royal Academy, Summer Exhibition (no. 474)
?1857, London, Society of Arts
1978, London, The Fine Art Society, *Eastern Encounters* (no. 58)

REFERENCES
Seddon 1858, pp. 32, 141, 146
*The Spectator*, 14 April 1855, p. 392 (review of Seddon's private exhibition)
A. Staley, *The Pre-Raphaelite Landscape*, Oxford, 1973, p. 98
M. Verrier, *The Orientalists*, New York and London, 1979, no. 9, illus.

95

## 95*
## 'Arab Shaykh' (probably Richard Burton) 1854

Top corners rounded: 45·7 × 35·6 cm
Signed [initials in monogram] and dated bottom right: *TSeddon Egypt/1854*
Private Collection, Houston, Texas
[*repr. in colour on p. 86, plate 117*]

As early as 12 December, only a few days after arriving in Cairo on his first trip to Egypt, Seddon noted in his diary that he had 'met a Mr Burton, who, knowing the Arabic language thoroughly, has taken the dress' (Seddon 1858, pp. 31–32). Soldier, diplomat, poet, linguist, translator, anthropologist, explorer and student of Islam, Richard Burton (1821–1890) was a key figure in European-Near Eastern relations in the nineteenth century. When Seddon met him he had just undertaken the boldest of the many adventures for which he became famous. Earlier in the year he had managed to pass himself off as a Muslim, posing as a doctor from India to excuse his foreign pronunciation of Arabic, and enter the sacred city of Mecca. He commissioned Seddon to make a watercolour sketch of him to be used as an illustration in his description of his experiences, *The Personal Narrative of a Pilgrimage to El-Medinah and Meccah* (1855–56). In his letter to Emmeline Bulford of 30 December 1853, Seddon reported that he had made 'a portrait of Lieutenant Burton in full Arab costume, with a camel, for an account he is going to publish of his travels in Arabia, and his journey to Mecca' (*ibid.*, p. 32). The watercolour, now in a private collection (1983, Brighton Museum and Art Gallery, *The Inspiration of Egypt*, no. 329), was reproduced as a lithograph in volume I of Burton's book, facing page 228, with the caption 'An Arab Shaykh in his Travelling Dress'. It is similar to *Arab Shaykh*, and in the private exhibition Seddon held in 1855 to show the results of his Near Eastern journey, the watercolour of Burton seems to have been given the title *Shaykh with Camel lying down* (*The Spectator*, 1855). It is plausible, then, that the *Arab Shaykh* should also be a portrait of Burton. On the other hand, it shows marked differences from the watercolour portrait; the pose is similar but the outfit is different, the face looks older in the oil and the beard is shorter and greyer. These allow considerable room for the possibility that it may be intended to represent nothing more than a *shaykh*. Perhaps Seddon was pleased with his portrait of Burton and decided to make a larger, more finished variation in oil, cast virtually in the same mould as the watercolour portrait but intended to pass, and be sold, as a study of a real Arab. In which case, it may well be identifiable as the 'Shaykh' Seddon was finishing from an Arab model in Paris on his return journey in January 1855 (see Seddon 1858, p. 131). M.W.

PROVENANCE
*c.* 1950, Priv. Coll., Egypt; 1979, March, acquired by The Fine Art Society, London, from whom acquired by Kurt E. Schon Ltd, New Orleans; Priv. Coll., Houston, Texas

EXHIBITIONS
?1855, London, the artist's room, 14 Berners Street (as *Arab Shaykh*)
?1856, London, Royal Academy, Summer Exhibition (no. 9, as *An Arab shaykh and tents in the Egyptian desert Painted on the spot*)
?1857, London, Society of Arts
1980, London, The Fine Art Society, *Travellers Beyond the Grand Tour* (no. 90)

REFERENCES
?Seddon 1858, p. 131
*The Spectator*, 14 April, 1855, p. 392 (review of Seddon's private exhibition)
*Connoisseur*, July 1980, 204, no. 821, ill. (cover)
Coral Petroleum, *A Near Eastern Adventure*, n.d., ill. (cover)

# Tissot, James   1836–1902

Born in Nantes to parents both of whom were involved in the clothing business, Tissot left home at about the age of twenty to study at the Ecole des Beaux-Arts in Paris, where he became a pupil of the neo-classical painters Lamothe and Flandrin. In the early 1860s he painted a number of historical subjects, several on the theme of Faust and Marguerite. He achieved fame and a considerable fortune with the scenes from modern life in high society that he exhibited from 1864. In 1871, after the Franco-Prussian War and the fall of the Commune, Tissot moved to London, where his studies of contemporary manners and customs, courtship and flirtation, usually featuring pretty young women in flouncy dresses, won him continuing success. Following the death of his Irish mistress Kathleen Newton in 1882, he returned to Paris to paint a series of large oils on the theme of *La Femme à Paris*. While working on the last of these, which showed a Parisian woman singing in church with a nun, he had a vision of Christ and became fervently religious, devoting the rest of his life to painting biblical subjects.

## 96

## The Journey of the Magi   *c.1894*
*Les Rois mages en voyage*

68·6 × 99·1 cm
Signed bottom left: *J. J. Tissot*
Minneapolis Institute of Arts
[*repr. in colour on p. 95, plate 118*]

Tissot believed he could forge a new and better religious art by undertaking extensive research to determine how sacred figures and events might actually have looked. In pursuance of this idea he travelled to the Holy Land in 1886–87, 1889 and 1896, making sketches and taking photographs. His interpretations of biblical scenes appeared as the illustrations to voluminous New and Old Testaments published in 1896–97 and 1904 respectively. (For a fuller discussion of Tissot and his desire for authenticity in biblical painting, see Warner pp. 33–34.) The idea of showing the Magi mounted on camels at the head of a desert caravan is typical of his approach. This work is a version of an original watercolour now in the Brooklyn Museum, which is reproduced in colour in the *New Testament* (I, 1896, p. 28). Tissot painted a number of oil versions of his Bible illustrations. According to the inventory for probate of his house, there were seven New Testament subjects in his possession at his death (see Willard Erwin Misfeldt, 'James Jacques Tissot: a Bio-Critical Study', Ph.D. thesis, Washington University, 1971, p. 327); and four, not including the present exhibit, appeared in the Vente Tissot in 1903 (9–10 July, Hôtel Drouot, Paris, lots 6–9). In addition, there are photographs showing five Old Testament subjects (there may originally have been seven) in the albums the artist kept as a record of his work. However, only two of the documented oils of biblical subjects have been traced: this painting and *The Sojourn in Egypt*, now in the National Gallery of Ireland, Dublin. With its dry, rough surface and predominantly pale colour, *The Journey of the Magi* is characteristic of the artist's late work in this medium.   M.W.

PROVENANCE
Possibly given by the artist or his heirs to the publisher of his illustrated *Old Testament*, Maurice de Brunhoff; 1970, 6 March, Christie's, London (lot 139) acquired by the Schweitzer Gallery, New York; 1970, acquired by the Minneapolis Institute of Arts
REFERENCE
M. Wentworth, *James Tissot*, Oxford, 1984, pp. 188–89, ill. col. pl. VI

96

# Vedder, Elihu  1836–1923

Born in New York City, the American visionary painter Elihu Vedder was raised both there and with his relations in Schenectady, New York and Cuba. At the age of sixteen or seventeen he received his first formal artistic training from the genre painter Tompkins Harrison Matteson. In 1856 Vedder left the United States to study in Italy and France, returning to New York in 1860. He exhibited six works at the National Academy of Design in 1862 and within three years was admitted as a member. Some of Vedder's earliest successes were paintings of enigmatic or mysterious themes such as *The Questioner of the Sphinx* (Cat. 97) and *The Roc's Egg* (both 1863), and *The Lair of the Sea Serpent* (1864; all three works in the Museum of Fine Arts, Boston) and it is for this type of fantastic or mystical work that he became best known.

Vedder returned to Europe in 1865 and except for frequent visits to America in the 1880s and 1890s lived in Rome or on Capri for the rest of his life. Although he considered himself primarily a landscape painter, his repertoire included not only directly studied scenes of the Italian countryside, but studio pieces of models in Renaissance dress, and several important narrative or allegorical figure paintings. In 1884, he illustrated a volume of the *Rubaiyat of Omar Khayyam*, which received widespread public attention. This vehicle was well-suited to the artist's extensive philosophical and spiritual ruminations and to the decorative aspects of his style which tended toward the sinuous line of Art Nouveau.

Later in his career Vedder executed murals for the Walker Art Building at Bowdoin College, and for the Library of Congress, and had a brief interest in the design of stained-glass windows, greeting cards, tiles and firebacks. For his large following of friends and admirers, which was particularly strong in Boston, he produced a collection of remembrances entitled *The Digressions of V* (1910) and the year before his death he published a volume of poetic musings called *Between Faith and Doubt* (1922).

## 97*

# The Questioner of the Sphinx  1863

92·4 × 107 cm
Signed and dated bottom right : *Elihu Vedder / 1863*
Museum of Fine Arts, Boston
*[repr. in colour on p. 157, plate 128]*

Although Vedder did not visit Egypt until 1889, he had ample inspiration from many sources for his chosen theme. Many travel books recommended Egypt as an appendage to the 'Grand Tour'. William H. Bartlett, whose popular engravings of the United States made the wonders and landmarks of the New World accessible to Europeans and Americans alike, published a volume in 1849 entitled *The Nile Boat or Glimpses of the Land of Egypt*. Among his illustrations was one of the Great Sphinx at Gizah at night.

Vedder's grand monument in *The Questioner of the Sphinx* appears not to have been based directly on the Great Sphinx. The artist may have been aware of the collection of Egyptian antiquities, belonging to Dr. Henry Abbott, which were under consideration for purchase by the New-York Historical Society the year he painted his impressive work. He also may have absorbed certain images from the collection of the Louvre which he had visited during his sojourn in Europe. The statue depicted is almost certainly a combination of remembered fragments of existing works and Vedder's own amazingly fertile imagination.

*The Questioner of the Sphinx*, which was exhibited at the National Academy of Design in 1863, comes from a period early in Vedder's life, in which he produced several remarkable works that explored inexplicable, powerful forces in the universe. It was these intangible aspects of the Near East, rather than its colourful or exotic customs, which intrigued Vedder. The Arab who crouches at the mouth of the unyielding Sphinx seeks knowledge that transcends ordinary thought and time.

The subject of the Sphinx is one which continued to interest Vedder. He produced a smaller version of *The Questioner of the Sphinx*, including an older, more care-worn human figure, in 1875 (Worcester Museum of Art), a fearsome, predatory, female tiger/beast in *The Sphinx of the Seashore* (1879–80, Fine Arts Museums of San Francisco) and at least one direct archaeological record of the Great Sphinx painted on site in 1890 (Mr and Mrs Edgar P. Richardson, Philadelphia).    D.C.

PROVENANCE
c. 1863, acquired by Martin Brimmer, Boston, from the artist; 1906, bequeathed by Mrs Martin Brimmer to the Museum of Fine Arts, Boston

EXHIBITIONS
1863, National Academy of Design, New York (no. 173)
1868, Boston Athenaeum (no. 286)
1933, Wadsworth Atheneum, Hartford (no. 75)
1966, Smithsonian Institution, Travelling Exhibition, *Paintings and Drawings by Elihu Vedder* (no. 7)
1970, Metropolitan Museum of Art, *Nineteenth Century America* (no. 126)
1974, Los Angeles County Museum of Art, *American Narrative Painting* (no. 70)
1978, National Collection of Fine Arts, Washington, *The Art of Elihu Vedder* (no. 28)
1980, Museum of Fine Arts, Boston, *The Boston Tradition* (no. 49)

REFERENCES
H. T. Tuckerman, *Book of The Artists*, New York, 1870, p. 451
E. Radford, 'Elihu Vedder and His Exhibition', *Art Journal*, April 1899, p. 102
E. Vedder, *Digressions of V*, Boston, 1910, p. 460
*American Paintings in the Museum of Fine Arts*, Boston, 1969, no. 991
R. Soria, *Elihu Vedder: American Visionary Artist in Rome*, Rutherford, New Jersey, 1970, pp. 38, 40, 283
P. D. Pierce, 'Deciphering Egypt : Four Studies in the American Sublime', Ph.D thesis, Yale University, 1980, pp. 55–76

97

# Vernet, Horace-Emile-Jean    1789–1863

Born in his family's apartments in the Louvre, Vernet came from a line of distinguished painters. As grandson of the marine painter Claude-Joseph Vernet and son of Carle, who specialised in historical and biblical scenes, he received his early training at home, supplemented by tuition from François Vincent (1746–1813). He made his debut at the Salon of 1800. A loyal supporter of Napoleon I, he was enrolled as Chevalier de la Légion d'Honneur in 1814 for his part in the defence of Paris. From 1819 he attached himself to the Orléans branch of the royal family. Though mistrusted for his liberal sentiments by the restored Bourbon monarchy, Vernet was nevertheless patronised by Charles X, who appointed him Professor at the Ecole des Beaux-Arts in 1826 and successor to Pierre Guérin at the Villa Medici Française in Rome in 1828.

Vernet's reputation was thus firmly established by 1833, when he travelled for the first time to Algeria with the French army. Further voyages were made in 1837, 1839–40, 1845, and finally in 1853. Together with his nephew, Frédéric Goupil-Fesquet, Vernet was one of the first Oriental travellers to make use of the daguerreotype and in November 1839 recorded views of Alexandria, Cairo and Jerusalem, only months after the process had been made public.

Best known for his numerous large-scale battle-pieces and scenes of army life, Vernet worked with a wide range of subject-matter and in a variety of media. He made illustrations and caricatures for books and journals, paintings inspired by literature and the Bible and a sequence of popular lithographs executed in the 1820s, as well as Oriental genre scenes.

98

## 98†

# The Battle of Somah    1839
*Le Combat de Somah*

145 × 112 cm
Signed and dated bottom right: *H. Vernet 1839*
Musée Rolin, Autun
[*repr. in colour on p. 60, plate 119*]

This painting, which commemorates the patriotic action of General Charngarnier, a native of Autun, at the Battle of Somah, was commissioned following a subscription raised by the citizens of the town. Fought on 24 November 1836, the battle was one of the decisive engagements in the French colonial wars in North Africa. According to a report issued by General Clauzel (de Fontenay, 1877, p. 26), Charngarnier, heavily under siege by the enemy, appealed to the patriotism of his men at a critical moment in the fighting and led the French army to victory. Vernet shows General Charngarnier rising above the surrounding carnage, calm in the face of impending death. The pose of the figure, though slightly larger in scale, echoes Gros's depiction of General Murat at the Battle of Abū Qīr (see Cat. 50). Yet, unlike Gros, Vernet's concern here is less with the dramatic evocation of battle than with documentary accuracy, and he accepted the commission only on the condition that he had the episode recounted to him by the leader of the second batallion, who had witnessed the scene.

Vernet had painted battle scenes from the beginning of his career, exhibiting the first, *Prise d'un camp retranché*, at the Salon of 1812. Many were bought by the Duc d'Orléans for the Palais Royale, but it was in the decoration of the Galerie des Batailles in Versailles that Vernet's most grandiose schemes were realised. His contribution to this project, instigated by King Louis-Philippe, included the enormous *Prise de la Smala d'Abd-el-Kader par le duc d'Aumâle* (1845; Versailles), and a variant of *The Battle of Somah*, executed as an *au-dessus de porte* with surrounding decorative borders. The voyages to North Africa allowed Vernet to enhance the pictorial interest of his paintings by including exotic physiognomies, Oriental weapons and costumes, as seen here in the fallen Arab horse and rider.

More than any other aspect of his oeuvre, the battle-piece aroused the critics' aversion to his pleasing, if characterless style. They considered his art to be non-intellectual and trivial, aimed solely at gratifying public taste and advancing his own personal success. Delacroix himself made reference to Vernet's remarkable ease of composition and noted in his journal that the main example to be learned from Vernet's popular success was 'to finish something when one had it in hand. the [*sic*] only means of creating a lot' (*Journal*, I, 19 August 1824, p. 118).

Even the most hostile of critics, however, had to concede the concern for authenticity and the in-depth military knowledge of this '*Raphael des cantines*' (Silvestre, 1862, p. 347). The characteristic features of Vernet's battle-pieces are perhaps best evaluated by Paul Mantz in *L'Artiste*, 1858: 'Horace Vernet's battles are not terrible, nor are they heroic, but they possess the clarity of a simple, carefully considered bulletin' (p. 81).    J.M.

PROVENANCE
1837, 3 March, subscription fund opened on the initiative of the Mayor of Autun to commission a painting from Horace Vernet; 1838, 9 December, letter from Horace Vernet to the Mayor, explaining the delay in the delivery of the painting; 1839, 28 September, payment of 4000 francs from Ville d'Autun to Horace Vernet

EXHIBITIONS
1974, Castres, Musée Goya, *Fortuny et son temps* (no. 148)
1980, Paris, Ecole des Beaux-Arts, *Horace Vernet (1789–1863)* (no. 73)

REFERENCES
P. Mantz, 'Galerie du XIXᵉ siecle. Horace Vernet', *L'Artiste*, 1857, pp. 177–82
P. Mantz, *L'Artiste*, 1858, p. 81
Th. Silvestre, *Histoire des Artistes vivants. Les Artistes français*, 1862, p. 347
H. de Fontenay and Ph. Mariller, *Notice des tableaux, dessins, estampes, lithographes, photographes et sculptures exposés dans les salles du Musée de l'Hôtel de Ville d'Autun*, Autun, 1877, pp. 26–27
Ch. Blanc, *Une Famille d'artistes. Les trois Vernet. Josephe – Carle – Horace*, Paris, 1898, p. 19
A. Dayot, *Les Vernet*, Paris, 1898, p. 219

## 99†

## The First Mass in Kabylia   1854

*La Première Messe en Kabylie*

194 × 123 cm
Signed and dated bottom right: *Horace Vernet 1854*
Musée cantonal des Beaux-Arts, Lausanne

The Mass in the Kabylia mountain range to the south-east of Algiers, was celebrated on 14 June 1853, to mark the anniversary of the French landing in Algeria, and the submission of the native tribes. Vernet participated in the ceremony during the course of his final visit to North Africa, personally seeing to the construction of the altar; as a devout Catholic, the religious significance of the glorification of a Christian deity in a land of infidels did not escape him. He was deeply moved by the scene, and felt his painting to be by far the most important and sincere of the thirty exhibited at the Salon of 1855. Indeed, apart from the presence of some Arab soldiers, and the token inclusion of *burnūses* and *babushes* in the foreground, there is little to suggest the North African location of the scene.

From his accounts published in *L'Illustration* (8 and 12 April 1856), Vernet appeared singularly unimpressed by Arab culture. He showed little enthusiasm for the mosques, pyramids or cities of Egypt and Algeria: 'Cairo', he wrote, 'is bigger than Algiers, only more wretched still' (quoted L. Lagrange, 1863, p. 453). The Holy Cities of Bethlehem and Jerusalem were, for him, the highlights of the tour, and he was especially inflamed by the sight of a cavalry encampment in the plains around El-Arisha and Gaza. According to one English biographer (*Art-Union*, 1844, p. 119), Vernet's desire to visit these countries was largely inspired by his reading of the Scriptures, which also seem to have coloured his actual experiences in the Orient. In particular, he was struck by the similarity between the costume of the Arabs and that worn in biblical times; the country, on both a superficial and a moral level, for him became *'la bible arabifiée'* (L. Lagrange, 1863, p. 455). In *The First Mass in Kabylia*, it is the profound religiosity of the occasion which Vernet chose to emphasise. The *repoussoir* foreground figures, the soldiers' rifles, and the abbot's clasped hands, all contrive to lead the eye up to the brightly-lit altar and cross, swathed in a mystic puff of cloud. The awesome grandeur of the Kabylia mountains hints at the presence of the deity and the humility of Man before the Almighty, though the force of expression is somewhat lost through Vernet's disposition towards the anecdotal and the picturesque.   J.M.

PROVENANCE
Gift of E. Kaufmann to the Musée cantonal des Beaux-Arts

EXHIBITION
1930, Paris, Petit Palais, *L'Exposition du Centenaire de la conquête de l'Algérie* (no. 394, ill.)

REFERENCES
Anon., 'Living Artists of Europe No. IV. Horace Vernet', *Art-Union*, VI, May 1844, pp. 119–120
H. Delaborde, 'Horace Vernet, ses oeuvres et sa manière', *Revue des Deux Mondes*, 1863, 44, pp. 76–98
L. Lagrange, 'Artistes Contemporains – Horace Vernet', *Gazette des Beaux-Arts*, November 1863, p. 453

## Wilkie, David   1785–1841

Born in the small town of Cults, Fife, Wilkie was initially trained at the Trustees' Academy in Edinburgh before moving to London to enrol at the Royal Academy Schools. Although he spent the rest of his life based in London, his early works depicted genre scenes of Scottish rural life; executed in a manner reminiscent of Dutch and Flemish masters, they earned him considerable praise. His fame in this field led to a series of important commissions, such as *Chelsea Pensioners Reading the Gazette of the Battle of Waterloo* (1822; Apsley House, London) painted for the Duke of Wellington. Though a genre scene, its celebration of a specific moment in recent history heralded Wilkie's interest in history painting. At the same time, Wilkie was developing a taste for travel, which led to a three-year tour of Europe from 1825 to 1828 and a six-month tour of the Near East in 1840–41. The object of this second journey was to investigate the possibility of painting biblical subjects in their authentic surroundings. Wilkie was detained in Constantinople and, after visiting the Holy Land, spent only a short time in Egypt at Alexandria while waiting for the boat home. He sketched many portraits of local dignitaries and started a number of Eastern and biblical scenes, none of which was completed owing to his untimely death on the return journey. Wilkie's funeral off the Straits of Gibraltar is commemorated in J. M. W. Turner's *Peace: Burial at Sea* (1841; Tate Gallery, London).

ABBREVIATED REFERENCE
Cunningham 1843  A. Cunningham *The Life of Sir David Wilkie*, London, 1843, 3 vols.

99

## 100†

### The Turkish Letter Writer    1840

Oil on panel: 68·6 × 53·4 cm
Signed and dated on frame of scribe's platform: *D Wilkie F. Constantinople, 1840*
Aberdeen Art Gallery and Museums
[*repr. in colour on p. 73, plate 121*]

Sir David Wilkie set off on his tour of the Near East on
15 August 1840. He sailed down the Danube to his first
destination, Constantinople, where he had the leisure to wander
round the city, inspecting the bazaars and coffee shops and to
learn about Turkish daily life. At Topkanah, the suburb outside
Pera, he was struck by a scene in the outer court of a mosque.
His journal records 'a scribe of most venerable appearance. He
was reading a letter or a paper he had been writing for two
Turkish young women – one very handsome; the way they were
placed made an excellent composition for a picture' (Cunningham
1843, III, p. 220). Soon afterwards, he took up the idea suggested
by this vignette, and began work on *The Turkish Letter Writer*.
Wilkie did not spend long on the picture. He started painting
it on 28 October and by 19 November he had commenced work
on *The Tartar Messenger* (Cat. 101), which may imply that by that
date he had finished all he was intending to do on the former
work. The painting was sent back to Britain screwed to the lid
of a packing case on 12 January 1841.

According to the letterpress in *The Wilkie Gallery*, the picture
shows two young women and a scribe to whom they have
dictated a love letter. Public scribes provided an essential service
in a largely illiterate country, and they offered a pictorial subject
rich in anecdote and innuendo. Both David Roberts (eg. *The
Letter Writer*; *The Holy Land, Syria, Idumea, Arabia and Nubia*,
London, 1842–49, III, pl. 31) and J. F. Lewis (eg. *The Scribe*;
present location unknown) found the subject irresistible. Wilkie
himself had already treated the theme of a narrative suggested
by a letter in *The Letter of Introduction* (1813; National Gallery
of Scotland, Edinburgh).

Wilkie's painting departs from the scene which he had
witnessed in one important respect: it shows a Turkish woman
and a Greek woman, rather than the two Turkish ladies Wilkie
had actually seen. Given the strained relationship between these
two countries at that date, it was unlikely that a Muslim and a
Christian would have been seen together and their juxtaposition
puzzled some observers. Even the letterpress to the engraving
of the painting in *The Wilkie Gallery* complained that 'while it
certainly adds to the picturesque variety of the composition, it
is rather inaccurate as to local usages.' It may be that Wilkie
wished to comment in this work not only on the variety of races
within the Turkish Empire, as he did in *The Tartar Messenger*
(Cat. 101), but also on the possibilities for peaceful co-existence
between Greek and Turk in the wake of the Greek War of
Independence (1821–29).    C.B.

PROVENANCE
1842, 25–30 April, Christie's, London, Wilkie sale (lot 667); Lord Charles Townshend; Lord
Northbrook; James Price; 1895, Mrs M. V. Smith Cunninghame; Aberdeen Art Gallery and
Museums

EXHIBITIONS
1842, London, Royal Academy, Summer Exhibition (no. 714)
1842, London, British Institution (no. 98)
1874, London, International Exhibition (no. 202 or 203)
1887, Manchester, Jubilee Exhibition (no. 710)
1967, Paisley Museum and Art Gallery, *Ramsay and Wilkie*

REFERENCES
Cunningham 1843, III, p. 320
*The Wilkie Gallery*, n.d., n.p., engr. by R. Staines
*Sketches in Turkey, Syria and Egypt, 1840–41* (no pl. no.), 1843, engr. by R. Staines
K. Bendiner, 'Wilkie in Turkey: "The Tartar Messenger Narrating the News of the Victory
    of St. Jean d'Acre"', *Art Bulletin*, June 1981, LXIII, p. 267, ill. fig. 9

## 101†

### The Tartar Messenger Narrating the News
### of the Victory of St. Jean d'Acre    1840

Oil on panel: 68·6 × 53·3 cm
Private Collection
[*repr. in colour on p. 72, plate 122*]

Wilkie began *The Tartar Messenger* while in Constantinople. It
was never finished since it was sent home to await completion
on his return from the Near East. It is closely related to *The
Turkish Letter Writer* (Cat. 100) in size, colour and approach, and
for most of their subsequent histories the two pictures belonged
to the same collections. In both paintings, Wilkie concentrated
on the figures, their inter-relationships and costume details. He
was fascinated by the mixture of racial types found within the

100

101

Turkish Empire, and in *The Tartar Messenger* he shows a Turk, a Greek, an Armenian and a Jew. He regretted, however, that since this was a Turkish subject, he could not introduce a female figure amongst the men. He resolved this problem by including the female children. The dramatic incident in this picture is heightened by fixing the eyes of everyone in the coffee shop on the narrator, though Wilkie could not resist the amusing episode of the barber filling the mouth of his customer with shaving foam on the left of the picture.

The painting is not based on any observed incident, but is an imaginary scene showing a messenger relaying to the men in a Turkish café news of the recent Anglo-Turkish victory over the Egyptians at St. Jean d'Acre. The battle was the outcome partly of expansionist policies pursued by the Egyptians in Syria, and partly of Muḥammad 'Alī's desire to create a hereditary Pashalik in Egypt (see Cat. 102). Notwithstanding her interests in Egypt, Britain's sympathies were largely with the Turks on this issue, reflecting widespread concern over the gradual dissolution of the Ottoman Empire and the political vacuum which this was to create in the Near East. The painting was also Wilkie's personal celebration of the end of a war which had detained him in Constantinople, delaying his planned visit to the Holy Land.

Kenneth Bendiner has underlined the picture's significance as a reflection of changing British attitudes towards Turkey. It exhibits a far more favourable attitude towards the Turks than previous works by other artists, which had stressed the Turks' role as the oppressors of the Greeks in their struggle for freedom. By placing the reference to the Turkish victory in a domestic rather than a military setting, which removed the need for violence and melodrama in his portrayal, Wilkie indicated his sympathy for the Turks. His highly acclaimed *Chelsea Pensioners Reading the Gazette of the Battle of Waterloo* (1822; Apsley House, London) had treated a similar theme of news of military victory in the same informal, anecdotal way. In that picture, however, the news is relayed by written word, rather than by word of mouth, upon which illiterate Turks relied.   C.B.

PROVENANCE
1842, 25–30 April, Christie's, London, Wilkie sale (lot 666); Mr. Farren; Lord Northbrook; James Price; 1895, Mrs M. V. Smith Cunninghame; Agnew's; 1955, acquired by the present owner

EXHIBITIONS
1874, London, International Exhibition (nos. 202 or 203)
1887, Manchester, Jubilee Exhibition (no. 715)

REFERENCES
Cunningham 1843, III, p. 338–39, 363
*Sketches in Turkey, Syria and Egypt, 1840–41*, 1843, engr. by R. Staines
*The Wilkie Gallery*, n.d., n.p., engr. by W. Greatbach
K. Bendiner, 'Wilkie in Turkey: "The Tartar Messenger Narrating the News of the Victory of St. Jeane d'Acre"', *Art Bulletin*, June, 1981, LXIII, pp. 259–68, ill. fig. I

## 102

# Muḥammad 'Alī, Pasha of Egypt   1841

Oil on millboard: 61 × 51 cm
Inscribed bottom left: *David Wilkie ft/Alexandria May 11th 1841*
The Trustees of the Tate Gallery

Muḥammad 'Alī, Pasha of Egypt from 1805 to 1848, was something of a legend in his own lifetime, earning praise for his Westernisation and modernisation policies at home, and notoriety abroad for his military aggression against the Turks. This portrait was painted in the wake of Egypt's defeat at the Battle of St. Jean d'Acre, an event which Wilkie had celebrated in *The Tartar Messenger* (Cat. 101). Notwithstanding his sympathies with Muḥammad 'Alī's adversaries, Wilkie was

happy to accept the invitation to paint the Pasha's likeness while he was waiting in Alexandria for the ship on which he was to return to England. News of this project travelled fast to London; by 29 May J. M. W. Turner was discussing Wilkie in a letter to a friend, saying, 'I heard last Eving [*sic*] that he is now painting the Pasha's Portrait alias Mahogany face'.

In spite of warnings to the contrary, the artist found his sitter pleasant and co-operative, and was able almost to complete the picture in three sittings. Muḥammad 'Alī was quite pleased with the result, although he felt that Wilkie had made him look too young by his tactful suppression of certain lines around the brows and eyes. Unlike David Roberts and J. F. Lewis, who also drew the Pasha, Wilkie chose to pose Muḥammad 'Alī in a Western-style chair rather than on his customary divan. This may have been to enhance his subject's dignity in Western eyes, a point of crucial importance in the light of British attitudes towards him at the time.

The review which the painting received in the *Athenaeum*, when it was exhibited at the Royal Academy in 1842, referred to Muḥammad 'Alī as 'the absolute troubler of modern Europe . . . There is force and despotism, not merely in his shrewd eyes and firm lips, but in the attitude and in the hands which grasp nervously, with scimitar-like fingers, the elbows of his chair.' The reviewer was probably unaware that Wilkie had originally made a sketch of the Pasha holding his sword in a far more menacing manner, to which Muḥammad 'Alī had objected, saying, 'the British have deprived me of my sword!' Indeed, the image presented here appears to modern eyes as that of a placid man, tallying with the artist Gleyre's description of him as 'anything but heroic'.   C.B.

PROVENANCE
1860, 21 June, Christie's, London, David Wilkie sale (lot 388), acquired by Edinburgh; 1909, 4 December, Christie's, London (lot 134), acquired by Sampson; 1919, 28 November, Christie's, London, Rt. Hon. Earl Brassey sale (lot 117), acquired by Permain; 1927, bequeathed by Henry Alexander Gordon, 4th Earl of Effingham, to the Tate Gallery, London

EXHIBITIONS
1842, London, Royal Academy Summer Exhibition (no. 116)
1958, London, Royal Academy, *Wilkie R.A.* (no. 43)
1983, Brighton Museum and Art Gallery; Manchester City Art Gallery, *The Inspiration of Egypt* (no. 292)

REFERENCES
Cunningham 1843, III, pp. 460, 462–9, 532
*Athenaeum*, 1842
J. Maas, *Victorian Painters*, London, 1970, ill. p. 93
K. Bendiner, 'Wilkie in Turkey', *Art Bulletin*, June 1981, pp. 264–65, ill. fig. 7

102

## North Africa and the Near East:
## A Chronology of Events, Personalities and Publications c. 1798–c. 1922 *Compiled by Briony Llewellyn**

| HISTORICAL EVENTS | ARTISTS |
|---|---|

**1770**

**1776**
to 1794: Luigi Mayer (d. 1803) in Constantinople and elsewhere in the Ottoman Empire as draughtsman to Sir Robert Ainslie, British Ambassador

**1780**

*after* **1787**
Thomas Hope (1769–1831) in Constantinople for an extended period?

**1790**

**1798**
French conquest of Egypt: 'the most seminal event in the history of the modern Islamic world' (M. S. Anderson)
2 July: Napoleon Bonaparte lands his forces at Alexandria
21 July: 'Battle of the Pyramids' (actually at Imbaba, 9 miles away): Cairo occupied by the French
1–2 August: 'Battle of the Nile': Nelson destroys French fleet in Abū Qīr Bay
4–20 October: General Divan sits as advisory council with delegations from all parts of Egypt
21 October: Muslim insurrection against the French in Cairo; quelled

**1797**
Hope in Egypt and possibly elsewhere in Near East

**1798–99**
November–July: Dominique Vivant, Baron Denon (1747–1825) in Egypt with the French Commission on the Sciences and Arts; accompanies General Belliard to Upper Egypt to aid General Desaix's pursuit of fleeing Mamlūks; August: leaves Egypt with Napoleon

**1799**
Napoleon attacks Syria from Egypt
16 April: Battle of Mount Tabor: French victory over Turks
May: French attempts to take Acre defeated; retreat to Cairo
25 July: Ottoman Turks defeated by French at Abū Qīr
23 August: Napoleon leaves secretly for France, from Alexandria, with a few close associates, including Denon; Kléber left in command

**1800**

**1800**
28 January: Kléber ratifies treaty with Turks at El Arisha for evacuation of French troops from Egypt; 20 March: Kléber defeats Turkish army at Heliopolis; 14 June: Kléber assassinated in Cairo; succeeded by Menou

**1801**
21 March: British defeat French at Canopus near Alexandria
3 September: French surrender Alexandria and evacuate
Muḥammad 'Alī arrives in Egypt with Albanian troops as part of Ottoman force attempting to re-establish authority
Bay of Tripoli insists on increase of payment of safe-conduct money by USA; Four Years War ensues (1801–05)

**1803**
Mecca taken by Wahhabi forces

**1804**
March: Muḥammad 'Alī, now commander of Albanian troops in Egypt, expels Mamlūks from Cairo

**1805**
12 May: Muḥammad 'Alī declares himself Pasha of Egypt (confirmed by Ottoman Porte November 1806); ruler of Egypt, to 1848: virtually independent of Turkey; gradual modernisation of the country

**1807**
29 May: Selim III, Sultan of Turkey, deposed
British abolition of slave trade

**1808**
United States prohibits import of slaves
Mahmud II, Sultān of Turkey (accession 28 July); reputed to be the son of a French girl, Aimée Dubecq de Rivery, living in the Harem since 1784; to 1839: initiates process of westernisation with extensive programme of reforms
Stratford Canning (1786–1880) on British Government service in Constantinople

*c.* **1807**
to 1812: Sir William Allan (1782–1850) in the Ukraine for several years; excursions to neighbouring regions to observe the Cossacks, Circassians and Tartars

*With acknowledgements to all contributors to the catalogue, and to Peter Stocks and to Rodney Searight

**1782**
Prémiére of Mozart's *Die Entführung aus dem Serail*, in Vienna

**1786**
W. Beckford, *Vathek*; Oriental fantasy inspired by *The Arabian Nights*

*c.* **1787**
Napoleon, 'Le prophète masquée' MS; grotesque Oriental fantasy found amongst his papers after his death

1780

**1791**
Prémiére of Mozart's *Die Zauberflöte*, in Vienna

**1798**
Panorama theatres opened in Leicester Square and the Strand; cycloramas of current events and interesting places from the work of famous artists displayed; many Near Eastern subjects (until 1856)
July: The French Commission on the Sciences and Arts accompanies Napoleon's forces to Egypt; consists of civil engineers, surveyors, cartographers, astronomers, botanists, surgeons, pharmacists, antiquarians, architects, artists, mathematicians, chemists, mineralogists, zoologists
22 August: Napoleon creates the Institut d'Egypte for the purposes of '(1) the progress and propagation of the sciences in Egypt; (2) research, study, and publication of natural, industrial, and historical data on Egypt; (3) advising on various questions concerning which the Government shall consult it'; it has four sections: mathematics, physics, political economy, literature and art

**1799**
July: discovery at Rosetta, by a French officer, of a black basalt stone with three scripts: Greek, Egyptian demotic and hieroglyphic; the key to the ancient Egyptian language
to 1803: Lord Elgin (1786–1841) ambassador to the Ottoman Porte; removes sculptures from the Parthenon in Athens for transportation to England (arrival 1804)

**1790**
J. Bruce, *Travels to Discover the Source of the Nile in the Years 1768, 1769, 1770, 1771, 1772, and 1773*

**1792**
C. Niebuhr (illus.), *Travel through Arabia and other countries in the East* (trans. R. Heron); description by the only survivor of a Danish expedition to the Yemen via Constantinople and Egypt.

**1799**
L-F. Cassas (illus.) *Voyage pittoresque de la Syrie, de la Phoenicie, de la Palestine et de la Basse Egypte*; 180 plates engraved from drawings by one of several artists employed by Comte de Choiseul-Gouffier, French Ambassador to the Ottoman Porte

1790

**1800**
J. M. W. Turner's *Fifth Plague of Egypt* exhibited at the Royal Academy, London; in fact represents the seventh plague

1800

**1801**
R. Southey, *Thalaba the Destroyer*; 'an Arabian tale'
L. Mayer (illus.), *Views in Egypt*; first of a series of volumes of views in the Ottoman Empire, for Sir Robert Ainslie, British Ambassador in Constantinople

**1802**
Baron Denon, *Voyage dans la Basse et la Haute Egypte*; widely circulated and influential series of views of the monuments of ancient Egypt

**1806**
to 1807: Vicomte de Chateaubriand (1868–1848) travels to Greece, Constantinople, Syria, Palestine, Egypt and Tunis

**1807**
T. Hope, *Household Furniture and Interior Decoration*; includes Egyptian interiors

**1809**
to 1810: Lord Byron (1788–1824) and John Cam Hobhouse (1786–1869) tour Greece, Albania, Asia Minor, and Constantinople
to 1817: John Lewis Burckhardt (1784–1817) exploring in Syria, Egypt and Arabia, as Shaykh Ibrahim ibn 'Abd Allah

**1809**
–1829: *Description de l'Egypte*; 24 volumes of plates and text representing the accumulated researches of Napoleon's Institut d'Egypte on that country's history, geography, science and culture

**1810**

**1811**
1 March: Massacre of the Mamlūks in Cairo; survivors flee to Sudan
to 1818: Egyptian War against the Wahhabis

**1812**
Algiers declares war on USA
Stratford Canning leaves Constantinople after four years

**1813**
Egyptian forces take Mecca

**1814**
to 1824: Muḥammad, Bay of Tunis

**1815**
United States victory over Tripoli and Tunis

**1815**
Jules-Robert Auguste (1789–1850) wealthy artist and collector of Oriental art and curiosities in Syria

**1820**

**1820**
to 1822: Sudan conquered by Muḥammad 'Alī as private venture; under Egyptian administration until 1883

*c.* **1821**
Cotton link between Egypt and Lancashire established

**1821**
Greek War of Independence (to 1830)

**1822**
to 1830: Muḥammad 'Alī intervenes in Greek War
to 1859: Mawlāy 'Abd al-Rahman, Sultān of Morocco

**1824**
Demise of The Levant Company

**1825–27**
to 1827: Canning's second mission to Constantinople

**1826**
'The Auspicious Event': massacre of Janisseries in Constantinople; results in modernisation of Turkish army

**1827**
20 October: Battle of Navarino: Turkish fleet destroyed
Fly-whisk incident: Day of Algiers strikes French consul: pretext for French invasion

*c.* **1827**
to 1829: Allan in Greece, Constantinople, Asia Minor

**1828**
to 1829: Alexandre-Gabriel Decamps (1803–1860) in Greece and Asia Minor: Smyrna; commissioned by French government to paint picture commemorating Battle of Navarino

**1829**
14 September: Treaty of Adrianople: end of Russo-Turkish War; results in growth of Russian influence in the Balkans

**1810**

to 1813: Lady Hester Stanhope (1776–1839) travels from Constantinople to Palmyra; presides over Bedouin encampment there

**1812**

Burckhardt discovers Petra
Burckhardt discovers Abu Simbel
Première of Rossini's *L'Italiana in Algeri*, in Venice

**1814**

Summer: Lady Hester builds a house at Djoun in Lebanon, and lives there until her death (1839)
to 1815: Burckhardt on pilgrimage to Mecca and Medina

**1815**

to 1819: Giovanni Battista Belzoni (1778–1823) excavating in Egypt

**1816**

The Elgin Marbles are acquired by the British Museum
Belzoni sponsored by the British consul, Henry Salt (1780–1827) removes the head of the 'Young Memnon' ('Ozymandias') from the Ramasseum at Thebes

**1817**

Belzoni and others find opening into the Temple of Rameses II at Abu Simbel
Belzoni discovers the tomb of Seti I in the Valley of the Kings, Thebes

**1818**

Belzoni finds an entrance into the Second Pyramid at Gizah (Chephren)

**1820**

to 1821: Belzoni's exhibition of copies and casts from the tomb of Seti I held in the Egyptian Hall, Piccadilly
London Society for Promoting Christianity among the Jews sends first mission to Jerusalem

**1821**

John Martin's *Belshazzar's Feast* exhibited in London
to 1833: John Gardner Wilkinson (1797–1875) in Egypt and Nubia; excavating at Thebes, 1824, 1827, 1828

**1822**

Linant de Bellefonds, French engineer and explorer, travels to Meroe in Nubia, the first European to see sites of Musawarat and Nagia;
one of his many expeditions in Egypt and Nubia

**1822**

Jean François Champollion (1790–1832) deciphers the Egyptian hieroglyphs
Donizetti's brother court *Kappelmeister* to Ottoman Sultān Mahmud II

**1824**

19 April: Byron's death at Missolonghi
to 1828: Robert Hay of Linplum (1799–1863) making a systematic survey of monuments in Upper Egypt, aided by scholars and draughtsmen

**1825**

to 1828: Edward William Lane's (1801–1876) first residence in Egypt: Cairo and two Nile trips

**1827**

E. Delacroix's *Death of Sardanapalus* exhibited at the Salon, Paris

**1828**

to 1829: Champollion and Ippolito Rossellini (1800–43) studying ancient monuments and inscriptions in Egypt on joint Franco-Tuscan mission

**1829**

to 1834: Hay's second expedition to Upper Egypt

---

**1811**

F. R. de Chateaubriand, *Itinéraire de Paris à Jérusalem* (Eng. trans. 1814); personal account of a pilgrimage to the Near East; influential

**1812**

–1818: Lord Byron, *Childe Harold*; established the Near East as a setting for romantic experience: 'Oh! that the Desert were my dwelling-place '

**1813**

Lord Byron, *The Giaour* and *The Bride of Abydos*; two of the poet's tales in Oriental settings
J. C. Hobhouse, *A journey through Albania and other provinces of Turkey in Europe and Asia, to Constantinople*; with Byron, 1809–10

**1814**

'Alī Bay el Abbassi, *Voyages en Asie et en Afrique* (Eng. trans. 1816); ?earliest published account of a European (Domingo Badia y Leblich) in disguise in the holy places of Islam

**1817**

P. B. Shelley, *Ozymandias*; sonnet inspired by imminent arrival in London of the head of the 'Young Memnon' (Ramesses II) from Thebes
T. Moore, *Lalla Rookh*; collection of poems with Oriental settings

**1819**

J. L. Burckhardt, *Travels in Nubia*; first of the explorer's posthumously published accounts of his extensive travels in Egypt and the Levant

**1820**

G. B. Belzoni, *Narrative of the Operations and Recent Discoveries . . . in Egypt and Nubia* (Plates, 1820–22)

**1821**

J. S. Buckingham, *Travels in Palestine*; first of his several narratives of travel in the Near East

**1822**

J. L. Burckhardt, *Travels in Syria and the Holy Land*
J. F. Champollion, *Lettre à M. Dacier*; Egyptian hieroglyphs deciphered

**1823**

C. L. Irby and J. Mangles, *Travels in Egypt and Nubia, Syria and Asia Minor*; account of travels 1817–18, among earliest Europeans to see Petra and Abu Simbel

**1824**

J. J. Morier, *Hajji Baba of Isphahan*; popular picaresque tale with Persian characters and setting

**1826**

J. Carne, *Letters from the East*; early tourist's account of travels in the Near East; a further vol. pub. 1830

**1827**

J. C. Pacho, *Relation d'un Voyage dans la Marmarique, la Cyrendique et les oasis d'Andjelah et de Maradéh*

**1828**

J. J. Morier, *Hajji Baba of Isphahan, in England*

**1829**

J. L. Burckhardt, *Travels in Arabia*
V. Hugo, *Orientales*; collection of poems on Orientalist themes

**1830** **1830**

**1830**

4 February: Declaration of Greek Independence

14 June: French invade Algeria: Algiers, and later Boué, Bougie and Oran taken;
6 July: Day of Algiers signs Act of Capitulation

**1830**

April–October: Dauzats in Egypt, Sinai, Palestine, Syria, Asia Minor;
as lithographer to expedition of Baron Taylor, in part to procure obelisk of Luxor

**1831**

Foundation of French Foreign Legion

Muḥammad 'Alī despatches his son, Ibrahim Pasha, to conquer Syria; occupied until 1840

**1831**

from April: Marilhat in Greece, Egypt, Palestine, Syria, Lebanon with scientific expedition led by Baron Charles von Hügel; late 1832–May 1833: in Alexandria and Lower Egypt, painting portraits; returns to France on ship with Luxor obelisk

**1832**

Abd al-Qādir assumes title of Amir; leads resistance to French until 1847
Greece established as an independent state with Otto of Bavaria as king

**1832**

January–June: Delacroix accompanies diplomatic mission of Comte de Mornay to Sultān of Morocco: Tangier, Meknes; also in Algiers; notebooks provide material for next thirty years; profound impact on Orientalism
to 1833: Owen Jones (1809–1874) with Jules Goury (1803–1834) in Egypt

**1833**

8 July: Treaty of Unkiar-Skelessi: Russia and Turkey close the Dardanelles to foreign ships

**1833**

March–April: Roberts visits Tangier and Tetuan
May: Lewis visits Tangier
Vernet and William Wyld (1806–1889) to Algeria

**1834**

French military régime in Algeria; establishment of 3 divisions under a Governor General: Algiers, Oran, Constantine, each with a Service des Bureaux Arabes

**1834**

Allan in Morocco
June–late 1837: Gleyre travels extensively in Near East as draughtsman to John Lowell Jr.: Albania, Greece, Constantinople, Smyrna, Rhodes, Alexandria, Cairo, Upper Egypt, Khartoum; returns without Lowell via Syria, Lebanon
to 1835: William Henry Bartlett (1809–1854) in Palestine and Lebanon; first of six visits to Near East

**1836**

November: Chauzel, Governor-General of Algeria, attempts to take Constantine;
24 November: Battle of Somah (Algeria): French victory

*c.* **1836**

to 1838: Thomas Allom (1804–1872) in Constantinople, Asia Minor, Holy Land: Jerusalem

**1837**

October: Constantine taken by the French
Overland Route in Egypt established; Peninsular and Orient Steam Navigation Company receives contract from British Government to carry mails to India (to 1840)

**1837**

Vernet in Algeria
Eugène Flandin (1803–1876) accompanies French army to Algeria
to 1839: Frère in Algeria; witnesses taking of Constantine

**1838**

British occupy Aden (to 1839)
Abdul Mejid, Sultān of Turkey (to 1861)

**1838**

September–May 1839: Roberts tours the Levant: Egypt: Alexandria to Wadi Halfa; Sinai, Petra; Holy Land: Hebron, Jaffa, Jericho, Dead Sea, Bethlehem, Jerusalem, Nazareth Tyre, Sidon; Baalbec, Beirut; Alexandria
November–January 1839: W. J. Müller in Egypt: Alexandria to Luxor

**1839**

24 June: Battle of Nezib (Syria): defeat of Turkish army by Egyptian army;
Mahmud II tries to expel Ibrahim Pasha; European powers pledge support
3 November: Hatt-i Sharif of Gulhane promulgated: equality of all religions before the law: first of Turkish reforming edicts – the *Tanzimat*

**1839**

Dauzats accompanies military expedition of Duc d'Orléans to Algeria: Oran, Algiers, Bougie, Stora, Philippeville, Setif, Portes de Fer in Djurdjura mountains
to 1840: Vernet in Algeria, Egypt, Palestine with Frédéric Goupil-Fesquet; uses daguerreotypes to record views of Alexandria, Cairo, Jerusalem (P. G. J. de Lotbinère independently making daguerreotypes on the Nile)

**1840** **1840**

15 July: Convention of London for the pacification of the Levant. European powers persuade Muḥammad 'Alī to withdraw forces from Syria; in return the pashalik of Egypt is made hereditary; he is created Pasha of Acre for his lifetime

**1840**

to 1842: Flandin with Pascal Coste (1787–1879) on French diplomatic mission to Persia
Summer–Autumn 1841: Lewis in Greece, Constantinople, Asia Minor: Brussa
October–May 1841: Wilkie in Constantinople, Jerusalem, Alexandria; dies at sea off Malta in June

**1830**

L. de Laborde, *Voyage de l'Arabie Pétrée*; account of travels with Linant de
Bellefonds in 1828, illustrated mainly by the author
J. L. Burckhardt, *Notes on the Bedouins and Wahabys*

**1832**

to 1833: Alphonse de Lamartine (1790–1869) travels to Syria and Egypt, via
Constantinople

**1832**

L. de Laborde, *Voyage en Orient de l'Asie, de la Syrie*; magnificently illustrated
W. Scott, *The Talisman*; popular novel set in the time of Richard the Lionheart's
Crusades
−1844: N. I. Rosellini, *I Monumenti dell' Egitto e della Nubia*; 3 multi-volume parts,
395 plates; the results of the author's expedition with Champollion

**1833**

Removal of an obelisk from the Temple of Luxor to the Place de la Concorde,
Paris
to 1834: Robert Curzon (1810–73) tours Egypt, Syria, Asia Minor and Greece
to 1835: Lane's second residence in Egypt: lives in Cairo as Mansour Effendi

**1833**

C. F. Head, *Eastern and Egyptian Scenery*; illustrations with notes of journey from
India to England via Egypt on the Overland Route 'to reveal the advantages of
steam navigation'
J. E. De Kay, *Sketches of Turkey in 1831 and 1832 by an American*

**1834**

to 1835: Alexander Kinglake (1809–91) tours Constantinople, Asia Minor,
Lebanon, Palestine, Egypt and Syria

**1835**

A. de Lamartine, *Souvenirs, impressions, pensées et paysages pendant un Voyage en
Orient 1832–3* (Eng. trans. 1848); in the footsteps of Chateaubriand
W. Wyld and E. Lessore, *Voyage Pittoresque dans la Régence d'Alger exécuté en 1833
et lithographié*; dedicated to Vernet with whom Wyld travelled
−1847: J. F. Champollion, *Monuments de l'Egypte et de la Nubie*; 4 vols, 446 plates

**1836**

E. W. Lane, *An Account of the Manners and Customs of the Modern Egyptians*; first
comprehensive and sympathetic survey of a particular Islamic society
T. H. Horne, *Landscape Illustrations of the Bible*; engravings by W. & E. Finden
after various artists based on travellers' topographical sketches
−1838: J. Carne, *Syria, the Holy Land, Asia Minor etc.*; illustrated by Bartlett,
Purser and Allom

**1837**

to 1838: Curzon in Albania, Egypt (Wadi Natrun) and Constantinople

**1837**

F. Arundale, *Illustrations of Jerusalem and Mount Sinai*; the author's journey with
F. Catherwood and J. Bonomi in 1833; probably the first 'infidels' to sketch in
the *haram* area of Jerusalem
J. Pardoe, *The City of the Sultans*; portrait of Constantinople life compiled from
her residence there
J. G. Wilkinson, *The Manners and Customs of the Ancient Egyptians*; a revised edn.
of *Thebes and a general view of Egypt* (1834), for half a century the standard work
on life in ancient Egypt
J. F. Lewis (illus), *Illustrations of Constantinople from drawings by Coke Smyth*;
lithographs from before the artist's visit to the Near East
−1839: P. Coste (illus.), *Architecture arabe, ou Monuments du Kaire*; detailed early
study of the Islamic architecture of Cairo

**1838**

to 1844: Charles Fellows (1799–1860) initiates a series of expeditions to south-
west Turkey, mainly Lycia, and removes sculptured stones from Xanthus to the
British Museum (eg. the Nereid Monument)

**1838**

Lord Lindsay, *Letters on Egypt, Edom and the Holy Land*; aristocratic Englishman's
tour of the Levant, 1836–37
M. C. F. Volney, *Travels through Syria and Egypt in the Years 1783–4 and 1795*
−1839: J. Pardoe, *The Beauties of the Bosphorus*; popular series of views by Bartlett
of Constantinople and environs
−1841: E. W. Lane, *The Thousand and One Nights*; first accurate though censored
translation, with explanatory notes revealing Islam as a real and living culture

**1839**

Baron Taylor, *La Syrie, l'Egypte, la Palestine, et la Judée*; illustrated by Dauzats
Rev. R. Walsh, *Constantinople and the Scenery of the Seven Churches of Asia Minor*;
illustrated by Allom
Vicomte de Marcellus, *Souvenirs de l'Orient*; based on a trip undertaken in 1820
−1849: C. Texier, *Description de l'Asie Mineure*; contains elaborate chromo-
lithographs of Islamic architecture in Turkey, the result of journeys 1833–37

**c. 1840**

T. Allom (illus.), *Character and Costume in Turkey and Italy*

**1840**

R. Hay, *Illustrations of Cairo*; lithographs by several artists; the study of Egyptian
antiquities revolved around Hay for nearly 10 years, 1824–34
E. Blondel, *Deux ans en Syrie et en Palestine, 1838–9*
T. Carlyle, *On the Hero as Prophet: Mahomet*; lecture rejecting the popular image
of Muḥammad as a 'falsehood incarnate' (pub. in *On Heroes*, 1841)
J. Murray (pub.), *A Handbook for Travellers in the Ionian Islands, Greece, Turkey,
Asia Minor and Constantinople*

**1841**
February: Battle of St. Jean d'Acre: peace between Turkey and Egypt

**1841**
?November: Lewis arrives in Cairo and lives there as an Ottoman Turk
for nearly a decade

**1842**
to 1846; 1848–58: Canning (later Viscount Stratford de Redcliffe) British
Ambassador in Constantinople, the 'Great Elchi'

*c.* **1842**
to 1882: Amadeo, Count Preziosi (1816–1882) living in Constantinople, drawing
its people and scenery for European residents and visitors; visits Egypt
*c.* 1861–62

**1842**
to 1843: Richard Dadd (1817–1886) accompanies his patron Sir Thomas Phillips
on a tour of the Near East: Greece, Constantinople, Asia Minor, Rhodes,
Lebanon, Syria, Holy Land, Egypt

**1843**
Alexandre Bida (1823–1895) visits Constantinople, Syria
October–February 1844: W. J. Müller with pupil H. J. Johnson (1822–1884) in
Asia Minor: Lycia; with archaeological expedition of Charles Fellows

**1844**
August: French war with Morocco: Tangier bombarded; 14 August: Battle of
Isly: defeat of Moroccan army; Sultān of Morocco recognises French
occupation of Algeria

**1844**
Flandin in Mesopotamia with archaeologist Paul Botta

**1845**
Vernet in Algeria

*c.* **1845**
to 1856: Félix Ziem (1821–1911) makes series of journeys to North Africa and
Near East

**1846**
May: Biskra (Algeria) captured by Duc d'Aumâle

**1846**
May–July: Chassériau in Algeria: Constantine to visit Caliph 'Alī ben Ahmed;
Algiers
Fromentin on brief secret trip with Charles Labbé to Algeria: Algiers, Blidah

**1847**
Fromentin returns to Algeria after successful exhibition of Orientalist work at
Salon; Constantine and Biskra for eight months

**1848**
to 1854: Abbas I, Viceroy of Egypt

**1848**
July–October: Lear in Constantinople, northern Greece, Albania

**1849**
2 August: death of Muḥammad 'Alī in Alexandria

**1849**
February: Lear briefly visits Cairo and Sinai
to 1850: Narcisse Berchère (1819–1891) in Egypt, Asia Minor, Greece

**1841**

to 1844: Curzon on British Government service in Constantinople and Erzerum

**1842**

Literary Association founded in Cairo by Dr. Henry Abbott (1812–59), Emile Prisse d'Avennes (1807–79) and others
to 1843: Wilkinson returns to Egypt
to 1845: Prusssian expedition to Egypt, led by Karl Richard Lepsius (1810–84) and including James Wild (architect), Joseph Bonomi and Ernst Weidenbach (artists)
to 1849: Lane's last residence in Egypt: lives as before in Cairo, with wife and sister; working on *Lexicon*

**1843**

Gérard de Nerval (1808–55) in Egypt, Lebanon, Constantinople and Asia Minor
Eliot Warburton (1810–52) tours Egypt, Palestine and Syria

**1844**

William Thackeray (1811–63) visits Athens, Constantinople, Jerusalem and Cairo, under the auspices of the Peninsular and Orient Steam Navigation Company

**1845**

Théophile Gautier (1811–72) in Algeria
Prisse d'Avennes, French scholar and artist working in Egypt, first for Muḥammad 'Alī and then independently, removes the Table of Kings from Karnac to France
to 1847: Henry Layard (1817–94) excavating at Nimrud, Nineveh and other Assyrian sites; discovery of winged bull and transportation to the British Museum

**1846**

Halicarnassus frieze removed from Bodrum, south-west Turkey, to the British Museum, by John Alison, sponsored by Canning

**1847**

De Goncourt brothers (Edmond 1822–96; Jules 1830–70) in Algeria

**1848**

to 1851: Wilkinson in Egypt and Nubia

**1849**

to 1851: Layard's second expedition to Assyrian sites
to 1851: Gustave Flaubert (1821–80) and Maxime du Camp (1822–94) travel in Egypt, Palestine, Lebanon, Syria, Constantinople and Greece

---

**1841**

E. Robinson, *Biblical Researches in Palestine, Mount Sinai and Arabia Petraea*; travels in 1838 in first attempt to establish the true location of biblical sites; widely read
J. G. Kinnear, *Cairo, Petra and Damascus, in 1839*; author accompanied David Roberts between Cairo and Jaffa
A. Dauzats and A. Dumas père, *Quinze Jours au Sinai*; record of a trip undertaken in 1839

**1842**

–1849: D. Roberts (illus.), *The Holy Land, Syria, Idumea Arabia, Egypt and Nubia*; 6 vols. of lithographs; first widely available large-scale illustrations of the Near East

**1843**

O. Jones and J. Goury, *Views on the Nile from Cairo to the Second Cataract*
E. W. Lane, *Selections from the Kur-án*
Sir D. Wilkie (illus.), *Sketches in Turkey, Syria and Egypt 1840 & 1841*; posthumously published
F. Goupil-Fesquet, *Voyage en Orient fait avec Horace Vernet en 1839 et 1840*; illustrated by the author

**1844**

W. H. Bartlett, *Walks about the City and Environs of Jerusalem*; first of several books of travel in the Near East written and illustrated by Bartlett from personal experience
C. Nodier, *Journal de l'Expédition des Portes de Fer*; illustrated by Dauzats, Auguste Raffet (1804–60) and others; the expedition in 1839
A. Kinglake, *Eothen*; whimsical and subjective account of travel in the Levant in 1835
S. Lane-Poole, *The Englishwoman in Egypt: Letters from Cairo, written during a residence there in 1842, 3, & 4, with E. W. Lane . . . by his sister*

**1844/5**

E. Warburton, *The Crescent and the Cross; or, romance and realities of eastern travel*

**1845**

W. H. Bartlett, *Views Illustrating the Topography of Jerusalem, Ancient and Modern*
Dr. C. L. Meryon (ed.), *Memoirs of Lady Hester Stanhope*
W. M. Thackeray, *Notes of a Journey from Cornhill to Cairo*; witty account of tour of the Levant in 1844

**1846**

J. P. Girault de Prangey (illus.), *Monuments arabes d'Egypt de Sinai et d'Asie mineur . . . de 1842 à 1845*
–1848: J. J. Ampère, 'Voyage et recherches en Egypt et en Nubie', series of articles in *Revue des Deux Mondes*

**1847**

Lord Castlereagh, *A Journey to Damascus through Egypt, Nubia, Arabia Petraea, Palestine and Syria*; aristocratic Englishman's 'Grand Tour' through the Levant, 1841–42, accompanied by a hired draughtsman, Anton Schranz
X. Marmier, *Lettres sur l'Algérie*
B. Disraeli, *Tancred, or the New Crusade*; novel recounting the modern 'crusade' of an idealistic young English nobleman; Disraeli toured the Levant 1830–31
J. Murray (pub.), *A Handbook for Travellers in Egypt*; written by J. G. Wilkinson, originally pub. as *Modern Egypt and Thebes* (1843)

**1848**

H. Martineau, *Eastern Life Present and Past*; personal travel narrative and history, by a noted writer
W. H. Bartlett, *Forty Days in the Desert*; journey across Sinai to Petra, 1845
–1851: J. A. St. John, *Oriental Album*; plates by E. Prisse d'Avennes illustrating the people and costumes of Egypt
–1851: A. Dumas père, *Le Véloce ou Tangier, Alger et Tunis*

**1849**

W. H. Bartlett, *The Nile Boat*; voyage on the Nile, 1845
R. Curzon, *Ancient monasteries of the Levant*; entertaining account of visits in 1833–34 and 1837–38 in search of manuscripts
J. Bonomi, *Grand moving panoramic picture of the Nile*; notes to accompany a popular entertainment
W. F. Lynch, *Narrative of the United States expedition to the River Jordan and the Dead Sea*
Sir A. H. Layard, *Nineveh and its Remains*; account of the author's first expedition to Assyria, 1845–47
–1859: K. R. Lepsius (ed.), *Denkmäler aus Aegypten und Aethiopien*; 12 folio volumes, 894 plates by Ernst Weidenbach, the result of an archaeological expedition, 1842–45, one of largest Egyptological works ever produced
Sir A. H. Layard, *Monuments of Nineveh*, 1st series; vols. of coloured plates of the archaeologist's discoveries in Assyria; 1853, second series

1850

*c.* **1850**
Bida in Egypt

**1850**
Belly with Léon Loysel on scientific expedition led by F.-F. Caignart de Saulcy to Syria, Palestine: Dead Sea; April 1851: Lebanon; Alexandria, Cairo

**1851**
to 1853: Frère in Greece, Smyrna, Constantinople (for 18 months); continues on to Syria, Palestine, Egypt
Spring: Lewis and wife Marian leave Cairo for England, after wide acclaim for *The Hhareem* in London

**1853**
14 June: Mass celebrated at Kabylia to mark anniversary of French landing in Algeria

**1853**
Fromentin spends nearly a year in Algeria: Mustapha, Blidah, travels south to El-Agouat
Vernet in Algeria
Fromentin returns to Algeria
Alfred Dehodencq (1822–1882) in Morocco: Tangier, Tetuan, Mogador, Rabat, Salé
December–April 1854: Lear in Egypt: Alexandria to Philae
December–October 1854: Seddon in Cairo and Holy Land; joined by Holman Hunt, travels via Damietta and Jaffa to Jerusalem

**1854**
Ottoman Sultān prohibits white slave trade
13 July: Abbas I of Egypt murdered; Muḥammad Said Pasha, Viceroy of Egypt (to 1863)
Ferdinand de Lesseps obtains concession for construction of Suez Canal from Muḥammad Said
Crimean War between Russia and Turkey, aided by Britain and France, initially over protection of Orthodox Christians in Ottoman Empire (to 1856)

**1854**
February: Holman Hunt to Cairo; June 1855; with Seddon to Jerusalem; trips to Dead Sea and elsewhere in Holy Land; travels through Holy Land, Syria, Lebanon and by sea to Constantinople, December, January 1856: visits Crimea to 1863: Dehodencq lives in Cadiz and Tangier
Gérôme visits Greece and Constantinople
to 1855: William Simpson (1823–1899) artist-reporter in the Crimea; visits Circassia with Duke of Newcastle
to 1856: Schreyer in Turkey

**1855**
Pasini to Persia, attached to French legation, via Arabia
Bida in Athens, Constantinople, Crimea, Beirut, Holy Land: Jerusalem
Belly to Egypt: Cairo; Spring 1856: to Sinai with Berchère

**1856**
18 February: Hatt-i Humayun promulgated at end of Crimean War: second *Tanzimat* reform
Capitulatory treaty signed by Morocco with Britain

**1856**
Gérôme in Egypt with Berchère, Belly, Bartholdi, and Edouard Imer: July–October: Upper Egypt; November–February 1857: Cairo
Autumn: Seddon returns to Cairo after success of his Orientalist pictures; dies there in November
?Schreyer in Syria and Egypt

**1857**
Ottoman Sultān prohibits black slave trade
The Indian Mutiny
Battle of Ischeriden: French Foreign Legion takes Kabylia region of Algeria

**1858**
Alexandria-Suez railway, via Cairo, opened

**1857**
Belly returns to Egypt to make studies for *The Pilgrimage to Mecca*
Leighton visits Algiers
?Schreyer in Syria and Egypt

**1858**
March–May: Lear to Egypt; Palestine: Jerusalem, Petra; Lebanon; Syria: Damascus
September–April 1859: Goodall in Cairo, visits Suez; shares studio in Coptic house with Haag
Carl Haag (1820–1916) in Egypt with Goodall; from April 1859 travels to Jerusalem and on to Syria where lives with Bedouins; returns to Cairo for winter 1859–60

**1859**
25 April: construction of Suez Canal begun
Muḥammad ʿAbd al-Rahmān, Sultān of Morocco (to 1873)
to 1860: Spanish war with Morocco

**1850**

J. F. Lewis's *The Hhareem* exhibited at the Old Water Colour Society, London
to 1854: Auguste Mariette (1821–81) discovers Serapeum at Memphis; the
beginning of many years excavating in Egypt; from his discoveries the first
national museum of antiquities in the Near East is formed

**1851**

Great Exhibition, London: several Islamic displays and works of art
to 1852: Bayard Taylor, the first American tourist in the Sudan

*c.* **1853**

Jane Digby (1807–81) marries Shaykh Medjuel El Mezrab; remains with him in
Syria until her death

**1853**

Richard Burton (1821–90) in Arabia; July-September in Mecca and Medina
disguised as a Pathan doctor
Gautier in Constantinople and Asia Minor
to 1861: W. Gifford Palgrave (1826–88) working as a missionary in Syria
(Zahleh)

**1855**

Wilkinson's last visit to Egypt: Thebes
Exposition Universelle, Paris: Islamic items included

**1858**

Anthony Trollope (1815–82) in Cairo on behalf of the General Post Office
negotiating with the Egyptian Government for a contract to convey mail through
Egypt by railway

*c.* **1850**

A. Bida and E. Barbot, *Souvenirs d'Egypte*; vol. of lithographs

**1850**

F. R. Chesney, *The expedition for the survey of the rivers Euphrates and Tigris, carried
on by order of the British Government in the years 1835, 1836, and 1837*; an attempt
to establish an overland route to India via Mesopotamia
G. de Nerval, *Scènes de la vie Orientale*; concentrates mainly on Egypt

**1851**

J. P. Girault de Prangey (illus.), *Monuments et Paysages de l'Orient*; coloured lithographs
W. H. Bartlett, *In the Footsteps of Our Lord and His Apostles in Syria, Greece and Italy*

**1852**

Sir C. Fellows, *Travels and Researches in Asia Minor more particularly in the province
of Lycia*; the archaeologist's excavations and discoveries, 1838–44; an
abridgement of earlier accounts
J. Bonomi, *Nineveh and its Palaces. The discoveries of Botta and Layard applied to
the elucidation of Holy Writ*
M. du Camp. *Egypte, Nubie, Palestine et Syrie*; account of travels with Flaubert,
1849–51, illustrated with the author's photographs

**1853**

Th. Gautier, *Voyages pittoresques en Algérie*
L. F. Caignart de Saulcy, *Voyage autour de la mer morte et dans les terres bibliques*;
account of journey undertaken 1850–51
Th. Gautier, *Constantinople*

**1855**

Princesse Christine Trivulzio-Belgiojoso, *La Vie intime et la vie nomade en Orient*;
based partly on personal experience
B. Taylor, *Pictures of Palestine, Asia Minor, Sicily and Spain or The Lands of the
Saracens*; impressions of Oriental life, based on a journey, 1852
–1856: R. Burton, *Personal Narrative of a Pilgrimage to Al-Madinah and Meccah*;
account of his visit in disguise to the sacred precincts of Islam
–1856: W. Simpson, *The Seat of War in the East*, 1st and 2nd series; lithographs
of the Crimea, establishing Simpson's reputation as an artist-reporter

**1856**

G. Meredith, *The Shaving of Shagput*; tale in 'Arabian Nights' style
P. de Molènes, *Aisha Rosa, souvenirs des rives du Bosphore*; tale in Oriental mode
P. Merimée, *Ballades et chants populaires de la Roumanie* reflects widespread interest
in popular cultures
C. Bossoli (illus.), *The Beautiful Scenery & Chief Places of Interest Throughout the Crimea*
E. Fromentin, *Un Eté dans le Sahara*
–1858: Princesse Belgiojoso, *Recits turco-asiatiques*

**1857**

C. Didier, *Séjour chez le grand-chérif de la Mekke*

**1858**

E. Fromentin, *Une Année dans le Sahel*
J. Murray (pub.), *A Handbook for Travellers in Syria and Palestine*; written by J. L
Porter
Count Preziosi, *Stamboul: Recollections of Eastern Life*; coloured lithographs
portraying the people of Constantinople
–1859: F. Frith, *Egypt and Palestine photographed and described*; series of
photographs taken in 1856–57

**1859**

E. Fitzgerald (trans.), *The Rubáiyàt of Omar Khayyam*

**1860**

**1860**
Muslim and Druze massacre of Christians in Damascus and Lebanon

*c.* **1860**
Hercules Brabazon Brabazon (1821–1906) in Cairo, Syria, Palestine, Lebanon, Constantinople

**1860**
Berchère in Suez to record stages of cutting of Canal
Mario Fortuny y Marsal (1838–1874) to Morocco with Spanish military expedition

**1861**
The Organic Regulation negotiated by France, Britain and Turkey, establishing internationally guaranteed régime in Lebanon under Christian administrator responsible to the Sultān
to 1876: Abdul Aziz, Sultān of Turkey

**1861**
Shreyer in North Africa: Algiers; and Near East?

**1862**
Gérôme in Egypt
Fortuny returns to Morocco to paint panorama commemorating Spanish victory at Tetuan
First of Guillaumet's ten trips to Algeria and Morocco (last trip 1883/4)
to 1864: Carl Werner (1808–1894) in Egypt and Palestine

**1863**
to 1879: Ismail Pasha, Khedive of Egypt

**1865**
Lecomte-du-Nouÿ in Egypt with Félix Clément

mid **1860s**
Brabazon visits Algiers

**1866**
Establishment of Syrian Protestant College, later the American University in Beirut

**1866**
December–April 1867: Lear in Egypt: Alexandria to Wadi Halfa; to Jerusalem via Gaza

**1867**
Sultān of Turkey visits London and Paris

**1867**
to 1869: Church in Alexandria, Beirut, Jerusalem, Petra, Damascus, Baalbec, Constantinople and Athens
Leighton to Constantinople, Brussa, Smyrna, Rhodes

**1868**
October–November: Leighton in Egypt: on Khedive's steamer to Philae
to 1869: Pasini in Constantinople
Brabazon on first of three trips to Upper Egypt (also 1874 and 1877)

**1868–69**
January–1869: Gérôme with Paul Lenoir (d. 1881), Edmond About, Frédéric Masson and Bonnat (?) to Egypt: travel from Cairo to Fayoum; across Sinai to Palestine: Petra, Jerusalem.
Gérôme returns to France, the rest to Turkey and Greece

**1869**
November: Opening of Suez Canal; ceremonies attended by European royalty including Empress Eugénie of France, Emperor of Austria, Crown Prince of Prussia and Crown Prince of Denmark

**1869**
November: Gérôme, Bonnat, Lenoir, About and Masson attend opening of Suez Canal; Fromentin, Berchère, Vacher de Tournemine (1812–1872) and Frère (in suite of Empress Eugènie), also attend inauguration ceremony, as official guests
January–February: Simpson in Cairo for visit of Prince and Princess of Wales; March: to Jerusalem to see excavations of Charles Warren for Palestine Exploration Fund; April: Constantinople and Crimea; November: returns to Egypt for Suez Canal opening ceremonies
Gifford in Egypt and elsewhere in Near East?
to 1870: Henri Regnault (1843–1871) and Georges Clairin (1843–1919) in Morocco
August–June 1872: Holman Hunt returns to Jerusalem; excursions to Bethlehem and elsewhere in Holy Land

**1860**

A. Trollope, *An Unprotected Female at the Pyramids*; short story parodying contemporary tourism in Egypt
D. Urquhart, *The Lebanon*; by a diplomat and Turcophile based in Constantinople; travelled in Lebanon 1849–50

**1861**

Librairie Hachette (pub.), *Itinéraire descriptif, historique et archéologique de l'Orient*

*c.* **1862**

Count Preziosi, *Souvenir du Caire*; coloured lithographs portraying the people of Cairo

**1862**

International Exhibition, London: includes Islamic Art
Prince of Wales visits Egypt: Alexandria to Aswān; Palestine, Syria, Lebanon, Constantinople
to 1863: Palgrave travels in Arabia as a Syrian Christian doctor
Lady Lucie Duff Gordon lives in Egypt (Luxor) until her death (1869)

**1862**

G. Flaubert, *Salammbô*; historical novel set in Carthage; detail drawn from author's travels in Near East 1849–51

**1863**

E. Renan, *Vie de Jésus*; written in the Holy Land, 1860–61; portrays Christ in strictly human terms
N. Berchère, *Le Désert de Suez. Cinq mois dans l'isthme*; record of the artist's observations of work on the cutting of the Suez Canal
–1893: E. W. Lane, *Arabic-English Lexicon*; the Arabic scholar's monumental work to which he devoted more than thirty years of his life; an exhaustive thesaurus of the Arabic language

**1864**

to 1868: Topographic Survey of Jerusalem by Captain Charles Wilson and the Royal Engineers

**1865**

Palestine Exploration Society founded
to 1866: Palgrave in Abyssinia and Egypt

**1865**

C. Werner (illus.), *Jerusalem, Bethlehem and The Holy Places*; vol. of coloured lithographs
*Ordnance Survey of Jerusalem*; maps, plans and photographs of the city for Coutts Bank
Lady Duff Gordon, *Letters from Egypt, 1863–65*; a consumptive English lady who lived the last years of her life in Egypt, 1862–69; her letters reveal her sympathetic attitude to the ordinary people of the country; republished with additions from 1865–69, in 1875
W. G. Palgrave, *Narrative of a year's journey through central and eastern Arabia (1862–63)*

**1866**

Lepsius discovers Edict of Canopus at Tanis (Lower Egypt), bilingual stone confirming Champollion's system

**1866**

E. Lott, *The English Governess in Egypt*; popular and unsensational account of life in the royal harem of Egypt and Turkey
Gustave Doré's illustrated Bible published in Paris

**1867**

Mark Twain (1835–1910) visits the Near East as part of first American Mediterranean cruise
Felix Bonfils (1831–85) opens photographic studio in Beirut with his wife; one of finest and most prolific photographers of the Near East
Exposition Universelle, Paris: Islamic items included
to 1873: Palgrave British Consul at Trebizond; travels in Asia Minor

**1868**

to 1869: Prince and Princess of Wales visit Egypt: Cairo and Upper Egypt, Suez, Alexandria; also Constantinople, Crimea, Athens

**1868**

F. Bedford (illus.), *The Holy Land, Egypt, Constantinople, Athens, etc.*; series of photographs taken during a visit to the Near East in 1862 in the entourage of the Prince of Wales

**1869**

Cairo opera house opens, with Verdi's *Rigoletto*
to 1870: First Cook's Tour of Egypt and the Holy Land
to 1871: Burton British Consul in Damascus

**1869**

E. About, *Le Fellah: souvenirs d'Egypte*; dedicated to Gérôme with whom he travelled
Sir W. H. Russell, *A Diary in the East during the tour of the Prince and Princess of Wales*; chronicle of the royal tour in 1869 of Egypt, Constantinople and the Crimea
M. Twain, *The Innocents Abroad*; popular, humorous narrative of travel to Europe, Asia Minor, Lebanon, Syria, Palestine and Egypt in 1867

## 1870

**1870**
Attempts by settlers to govern Algeria through Commune d'Alger

**1871**
Resistance by Algerian tribesmen against the French

**1872**
Indo-European Telegraph Company links Europe with India across Black Sea to Tiflis, Tabriz and Tehran
British lay overland cable from Bushire to Karachi

**1873**
to 1895: Mawlāy al-Hasan, Sultān of Morocco

**1875**
November: Disraeli purchases Khedive of Egypt's holding of Suez Canal shares

**1876**
Egypt bankrupt: establishment of Caisse de la Dette Publique:
dual control by French and British
Bulgarian massacres by Turks
to 1909: Abdul Hamid II, Sultān of Turkey

**1877**
Russo-Turkish War

**1878**
Congress and Treaty of Berlin between European powers; several areas in Near East affected: Bulgarian independence; understanding on spheres of influence in North Africa

**1879**
to 1892: Muḥammad Tewfiq, Khedive of Egypt

**1870s**
Lecomte-du-Nouÿ visits Morocco
Frederick Arthur Bridgeman (1847–1928) visits Egypt and Algeria several times

*c.* **1870**
to 1873: Constant in Morocco for two years with C. J. Tissot's diplomatic mission

**1870**
to 1871: Goodall returns to Egypt: Cairo, Sakkara

**1871**
Gérôme in Egypt and Constantinople
Fortuny and Clairin in Morocco: Tangier, Tetuan

*c.* **1872**
Clairin accompanies Tissot's envoy in Morocco: Tangier, Tetuan, Fez

**1872**
Lecomte-du-Nouÿ in Greece, Egypt, Asia Minor
October: Lear in Cairo and Suez
Gérôme in Egypt

**1873**
Pasini in Asia Minor, Syria
Leighton in Damascus
to 1874: L. C. Müller in Smyrna, Constantinople; on to Egypt, the first of nine visits there (last trip 1886)
to 1874: Haag returns to Cairo

**1874**
Gérôme in Egypt
Girardet in Morocco; first of eight visits to North Africa

**1875**
Gérôme in Constantinople
to 1876: L. C. Müller working in Cairo with Makart and several other Austrian painters
December–March 1878: Holman Hunt returns to Jerusalem and Holy Land

**1877**
Simpson to Asia Minor: Mycenae, Troy, Ephesus; as artist-reporter on Schliemann's excavations

*c.* **1870**
E. Riou (illus.), *Voyage pittoresque à travers l'Isthme de Suez*; commemmorative vol. of lithographs for inauguration of the Suez Canal, November 1869

**1871**
First performance of Verdi's *Aida*, in Cairo; commissioned by Khedive Ismail Pasha, libretto by du Locle from synopsis by Mariette
to 1890: Heinrich Schliemann (1822–90) excavating in Asia Minor and Greece; discovers site of Troy

**1871**
J. Murray (pub.), *A Handbook for Travellers in Constantinople, the Bosphorus, Dardanelles, Broussa and Plain of Troy*
E. H. Palmer, *The Desert of the Exodus*; the author participated in the Ordnance Survey expedition to Sinai, 1868–69, and visited El-Tih, Idumea and Moab for the Palestine Exploration Fund, 1869–70
–1875: C. Werner (illus.), *Nile Sketches*

**1872**
to 1878: Wilfrid Scawen Blunt (1840–1922) and his wife Lady Anne, travelling in North Africa, Egypt, Palestine, Asia Minor and (1878) Mesopotamia

**1872**
Comte de Gobineau, *Souvenirs de Voyage*
P. Lenoir, *Le Fayoum, le Sinaï et Pétra*, (Eng. trans. 1873); the author's journey with Gérôme, About and Masson in 1868

**1873**
First International Congress of Orientalists held in Paris; every two to three years thereafter in various capitals

**1873**
J. Murray (pub.), *A Handbook for Travellers in Algeria*
J. Bourgoin, *Les Arts arabes*

**1874**
to 1875: Charles Doughty (1843–1926) travels in Syria, Holy Land, Sinai and Egypt

**1875**
I. Burton, *The Inner Life of Syria, Palestine and the Holy Land*; the author's experience of the Levant when her husband, Richard Burton, was consul in Damascus, 1869–71

**1876**
to 1878: Doughty in Damascus; travels from there to north-west Arabia: Madain Salih (Nabataean ruins), Nejd; with the Bedouin

**1876**
K. Baedeker (ed.), *Palestine and Syria. Handbook for Travellers* (German edn. 1880)
C. Warren, *Underground Jerusalem*; the results of surveys in the Holy City, 1867–70
E-M. de Vogüé, *Syrie, Palestine, Mont Athos: Voyage aux pays du passé*; journey by an influential man of letters and positivist

*c.* **1877**
–1885: C. Warren. (ed.), *Picturesque Palestine, Sinai & Egypt*; 4 vols., illustrated by Roberts, Goodall, Poynter, Werner, Alma-Tadema and other artists: lavish pictorial coverage of Palestine; text by eminent Palestine explorers

**1877**
to 1881: Layard British Ambassador in Constantinople

**1877**
F. G. Burnaby, *On horseback through Asia Minor*; account of travels, 1876–77
A. B. Edwards, *A Thousand Miles up the Nile*; novelist and Egyptologist, an account of her first voyage up the Nile, 1874
E. Prisse d'Avennes, *L'Art Arabe*; published in parts from 1869, coloured lithographs of every aspect of Islamic art and architecture, studied in Cairo

**1878**
Arrival of Cleopatra's Needle (from Alexandria) in London; erected on Thames Embankment
to 1879: Blunt's journey to Nejd in Arabia

**1878**
K. Baedeker (ed.), *Egypt. Handbook for Travellers. Part first: Lower Egypt etc.* (German edn. 1877)

**1879**
P. Loti, *Aziyadé*; novel based on his romantic entanglement with a lady of the harem during a visit to Salonika and Constantinople, May 1876–November 1877
Lady Anne Blunt, *Bedouin Tribes of the Euphrates*; wife of W. S. Blunt, travelled with him in Syria, Mesopotamia and Arabia, late 1870s
F. Bonfils, *Architecture antique: Egypte, Grèce, Asie Mineure*; first of many photographic albums of the Near East by this talented family
–1880: G. M. Ebers, *Ägypten in Bild und Wort*; profusely illustrated with both topographical and fanciful views by several different artists

## 1880

**1880**
Last major revolt in Algeria quelled by French

**1881**
First wave of Jewish immigration into Palestine
Uprising in Sudan, led by the Mahdi
Public Debt Administration established by European banks:
many areas of Turkish finance under foreign supervision
French army invades Tunisia from Algeria: navy seizes Biserta;
Bay of Tunis accepts French protectorate

**1882**
June: riots in Alexandria; Arabi Pasha takes control; July: British fleet bombard
Alexandria; 13 September: British troops defeat Arabi Pasha at Tel el Kebir; 2
days later enter Cairo

**1883**
Evelyn Baring, later Lord Cromer (1841–1917), British Agent and Consul-General
in Egypt (to 1890)

**1885**
Death of General Gordon at Khartoum

**1888**
to 1893: Extension of railway from Balkans to Ankara, built by German-backed
Anatolian Railway Company

**1880s**
F. A. Bridgeman (1847–1928) visits Egypt and Algeria on several occasions
to 1914: Robert Talbot Kelly (1861–1934) spends many years painting in Egypt
Ludwig Deutsch visits Cairo on several occasions

**1880**
January: John Singer Sargent (1856–1925) in Morocco
to 1882: Bauernfeind's first visit to the Near East: Cairo, Jaffa, Jerusalem, Damascus
Autumn–1882: Melville living in Cairo; visits Luxor; March 1882: by sea to
India; returns from Baghdad to Black Sea on horseback

**1881**
?Gérôme in Constantinople, ? with Aublet (1851–1938)
March–April: Renoir in Algiers

**1882**
Leighton on fleeting visit to Cairo
March–April: Renoir returns to Algiers

**1883**
to 1884: Theodore van Rysselberghe (1862–1926) in Morocco: Tangier
to 1884: Last of Guillaumet's ten trips to the Near East

**1884**
Etienne Dinet (1861–1929) with Lucien Simon (1861–1945) and brother to
Algeria: live in Bou-Saada, Biskra and El Agouat
Vasily Vasilievtch Vereshchagin (1824–1904) in Jerusalem and elsewhere in
Holy Land, making studies for fifty-four large paintings with biblical subjects,
subsequently exhibited in major European cities
Brabazon in Morocco: Tangier

**1886**
Last of L. C. Müller's nine visits to Egypt
October–March 1887: James Tissot to Holy Land: Jerusalem,
to collect material for his illustrated Bible

**1887**
George Frederick Watts (1817–1904) on honeymoon with second wife in Egypt:
Nile voyage in Cook's dahabiyyah

**1888**
Bauernfeind in Syria: Damascus, Palmyra
Brangwyn on a cargo ship to Dardanelles, Constantinople and Black Sea

**1889**
Brangwyn on a cargo ship to Tunis, Smyrna, Trebizond
J. Tissot returns to Holy Land
November–April 1890: Vedder in Egypt with American manufacturer George Corliss

## 1890

**1892**
to 1914: Abbas II Hilmi, Khedive of Egypt

**1895**
Nationalist Party in Egypt founded by Mustafa Kamel (1874–1901),
champion of Egyptian nationalism, and others
to 1896: Armenian massacres by Turks
to 1907: Mawlāy 'Abd al-'Aziz, Sultān of Morocco

**1890s**
Melville visits Algeria
Ludwig Deutsch visits Cairo on several occasions

**1890**
December–1891: Sargent in Egypt, Palestine, Constantinople, Greece

**1892**
Holman Hunt returns to Cairo (February) and to Jerusalem (March–May)
Charles Cottet (1863–1925) in Algeria; Tunisia?
to 1893: Sargent in Tunis

**1893**
Spring: Brangwyn in Morocco: Tangier, with colourist Dudley Hardy
Emile Bernard (1868–1941) visits Samos, Smyrna, Constantinople; Autumn:
Palestine: Jerusalem; Alexandria to Cairo;
October 1894–May 1895: Palestine; then settles in Cairo until 1904

**1894**
Albert Besnard (1849–1934) in Morocco

**1895**
Clairin in Egypt with Camille Saint-Saëns

**1880**
Jean Nicholas Rimbaud, gun-runner in Aden and Abyssinia
to 1882: M. Flinders Petrie (1853–1942) carries out detailed survey of the Great
Pyramid (of Cheops) at Giza; his first of many excavations in Egypt during which
he used novel methods to advance the whole approach to Egyptology

**1880**
*Dalziel's Bible Gallery Illustrations*, engraved by the Brothers Dalziel; illustrated
by Holman Hunt, Leighton, Poynter, Madox Brown, Watts and many others

**1881**
Blunt purchases an estate near Cairo (Shaykh Obeyd), spends several winters there
Second 'Needle' from Alexandria removed to New York; erected in Central Park
Gaston Maspero (1846–1916) succeeds Mariette as Director of the Bulaq
museum of Egyptian antiquities

**1881**
H. Schliemann, *Ilios: the city and country of the Trojans; the results of researches . . .
on the site of Troy . . . in the years 1871, 72, 73, 78, 79*
Lady Anne Blunt, *A Pilgrimage to Nejd, the cradle of the Arab race*; the Blunts'
travels, 1878–79
P. Loti, *Le Roman d'un Spahi*; novel based on his visit to Dakar and St Louis,
1873
–1885: Palestine Exploration Fund (pub.), *The Survey of Western Palestine*; 7 vols.;
papers written by eminent Palestine explorers; survey undertaken 1872–75 and
1877–79

**1882**
Egypt Exploration Fund founded in London by Amelia Edwards, Reginald Stuart
Poole and Sir Erasmus Wilson
Laurence Oliphant (1829–88) and his wife initiate scheme to colonise Palestine
with Jews

**1882**
W. S. Blunt, *The Future of Islam*; reveals the author's belief in Islamic nationalism
and his opposition to Western influences

**1884**
A. J. Butler, *The Ancient Coptic Churches of Egypt*

**1885**
–1888: R. Burton, *A Plain and Literal Translation of the Arabian Nights*; 10 vols.,
a critical and popular success; Burton attempted to capture the exotic spirit of
the original with archaisms and flowery phrases

**1886**
S. Lane-Poole, *The Art of the Saracens in Egypt*
Palestine Exploration Fund (pub.), *Twenty-one Years' Work in the Holy Land*

**1887**
E. Belhard and A. L. Palmiera, *Egypte et la Nubie: grand Album monumentals,
historique, architectural*; early collotype reproductions

**1888**
C. M. Doughty, *Travels in Arabia Deserta*; a record of the author's two years with
the Bedouin of Arabia, 1876–78
G. Guillaumet, *Tableaux algériens*; drawn from his frequent visits to Algeria,
notably the south

**1890**
E. Wallis Budge, *The Nile. Notes for travellers in Egypt*; Thos. Cook's guide book
to the principal monuments between Cairo and Khartoum

1890

**1891**
Howard Carter (1874–1939) begins his career in Egyptology

**1892**
Flinders Petrie becomes first professor of Egyptology in Britain (University
College, London), until 1933

**1892**
K. Baedeker, *Egypt. Handbook for Travellers. Part second: Upper Egypt etc.* (German
edn. 1891); repub. with sections on Lower Egypt, 1898

**1893**
Foundation of the Societé des Peintres Orientalistes; first official exhibiting body
for Orientalist painters
Exposition d'art musulman, Palais de l'Industrie, Paris; the first major exhibition
devoted solely to Islamic art; seen by Matisse
André Gide (1869–1951) in Algeria

**1894**
–1905: M. Flinders Petrie (ed.), *A History of Egypt*; 6 vols, contributions from
J. P. Mahally, J. G. Milne, S. Lane-Poole

**1895**
P. Loti, *Jerusalem* and *La Galilée*; poetic evocations of a visit to the Holy Land
–1908: H. E. Naville, *The Temple of Deir El Bahari*; record, in six parts, of
excavations sponsored by the Egypt Exploration Fund; the plates mainly from
drawings by Howard Carter

**1894**
First exhibition in Paris of Société des Peintres Orientalistes

**1896**
14 March: Lord Cromer despatches Anglo-Egyptian force to Sudan

**1897**
First Zionist congress

**1898**
2 September: Battle of Omdurman: collapse of Mahdist regime in Sudan
The Fashoda Incident: meeting between General Kitchener and Captain
Marchand in Sudan

**1899**
to 1956: Anglo-Egyptian Condominium in Sudan

**1896**
J. Tissot returns to the Holy Land
Cottet in Egypt, Turkey?

**1897**
Dinet in Egypt
October–May 1898: Henri Evenepoel (1872–1899) in Algeria: Blidah

**1898**
Girardet in Egypt and Palestine
Bauernfeind returns to Jerusalem to live: dies there in 1904

**1900**

**1903**
Levant Consular Service established

**1904**
8 April: Entente Cordiale between Britain and France

**1905**
31 March: Kaiser Wilhelm II visits Tangier; initiates Moroccan Crisis

**1906**
Dinshawai incident in the Nile Delta: symptom of British autocracy and Egyptian
resentment

**1908**
Hijāz railway between Medina and Damascus opened
July: Young Turks Revolution initiated

**1909**
27 April: Young Turks depose Sultān Abdul Hamid in favour of Muḥammad V
Turkish massacre of Armenians
to 1918: Muḥammad V, Sultān of Turkey

**1902**
to 1904: Sir Lawrence Alma-Tadema (1836–1912) in Egypt to attend
inauguration of first Aswān Dam

**From 1904**
Dinet makes a summer home in Bou-Saada

**1904**
December–April 1905: Kandinsky in Algeria, Tunisia: Biserta, Tunis, Carthage

**1905**
to 1906: Sargent in Palestine and elsewhere in Near East

**1906**
Matisse in Algeria: Biserta

**1910**   **1911**
April: Fez taken by the French
Franco-German Convention on Morocco
to 1913: Italian campaign in Libya

*c.* **1912**
Arab nationalism: formation of two secret societies, al Fatat and al-'Ahd

**1912**
30 March: Morocco becomes a French protectorate
to 1925: Gradual French infiltration and occupation of Morocco

**1913**
to 1914: Britain, Germany and Turkey agree on construction of Baghdad Railway

**1914**
18 December: Egypt declared a British protectorate; Khedive Abbas II deposed
World War I; Turkey enters on side of Germany (Treaty of Alliance, 2 August)

**1916**
Outbreak of Arab revolt against Ottoman rule
Sykes-Picot Agreement: British, French and Russian spheres of influence
in the Levant determined

**1917**
2 November: Balfour Declaration: in favour of Jewish homeland in Palestine

**1912**
Spring: Matisse in Algeria, Morocco; Autumn–Spring 1913: returns to Algeria,
Morocco

**1920**   **1920**
British and French mandates established in Near East

**1922**
End of Ottoman Sultānate; last Sultān exiled to San Remo

230

**1896**
−1897: J. Tissot, *La Vie de Notre Seigneur Jésus Christ*; 'Tissot's Bible'; Eng. trans.
1897–98
E. Muir, *The Mamluk or Slave Dynasty of Egypt 1200–1517*

**from 1897**
Isabelle Eberhardt (Si Mahmoud) (1877–1904) in the deserts of North Africa,
often dressed as a man; married to a Spahi Slimène Ehnni in 1901

**1898**
Kaiser Wilhelm's tour of Holy Land (arranged by Thos. Cook)

**1899**
Gertrude Bell (1868–1926) undertakes extensive travels and archaeological
research in Syria, Asia Minor, Mesopotamia; 1916–21, advisor to British
Government on Arab politics in Iraq, dies there 1926

**1902**                                                                    1900
R. Talbot Kelly, *Egypt, Painted and Described*

**1904**
J. Tissot, *La Sainte Bible*; the Old Testament, published posthumously

**1907**                                      **1907**
Maison de France established at Villa Abd el Tif in Algiers; an institute for artists    G. Bell, *The Desert and the Sown*; account of her journey through Syria to Asia
working in North Africa                                                  Minor, 1906

                                              **1908**
                                              Lord Cromer, *Modern Egypt*; Egypt as seen by its British residents
                                              C. M. Doughty, *Wanderings in Arabia*; an abridgement of *Arabia Deserta* which
                                              brought it the recognition it has maintained as one of the greatest of Near Eastern
                                              travel books

**1910**                                      **1911**                                     1910
Exhibition of Islamic art in Munich; seen by Matisse and Kandinsky       G. Bell, *Amurath to Amurath*; account of travels in Syria, Mesopotamia and Asia
                                              Minor in 1910

**1914**
to 1916: T. E. Lawrence (1888–1935) in Cairo, in Arab Bureau, part of military
intelligence

**1916**
to 1918: Lawrence in Arabia as liaison officer and adviser to Feisal, third son
of Sharif of Mecca, participating in Arab revolt against the Turks; enters
Damascus 1 October 1918

                                                                           1920

**1926**
T. E. Lawrence, *Seven Pillars of Wisdom*

# Bibliography

*Works which themselves contain substantial bibliographies are marked with an asterisk.*

## GENERAL

*Jean Alazard, *L'Orient et la peinture française au XIXe siècle, d'Eugène Delacroix à Auguste Renoir*, Paris, 1930

Jean Alazard, 'L'Algérie et les arts de 1830 à nos jours', *Histoire et historiens de l'Algérie, 1830–1930*, Collection du Centenaire de l'Algérie, Paris, 1931, pp. 349–62

*Kenneth Paul Bendiner, 'The Portrayal of the Middle East in British Painting, 1835–1860', Ph.D. dissertation, Columbia University, 1979

Léonce Bénédite, 'Les Peintres orientalistes français', *Gazette des Beaux-Arts*, 3e période, vol. XXI, 1899, pp. 239–47

P. and V. Berko, *Peinture Orientaliste*, Brussels, 1982

Roger Bezombes, *L'Exotisme dans l'art et la pensée*, Paris, 1953

A. Boppe, *Les Introducteurs des ambassadeurs*, Paris, 1907

A. Boppe, *Les Peintres du Bosphore au XVIIIe siècle*, Paris, 1911

*James Stevens Curl, *The Egyptian Revival, an Introductory Study of a Recurring Theme in the History of Taste*, London, 1982

Gerbert Frodl, 'Wiener Orientmalerei im 19. Jahrhundert', *Alte und Moderne Kunst*, vol. 26, nos. 178–9, 1981, pp. 19–25

Peter Hughes, *Eighteenth-Century France and the East*, Wallace Collection Monographs, London, 1981

Philippe Jullian, *The Orientalists. European Painters of Eastern Scenes*, Oxford, 1977

André Maubert, 'L'Exotisme dans la peinture française du XVIIe siècle', thesis, Université de Paris, 1943

Linda Nochlin, 'The Imaginary Orient', *Art in America*, May 1983, vol. 71, pp. 118–31, 187–91

Hassan El-Nouty, 'Les Peintres français en Egypte au XIXe siècle', complementary thesis, Université de Paris, 1953

Ary Renan, 'La Peinture orientaliste', *Gazette des Beaux-Arts*, 3e période, vol. XI, 1894, pp. 43–53

*Valerie M. Romaya, 'Nineteenth-Century British Artists in the Middle East', M. Phil. thesis, University of Nottingham, 1977

*Lynne Thornton, *Les Orientalistes. Peintres voyageurs 1828–1908*, Paris, 1983

Michelle Verrier, *The Orientalists*, New York and London, 1979

## ORIENTALIST EXHIBITIONS

Baltimore Museum of Art, *The Cult of Arabia*, 1972

Brighton Museum and Manchester City Art Gallery, *The Inspiration of Egypt. Its Influence on British Artists, Travellers and Designers, 1700–1900*, 1983

Cairo, Société des Amis de l'Art, *Les Orientalistes français: l'Afrique du Nord dans l'art français du XIXe et XXe siècles*, 1936

Cambridge, Fogg Art Museum, *North Africa Interpreted by European Artists*, 1943

Edinburgh, Talbot Rice Art Centre, and Norwich, Sainsbury Centre for the Visual Arts, *A Middle-Eastern Journey: Artists on their Travels, from the collection of Rodney Searight*, 1980–1

London, The Fine Art Society, *North African Traveller, Casablanca to Cairo* 1974

*London, The Fine Art Society, *Eastern Encounters. Orientalist Painters of the Nineteenth Century*, 1978

London, The Fine Art Society, *Travellers Beyond the Grand Tour*, 1980

London, Leighton House, *The Middle East. Watercolours and Drawings by British and Foreign Artists and Travellers 1750–1900. From the collection of Rodney Searight* 1971

*London, Leighton House, *The Islamic Perspective. An aspect of British architecture and design in the nineteenth century*, 1983

*Marseille, Musée Cantini, *L'orient en question. De Missolonghi à Suez, ou l'Orientalisme de Delacroix à Flaubert*, 1975

Marseille, Musée de Beaux-Arts, *Les Orientalistes provinçaux*, 1982–3

Nantes, Musée des Beaux-Arts, *Orients*, 1980

New York, Metropolitan Museum of Art, *The Image of the Turk in Europe*, 1973

Paris, Galerie Charpentier, *Les Peintres orientalistes français*, 1933

*Paris, Galerie Jean Soustiel, *Mahmal et Attatichs. Peintres et Voyageurs en Turquie, en Egypte et en Afrique du Nord*, 1975–6

Paris, Petit Palais, *Centenaire de la conquête de l'Algérie, 1830–1930*, 1930

Pau, Dunkirk and Douai, Musées des Beaux-Arts, *Les Orientalistes de 1850 à 1914*, 1983

Providence, Rhode Island School of Design, *French Painting in Africa*, 1935

*Rochester, Memorial Art Gallery of the University of Rochester, *Orientalism. The Near East in French Painting, 1800–1880*, 1982

Tours, Musée des Beaux-Arts, *L'Orientalisme dans les collections des Musées de Tours*, 1980

## WORKS ON INDIVIDUAL ARTISTS

### Auguste
*Donald Rosenthal, 'Jules-Robert Auguste and the Early Romantic Circle', Ph.D. dissertation, Columbia University, 1978

### Bauernfeind
Hugo Schmid, *Der Maler Gustav Bauernfeind, 1848–1904*, Sulz, 1981

### Belly
J. K. Huysmans, 'Art contemporain – Belly', *Les Chefs-d'oeuvre d'art au Luxembourg*, Paris, 1881

Conrad de Mandach, 'Artistes contemporains. Léon Belly (1827–1877)', *Gazette des Beaux-Arts*, 4e période, vol. IX, 1913, pp. 73–84, 143–57

Saint-Omer, Musée de l'Hôtel Sandelin, *Léon Belly*, 1977

P. Wintrebert, 'Catalogue de l'oeuvre de Léon Belly', thesis, Université de Lille III, 1974

### Benjamin-Constant
C. D., 'Benjamin-Constant', *Les Arts*, no. 5, June 1902, pp. 26–8

William R. Johnston, 'Caliphs and Captives', *Bulletin du Musée de Montréal*, June 1972, pp. 11–16

J. Murray Templeton, 'Benjamin-Constant', *Magazine of Art*, 1891, pp. 181–8

### Bonnat
Léonce Bénédite, 'Léon Bonnat (1833–1922)', *Gazette des Beaux-Arts*, 5e période, vol. VII, 1923, pp. 1–15

M. Pouget, *Léon Bonnat*, Paris, 1977

Gabriel P. Weisburg, *The Realist Tradition: French Painting and Drawing 1830–1900*, Cleveland Museum of Art and Indiana University Press, 1981, pp. 271–3

### Brangwyn
Rodney Brangwyn, *Brangwyn*, London, 1978

Vincent Galloway, *The Oils and Murals of Sir Frank Brangwyn, R.A., 1867–1956*, Leigh-on-Sea, 1962

### Chassériau
Arthur Baignères, 'Théodore Chassériau', *Gazette des Beaux-Arts*, 2e période, vol. XXXIII, 1886, pp. 209–18

Léonce Bénédite, *Théodore Chassériau, sa vie et son oeuvre*, 2 vols., Paris, 1932

Valbert Chevillard, *Un Peintre romantique. Théodore Chassériau*, Paris, 1893

Raymond Escholier, 'L'Orientalisme de Chassériau', *Gazette des Beaux-Arts*, 5e période, vol. III, 1921, pp. 89–107

Paris, Musée de l'Orangerie, *Chassériau*, 1930

*Marc Sandoz, *Théodore Chassériau 1819–1856. Catalogue raisonné des peintures et des estampes*, Paris, 1974

### Church
D. C. Huntington, *The Landscapes of Frederic Edwin Church*, New York, 1966

### Dauzats
Alexandre Dumas (Père) and Adrien Dauzats, *Quinze jours au Sinaï*, Paris, 1841

Paul Guinard, *Dauzats et Blanchard. Peintres de l'Espagne romantique*, Paris, 1967

Henry Jouin, *Adrien Dauzats, peintre et écrivain*, Paris, 1896

### Decamps
Marius Chaumelin, *Decamps. Sa vie, son oeuvre, ses imitateurs*, Marseille, 1861

Charles Clément, *Les Artistes célèbres: Decamps*, Paris, 1866

Paul Mantz, 'Decamps', *Gazette des Beaux-Arts*, Ière période, vol. XII, 1862, pp. 97–128

*Dewey Mosby, *Alexandre-Gabriel Decamps*, New York, 1977

### Delacroix
Eugène Delacroix, *Oeuvres littéraires*, 2 vols., Paris, 1923

Eugène Delacroix, *Journal de Eugène Delacroix*, ed. André Joubin, 3 vols., Paris, 1932

Eugène Delacroix, *Correspondance générale d'Eugène Delacroix*, ed. André Joubin, 5 vols., Paris, 1936–8

Raymond Escholier, *Delacroix, peintre, graveur, écrivain*, 3 vols., Paris, 1926–9

Jean Guiffrey, *Le Voyage d'Eugène Delacroix au Maroc*, 2 vols., Paris, 1909

George Heard Hamilton, 'Eugène Delacroix and Lord Byron', *Gazette des Beaux-Arts*, 6e période, vol. XXIII, 1943, pp. 99–110

George Heard Hamilton, 'Delacroix, Byron and the English Illustrators', *Gazette des Beaux-Arts*, 6e période, vol. XXXVI, 1949, pp. 261–78

René Huyghe, *Delacroix*, London, 1963

Lee Johnson, 'Delacroix's *Rencontre de Cavaliers Maures*', *Burlington Magazine*, vol. CIII, 1961, pp. 417–23

*Lee Johnson, *The Paintings of Eugène Delacroix. A Critical Catalogue 1816–1831*, 2 vols., Oxford, 1981

Lee Johnson, 'Delacroix's road to the Sultan of Morocco', *Apollo*, vol. CXV, 1982, pp. 186–9

*Eve Kliman, 'Delacroix's lions and tigers: a link between man and nature', *Art Bulletin*, vol. LXIV, 1982, pp. 446–66

E. Lambert, *Histoire d'un tableau. "L'Abd er Rahman, Sultan du Maroc" de Delacroix*, Institut des Hautes Etudes Marocaines, no. XIV, Paris, 1953

London, Arts Council, *Delacroix*, 1964

Jonathan Mayne, 'Delacroix's Orient', *Apollo*, vol. LXXVIII, 1963, pp. 203–7

Paris, Atelier Delacroix, *Delacroix et l'orientalisme de son temps*, 1953

233

Paris, Musée de l'Orangerie, *Voyage de Delacroix au Maroc, et exposition rétrospective du peintre M. Auguste*, 1933

A. Robaut and E. Chesneau, *L'Oeuvre complète de Eugène Delacroix, peintures, dessins, gravures, lithographies*, Paris, 1885

Jack J. Spector, *Delacroix: The Death of Sardanapalus*, London, 1974

Frank Trapp, *The Attainment of Delacroix*, Baltimore and London, 1971

**Frère**
Eugène Montrosier, *Artistes Modernes. Les Peintres de Genre*, nouvelle série, Paris, 1896, pp. 9–12

**Fromentin**
*Jane Abbott, 'An Annotated Bibliography (1937–1970) of Commentary on the Life and Writings of Eugène Fromentin', Master's dissertation, University of North Carolina, 1973

Prosper Dorbec, *Eugène Fromentin*, Paris, 1926

Eugène Fromentin, *Un Eté dans le Sahara*, Paris, 1857

Eugène Fromentin, *Une Anneé dans le Sahel*, Paris, 1859

Eugène Fromentin, *Voyage en Egypte, 1869*, Paris, 1935

Eugène Fromentin, *Lettres de jeunesse*, ed. Pierre Blanchon, Paris, 1909

Eugène Fromentin, *Correspondance*, ed. Pierre Blanchon, Paris, 1911

Louis Gonse, *Eugène Fromentin Peintre et écrivain*, Paris, 1881

Henry Houssaye, 'Eugène Fromentin', *Revue des Deux Mondes*, 3e période, vol. 20, 1877, pp. 882–95

La Rochelle, Museé des Beaux-Arts, *Eugène Fromentin: le peintre et l'écrivain*, 1970

Fouad Marcos, *Fromentin et l'Afrique*, Paris, 1974

*Pierre Martino, 'Fromentin: essai de bibliographie critique', *Revue Africaine*, 1914, pp. 153–82

*Barbara Wright, *Eugène Fromentin: A Bibliography*, London, 1973

**Gérôme**
*Gerald Ackerman, 'Jean-Léon Gérôme', 1824–1904, Ph.D. dissertation, Pomona College, 1971

*Dayton Art Institute, Minneapolis Institute of Arts and Baltimore, Walters Art Gallery, *Jean-Léon Gérôme (1824–1904)*, 1972–3, with an essay by Richard Ettinghausen, 'Jean-Léon Gérôme as a painter of Near-Eastern life'

Emile Galichon, 'M. Gérôme. Peintre ethnographe', *Gazette des Beaux-Arts*, Ière période, vol. XXIV, 1868, pp. 147–51

Fanny Field Hering, *Gérôme, his life and works*, New York, 1892

Paul Lenoir, *Le Fayoum, Le Sinaï et Pétra. Expédition dans la Moyenne Egypte et l'Arabie Petrée sous la direction de J. L. Gérôme*, Paris, 1872

C. Moreau-Vauthier, *Gérôme, peintre et sculpteur, l'homme et l'artiste*, Paris, 1906

Edward Strahan, pseudonym for Evert Shinn, *Gérôme, a collection of the works of J. L. Gérôme in one hundred photogravures*, 2 vols., New York, 1881–3

Charles Timbal, 'Les Artistes contemporains. Gérôme', *Gazette des Beaux-Arts*, 2e période, vol. XIV, 1876, pp. 218–31, 334–46

**Gifford**
University of Texas at Austin, Texas, *Sanford Robinson Gifford 1823–1880*, 1970

L. J. Weiss, *Sanford Robinson Gifford (1823–1880)*, New York, 1977

**Girardet**
R. Burnard, *L'Etonnante histoire des Girardet, artistes suisses*, Neuchâtel, 1944

Paris, Hôtel Drouot, *Catalogue des tableaux provenant de l'atelier Eugène Girardet*, 20 March 1908 (preface by Léonce Bénédite)

**Gleyre**
Charles Clément, *Gleyre. Etude biographique et critique*, Geneva, Neuchâtel and Paris, 1878

*New York University, Grey Art Gallery and Study Center, and University of Maryland Art Gallery, *Charles Gleyre 1806–1874*, 1980, with an essay by Nancy Scott Newhouse, 'From Rome to Khartoum: Gleyre, Lowell and the Evidence of the Boston Watercolors and Drawings'

*Winterthur, Kunstmuseum, etc., *Charles Gleyre ou les illusions perdues*, 1974, with an essay by Jacques-Edouard Berger, 'Gleyre et l'Orient'

**Goodall**
Frederick Goodall, *The Reminiscences of Frederick Goodall, R.A.*, London, 1902

N. G. Slarke, *Frederick Goodall, R. A.*, Oundle, 1981

**Gros**
Anonymous, 'M. Gros', *L'Artiste*, Ière série, vol. IX, 1835, pp. 265–7

Anonymous, 'Vente des tableaux, dessins et esquisses de M. Gros', *L'Artiste*, Ière série, vol. X, 1835, pp. 197, 209–10

J. B. Delestre, *Gros, sa vie et ses ouvrages*, Paris, 1867

J. Tripier Le Franc, *Histoire de la vie et de la mort du baron Gros*, Paris, 1880

Pierre Lelièvre, 'Gros, peintre d'histoire', *Gazette des Beaux-Arts*, 6e période, vol. XV, 1936, pp. 289–304

Paris, Petit Palais, *Gros, ses amis, ses élèves*, 1936

Norman Schlenoff, 'Baron Gros and Napoleon's Egyptian Campaigns', *Essays in Honour of Walter Friedlaender*, New York, 1965

**Guillaumet**
Adolphe Badin, 'Gustave Guillaumet', *L'Art*, vol. XLIV, 1888, pp. 3–13, 39–45, 53–60

Léonce Bénédite, 'La Peinture orientaliste et Gustave Guillaumet', *Nouvelle Revue*, vol. L, 1888, pp. 326–43

Gustave Guillaumet, *Lettres d'un voyageur*, Paris, 1888

Gustave Guillaumet, *Tableaux algériens*, Paris, 1888

Paris, Galerie Georges Petit, *Vente de l'atelier de Gustave Achille Guillaumet*, 6–8 February 1888

Ary Renan, 'Gustave Guillaumet', *Gazette des Beaux-Arts*, 2e période, vol. XXXV, 1887, pp. 404–22

**Holman Hunt**
William Holman Hunt, *Pre-Raphaelitism and the Pre-Raphaelite Brotherhood*, 2 vols., London, 1905

*George P. Landow, *William Holman Hunt and Typological Symbolism*, New Haven, 1979

Liverpool, Walker Art Gallery and London, Victoria and Albert Museum, *William Holman Hunt*, 1969

London, Tate Gallery, *The Pre-Raphaelites*, 1984

**Ingres**
Henri Delaborde, *Ingres. Sa vie, ses travaux, sa doctrine*, Paris, 1870

Henri Lapauze, *Ingres, sa vie et son oeuvre*, Paris, 1911

J. Momméja, '"Le Bain turc" d'Ingres', *Gazette des Beaux-Arts*, September 1906, pp. 177–98

Paris, Musée du Louvre. *Le Bain turc d'Ingres*, Les dossiers du département des peintures, no. 1, 1971

Paris, Petit Palais, *Ingres*, 1967

*Robert Rosenblum, *Ingres*, New York, 1967

*Georges Wildenstein, *Ingres*, London, 1954

**Kandinsky**
Will Grohmann, *Wassily Kandinsky, Leben und Werk*, Cologne, 1958

Wassily Kandinsky, *Complete Writings on Art*, ed. Kenneth C. Lindsay and Peter Vergo, Boston and London, 1982

*Hans K. Roethel and Jean K. Benjamin, *Kandinsky. Catalogue Raisonné of the Oil Paintings. Volume One, 1900–1915*, London, 1982

**Lear**
Philip Hofer, *Edward Lear as a Landscape Draughtsman*, Cambridge, Mass., 1968

Edward Lear, *Journals of a Landscape Painter in Greece and Albania etc.*, London, 1851

Edward Lear, *Letters of Edward Lear*, ed. Lady Strachey, London, 1907

Edward Lear, *Later Letters of Edward Lear*, ed. Lady Strachey, London, 1911

Vivien Noakes, *Edward Lear: the Life of a Wanderer*, London, 1968

**Lecomte-du-Nouÿ**
Guy de Montgailhard, *Lecomte-du-Nouÿ*, Paris, 1906

V. Sisman, 'Lecomte-du-Nouÿ', thesis, Université de Nanterre, 1981

**Leighton**
A. L. Baldry, *Leighton*, 'Masterpieces in Colour' Series, London, 1908

Mrs Russell Barrington, *The Life, Letters and Work of Frederic Leighton*, 2 vols., London, 1906

Alice Corkran, *Frederic Leighton*, London, 1904

*Richard and Leonée Ormond, *Lord Leighton*, New Haven and London, 1975

Ernest Rhys, *Sir Frederic Leighton, Bart., P.R.A.*, London, 1895

John Edgcumbe Staley, *Lord Leighton of Stretton, P.R.A.*, London, 1906

**Lewis**
Anonymous, 'British Artists: Their Style and Character, No. XXXII – John Frederick Lewis', *Art Journal*, New Series, vol. IV, 1858, pp. 41–3

Anonymous, 'John Frederick Lewis, R.A.', *Art Journal*, New Series, vol. XV, 1876, p. 329

Randall Davies and Basil S. Long, 'John Frederick Lewis, R.A. (1805–76)', *Old Water-Colour Society's Club*, vol. III, 1925–6, pp. 31–50

John Frederick Lewis, *Lewis's Illustrations of Constantinople, made . . . in the years 1835–6. Arranged and drawn on stone from the original sketches of Coke Smyth, by John F. Lewis*, London, 1837

*Major-General Michael Lewis, C.B.E., *John Frederick Lewis, R.A.*, Leigh-on-Sea, 1978

Newcastle-upon-Tyne, Laing Art Gallery, *John Frederick Lewis*, 1971

Hugh Stokes, 'John Frederick Lewis, R.A. (1805–1876)', *Walker's Quarterly*, no. 28, 1929

**Marilhat**
Anonymous, 'Marilhat, paysagiste. Fragments de ses lettres inédites', *Le Magasin Pittoresque*, 1856, pp. 347–50, 370–1, 403–4

Clermont-Ferrand, Musée Bargoin, *Prosper Marilhat*, 1973

Théophile Gautier, 'Prosper Marilhat', *Revue des Deux Mondes*, 5e série, vol. 23, 1848, pp. 56–75

Hippolyte Gomot, *Marilhat et son oeuvre*, Clermont-Ferrand, 1884

*Danielle Menu, 'Prosper Marilhat: essai de catalogue', thesis, Université de Dijon, 1972

**Matisse**

*Alfred H. Barr, Jr., *Matisse, His Art and His Public*, New York, 1951, new ed., 1966

Jean Clair, 'La Tentation de l'Orient', *La Nouvelle Revue Française*, July 1970, pp. 65–71

Jack D. Flam, 'Matisse in Morocco', *Connoisseur*, vol. CCXI, 1982, pp. 74–86

Mario Luzi, *L'Opera di Matisse dalla rivolta 'fauve' all'intimismo, 1904–1928*, Milan, 1971

Henri Matisse, *Ecrits et propos sur l'art*, ed. Dominique Fourcade, Paris, 1972

Paris, Grand Palais, *Henri Matisse, Exposition du centenaire*, 1970

**Melville**

*Agnes E. Mackay, *Arthur Melville, Scottish Impressionist, 1855–1904*, Leigh-on-Sea, 1951

**L. C. Müller**

Adalbert Franz Seligmann, *Carl Leopold Müller. Ein Künstlerleben in Briefen, Bildern und Dokumenten*, Vienna, 1922

**W. J. Müller**

Bristol City Art Gallery, *William James Müller, 1812–1845*, 1962

Cyril G. E. Bunt, *The Life and Work of William James Müller of Bristol*, Leigh-on-Sea, 1948

*Briony Llewellyn, 'William James Müller and the Middle East', M.A. report, Courtauld Institute, University of London, 1981

William James Müller, 'An Artist's Tour in Egypt', *Art-Union*, vol. I, 1839, pp. 131–2

William James Müller, 'Letters from Xanthus', *Art-Union*, vol. VI, 1844, pp. 41–2, 209–11, 356–8

N. Neal Solly, *Memoir of the Life of William James Müller*, London, 1875

**Renoir**

*François Daulte, *Auguste Renoir: Catalogue raisonné de l'oeuvre peint*, vol. I, *Les Figures (1860–1890)*, Lausanne, 1971

*Renoir en Italie et en Algérie*, preface by Albert André, introduction by Georges Besson, Paris, 1955

Jean Renoir, *Renoir*, Paris, 1962

Ambroise Vollard, *Tableaux, Pastels et Dessins de Pierre-Auguste Renoir*, Paris, vol. I, 1918, vol. II, n.d.

Ambroise Vollard, *Renoir*, Paris, 1918

**Roberts**

Anonymous, 'British Artists: Their Style and Character, No. XXXVI – David Roberts', *Art Journal*, New Series, vol. IV, 1858, pp. 201–2

James Ballantine, *The Life of David Roberts, R.A., Compiled from his Journals and Other Sources*, Edinburgh, 1866

Helen Guiterman, *David Roberts, R.A., 1796–1864*, London, 1978

David Roberts, *The Holy Land, Syria, Idumea, Arabia, Egypt and Nubia*, with texts by the Rev. George Croly, L.L.D., and William Brockedon, F.R.S., 6 vols., 1842–9

*Scottish Arts Council, *David Roberts, Artist Adventurer, 1796–1864*, 1981–2

**Schreyer**

Oshkosh, Paine Art Center and Arboretum, *Adolf Schreyer*, 1972

**Seddon**

John Pollard Seddon, *Memoir and Letters of the Late Thomas Seddon, Artist, By His Brother*, London, 1858

**Tissot**

*New York, Jewish Museum, *J. James Tissot. Biblical Paintings*, 1982, with an essay by Gert Schiff, 'Tissot's Illustrations for the Hebrew Bible'

*Michael Wentworth, *James Tissot*, Oxford, 1984

**Vedder**

P. D. Pierce, 'Deciphering Egypt: Four Studies in the American Sublime', Ph.D. dissertation, Yale University, 1980

E. Radford, 'Elihu Vedder and His Exhibition', *Art Journal*, April 1899, p. 102

E. Vedder, *Digressions of V*, Boston, 1910

**Vernet**

Anonymous, 'Living Artists of Europe No. IV. Horace Vernet', *Art-Union*, vol. VI, 1844, pp. 119–20

Charles Blanc, *Une Famille d'artists. Les Trois Vernet. Joseph – Carle – Horace*, Paris, 1898

Armand Dayot, *Les Vernet*, Paris, 1898

Henri Delaborde, 'Horace Vernet, ses oeuvres et sa manière', *Revue des Deux Mondes*, vol. 44, 1863, pp. 76–98

Amédée Durande, *Joseph, Carle et Horace Vernet. Correspondance et biographies*, Paris, 1864

Frédéric Goupil-Fesquet, *Voyage en Orient fait avec Horace Vernet en 1839 et 1840*, Paris, 1843

Léon Lagrange, 'Artistes contemporains. Horace Vernet', *Gazette des Beaux-Arts*, Ière période, vol. XV, 1863, pp. 297–327, 439–65

Paul Mantz, 'Galerie du XIXe siècle. Horace Vernet', *L'Artiste*, 6e série, vol. II, 1857, pp. 177–82

Olivier Merson, 'Artistes contemporains. Horace Vernet', *Revue contemporaine*, vol. XXXI, 1863, pp. 553–89

*Rome, Académie de France, and Paris, Ecole nationale supérieure des Beaux-Arts, *Horace Vernet*, 1980

**Wilkie**

Kenneth Paul Bendiner, 'Wilkie in Turkey: "The Tartar Messenger Narrating the News of the Victory of St Jean d'Acre"', *Art Bulletin*, vol. LXIII, 1981, pp. 259–68

Allan Cunningham, *The Life of Sir David Wilkie with His Journals, Tours and Critical Remarks on Works of Art and a Selection from His Correspondence*, 3 vols., London, 1843

David Wilkie, *Sir David Wilkie's Sketches in Turkey, Syria and Egypt, 1840–1*, drawn on stone by Joseph Nash, London, 1843

## ORIENTALISM IN LITERATURE

J. M. Carré, *Voyageurs et écrivains français en Egypte*, Cairo, 1932

P. Jourda, *L'Exotisme dans la littérature française depuis Chateaubriand*, 2 vols., Paris, 1956

Marie de Meester, *Oriental Influences in the English Literature of the Nineteenth Century*, Heidelberg, 1915

Pierre Martino, *L'Orient dans la littérature française au XVIIe et au XVIIIe siècles*, Paris, 1908

Hassan El-Nouty, *Le Proche-Orient dans la littérature française de la fin du Romantisme à la mort de Pierre Loti*, thesis, Université de Paris, 1953

Hassan El-Nouty, *Le Proche-Orient dans la littérature française de Nerval à Barrès*, Paris, 1958

*Edward Said, *Orientalism*, New York, 1978

Byron Porter Smith, *Islam in English Literature*, Beirut, 1939

Francis Steegmuller (transl. and ed.), *Flaubert in Egypt: A Sensibility on Tour*, Boston, 1972

*Jean-Jacques Waardenburg, *L'Islam dans le miroir de l'Occident*, Paris, 1963

## EUROPEAN RELATIONS WITH NORTH AFRICA AND THE NEAR EAST

*Thomas J. Assad, *Three Victorian Travellers: Burton, Blunt, Doughty*, London, 1964

Lesley Blanch, *The Wilder Shores of Love*, London, 1965

Frederick Jones Bliss, *The Development of Palestine Exploration*, London, 1906

Fred Gladstone Bratton, *A History of Egyptian Archaeology*, New York, 1968

Deborah Bull and Donald Lorimer, *Up the Nile*, New York, 1979

*Peter Clayton, *The Rediscovery of Ancient Egypt*, London, 1982

*Norman Daniel, *Islam, Europe and Empire*, Edinburgh, 1966

Raoul Girardet, *L'Idée coloniale en France de 1871 à 1962*, Paris, 1972

Philip K. Hitti, *Islam and the West. A Historical Cultural Survey*, Princeton, 1962

D. S. Landes, *Bankers and Pashas*, London, 1958

Peter Mansfield, *The British in Egypt*, London, 1971

John Marlowe, *Anglo-Egyptian Relations, 1800–1953*, London, 1954

Sari J. Nasir, *The Arabs and the English*, London, 1976

G. N. Sanderson, *England, Europe and the Upper Nile*, Edinburgh, 1965

*Sarah Searight, *The British in the Middle East*, London, 1969, revised ed. 1979

*A. L. Tibawi, *British Interests in Palestine, 1800–1901*, Oxford, 1961

Kathryn Tidrick, *Heart-beguiling Araby*, Cambridge, 1981

*Fani-Maria Tsigakou, *The Rediscovery of Greece*, London, 1981

Louis Vaczek and Gail Buckland, *Travellers in Ancient Lands. A Portrait of the Middle East, 1839–1919*, New York, 1981

S. H. Weber, *Voyages and Travels in the Near East in the Nineteenth Century*, Princeton, 1952

## HISTORY OF NORTH AFRICA AND THE NEAR EAST

C. E. Bosworth, *The Islamic Dynasties*, Edinburgh, 1980

Shafik Ghorbal, *The Beginnings of the Egyptian Question and the Rise of Mehemet Ali*, London, 1928

J. Christopher Herold, *Bonaparte in Egypt*, London, 1963

Marshall G. S. Hodgson, *The Venture of Islam. Volume 3: The Gunpowder Empires and Modern Times*, Chicago, 1974

*P. M. Holt, *Egypt and the Fertile Crescent, 1516–1922. A Political History*, London, 1966

P. M. Holt (ed.), *Political and Social Change in Modern Egypt*, Oxford, 1968

Albert Hourani, *The Emergence of the Modern Middle East*, London, 1981

*Charles Issawi, *The Economic History of the Middle East, 1800–1914: A Book of Readings*, Chicago, 1966

Abdallah Laroui, *L'Histoire du Maghreb: un essai de synthèse*, Paris, 1970

*Reuben Levy, *The Social Structure of Islam*, Cambridge, 1969

Bernard Lewis, *The Muslim Discovery of Europe*, London, 1982

*Bernard Lewis, *The Emergence of Modern Turkey*, London, 1961

Afaf Lutfi al-Sayyid Marsot, *Egypt in the Reign of Muhammad Ali*, Cambridge, 1984

*Jamil M. Abun Nasr, *A History of the Maghrib*, Cambridge, 2nd ed., 1975

*Roger Owen, *The Middle East in the World Economy, 1800–1914*, London, 1981

V. J. Parry and M. E. Yapp, *War, Technology and Society in the Middle East*, London, 1975

*Francis Robinson, *Atlas of the Islamic World since 1500*, Oxford, 1982

*P. J. Vatikiotis, *The Modern History of Egypt*, London, 2nd ed., 1983

## CONTEMPORARY PUBLICATIONS

A selection of works from the vast nineteenth-century literature on North Africa and the Near East is given in the Chronology. For fuller bibliographies, see Richard Bevis, *Bibliotheca Cisorientalia. An Annotated Checklist of Early English Travel Books on the Near and Middle East*, Boston, 1973, and Reinhold Röhricht, *Bibliotheca Geographica Palestinae. Chronologisches Verzeichniss der auf die Geographie des Heiligen Landes bezüglichen Literatur von 333 bis 1878 und Versuch einer Cartographie*, Berlin, 1890.

FP Xtra